Nuft and the Last Dragons

by Freddy Milton

FANTAGRAPHICS
SEATTLE

Fantagraphics Books, Inc.
7563 Lake City Way NE
Seattle WA 98115
(800) 657-1100

Publisher: Gary Groth
Senior Editor: J. Michael Catron
Design: Chelsea Wirtz
Production: Paul Baresh
Associate Publisher: Eric Reynolds

Nuft and the Last Dragons logo by Ingo Milton.
Special thanks to Ingo Milton and Dwight Decker.

First printing: July 2021
ISBN: 978-1-68396-365-3
Printed in China
Library of Congress Control Number: 2020941297

The stories in this volume were originally published
in Denmark. "The Nufts Move In" ("Familien Gnuff:
Poltergeisterne") in *Søren Spætte* #2, 5, 6, and 9,
1983. "Trouble on George Street" in the graphic album
Familien Gnuff: Ballade I Nørregade, 1986. "The Great
Technowhiz" in the graphic album *Familien Gnuff: Den
Store Teknokrak*, 1986. "Gnuff" in *Sejd* #12, 1977.

Visit us at fantagraphics.com.
Follow us on Twitter at @fantagraphics
and on Facebook at facebook.com/fantagraphics.

All comics stories
written and drawn

by Freddy Milton

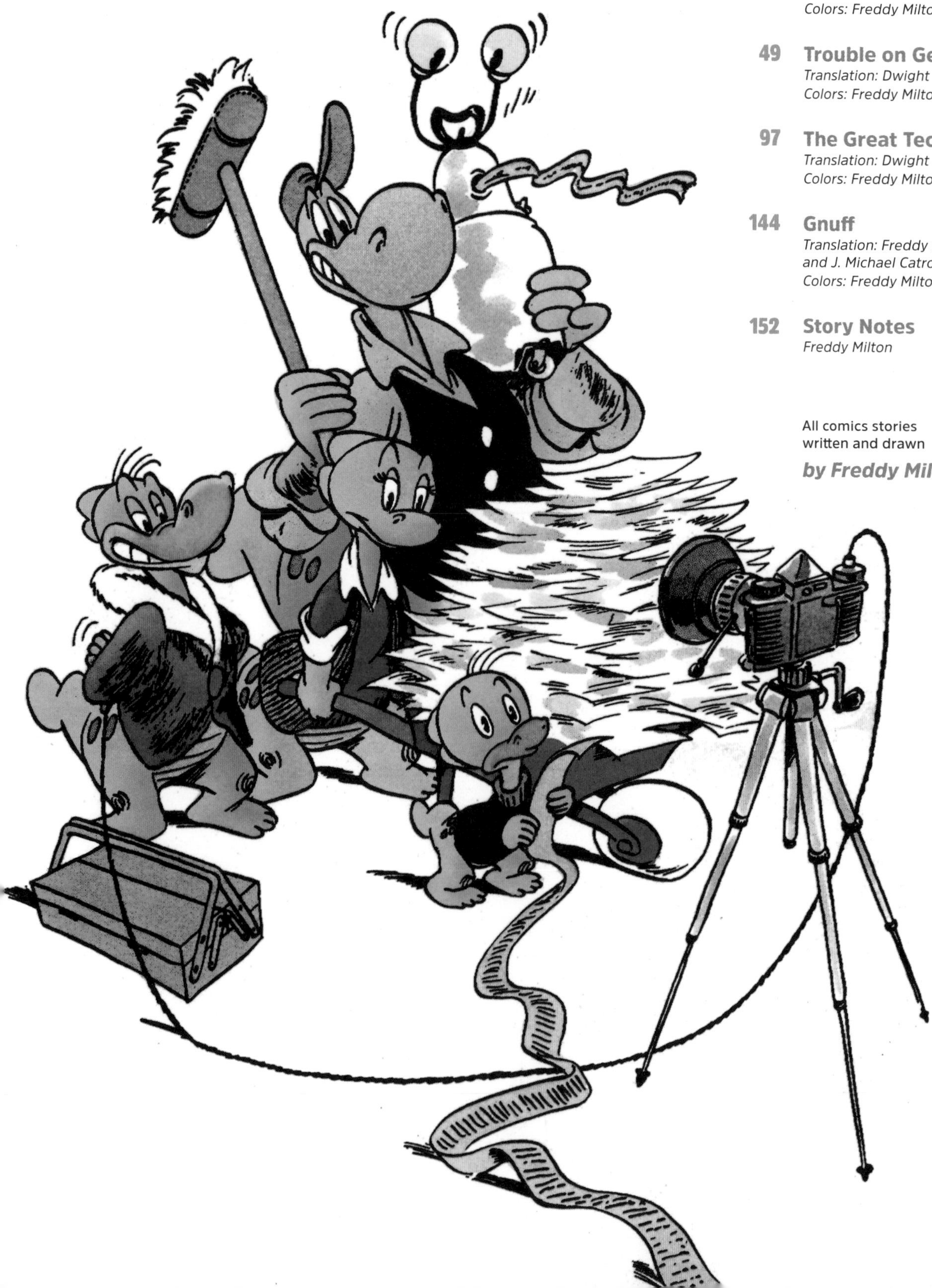

Just a Silly Cartoonist

Recently, my granddaughter, Selma, 6 years old, presented me with an illustrated story she had made about a little witch. It was a complete storybook — 32 pages plus covers, drawn on the front and back of each page and all taped together. Thirty-two is a magic number when it comes to publications. But I had never suggested to her that she try something like that.

What impressed me most was her dedication. How many children make long illustrated stories and carry them through to the end?

I didn't do that at her age. When my son, Thorbjoern, was young, he had begun creating books of his own, but he made only a few drawings before he lost interest. But I forgive him, for he now has a master's degree in IT, and he's off to a good start in an important career. (Besides, he helps me every now and then when I have computer problems.)

What launched me on a career in comics was a birthday present I got when I was 5 years old. It was the March 1953 issue of *Anders And & Co.*, the Danish monthly Disney comics magazine. Donald Duck wanted to impress his nephews with his prowess as a kite flyer. His giant kite lifts his car from the ground and carries it over the city — until Donald cuts the rope. He whomps down on the rooftop terrace of a swanky hotel where "the annual banquet of the *World's Greatest Men* is in progress!"

When they ask who he is, a woozy Donald answers that he was just a dumb duck who had bragged that he was the world's greatest kite maker...

...and the conference organizer rapidly picks up on that line and presents Donald to the other participants as the greatest kite maker in the world!

The creator of the story, whom we for many years called "The Good Artist," concluded that tale by hearkening back to the opening sequence where Huey, Dewey, and Louie had accidentally trampled Donald's newly planted cabbage. When they trepidatiously answer a phone call from their uncle at The Swelldorf-Castoria, he orders them to replant his cabbage patch, and they grumble off to repair the damage.

American readers know this story — by Carl Barks, of course — as "Donald's Monster Kite," from *Walt Disney's Comics and Stories* #68, May 1946.

My grandmother read that magazine aloud to me numerous times. And she read and reread the following issues, too, until they barely held together. As an adult, I had to replace them with better copies.

I identified with poor Donald, and for many years I thought I was just a silly cartoonist who thought he was something more. I really longed for a conference organizer who would invite me into a league of extraordinary gentlemen.

It took me years to arrive at the point of doing my own comics. Barks was an icon. It was impossible even to imagine that you could do anything to compare to what the Master himself had accomplished. Then, one fine day in 1994 in Copenhagen, in the less swanky Hotel Phoenix, I finally shook hands with Carl Barks, who was on his grand European Tour. (I wrote about that in my biography, *The Boy Who Loved Carl Barks*, Theme Park Press, 2018).

On my quest to define my own style, I experimented with different approaches to telling stories in comics. You can see that evolution for yourself on my homepage, www.freddymilton.dk, which, yes, has an extensive section in English.

Nuft and the Last Dragons (known in Europe as *Familien Gnuff*), my most ambitious and longest-running comics series, is the result of those years of experimentation and struggle.

Though conceived and developed well before I began my career drawing Donald Duck and Woody Woodpecker, *Nuft* didn't find a publisher in Europe until around the time I was working on Woody. My inspiration for *Nuft and the Last Dragons* comes from Carl Barks's Donald Duck stories and from my attempts to place Woody Woodpecker in a more contemporary setting.

Bucking a certain funny-animal convention, all my humans have five fingers and don't wear white gloves. I also like to vary the cast of supporting characters. In other funny-animal series, humans are often dog-faced, but I use rhinos, hippos, elephants, goats, pigs, and cats. You'll also find a lot of birds swooping around.

Ultimately, I did arrive at a style that, while inspired by Carl Barks, still has a definite Freddy Milton touch. That style has served me and my readers well over the many years that I have drawn the adventures of Donald Duck (and other Disney characters), Woody Woodpecker, and, of course, my own creation, which you can read in these very pages, *Nuft and the Last Dragons*. I hope you enjoy it.

— *Freddy Milton*

RIGHT: Freddy Milton with a copy of his first Nuft graphic album (look familiar?) at the Art Bubble Festival in Copenhagen, Denmark, November 9, 2019. Photo by Carsten Olsen.

OPPOSITE TOP: Freddy Milton at his drawing board, 1978.

OPPOSITE BOTTOM LEFT: Freddy Milton meets Carl Barks at the "less swanky" Hotel Phoenix in Copenhagen, 1994.

OPPOSITE BOTTOM RIGHT: The artist draws himself.

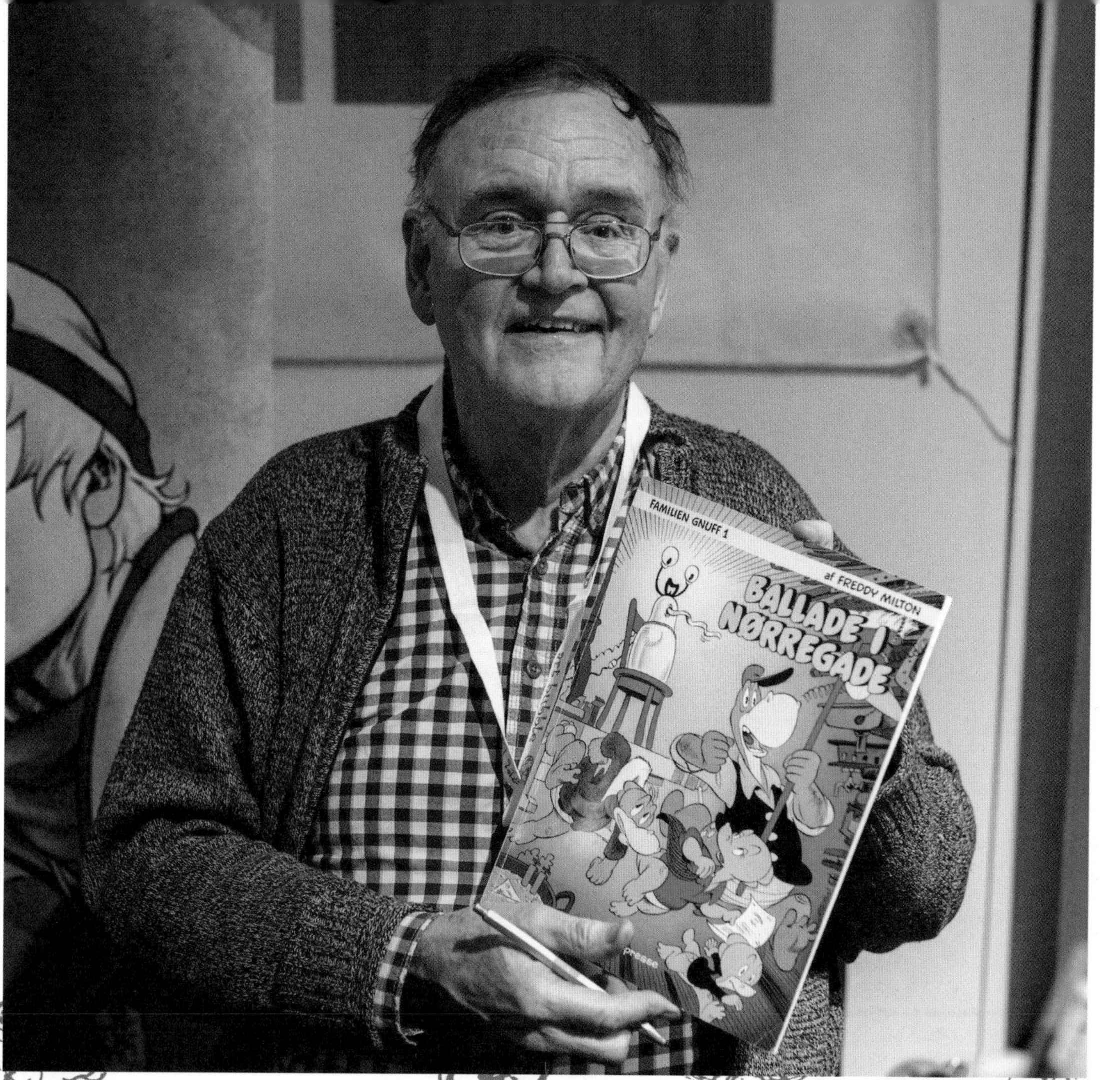
FAMILIEN GNUFF 1
af FREDDY MILTON
BALLADE I NØRREGADE

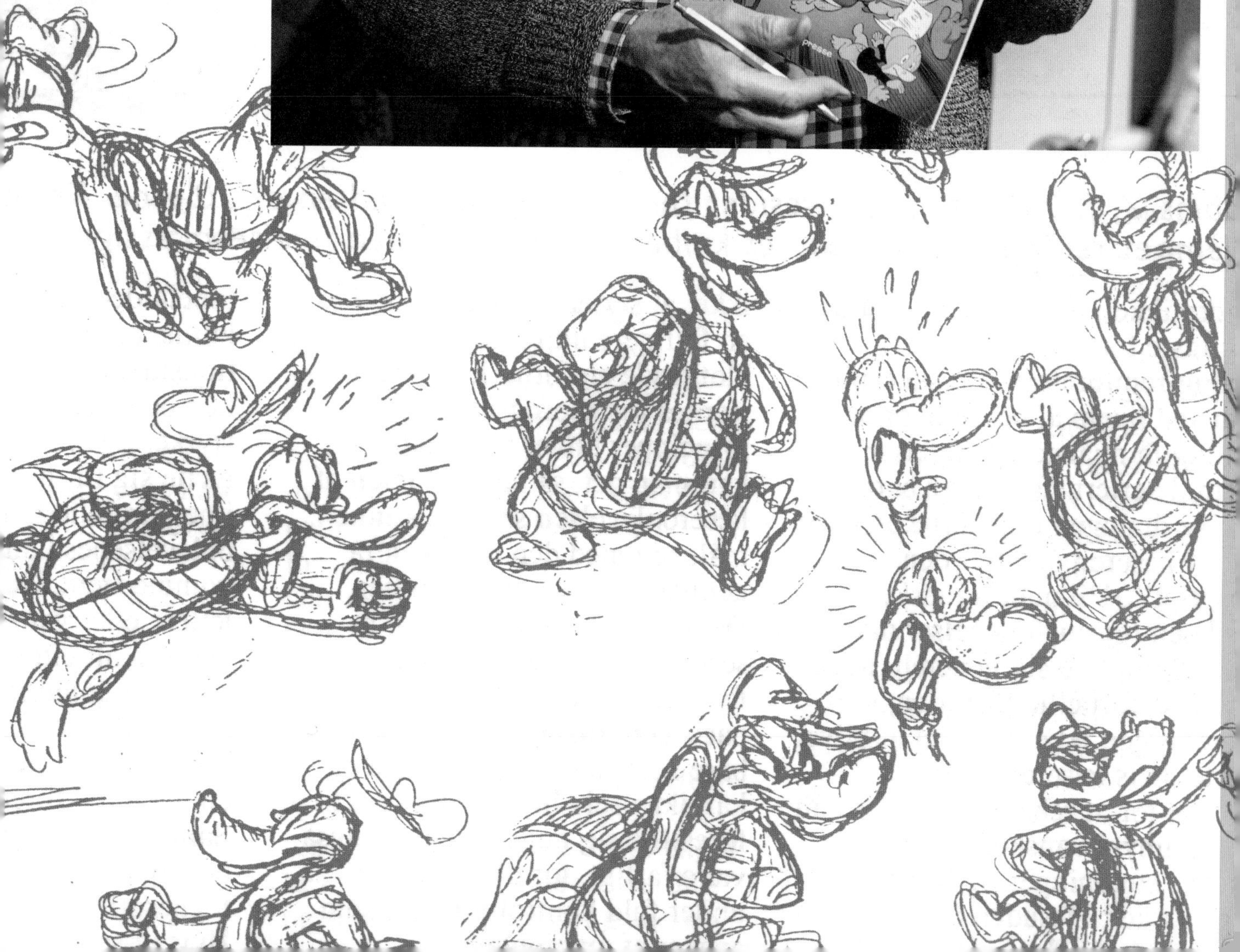

Who's Who

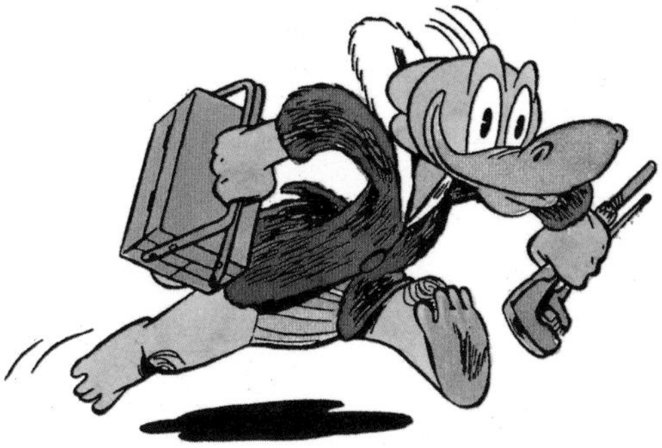

Nuft

Nuft, Nellie and Nicky's brother, is an ever-optimistic dragon who has a special talent for flying — off the handle. He usually works as a plumber, and he often ends up in hot water.

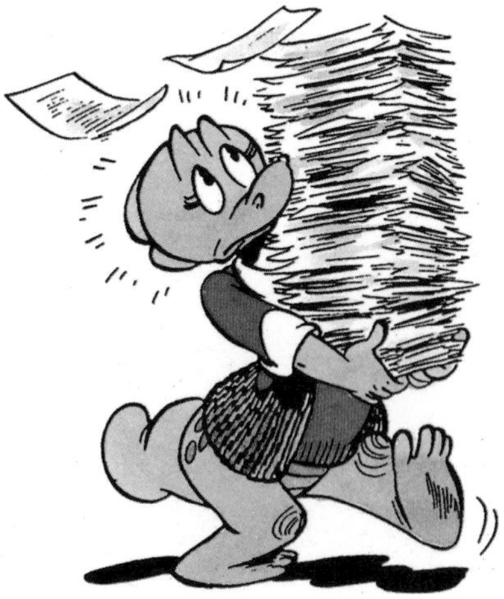

Nellie

Nellie, Nuft and Nicky's sister, is the responsible type, deeply immersed in the practical side of life. She would like to make the world a better place, but her daily obligations seldom leave her enough time for it.

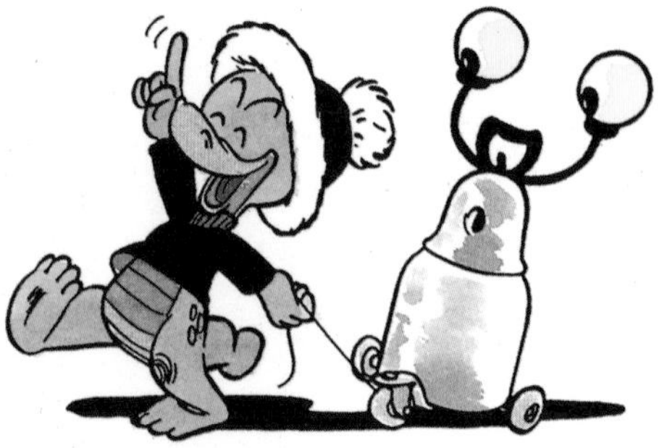

Nicky

Nicky, Nuft and Nellie's little brother, is the youngest member of the family. He's only 98 years old. He still goes to school, but sometimes the school changes faster than he can keep up.

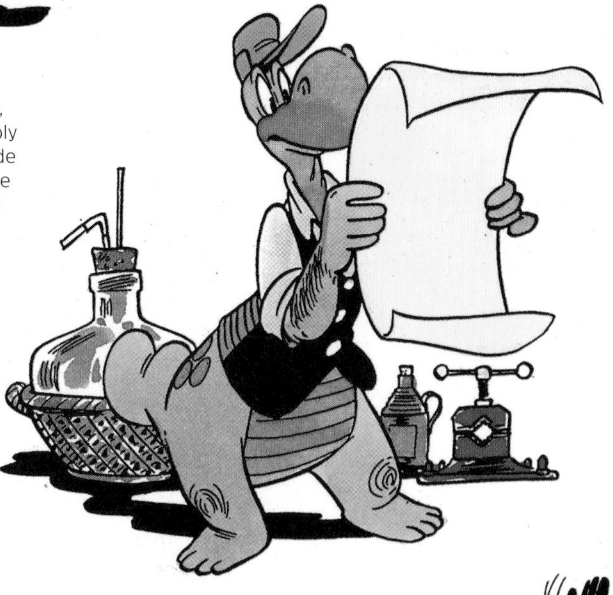

Norbert

Norbert, the Nufts' cousin, is the oldest member of the clan. He lives in town, and the city fathers often make use of his special talents.

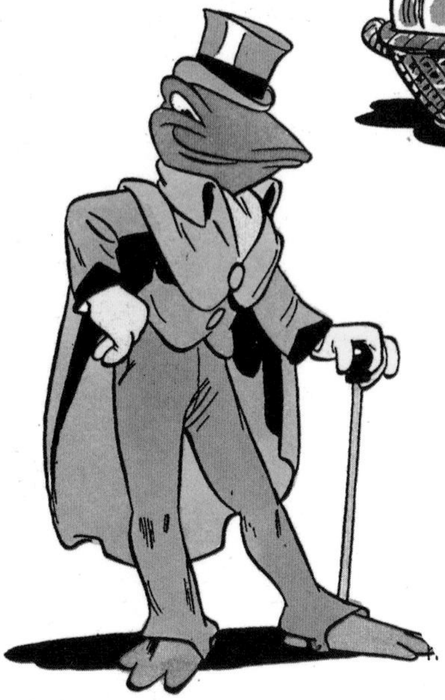

J.P. Phrogg

J.P. Phrogg is something of a mystery. Whenever weakness, greed, or misunderstanding give him an opening, he tries to use his dubious talents for personal advantage. His opponents are frequently deceived by his charm.

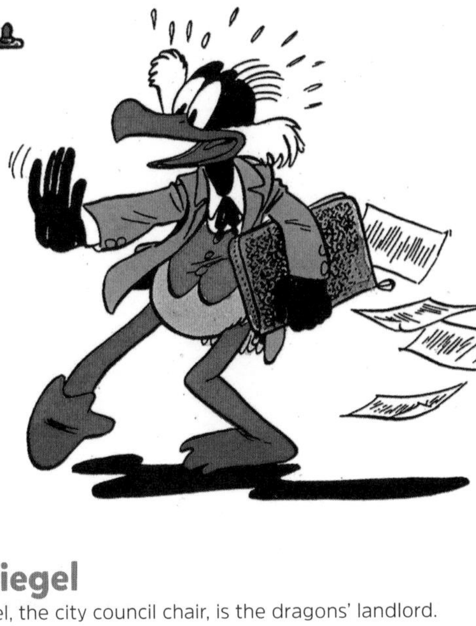

Siegel

Siegel, the city council chair, is the dragons' landlord. His various business and governmental activities are an endless source of conflicts of interests.

The Nufts Move In

by Freddy Milton
Translation: Kim Thompson
Colors: Freddy Milton

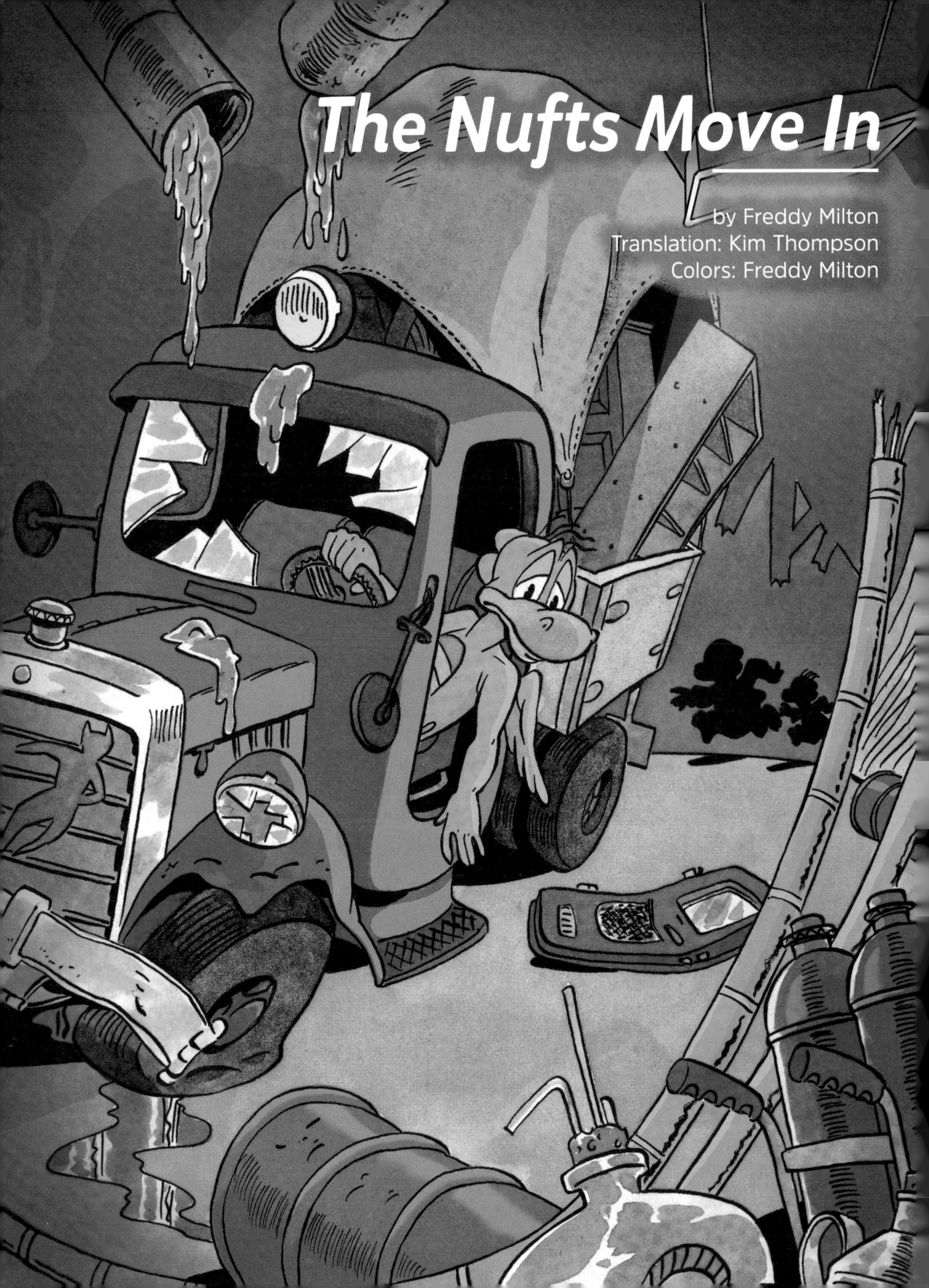

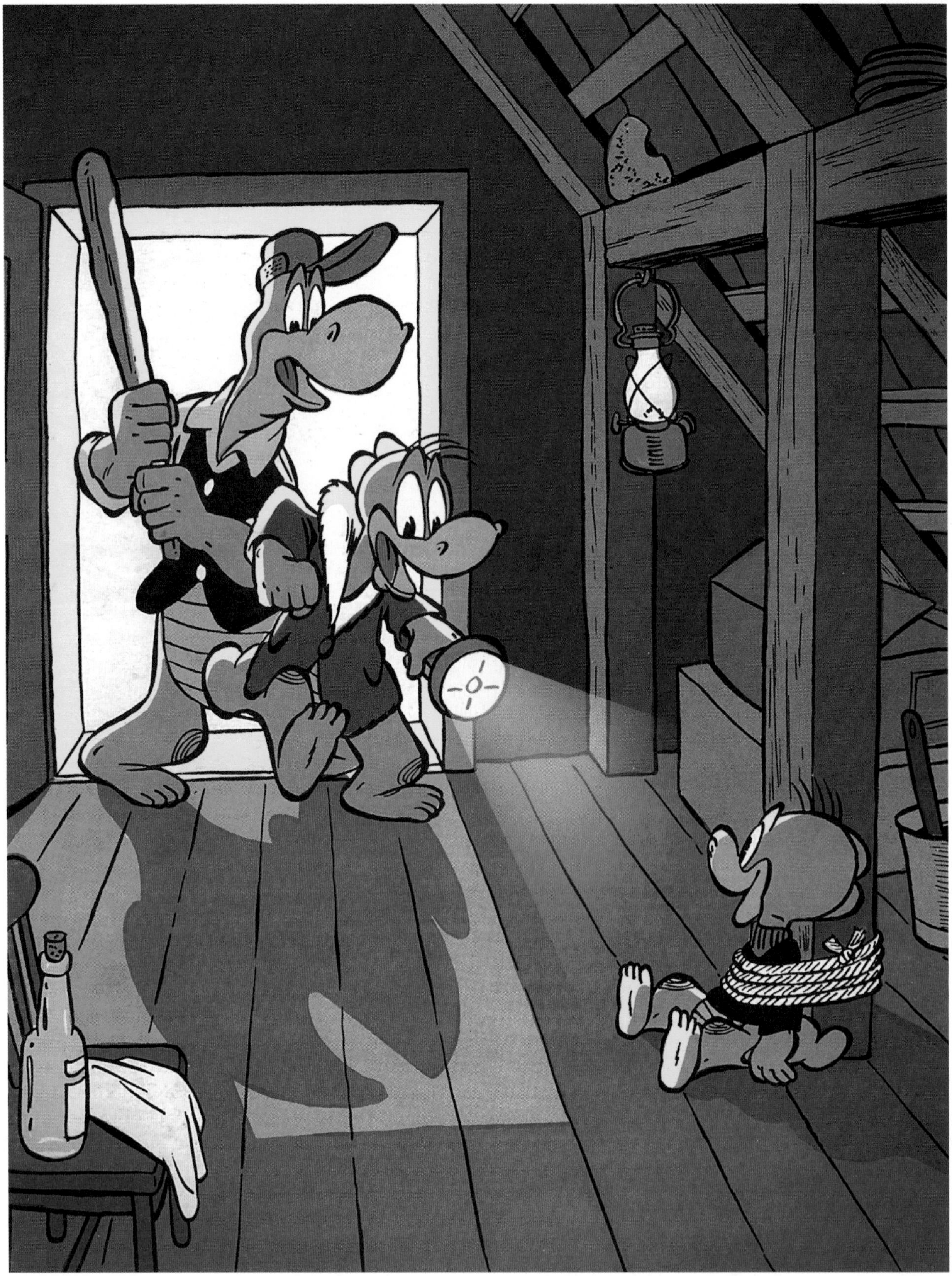

ABOVE: A slightly updated version of Freddy Milton's front cover art for *Critters #5*.

PREVIOUS PAGE: Freddy Milton's front cover art for the Danish edition of *The Nufts Move In*.

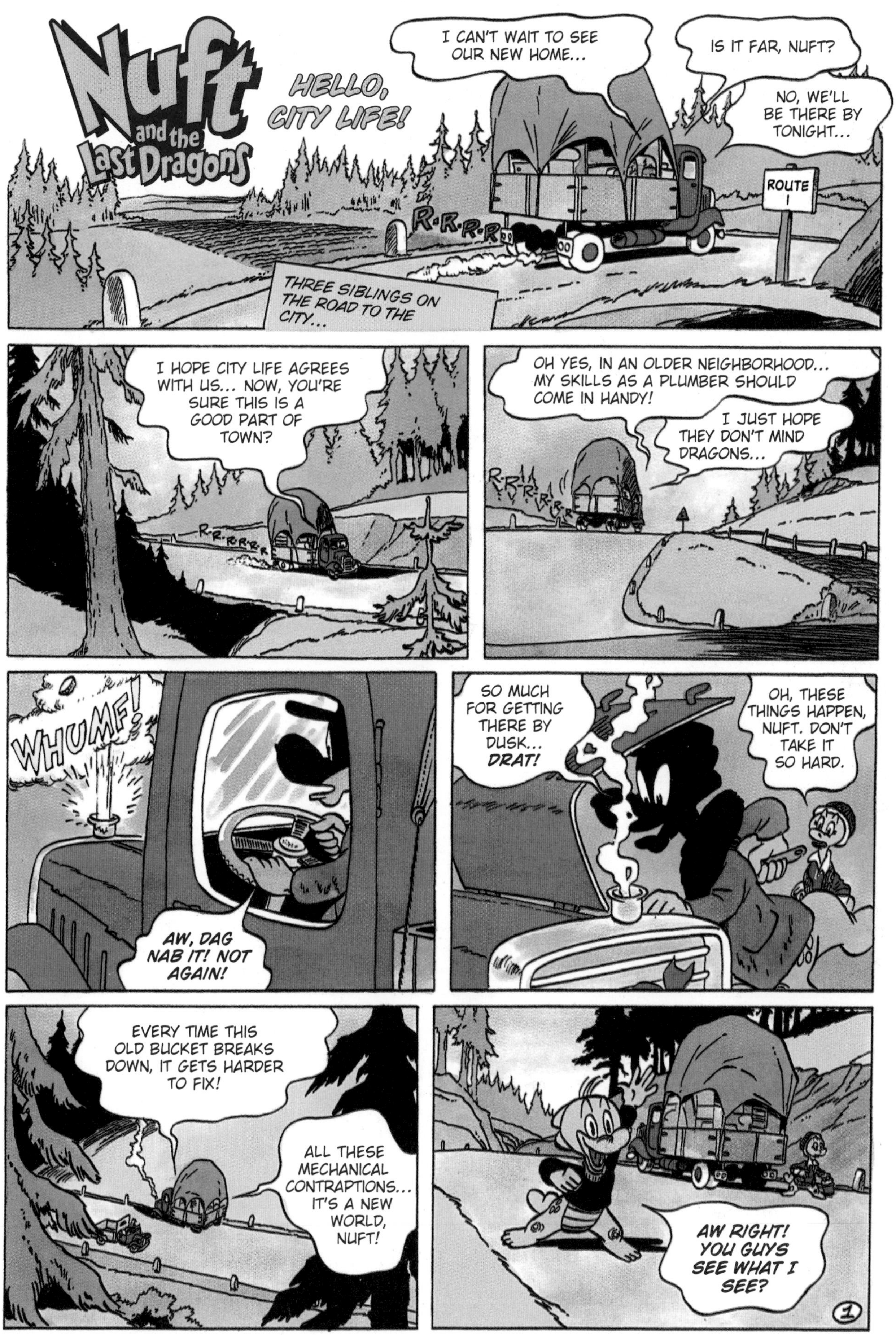
Nuft and the Last Dragons
HELLO, CITY LIFE!
I CAN'T WAIT TO SEE OUR NEW HOME...
IS IT FAR, NUFT?
NO, WE'LL BE THERE BY TONIGHT...
ROUTE 1
R-R-R-R
THREE SIBLINGS ON THE ROAD TO THE CITY...
I HOPE CITY LIFE AGREES WITH US... NOW, YOU'RE SURE THIS IS A GOOD PART OF TOWN?
R-R-R-R-R-R
OH YES, IN AN OLDER NEIGHBORHOOD... MY SKILLS AS A PLUMBER SHOULD COME IN HANDY!
I JUST HOPE THEY DON'T MIND DRAGONS...
WHUMF!
AW, DAG NAB IT! NOT AGAIN!
SO MUCH FOR GETTING THERE BY DUSK... DRAT!
OH, THESE THINGS HAPPEN, NUFT. DON'T TAKE IT SO HARD.
EVERY TIME THIS OLD BUCKET BREAKS DOWN, IT GETS HARDER TO FIX!
ALL THESE MECHANICAL CONTRAPTIONS... IT'S A NEW WORLD, NUFT!
AW RIGHT! YOU GUYS SEE WHAT I SEE?
1

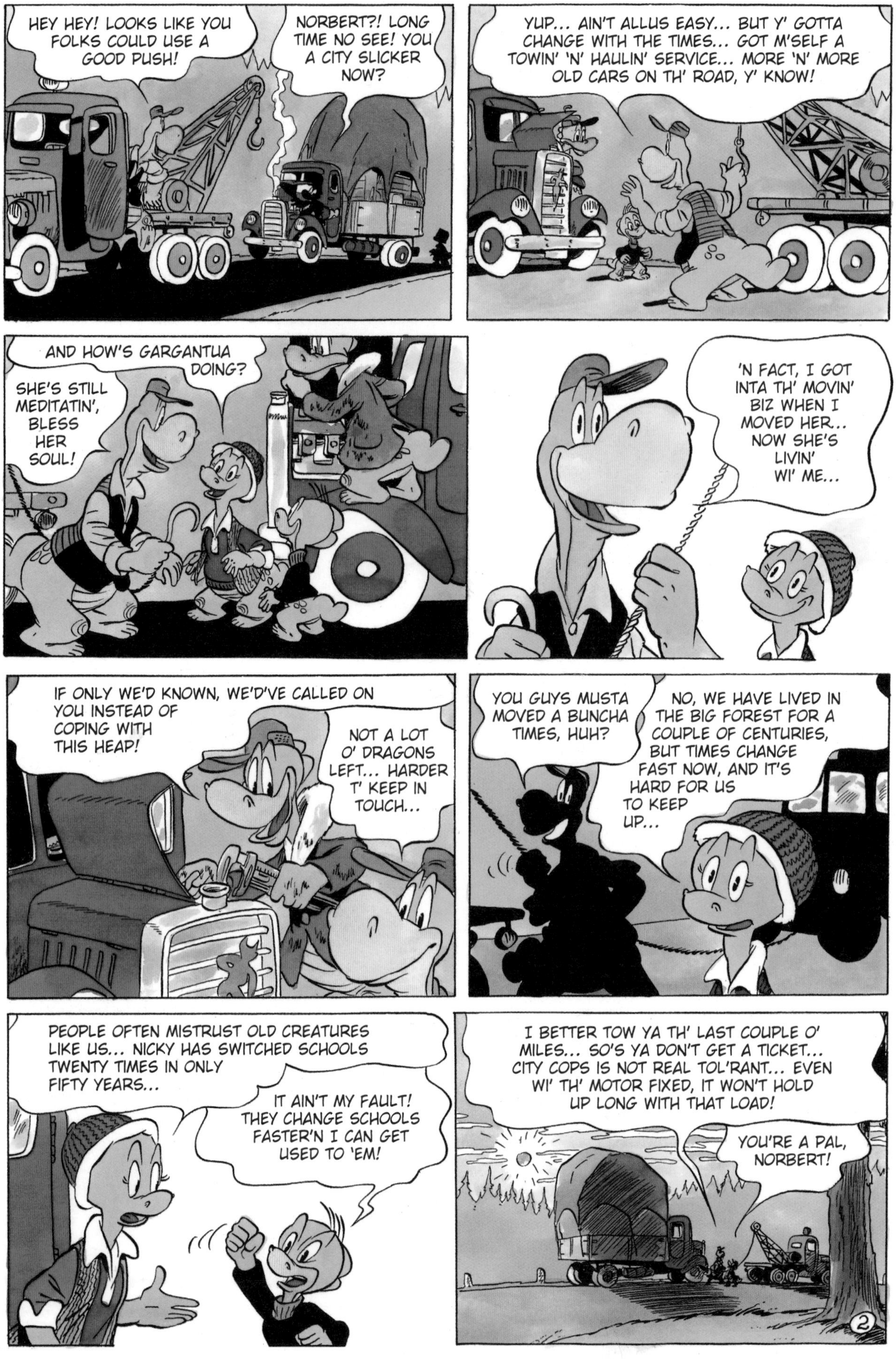
HEY HEY! LOOKS LIKE YOU FOLKS COULD USE A GOOD PUSH!
NORBERT?! LONG TIME NO SEE! YOU A CITY SLICKER NOW?
YUP... AIN'T ALLUS EASY... BUT Y' GOTTA CHANGE WITH THE TIMES... GOT M'SELF A TOWIN' 'N' HAULIN' SERVICE... MORE 'N' MORE OLD CARS ON TH' ROAD, Y' KNOW!
AND HOW'S GARGANTUA DOING?
SHE'S STILL MEDITATIN', BLESS HER SOUL!
'N FACT, I GOT INTA TH' MOVIN' BIZ WHEN I MOVED HER... NOW SHE'S LIVIN' WI' ME...
IF ONLY WE'D KNOWN, WE'D'VE CALLED ON YOU INSTEAD OF COPING WITH THIS HEAP!
NOT A LOT O' DRAGONS LEFT... HARDER T' KEEP IN TOUCH...
YOU GUYS MUSTA MOVED A BUNCHA TIMES, HUH?
NO, WE HAVE LIVED IN THE BIG FOREST FOR A COUPLE OF CENTURIES, BUT TIMES CHANGE FAST NOW, AND IT'S HARD FOR US TO KEEP UP...
PEOPLE OFTEN MISTRUST OLD CREATURES LIKE US... NICKY HAS SWITCHED SCHOOLS TWENTY TIMES IN ONLY FIFTY YEARS...
IT AIN'T MY FAULT! THEY CHANGE SCHOOLS FASTER'N I CAN GET USED TO 'EM!
I BETTER TOW YA TH' LAST COUPLE O' MILES... SO'S YA DON'T GET A TICKET... CITY COPS IS NOT REAL TOL'RANT... EVEN WI' TH' MOTOR FIXED, IT WON'T HOLD UP LONG WITH THAT LOAD!
YOU'RE A PAL, NORBERT!
2

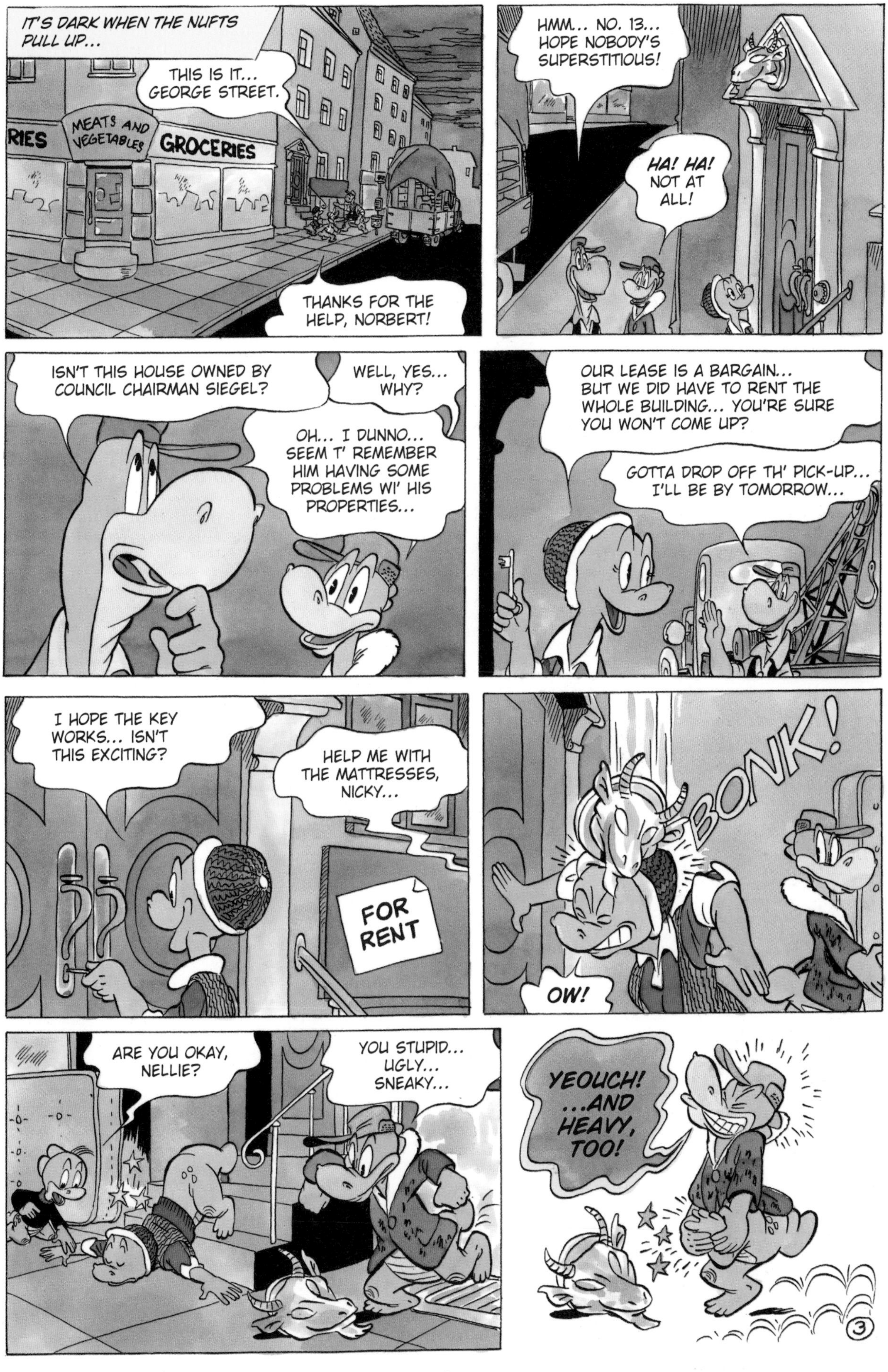
IT'S DARK WHEN THE NUFTS PULL UP...
THIS IS IT... GEORGE STREET.
MEATS AND VEGETABLES
RIES
GROCERIES
THANKS FOR THE HELP, NORBERT!
HMM... NO. 13... HOPE NOBODY'S SUPERSTITIOUS!
HA! HA! NOT AT ALL!
ISN'T THIS HOUSE OWNED BY COUNCIL CHAIRMAN SIEGEL?
WELL, YES... WHY?
OH... I DUNNO... SEEM T' REMEMBER HIM HAVING SOME PROBLEMS WI' HIS PROPERTIES...
OUR LEASE IS A BARGAIN... BUT WE DID HAVE TO RENT THE WHOLE BUILDING... YOU'RE SURE YOU WON'T COME UP?
GOTTA DROP OFF TH' PICK-UP... I'LL BE BY TOMORROW...
I HOPE THE KEY WORKS... ISN'T THIS EXCITING?
HELP ME WITH THE MATTRESSES, NICKY...
FOR RENT
BONK!
OW!
ARE YOU OKAY, NELLIE?
YOU STUPID... UGLY... SNEAKY...
YEOUCH! ...AND HEAVY, TOO!
3

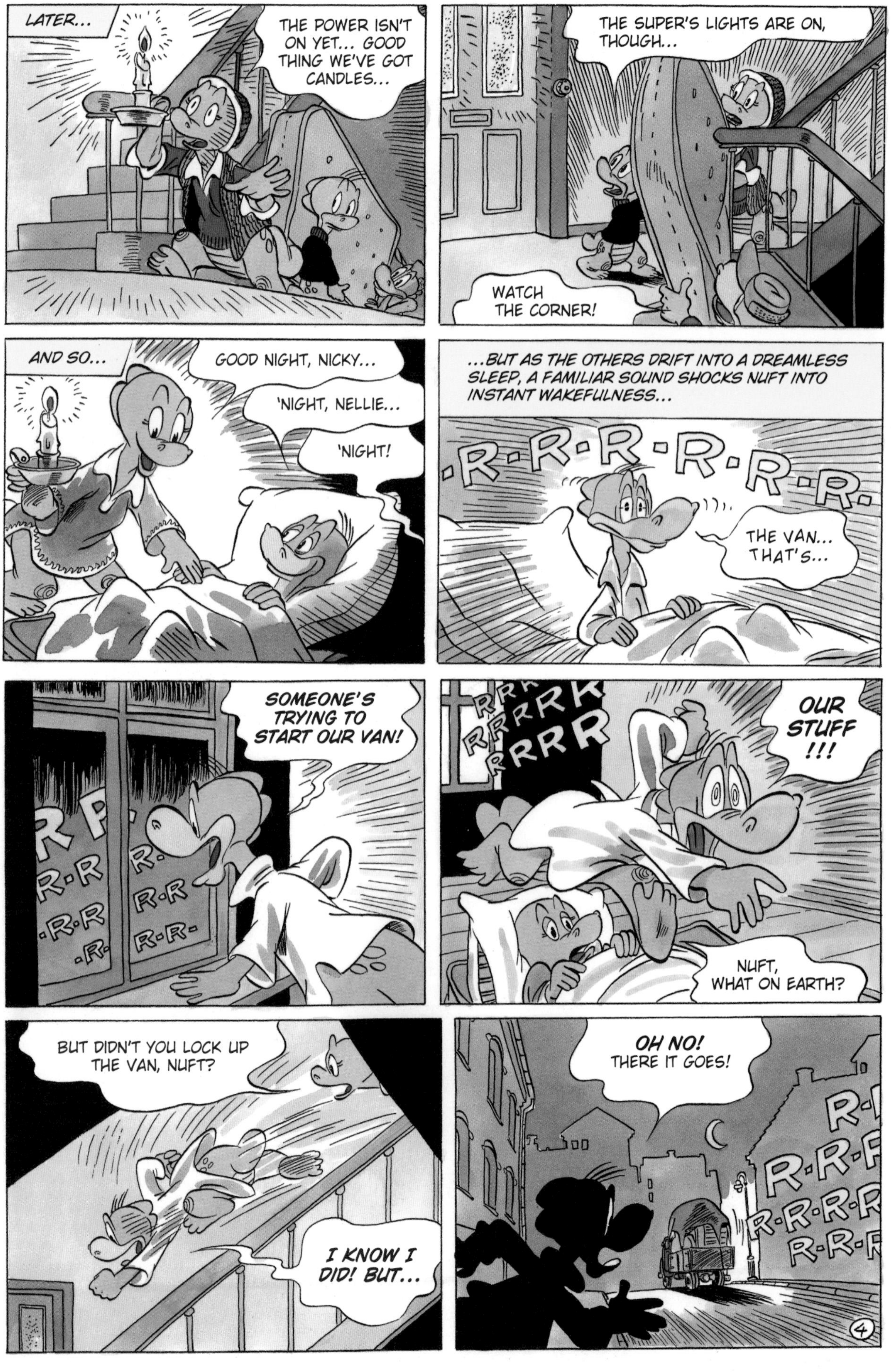
LATER...
THE POWER ISN'T ON YET... GOOD THING WE'VE GOT CANDLES...
THE SUPER'S LIGHTS ARE ON, THOUGH...
WATCH THE CORNER!
AND SO...
GOOD NIGHT, NICKY...
'NIGHT, NELLIE...
'NIGHT!
...BUT AS THE OTHERS DRIFT INTO A DREAMLESS SLEEP, A FAMILIAR SOUND SHOCKS NUFT INTO INSTANT WAKEFULNESS...
-R-R-R-R-R-R-
THE VAN... THAT'S...
SOMEONE'S TRYING TO START OUR VAN!
OUR STUFF !!!
NUFT, WHAT ON EARTH?
BUT DIDN'T YOU LOCK UP THE VAN, NUFT?
I KNOW I DID! BUT...
OH NO! THERE IT GOES!
4

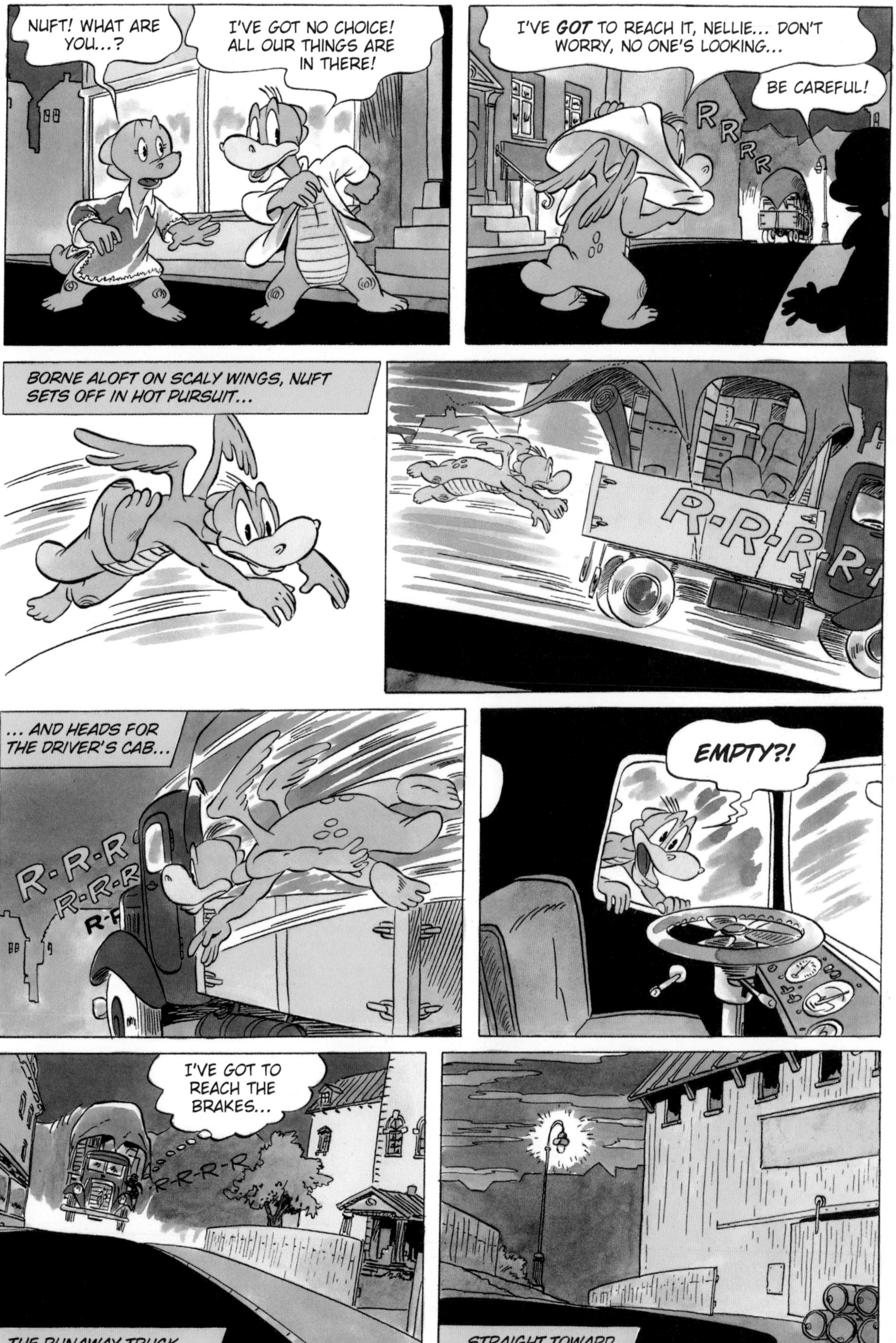
NUFT! WHAT ARE YOU...?
I'VE GOT NO CHOICE! ALL OUR THINGS ARE IN THERE!
I'VE GOT TO REACH IT, NELLIE... DON'T WORRY, NO ONE'S LOOKING...
BE CAREFUL!
RRRRR
BORNE ALOFT ON SCALY WINGS, NUFT SETS OFF IN HOT PURSUIT...
R-R-R-R-R-R
... AND HEADS FOR THE DRIVER'S CAB...
R-R-R
R-R-R
EMPTY?!
I'VE GOT TO REACH THE BRAKES...
R-R-R-R
THE RUNAWAY TRUCK BARRELS DOWN A HILL...
...STRAIGHT TOWARD AN OLD FACTORY!
5

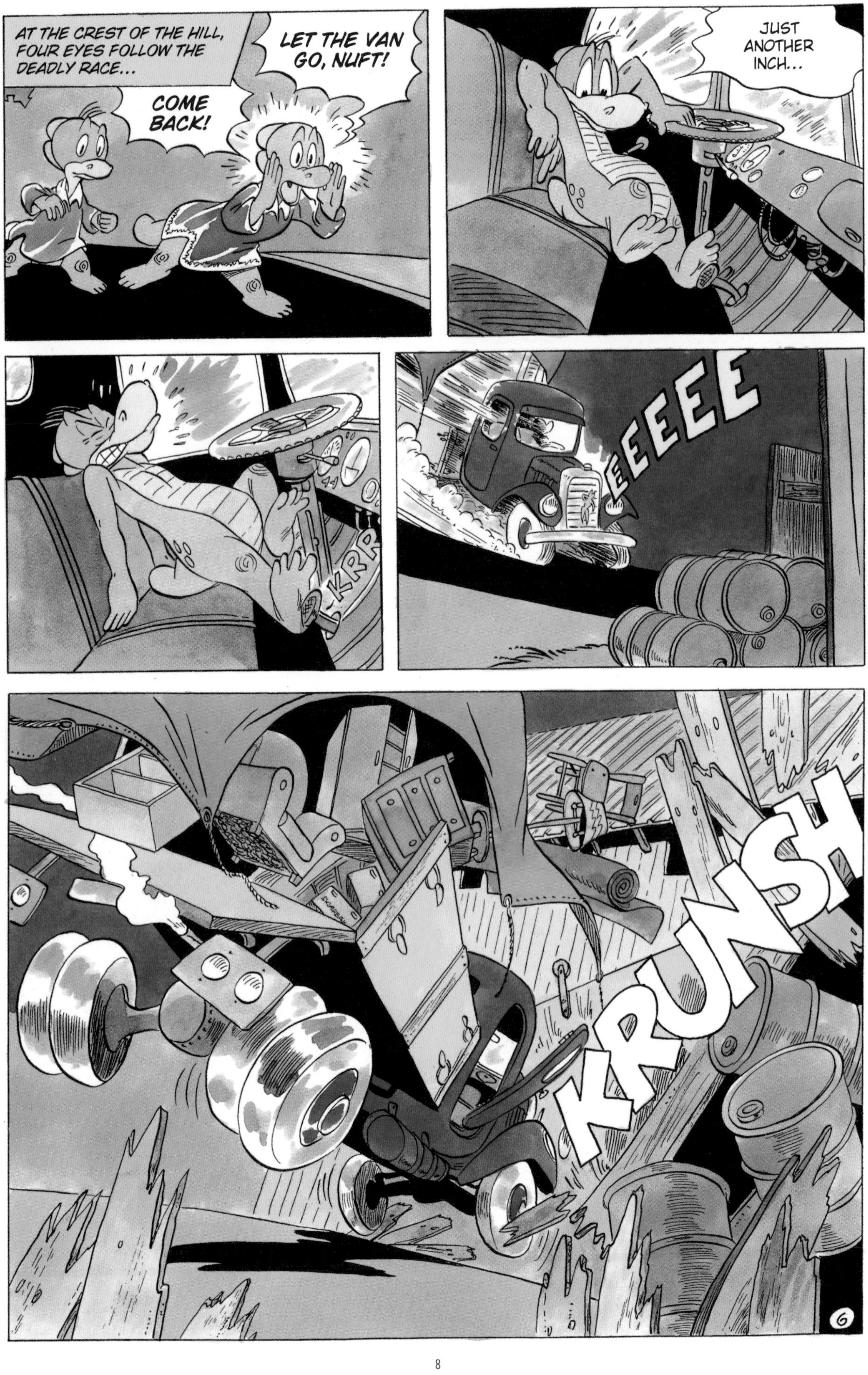
AT THE CREST OF THE HILL, FOUR EYES FOLLOW THE DEADLY RACE...
LET THE VAN GO, NUFT!
COME BACK!
JUST ANOTHER INCH...
KRR
EEEEE
KRUNSH

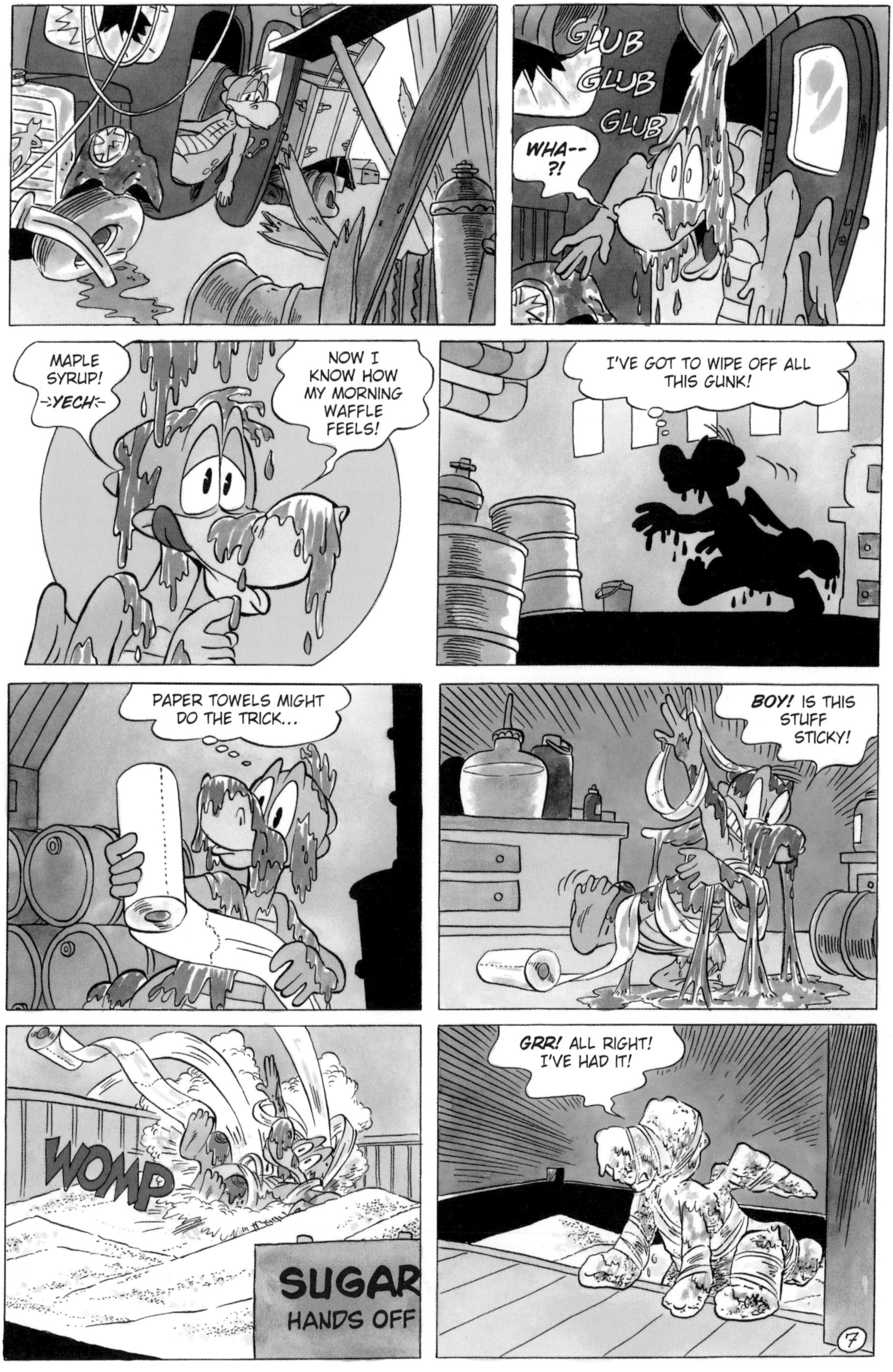
GLUB
GLUB
GLUB
WHA-- ?!
MAPLE SYRUP! -YECH-
NOW I KNOW HOW MY MORNING WAFFLE FEELS!
I'VE GOT TO WIPE OFF ALL THIS GUNK!
PAPER TOWELS MIGHT DO THE TRICK...
BOY! IS THIS STUFF STICKY!
WOMP
SUGAR
HANDS OFF
GRR! ALL RIGHT! I'VE HAD IT!
7

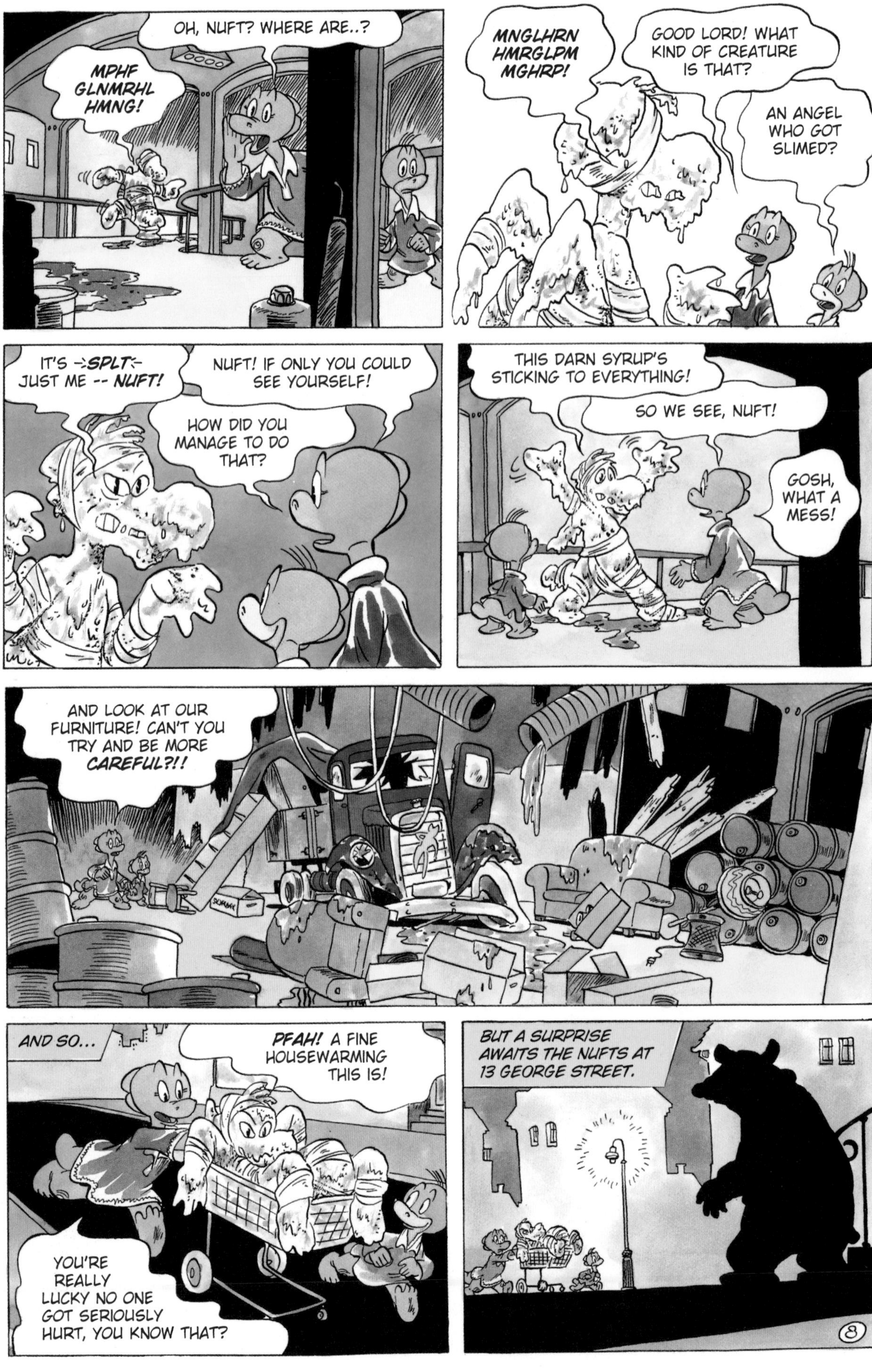
OH, NUFT? WHERE ARE..?
MPHF GLNMRHL HMNG!
MNGLHRN HMRGLPM MGHRP!
GOOD LORD! WHAT KIND OF CREATURE IS THAT?
AN ANGEL WHO GOT SLIMED?
IT'S -›SPLT‹- JUST ME -- NUFT!
NUFT! IF ONLY YOU COULD SEE YOURSELF!
HOW DID YOU MANAGE TO DO THAT?
THIS DARN SYRUP'S STICKING TO EVERYTHING!
SO WE SEE, NUFT!
GOSH, WHAT A MESS!
AND LOOK AT OUR FURNITURE! CAN'T YOU TRY AND BE MORE CAREFUL?!!
AND SO...
PFAH! A FINE HOUSEWARMING THIS IS!
YOU'RE REALLY LUCKY NO ONE GOT SERIOUSLY HURT, YOU KNOW THAT?
BUT A SURPRISE AWAITS THE NUFTS AT 13 GEORGE STREET.
8

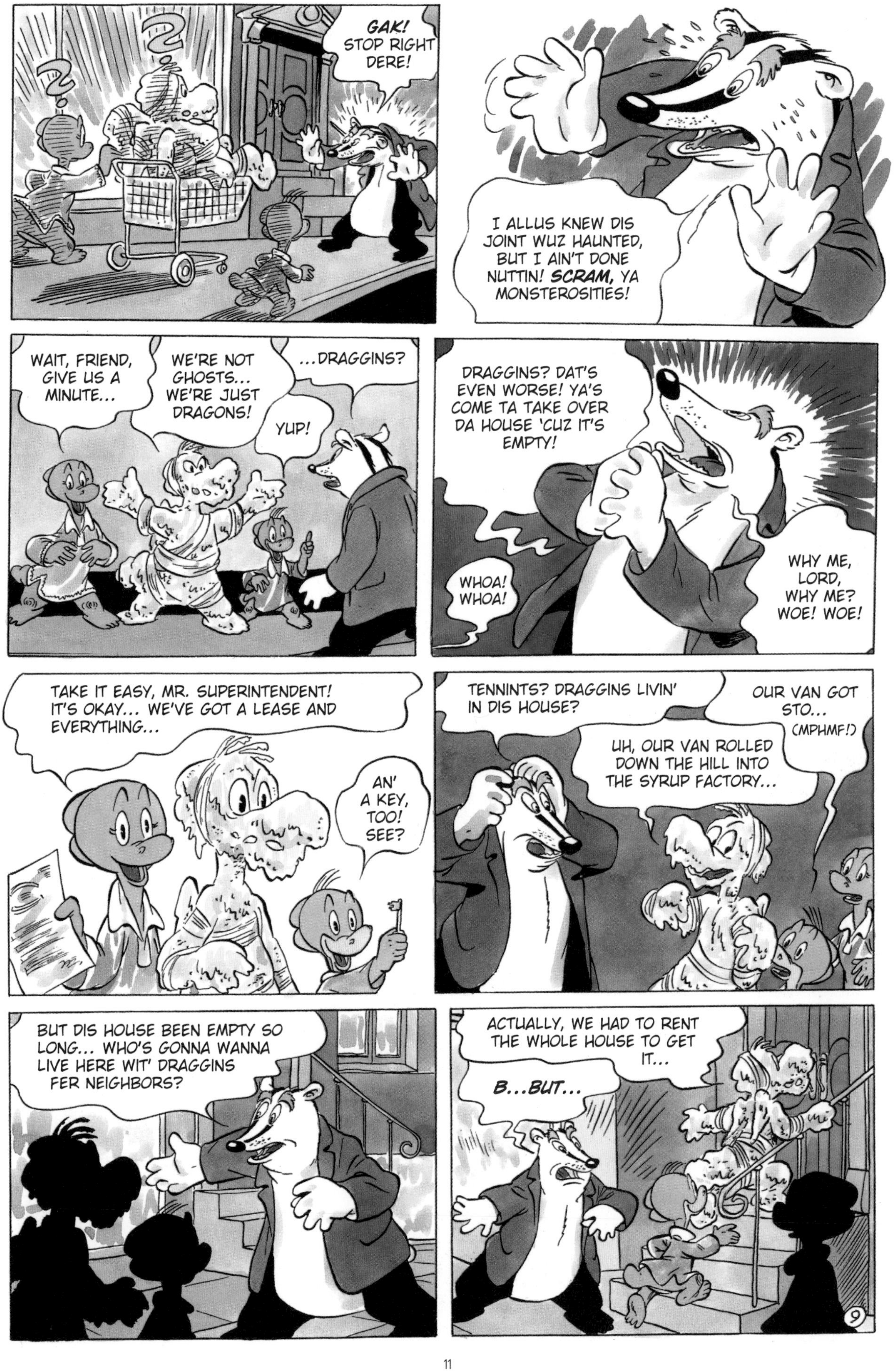
GAK! STOP RIGHT DERE!
I ALLUS KNEW DIS JOINT WUZ HAUNTED, BUT I AIN'T DONE NUTTIN! SCRAM, YA MONSTEROSITIES!
WAIT, FRIEND, GIVE US A MINUTE...
WE'RE NOT GHOSTS... WE'RE JUST DRAGONS!
...DRAGGINS?
YUP!
DRAGGINS? DAT'S EVEN WORSE! YA'S COME TA TAKE OVER DA HOUSE 'CUZ IT'S EMPTY!
WHOA! WHOA!
WHY ME, LORD, WHY ME? WOE! WOE!
TAKE IT EASY, MR. SUPERINTENDENT! IT'S OKAY... WE'VE GOT A LEASE AND EVERYTHING...
AN' A KEY, TOO! SEE?
TENNINTS? DRAGGINS LIVIN' IN DIS HOUSE?
OUR VAN GOT STO...
(MPHMF!)
UH, OUR VAN ROLLED DOWN THE HILL INTO THE SYRUP FACTORY...
BUT DIS HOUSE BEEN EMPTY SO LONG... WHO'S GONNA WANNA LIVE HERE WIT' DRAGGINS FER NEIGHBORS?
ACTUALLY, WE HAD TO RENT THE WHOLE HOUSE TO GET IT...
B...BUT...
9

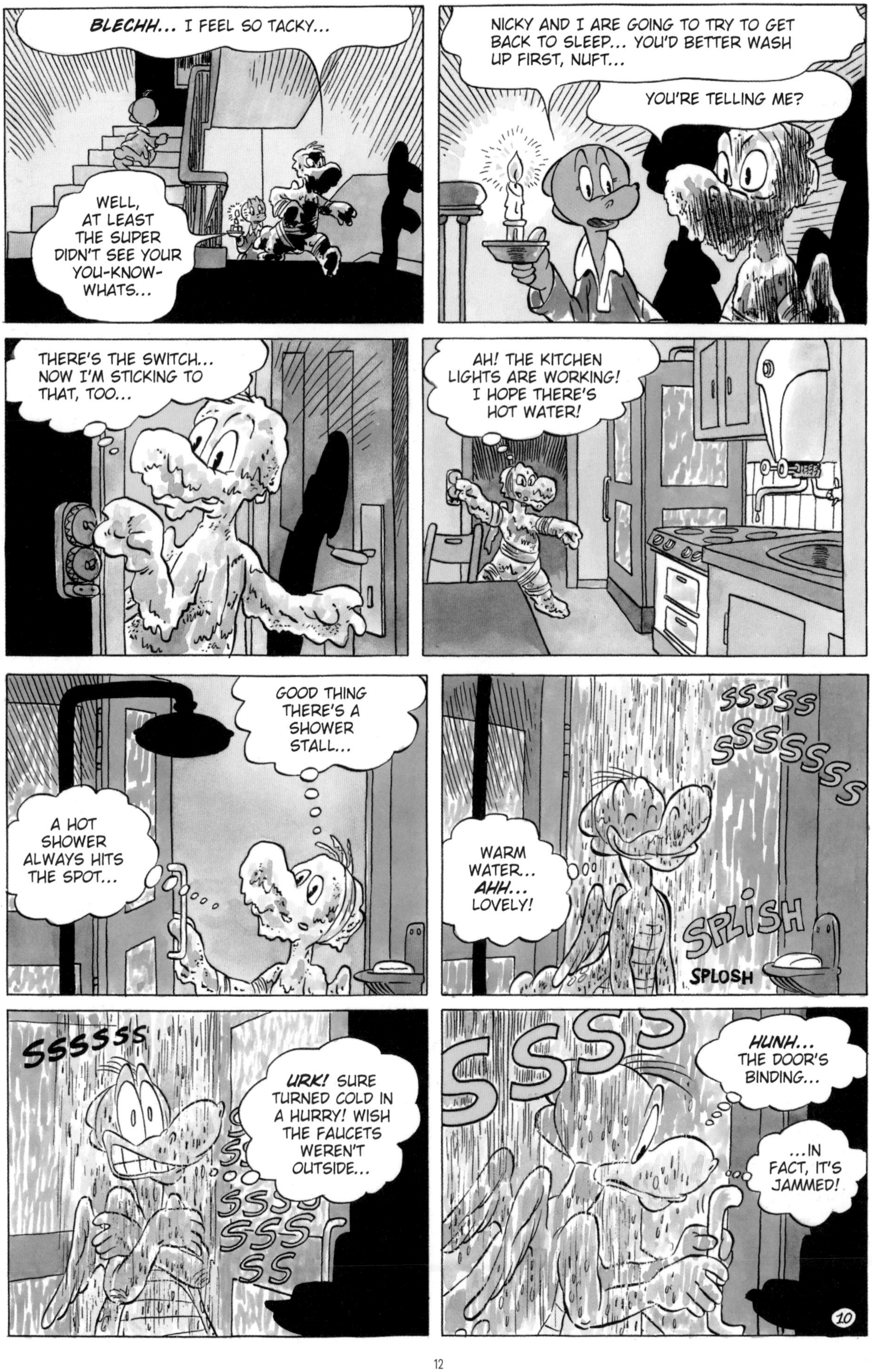
BLECHH... I FEEL SO TACKY...
WELL, AT LEAST THE SUPER DIDN'T SEE YOUR YOU-KNOW-WHATS...
NICKY AND I ARE GOING TO TRY TO GET BACK TO SLEEP... YOU'D BETTER WASH UP FIRST, NUFT...
YOU'RE TELLING ME?
THERE'S THE SWITCH... NOW I'M STICKING TO THAT, TOO...
AH! THE KITCHEN LIGHTS ARE WORKING! I HOPE THERE'S HOT WATER!
GOOD THING THERE'S A SHOWER STALL...
A HOT SHOWER ALWAYS HITS THE SPOT...
SSSSS SSSSSSSS
WARM WATER... AHH... LOVELY!
SPLISH
SPLOSH
SSSSSS
URK! SURE TURNED COLD IN A HURRY! WISH THE FAUCETS WEREN'T OUTSIDE...
SSSSSSSSS
SSSS
HUNH... THE DOOR'S BINDING...
...IN FACT, IT'S JAMMED!
10

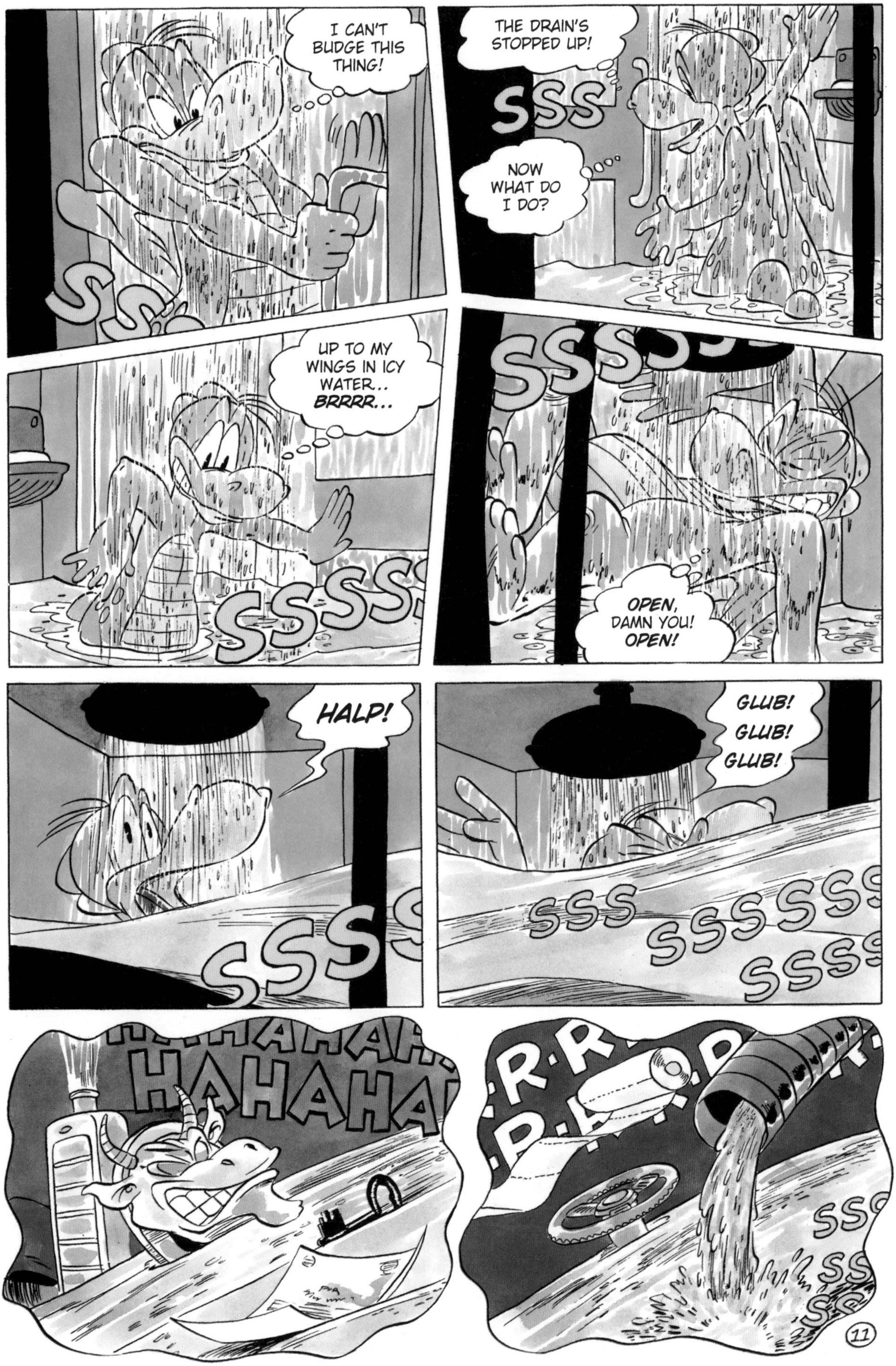
I CAN'T BUDGE THIS THING!
SSS
THE DRAIN'S STOPPED UP!
SSS
NOW WHAT DO I DO?
UP TO MY WINGS IN ICY WATER... BRRRR...
SSSSS
SSSSS
OPEN, DAMN YOU! OPEN!
HALP!
SSS
GLUB! GLUB! GLUB!
SSS
SSSSSS
SSSSS
SSSS
HAHAHAH
HAHAHAH
SSS

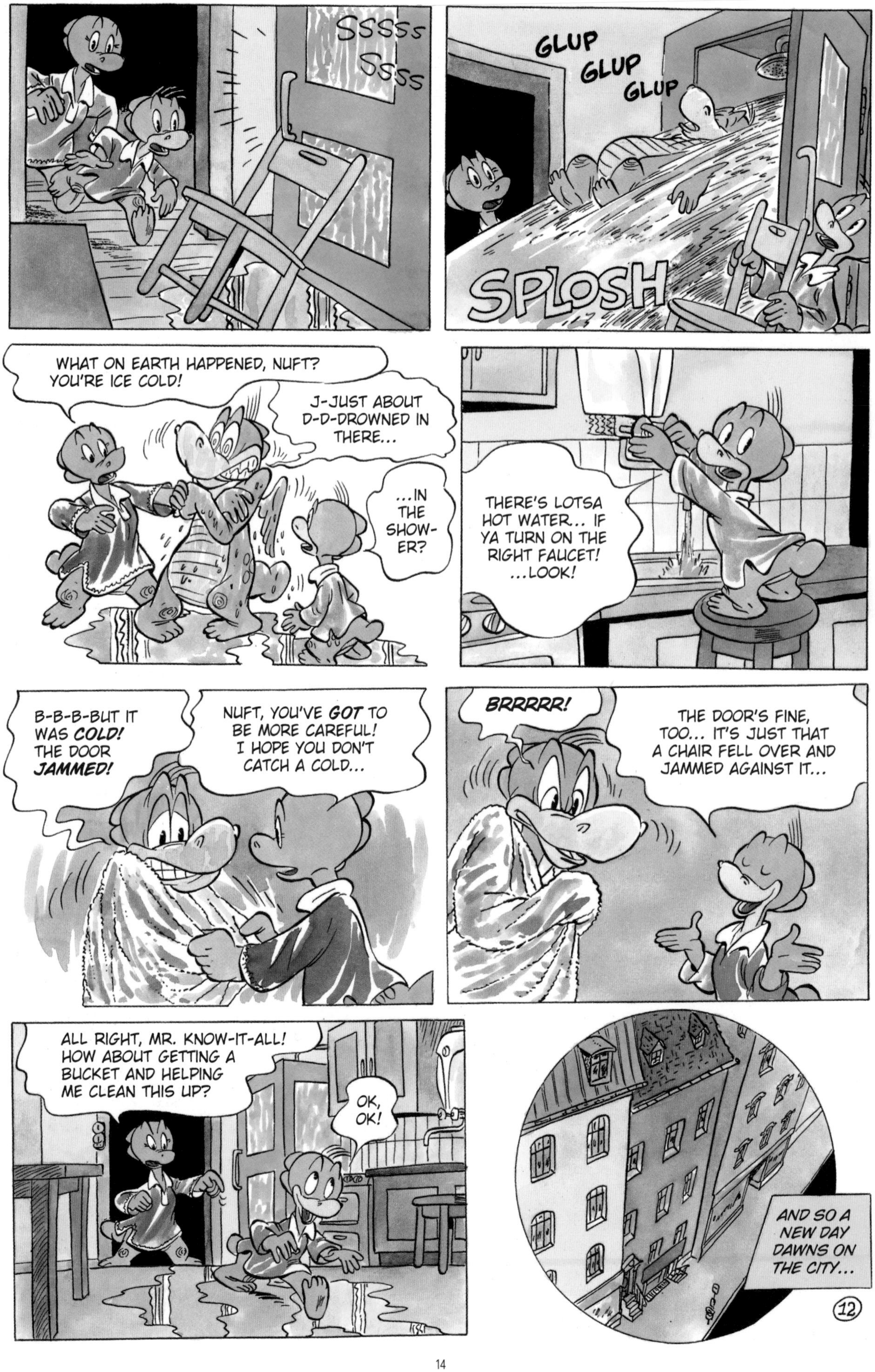
SSSSS
SSSS
GLUP
GLUP
GLUP
SPLOSH
WHAT ON EARTH HAPPENED, NUFT? YOU'RE ICE COLD!
J-JUST ABOUT D-D-DROWNED IN THERE...
...IN THE SHOW-ER?
THERE'S LOTSA HOT WATER... IF YA TURN ON THE RIGHT FAUCET! ...LOOK!
B-B-B-BUT IT WAS COLD! THE DOOR JAMMED!
NUFT, YOU'VE GOT TO BE MORE CAREFUL! I HOPE YOU DON'T CATCH A COLD...
BRRRRR!
THE DOOR'S FINE, TOO... IT'S JUST THAT A CHAIR FELL OVER AND JAMMED AGAINST IT...
ALL RIGHT, MR. KNOW-IT-ALL! HOW ABOUT GETTING A BUCKET AND HELPING ME CLEAN THIS UP?
OK, OK!
AND SO A NEW DAY DAWNS ON THE CITY...
12

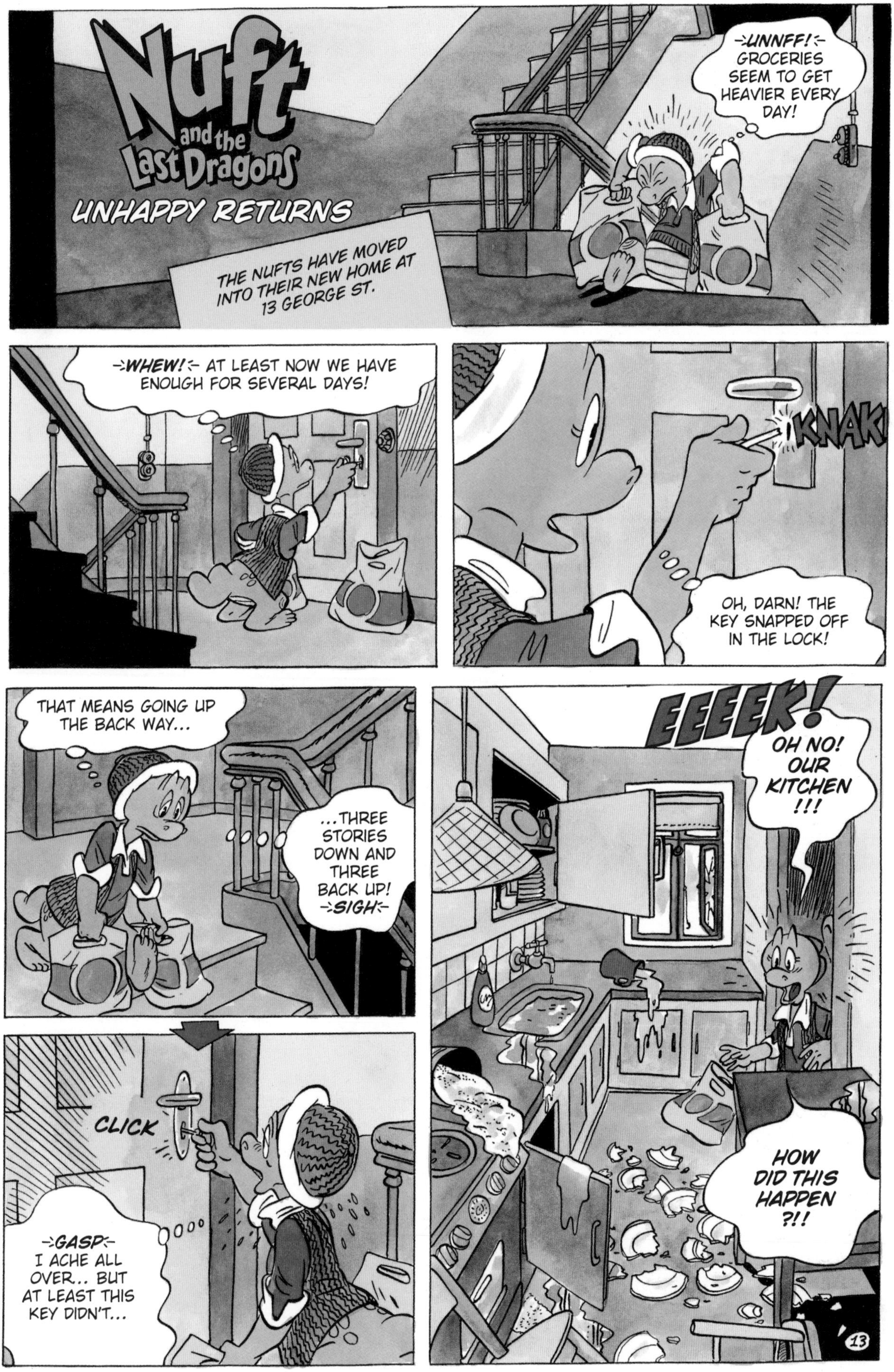
Nuft and the Last Dragons
UNHAPPY RETURNS
-UNNFF!- GROCERIES SEEM TO GET HEAVIER EVERY DAY!
THE NUFTS HAVE MOVED INTO THEIR NEW HOME AT 13 GEORGE ST.
-WHEW!- AT LEAST NOW WE HAVE ENOUGH FOR SEVERAL DAYS!
KNAK!
OH, DARN! THE KEY SNAPPED OFF IN THE LOCK!
THAT MEANS GOING UP THE BACK WAY...
...THREE STORIES DOWN AND THREE BACK UP! -SIGH-
CLICK
-GASP- I ACHE ALL OVER... BUT AT LEAST THIS KEY DIDN'T...
EEEEK!
OH NO! OUR KITCHEN !!!
HOW DID THIS HAPPEN ?!!
13

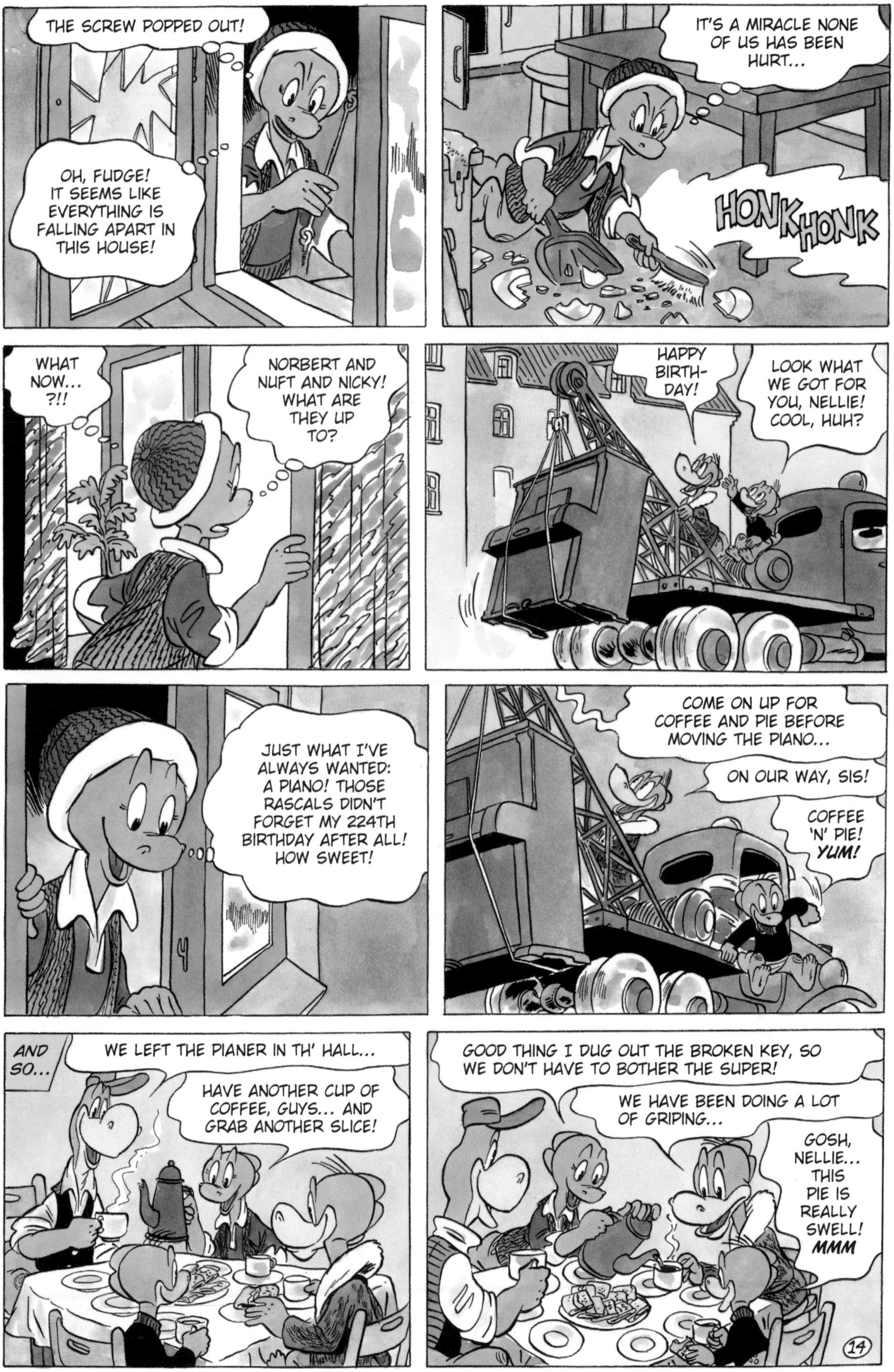
THE SCREW POPPED OUT!
OH, FUDGE! IT SEEMS LIKE EVERYTHING IS FALLING APART IN THIS HOUSE!
IT'S A MIRACLE NONE OF US HAS BEEN HURT...
HONK HONK
WHAT NOW... ?!!
NORBERT AND NUFT AND NICKY! WHAT ARE THEY UP TO?
HAPPY BIRTH-DAY!
LOOK WHAT WE GOT FOR YOU, NELLIE! COOL, HUH?
JUST WHAT I'VE ALWAYS WANTED: A PIANO! THOSE RASCALS DIDN'T FORGET MY 224TH BIRTHDAY AFTER ALL! HOW SWEET!
COME ON UP FOR COFFEE AND PIE BEFORE MOVING THE PIANO...
ON OUR WAY, SIS!
COFFEE 'N' PIE! YUM!
AND SO...
WE LEFT THE PIANER IN TH' HALL...
HAVE ANOTHER CUP OF COFFEE, GUYS... AND GRAB ANOTHER SLICE!
GOOD THING I DUG OUT THE BROKEN KEY, SO WE DON'T HAVE TO BOTHER THE SUPER!
WE HAVE BEEN DOING A LOT OF GRIPING...
GOSH, NELLIE... THIS PIE IS REALLY SWELL! MMM
14

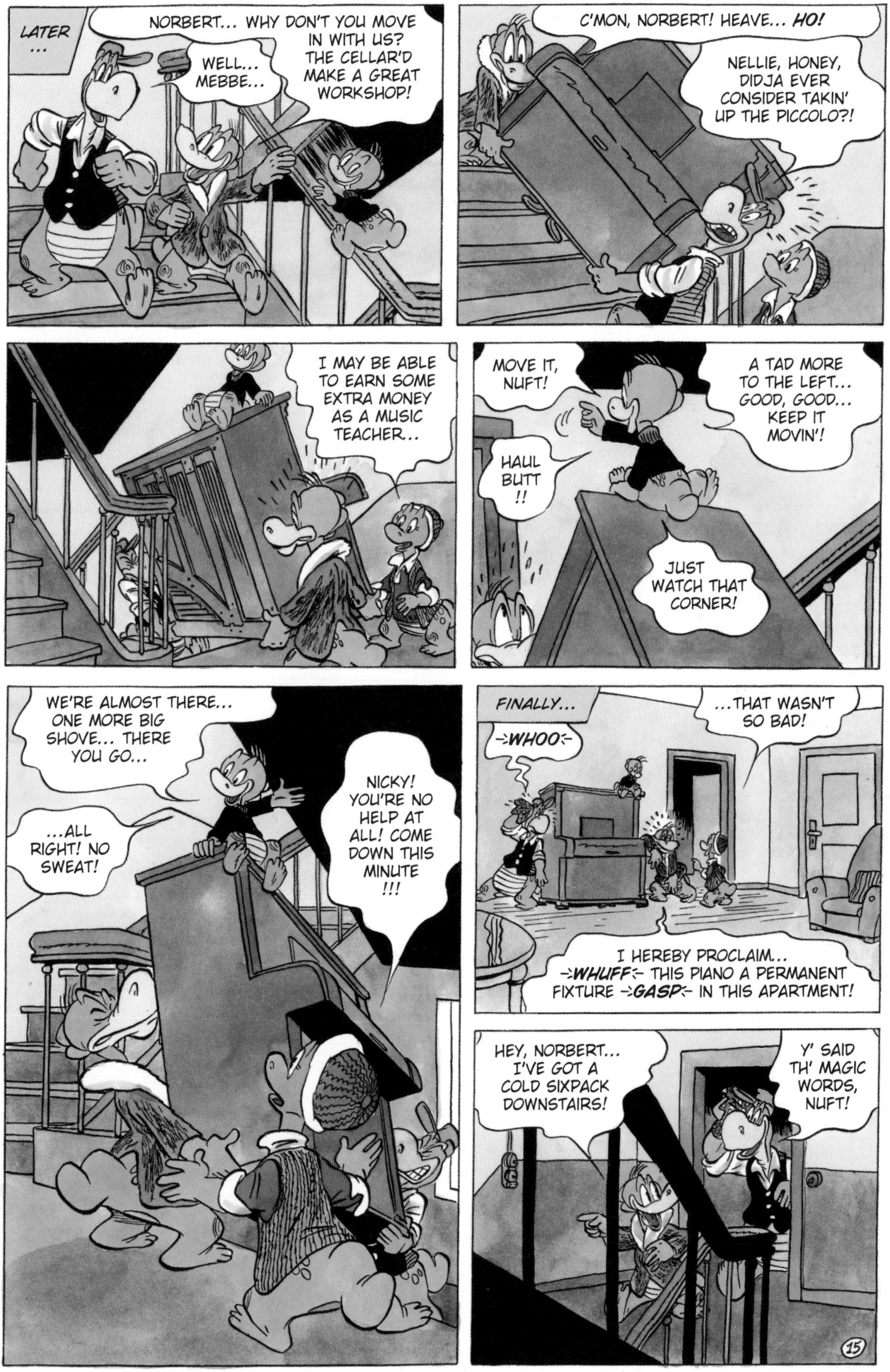
LATER...
NORBERT... WHY DON'T YOU MOVE IN WITH US? THE CELLAR'D MAKE A GREAT WORKSHOP!
WELL... MEBBE...
C'MON, NORBERT! HEAVE... HO!
NELLIE, HONEY, DIDJA EVER CONSIDER TAKIN' UP THE PICCOLO?!
I MAY BE ABLE TO EARN SOME EXTRA MONEY AS A MUSIC TEACHER...
MOVE IT, NUFT!
A TAD MORE TO THE LEFT... GOOD, GOOD... KEEP IT MOVIN'!
HAUL BUTT !!
JUST WATCH THAT CORNER!
WE'RE ALMOST THERE... ONE MORE BIG SHOVE... THERE YOU GO...
...ALL RIGHT! NO SWEAT!
NICKY! YOU'RE NO HELP AT ALL! COME DOWN THIS MINUTE !!!
FINALLY...
-WHOO-
...THAT WASN'T SO BAD!
I HEREBY PROCLAIM... -WHUFF- THIS PIANO A PERMANENT FIXTURE -GASP- IN THIS APARTMENT!
HEY, NORBERT... I'VE GOT A COLD SIXPACK DOWNSTAIRS!
Y' SAID TH' MAGIC WORDS, NUFT!
15

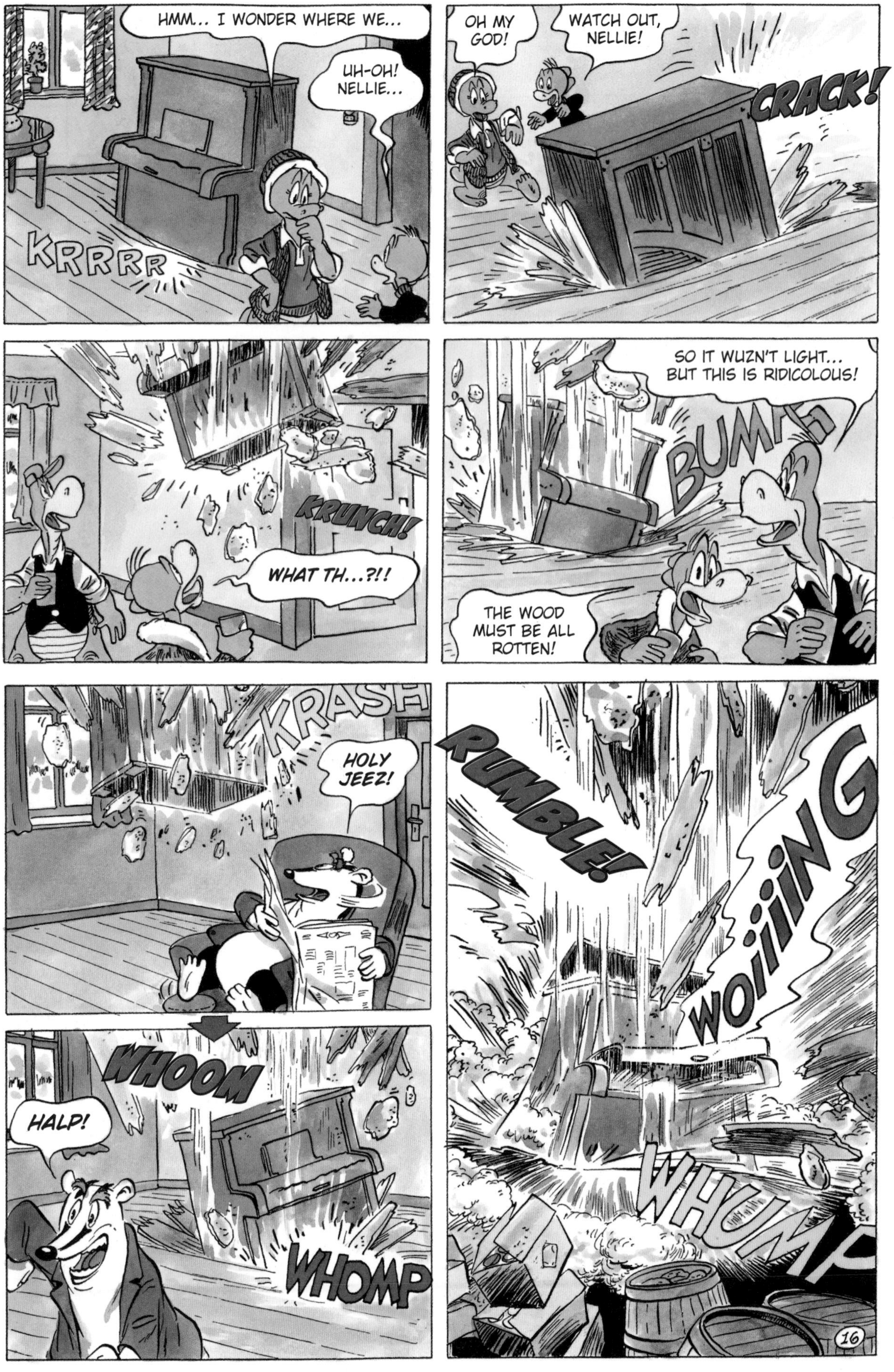
HMM... I WONDER WHERE WE...
UH-OH! NELLIE...
KRRRRR
OH MY GOD!
WATCH OUT, NELLIE!
CRACK!
KRUNCH!
WHAT TH...?!!
SO IT WUZN'T LIGHT... BUT THIS IS RIDICOLOUS!
BUMP
THE WOOD MUST BE ALL ROTTEN!
KRASH
HOLY JEEZ!
WHOOM
HALP!
WHOMP
RUMBLE!
WOiiiiNG
WHUMP
16

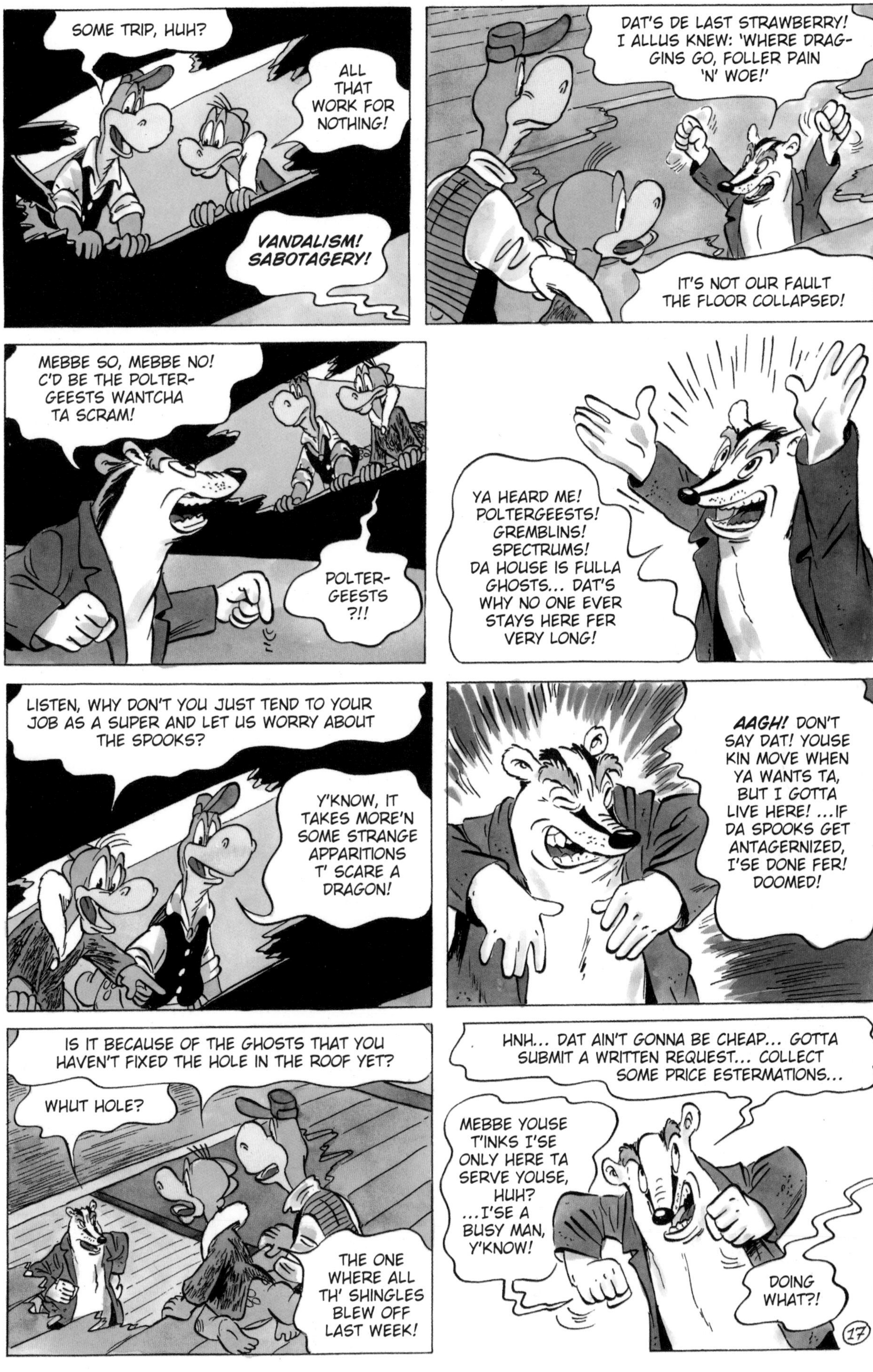
SOME TRIP, HUH?
ALL THAT WORK FOR NOTHING!
VANDALISM! SABOTAGERY!
DAT'S DE LAST STRAWBERRY! I ALLUS KNEW: 'WHERE DRAGGINS GO, FOLLER PAIN 'N' WOE!'
IT'S NOT OUR FAULT THE FLOOR COLLAPSED!
MEBBE SO, MEBBE NO! C'D BE THE POLTERGEESTS WANTCHA TA SCRAM!
POLTERGEESTS ?!!
YA HEARD ME! POLTERGEESTS! GREMBLINS! SPECTRUMS! DA HOUSE IS FULLA GHOSTS... DAT'S WHY NO ONE EVER STAYS HERE FER VERY LONG!
LISTEN, WHY DON'T YOU JUST TEND TO YOUR JOB AS A SUPER AND LET US WORRY ABOUT THE SPOOKS?
Y'KNOW, IT TAKES MORE'N SOME STRANGE APPARITIONS T' SCARE A DRAGON!
AAGH! DON'T SAY DAT! YOUSE KIN MOVE WHEN YA WANTS TA, BUT I GOTTA LIVE HERE! ...IF DA SPOOKS GET ANTAGERNIZED, I'SE DONE FER! DOOMED!
IS IT BECAUSE OF THE GHOSTS THAT YOU HAVEN'T FIXED THE HOLE IN THE ROOF YET?
WHUT HOLE?
THE ONE WHERE ALL TH' SHINGLES BLEW OFF LAST WEEK!
HNH... DAT AIN'T GONNA BE CHEAP... GOTTA SUBMIT A WRITTEN REQUEST... COLLECT SOME PRICE ESTERMATIONS...
MEBBE YOUSE T'INKS I'SE ONLY HERE TA SERVE YOUSE, HUH? ...I'SE A BUSY MAN, Y'KNOW!
DOING WHAT?!
17

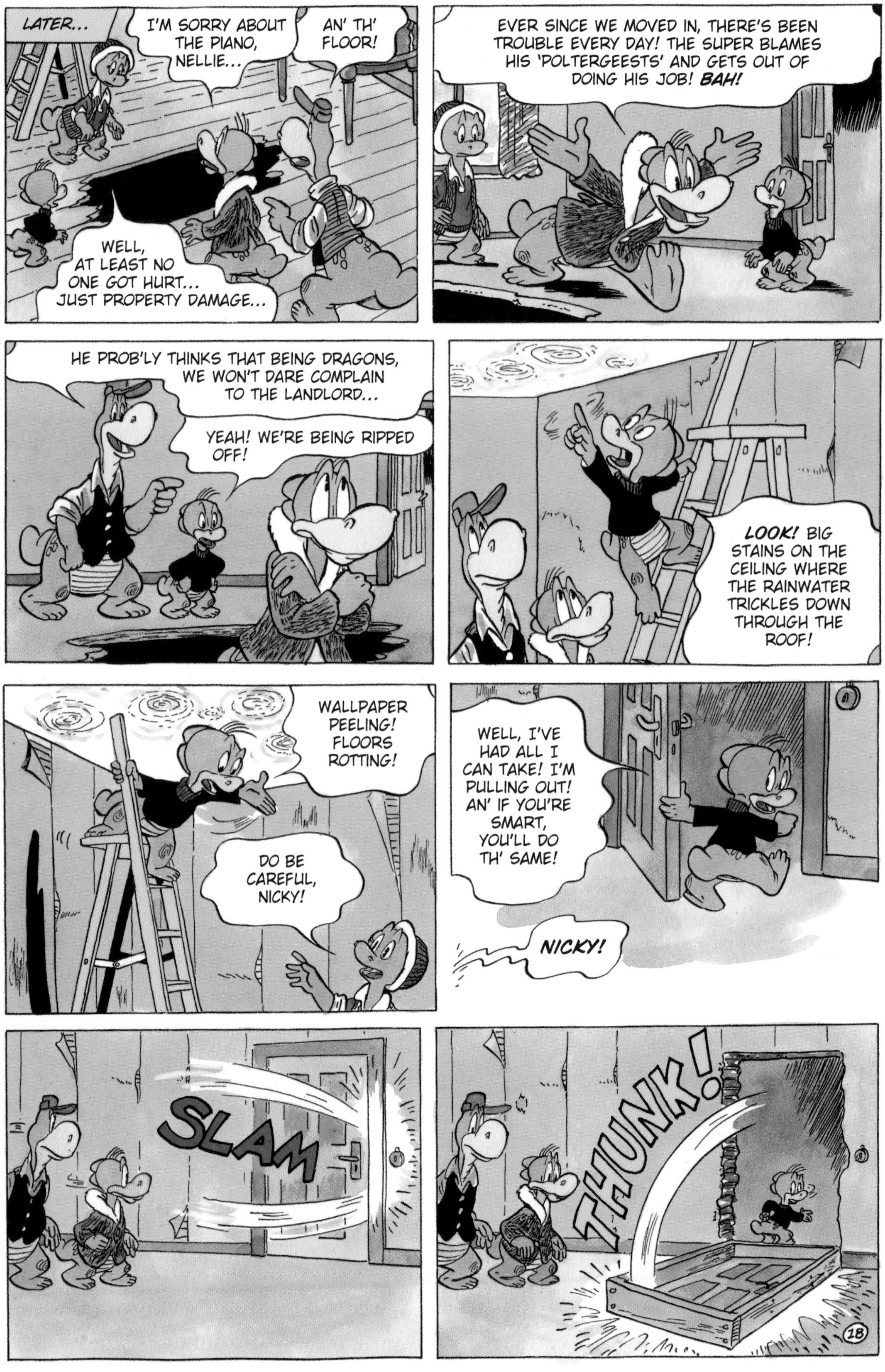
LATER...
I'M SORRY ABOUT THE PIANO, NELLIE...
AN' TH' FLOOR!
WELL, AT LEAST NO ONE GOT HURT... JUST PROPERTY DAMAGE...
EVER SINCE WE MOVED IN, THERE'S BEEN TROUBLE EVERY DAY! THE SUPER BLAMES HIS 'POLTERGEESTS' AND GETS OUT OF DOING HIS JOB! BAH!
HE PROB'LY THINKS THAT BEING DRAGONS, WE WON'T DARE COMPLAIN TO THE LANDLORD...
YEAH! WE'RE BEING RIPPED OFF!
LOOK! BIG STAINS ON THE CEILING WHERE THE RAINWATER TRICKLES DOWN THROUGH THE ROOF!
WALLPAPER PEELING! FLOORS ROTTING!
DO BE CAREFUL, NICKY!
WELL, I'VE HAD ALL I CAN TAKE! I'M PULLING OUT! AN' IF YOU'RE SMART, YOU'LL DO TH' SAME!
NICKY!
SLAM
THUNK!
18

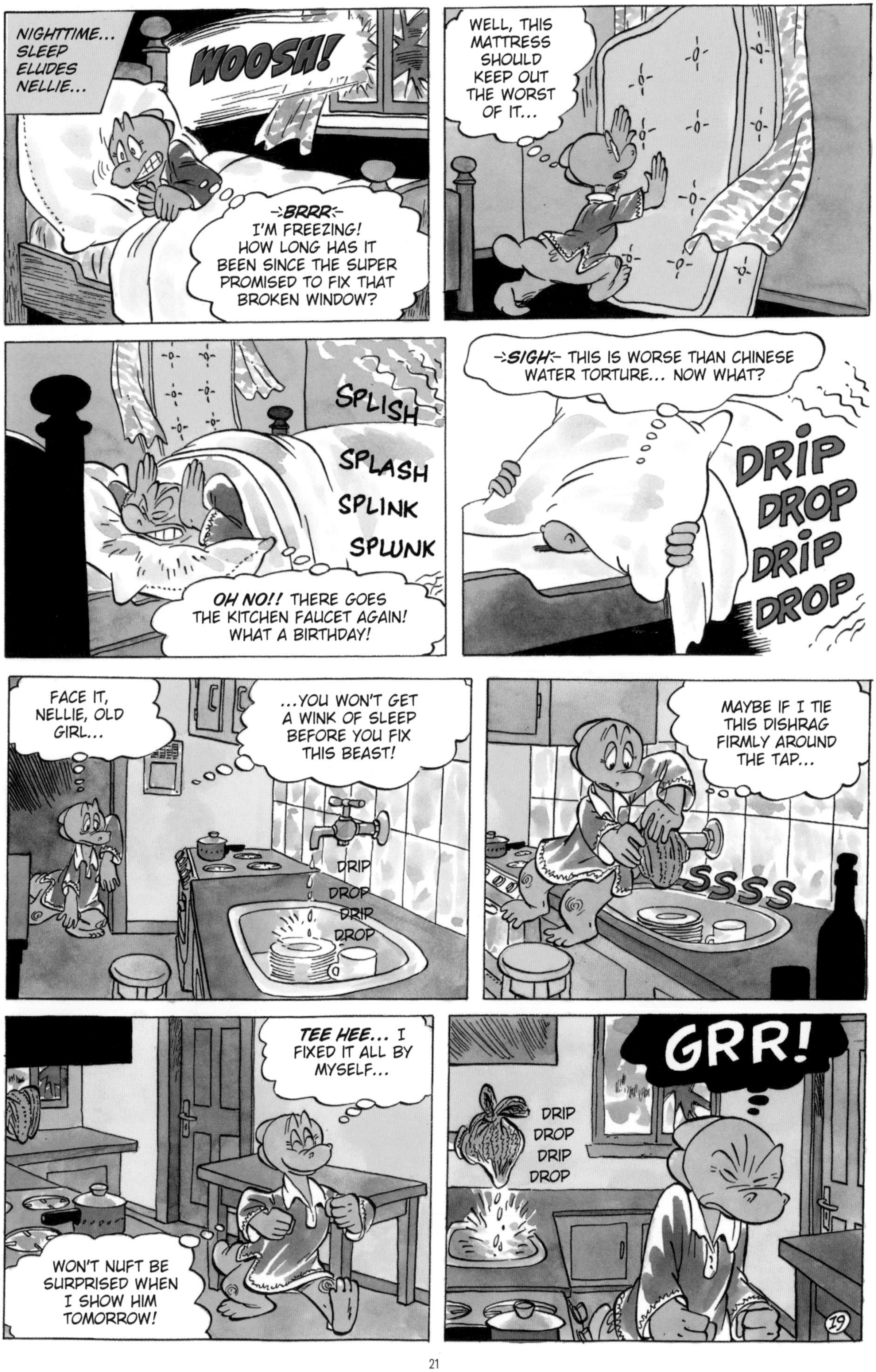
NIGHTTIME... SLEEP ELUDES NELLIE...
WOOSH!
BRRR
I'M FREEZING! HOW LONG HAS IT BEEN SINCE THE SUPER PROMISED TO FIX THAT BROKEN WINDOW?
WELL, THIS MATTRESS SHOULD KEEP OUT THE WORST OF IT...
SPLISH
SPLASH
SPLINK
SPLUNK
OH NO!! THERE GOES THE KITCHEN FAUCET AGAIN! WHAT A BIRTHDAY!
SIGH THIS IS WORSE THAN CHINESE WATER TORTURE... NOW WHAT?
DRIP
DROP
DRIP
DROP
FACE IT, NELLIE, OLD GIRL...
...YOU WON'T GET A WINK OF SLEEP BEFORE YOU FIX THIS BEAST!
DRIP
DROP
DRIP
DROP
MAYBE IF I TIE THIS DISHRAG FIRMLY AROUND THE TAP...
SSSS
TEE HEE... I FIXED IT ALL BY MYSELF...
WON'T NUFT BE SURPRISED WHEN I SHOW HIM TOMORROW!
GRR!
DRIP
DROP
DRIP
DROP
19

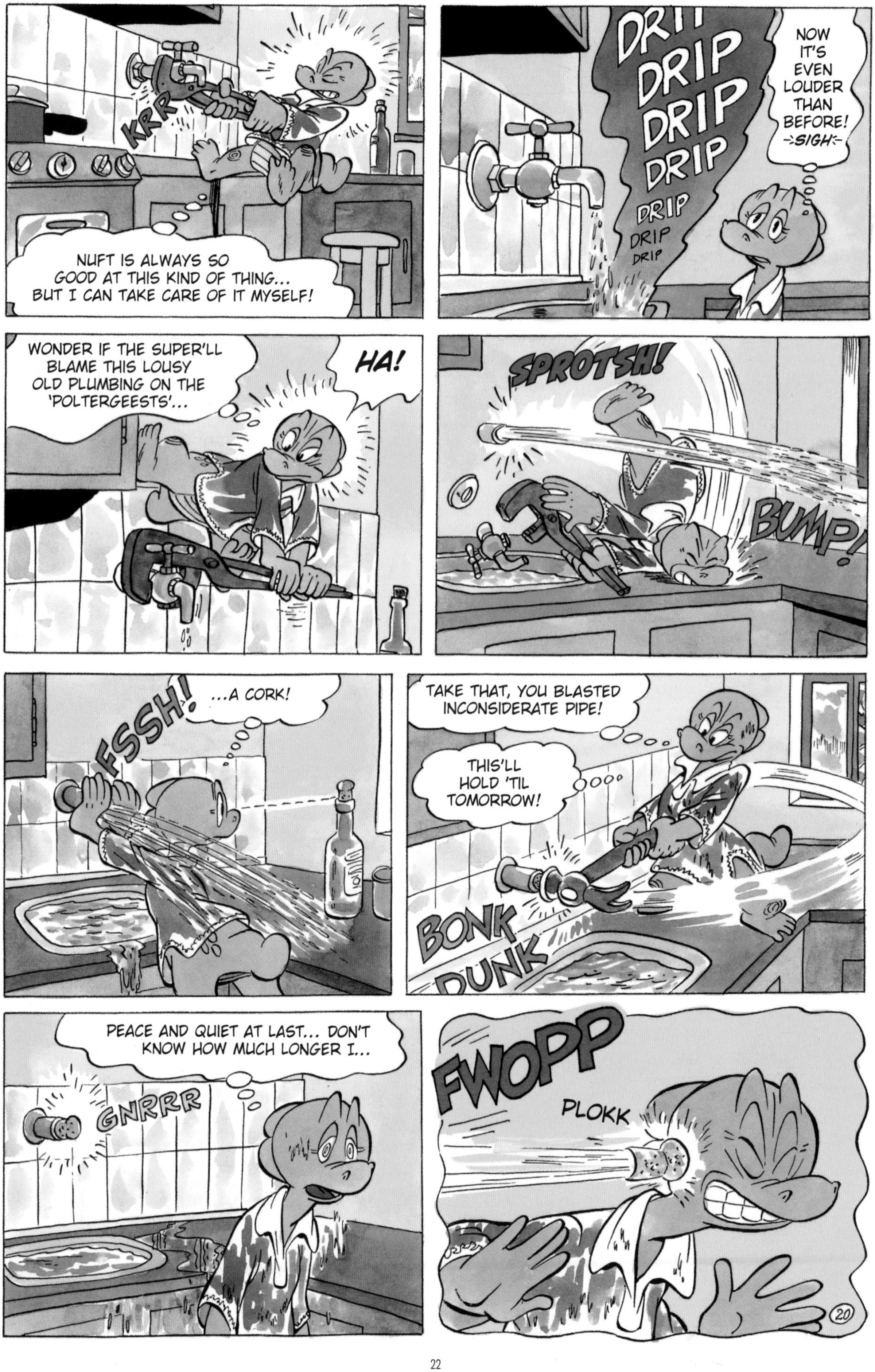
KRR
NUFT IS ALWAYS SO GOOD AT THIS KIND OF THING... BUT I CAN TAKE CARE OF IT MYSELF!
DRIP DRIP DRIP DRIP DRIP DRIP DRIP
NOW IT'S EVEN LOUDER THAN BEFORE! -SIGH-
WONDER IF THE SUPER'LL BLAME THIS LOUSY OLD PLUMBING ON THE 'POLTERGEESTS'...
HA!
SPROTSH!
BUMP!
FSSH!
...A CORK!
TAKE THAT, YOU BLASTED INCONSIDERATE PIPE!
THIS'LL HOLD 'TIL TOMORROW!
BONK
DUNK
PEACE AND QUIET AT LAST... DON'T KNOW HOW MUCH LONGER I...
GNRRR
FWOPP
PLOKK
20

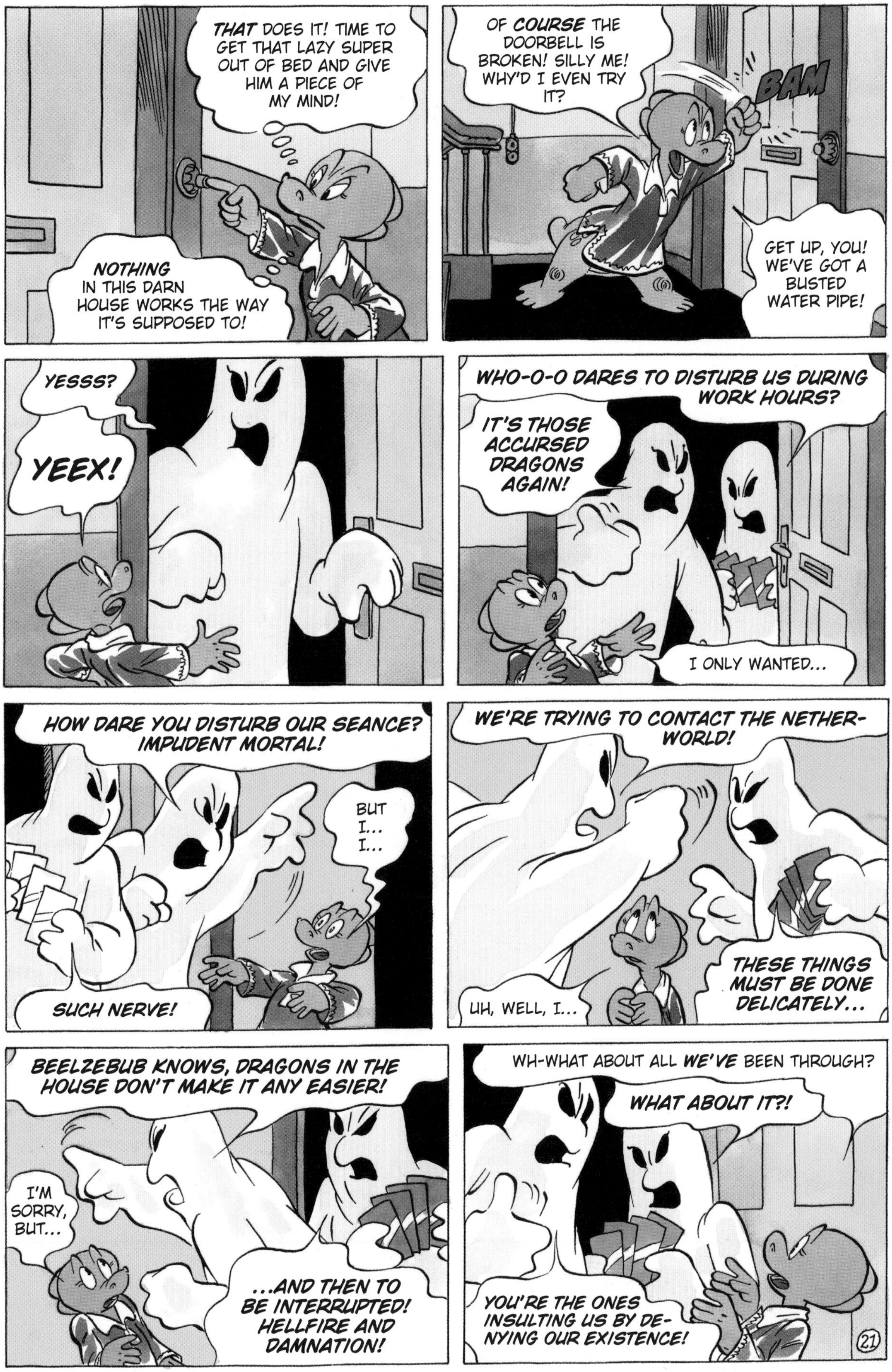
THAT DOES IT! TIME TO GET THAT LAZY SUPER OUT OF BED AND GIVE HIM A PIECE OF MY MIND!
NOTHING IN THIS DARN HOUSE WORKS THE WAY IT'S SUPPOSED TO!
OF COURSE THE DOORBELL IS BROKEN! SILLY ME! WHY'D I EVEN TRY IT?
BAM
GET UP, YOU! WE'VE GOT A BUSTED WATER PIPE!
YESSS?
YEEX!
WHO-O-O DARES TO DISTURB US DURING WORK HOURS?
IT'S THOSE ACCURSED DRAGONS AGAIN!
I ONLY WANTED...
HOW DARE YOU DISTURB OUR SEANCE? IMPUDENT MORTAL!
BUT I... I...
SUCH NERVE!
WE'RE TRYING TO CONTACT THE NETHER-WORLD!
UH, WELL, I...
THESE THINGS MUST BE DONE DELICATELY...
BEELZEBUB KNOWS, DRAGONS IN THE HOUSE DON'T MAKE IT ANY EASIER!
I'M SORRY, BUT...
...AND THEN TO BE INTERRUPTED! HELLFIRE AND DAMNATION!
WH-WHAT ABOUT ALL WE'VE BEEN THROUGH?
WHAT ABOUT IT?!
YOU'RE THE ONES INSULTING US BY DE-NYING OUR EXISTENCE!
21

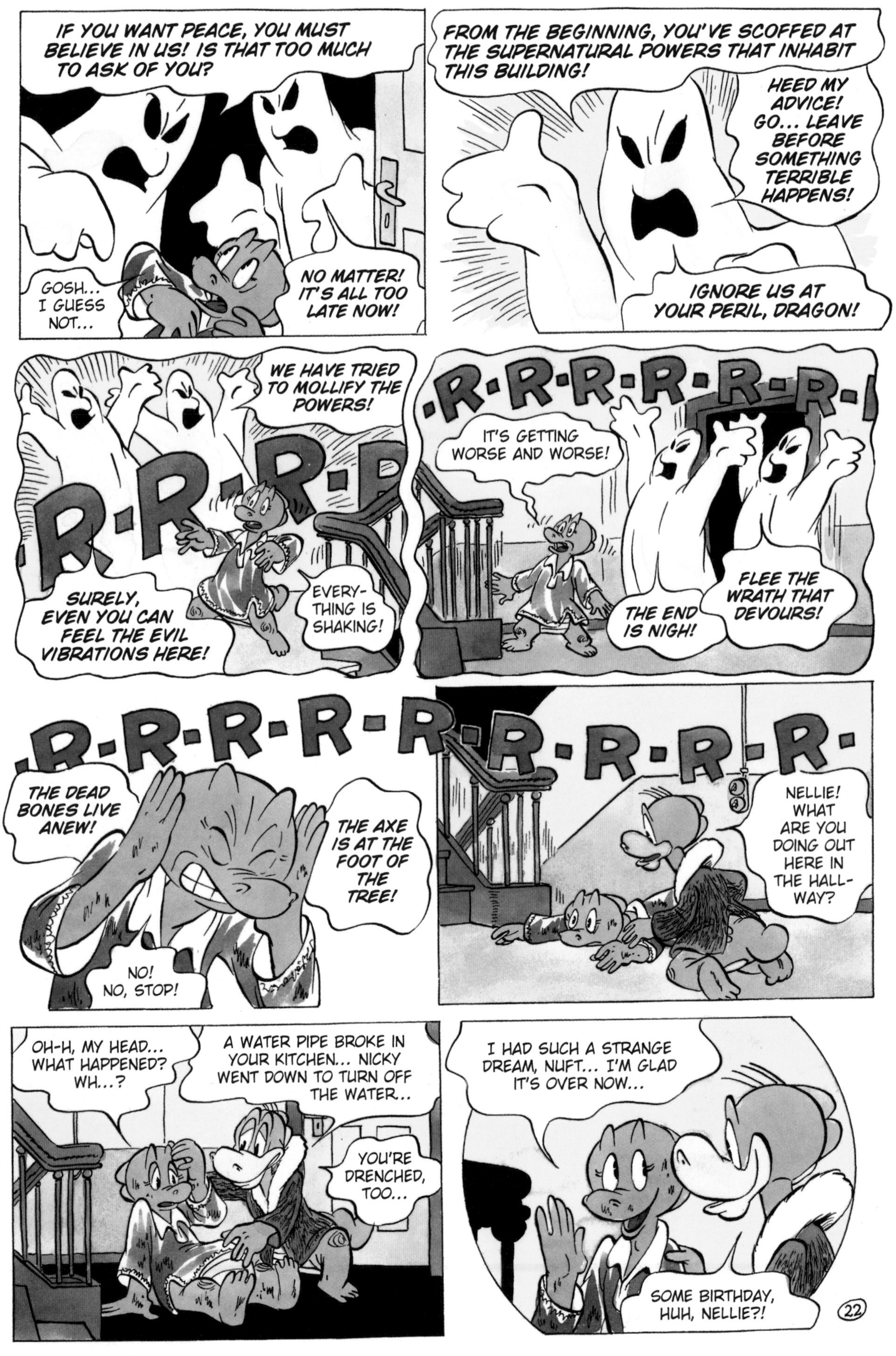
IF YOU WANT PEACE, YOU MUST BELIEVE IN US! IS THAT TOO MUCH TO ASK OF YOU?
GOSH... I GUESS NOT...
NO MATTER! IT'S ALL TOO LATE NOW!
FROM THE BEGINNING, YOU'VE SCOFFED AT THE SUPERNATURAL POWERS THAT INHABIT THIS BUILDING!
HEED MY ADVICE! GO... LEAVE BEFORE SOMETHING TERRIBLE HAPPENS!
IGNORE US AT YOUR PERIL, DRAGON!
WE HAVE TRIED TO MOLLIFY THE POWERS!
R-R-R-R
SURELY, EVEN YOU CAN FEEL THE EVIL VIBRATIONS HERE!
EVERY-THING IS SHAKING!
-R-R-R-R-R-R-
IT'S GETTING WORSE AND WORSE!
THE END IS NIGH!
FLEE THE WRATH THAT DEVOURS!
-R-R-R-R-R-
THE DEAD BONES LIVE ANEW!
THE AXE IS AT THE FOOT OF THE TREE!
NO! NO, STOP!
R-R-R-R-R-
NELLIE! WHAT ARE YOU DOING OUT HERE IN THE HALL-WAY?
OH-H, MY HEAD... WHAT HAPPENED? WH...?
A WATER PIPE BROKE IN YOUR KITCHEN... NICKY WENT DOWN TO TURN OFF THE WATER...
YOU'RE DRENCHED, TOO...
I HAD SUCH A STRANGE DREAM, NUFT... I'M GLAD IT'S OVER NOW...
SOME BIRTHDAY, HUH, NELLIE?!
22

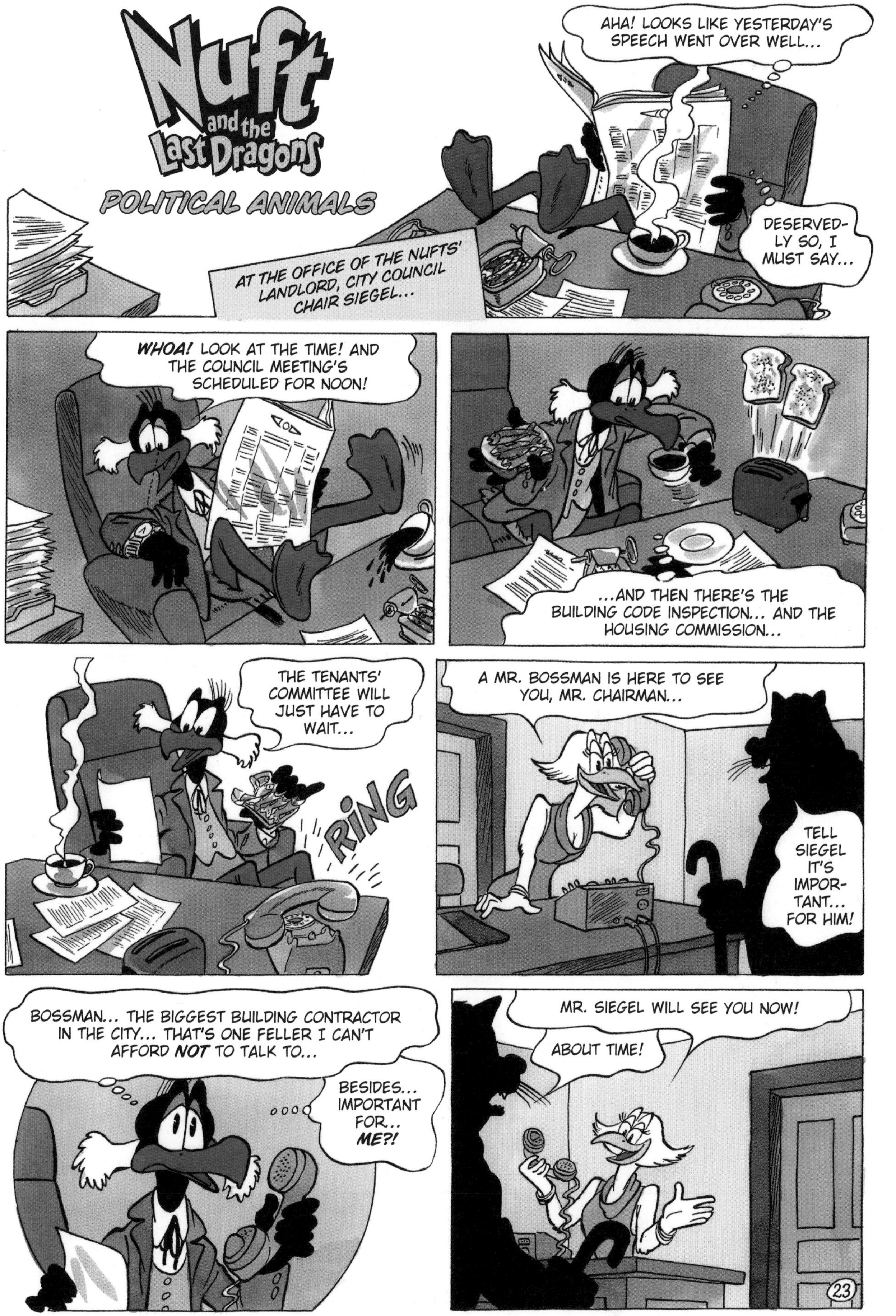
Nuft and the Last Dragons
POLITICAL ANIMALS
AT THE OFFICE OF THE NUFTS' LANDLORD, CITY COUNCIL CHAIR SIEGEL...
AHA! LOOKS LIKE YESTERDAY'S SPEECH WENT OVER WELL...
DESERVED-LY SO, I MUST SAY...
WHOA! LOOK AT THE TIME! AND THE COUNCIL MEETING'S SCHEDULED FOR NOON!
...AND THEN THERE'S THE BUILDING CODE INSPECTION... AND THE HOUSING COMMISSION...
THE TENANTS' COMMITTEE WILL JUST HAVE TO WAIT...
RING
A MR. BOSSMAN IS HERE TO SEE YOU, MR. CHAIRMAN...
TELL SIEGEL IT'S IMPOR-TANT... FOR HIM!
BOSSMAN... THE BIGGEST BUILDING CONTRACTOR IN THE CITY... THAT'S ONE FELLER I CAN'T AFFORD NOT TO TALK TO...
BESIDES... IMPORTANT FOR.. ME?!
MR. SIEGEL WILL SEE YOU NOW!
ABOUT TIME!
23

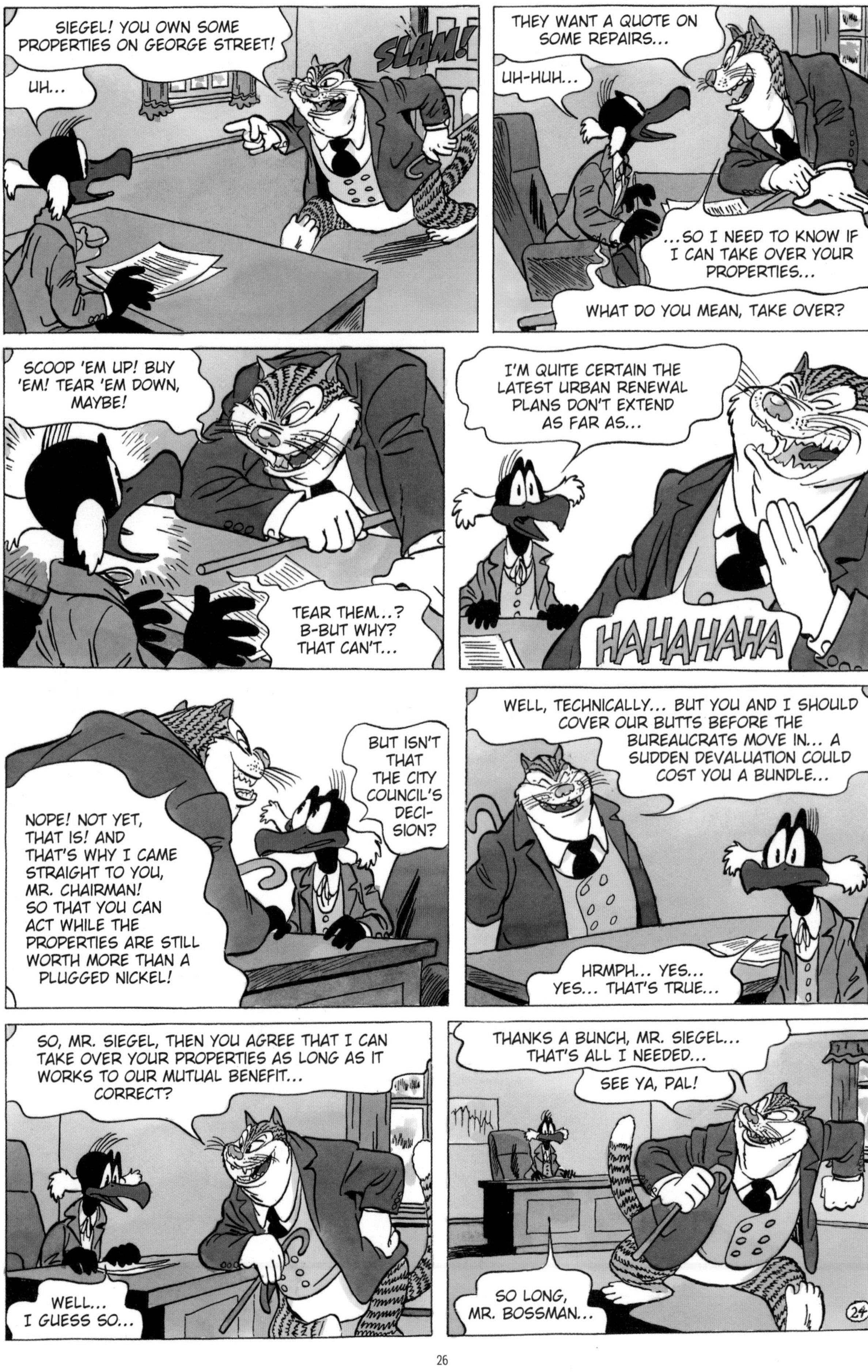
SIEGEL! YOU OWN SOME PROPERTIES ON GEORGE STREET!
SLAM!
UH...
THEY WANT A QUOTE ON SOME REPAIRS...
UH-HUH...
...SO I NEED TO KNOW IF I CAN TAKE OVER YOUR PROPERTIES...
WHAT DO YOU MEAN, TAKE OVER?
SCOOP 'EM UP! BUY 'EM! TEAR 'EM DOWN, MAYBE!
TEAR THEM...? B-BUT WHY? THAT CAN'T...
I'M QUITE CERTAIN THE LATEST URBAN RENEWAL PLANS DON'T EXTEND AS FAR AS...
HAHAHAHA
BUT ISN'T THAT THE CITY COUNCIL'S DECI-SION?
NOPE! NOT YET, THAT IS! AND THAT'S WHY I CAME STRAIGHT TO YOU, MR. CHAIRMAN! SO THAT YOU CAN ACT WHILE THE PROPERTIES ARE STILL WORTH MORE THAN A PLUGGED NICKEL!
WELL, TECHNICALLY... BUT YOU AND I SHOULD COVER OUR BUTTS BEFORE THE BUREAUCRATS MOVE IN... A SUDDEN DEVALUATION COULD COST YOU A BUNDLE...
HRMPH... YES... YES... THAT'S TRUE...
SO, MR. SIEGEL, THEN YOU AGREE THAT I CAN TAKE OVER YOUR PROPERTIES AS LONG AS IT WORKS TO OUR MUTUAL BENEFIT... CORRECT?
WELL... I GUESS SO...
THANKS A BUNCH, MR. SIEGEL... THAT'S ALL I NEEDED...
SEE YA, PAL!
SO LONG, MR. BOSSMAN...
24

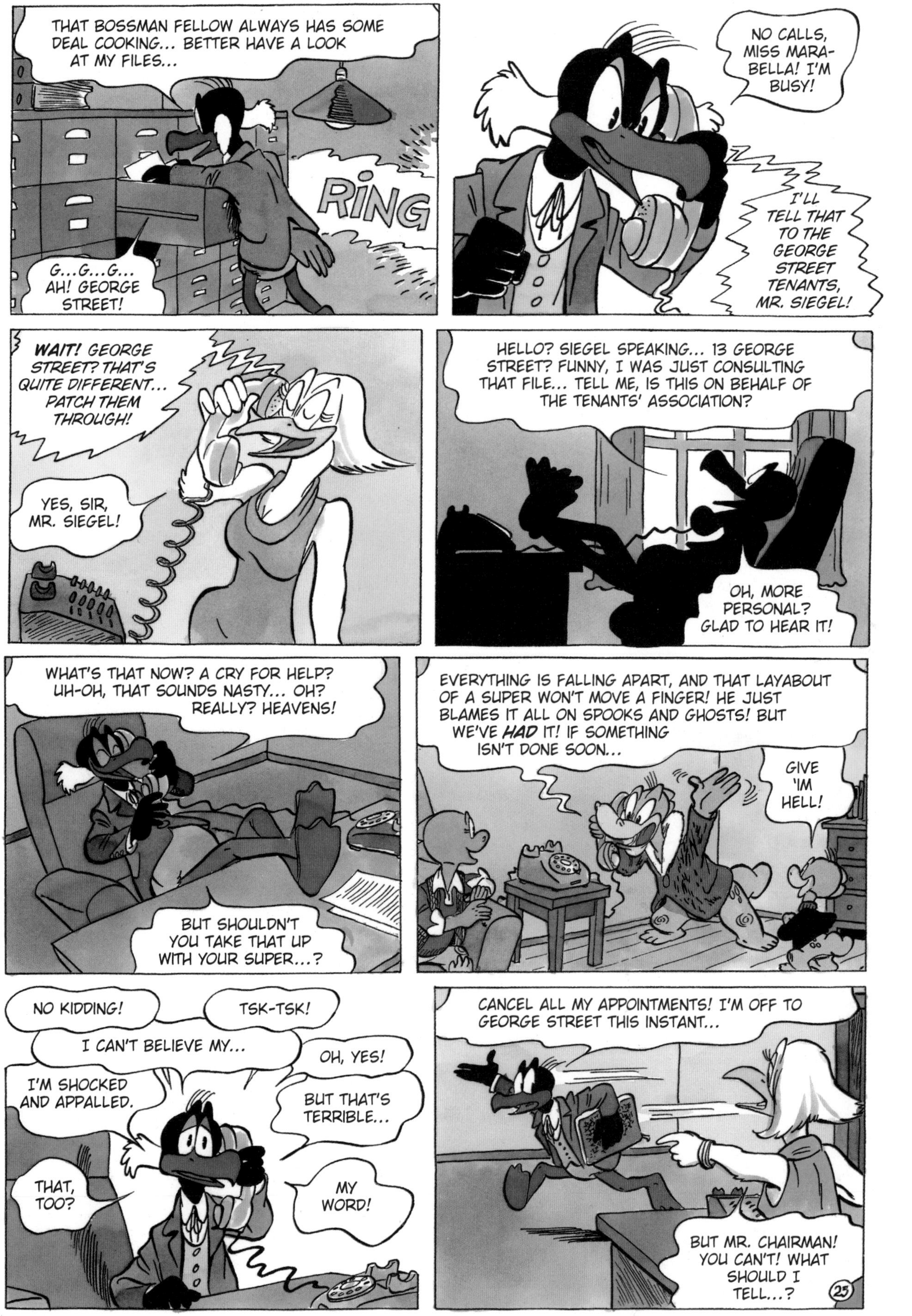
THAT BOSSMAN FELLOW ALWAYS HAS SOME DEAL COOKING... BETTER HAVE A LOOK AT MY FILES...
RING
G...G...G... AH! GEORGE STREET!
NO CALLS, MISS MARA-BELLA! I'M BUSY!
I'LL TELL THAT TO THE GEORGE STREET TENANTS, MR. SIEGEL!
WAIT! GEORGE STREET? THAT'S QUITE DIFFERENT... PATCH THEM THROUGH!
YES, SIR, MR. SIEGEL!
HELLO? SIEGEL SPEAKING... 13 GEORGE STREET? FUNNY, I WAS JUST CONSULTING THAT FILE... TELL ME, IS THIS ON BEHALF OF THE TENANTS' ASSOCIATION?
OH, MORE PERSONAL? GLAD TO HEAR IT!
WHAT'S THAT NOW? A CRY FOR HELP? UH-OH, THAT SOUNDS NASTY... OH? REALLY? HEAVENS!
BUT SHOULDN'T YOU TAKE THAT UP WITH YOUR SUPER...?
EVERYTHING IS FALLING APART, AND THAT LAYABOUT OF A SUPER WON'T MOVE A FINGER! HE JUST BLAMES IT ALL ON SPOOKS AND GHOSTS! BUT WE'VE HAD IT! IF SOMETHING ISN'T DONE SOON...
GIVE 'IM HELL!
NO KIDDING!
TSK-TSK!
I CAN'T BELIEVE MY...
OH, YES!
I'M SHOCKED AND APPALLED.
BUT THAT'S TERRIBLE...
THAT, TOO?
MY WORD!
CANCEL ALL MY APPOINTMENTS! I'M OFF TO GEORGE STREET THIS INSTANT...
BUT MR. CHAIRMAN! YOU CAN'T! WHAT SHOULD I TELL...?
25

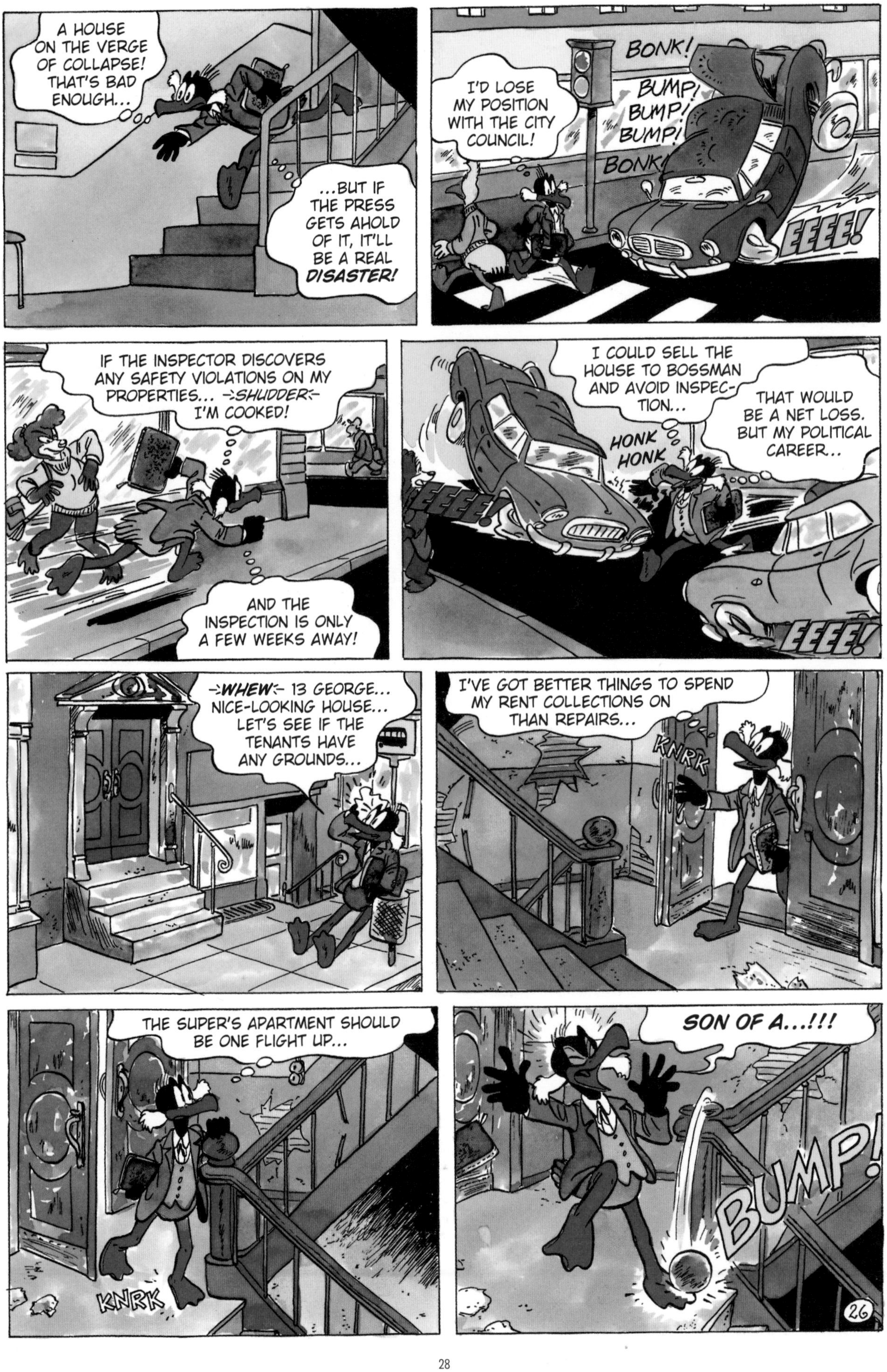
A HOUSE ON THE VERGE OF COLLAPSE! THAT'S BAD ENOUGH...
...BUT IF THE PRESS GETS AHOLD OF IT, IT'LL BE A REAL DISASTER!
BONK!
BUMP! BUMP! BUMP!
BONK!
I'D LOSE MY POSITION WITH THE CITY COUNCIL!
EEEE!
IF THE INSPECTOR DISCOVERS ANY SAFETY VIOLATIONS ON MY PROPERTIES... -SHUDDER- I'M COOKED!
AND THE INSPECTION IS ONLY A FEW WEEKS AWAY!
I COULD SELL THE HOUSE TO BOSSMAN AND AVOID INSPECTION...
THAT WOULD BE A NET LOSS. BUT MY POLITICAL CAREER...
HONK HONK
EEEE!
EEEE!
-WHEW- 13 GEORGE... NICE-LOOKING HOUSE... LET'S SEE IF THE TENANTS HAVE ANY GROUNDS...
I'VE GOT BETTER THINGS TO SPEND MY RENT COLLECTIONS ON THAN REPAIRS...
KNRK
THE SUPER'S APARTMENT SHOULD BE ONE FLIGHT UP...
KNRK
SON OF A...!!!
BUMP!
26

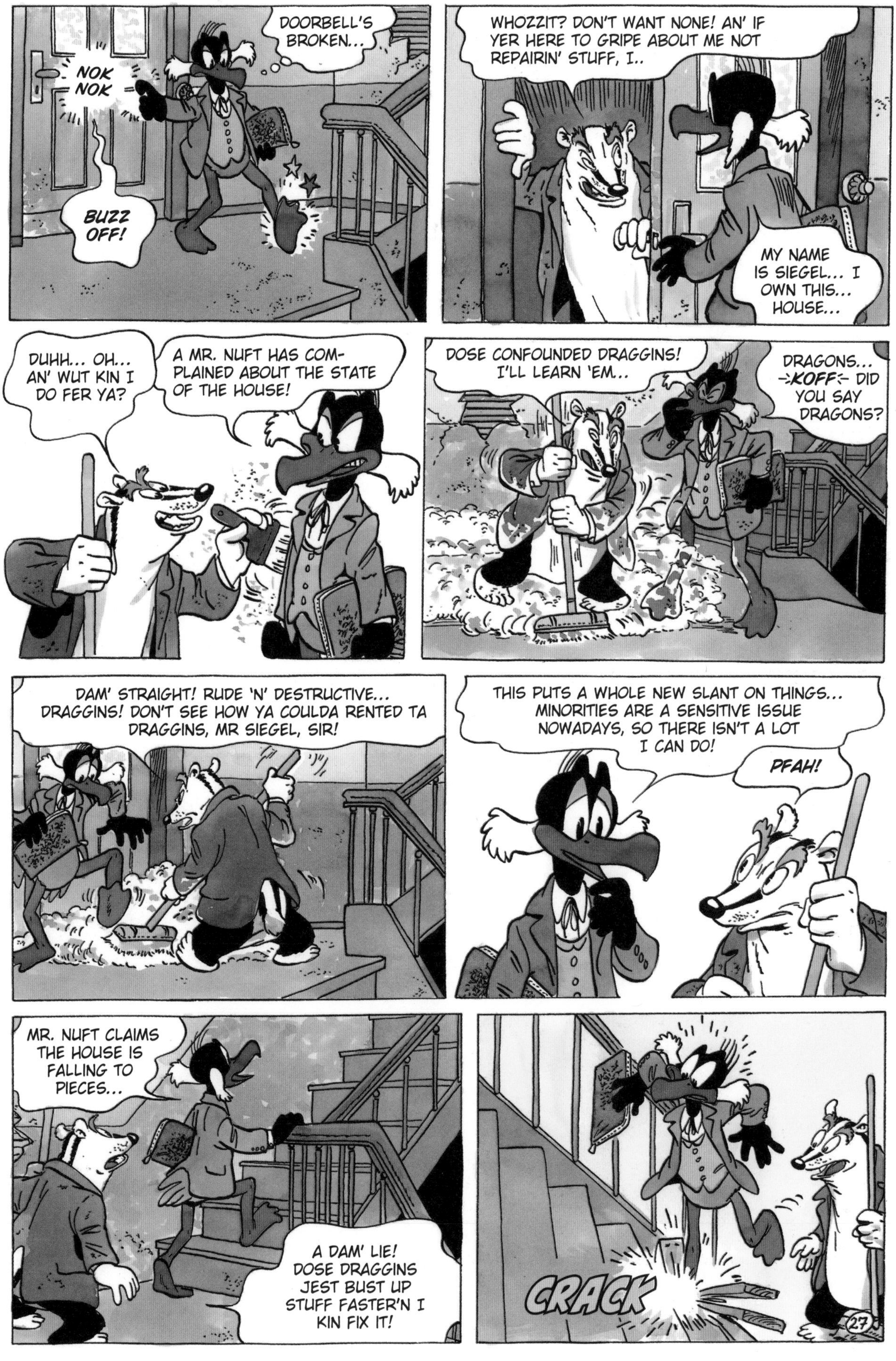

DOORBELL'S BROKEN...
NOK NOK
BUZZ OFF!
WHOZZIT? DON'T WANT NONE! AN' IF YER HERE TO GRIPE ABOUT ME NOT REPAIRIN' STUFF, I..
MY NAME IS SIEGEL... I OWN THIS... HOUSE...
DUHH... OH... AN' WUT KIN I DO FER YA?
A MR. NUFT HAS COMPLAINED ABOUT THE STATE OF THE HOUSE!
DOSE CONFOUNDED DRAGGINS! I'LL LEARN 'EM...
DRAGONS... KOFF DID YOU SAY DRAGONS?
DAM' STRAIGHT! RUDE 'N' DESTRUCTIVE... DRAGGINS! DON'T SEE HOW YA COULDA RENTED TA DRAGGINS, MR SIEGEL, SIR!
THIS PUTS A WHOLE NEW SLANT ON THINGS... MINORITIES ARE A SENSITIVE ISSUE NOWADAYS, SO THERE ISN'T A LOT I CAN DO!
PFAH!
MR. NUFT CLAIMS THE HOUSE IS FALLING TO PIECES...
A DAM' LIE! DOSE DRAGGINS JEST BUST UP STUFF FASTER'N I KIN FIX IT!
CRACK
27

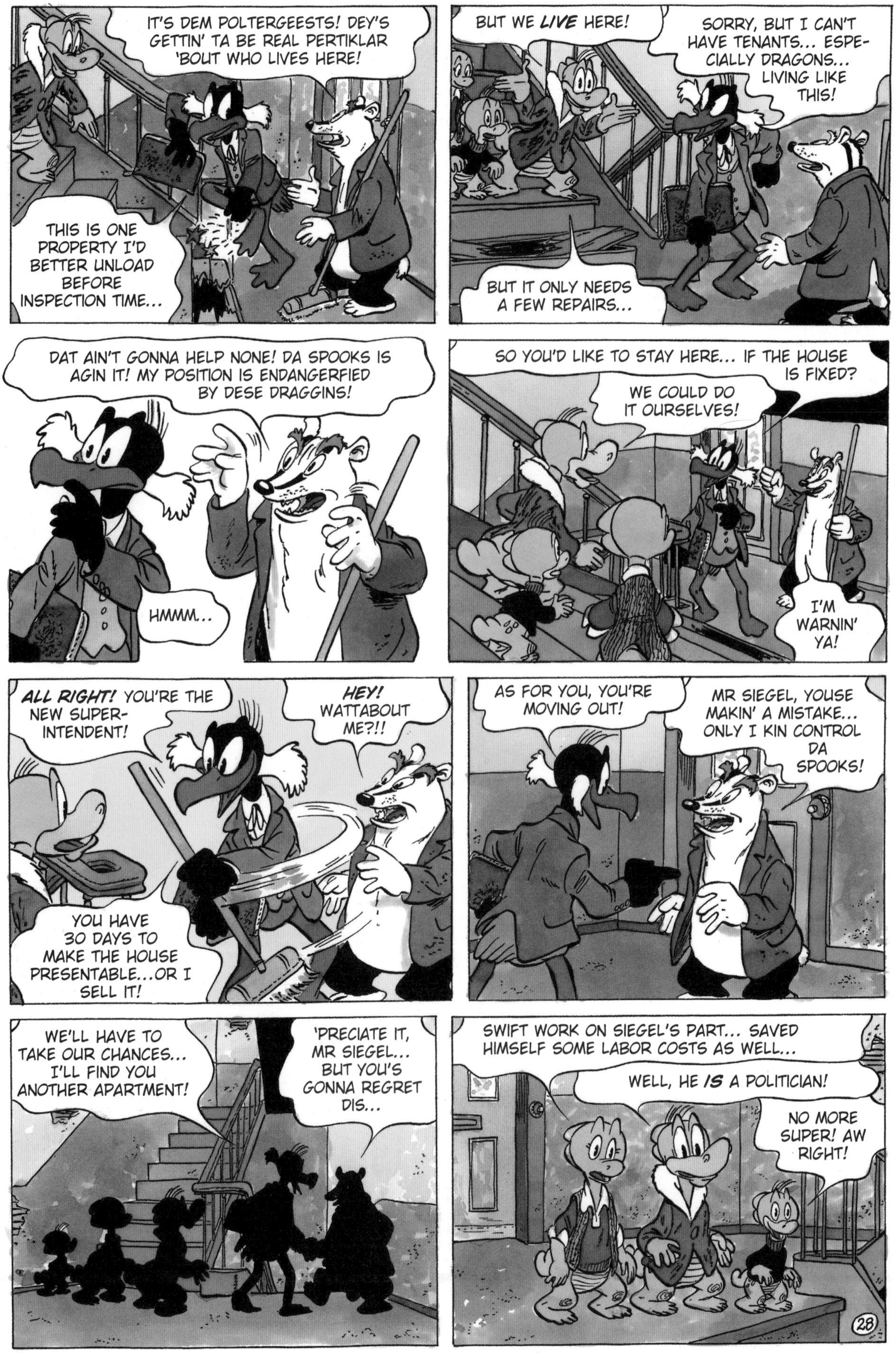
IT'S DEM POLTERGEESTS! DEY'S GETTIN' TA BE REAL PERTIKLAR 'BOUT WHO LIVES HERE!
THIS IS ONE PROPERTY I'D BETTER UNLOAD BEFORE INSPECTION TIME...
BUT WE LIVE HERE!
SORRY, BUT I CAN'T HAVE TENANTS... ESPECIALLY DRAGONS... LIVING LIKE THIS!
BUT IT ONLY NEEDS A FEW REPAIRS...
DAT AIN'T GONNA HELP NONE! DA SPOOKS IS AGIN IT! MY POSITION IS ENDANGERFIED BY DESE DRAGGINS!
HMMM...
SO YOU'D LIKE TO STAY HERE... IF THE HOUSE IS FIXED?
WE COULD DO IT OURSELVES!
I'M WARNIN' YA!
ALL RIGHT! YOU'RE THE NEW SUPER-INTENDENT!
HEY! WATTABOUT ME?!!
YOU HAVE 30 DAYS TO MAKE THE HOUSE PRESENTABLE...OR I SELL IT!
AS FOR YOU, YOU'RE MOVING OUT!
MR SIEGEL, YOUSE MAKIN' A MISTAKE... ONLY I KIN CONTROL DA SPOOKS!
WE'LL HAVE TO TAKE OUR CHANCES... I'LL FIND YOU ANOTHER APARTMENT!
'PRECIATE IT, MR SIEGEL... BUT YOU'S GONNA REGRET DIS...
SWIFT WORK ON SIEGEL'S PART... SAVED HIMSELF SOME LABOR COSTS AS WELL...
WELL, HE IS A POLITICIAN!
NO MORE SUPER! AW RIGHT!
28

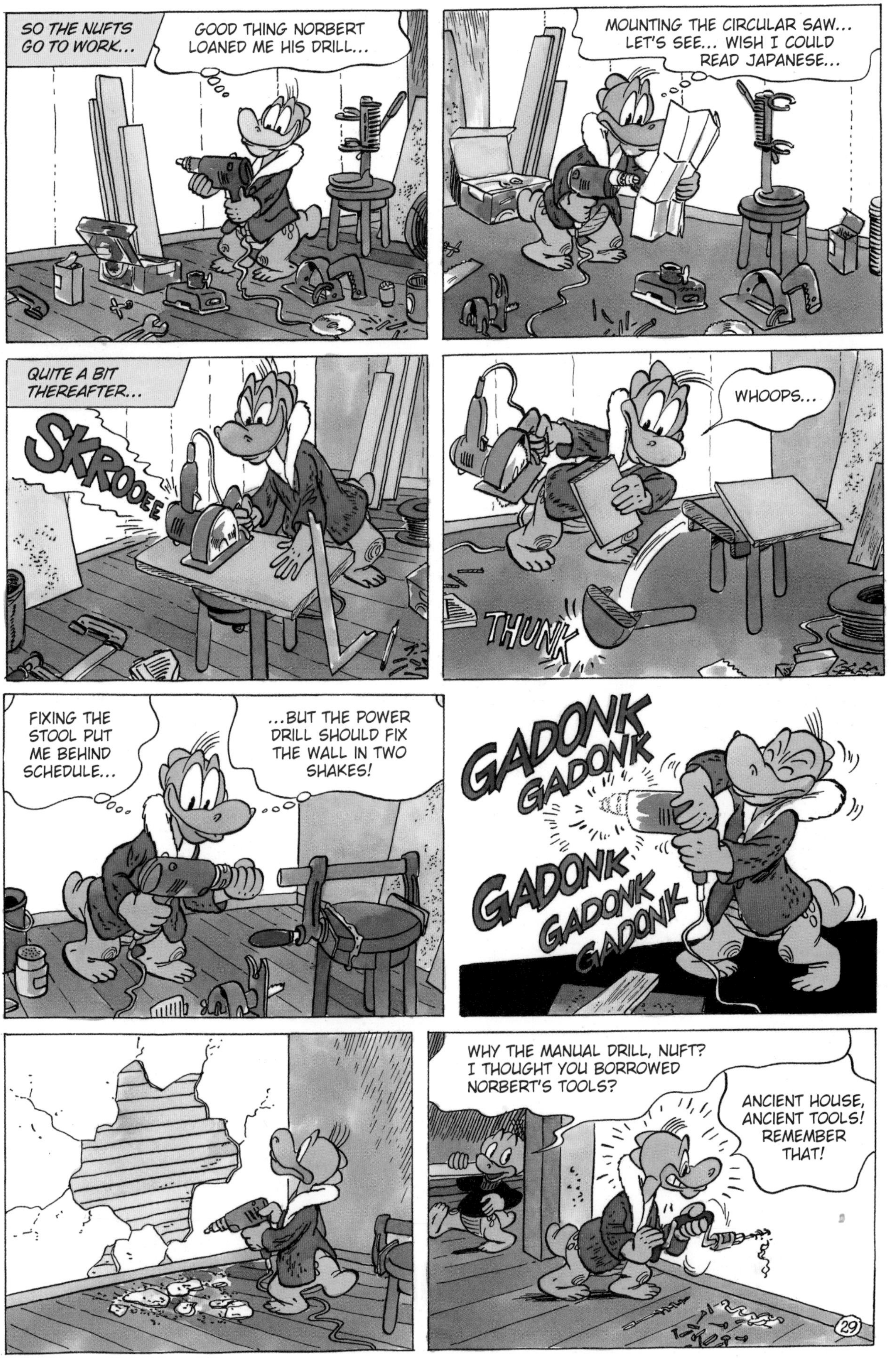
SO THE NUFTS GO TO WORK...
GOOD THING NORBERT LOANED ME HIS DRILL...
MOUNTING THE CIRCULAR SAW... LET'S SEE... WISH I COULD READ JAPANESE...
QUITE A BIT THEREAFTER...
SKROOOEEE
WHOOPS...
THUNK
FIXING THE STOOL PUT ME BEHIND SCHEDULE...
...BUT THE POWER DRILL SHOULD FIX THE WALL IN TWO SHAKES!
GADONK
GADONK
GADONK
GADONK
GADONK
WHY THE MANUAL DRILL, NUFT? I THOUGHT YOU BORROWED NORBERT'S TOOLS?
ANCIENT HOUSE, ANCIENT TOOLS! REMEMBER THAT!
29

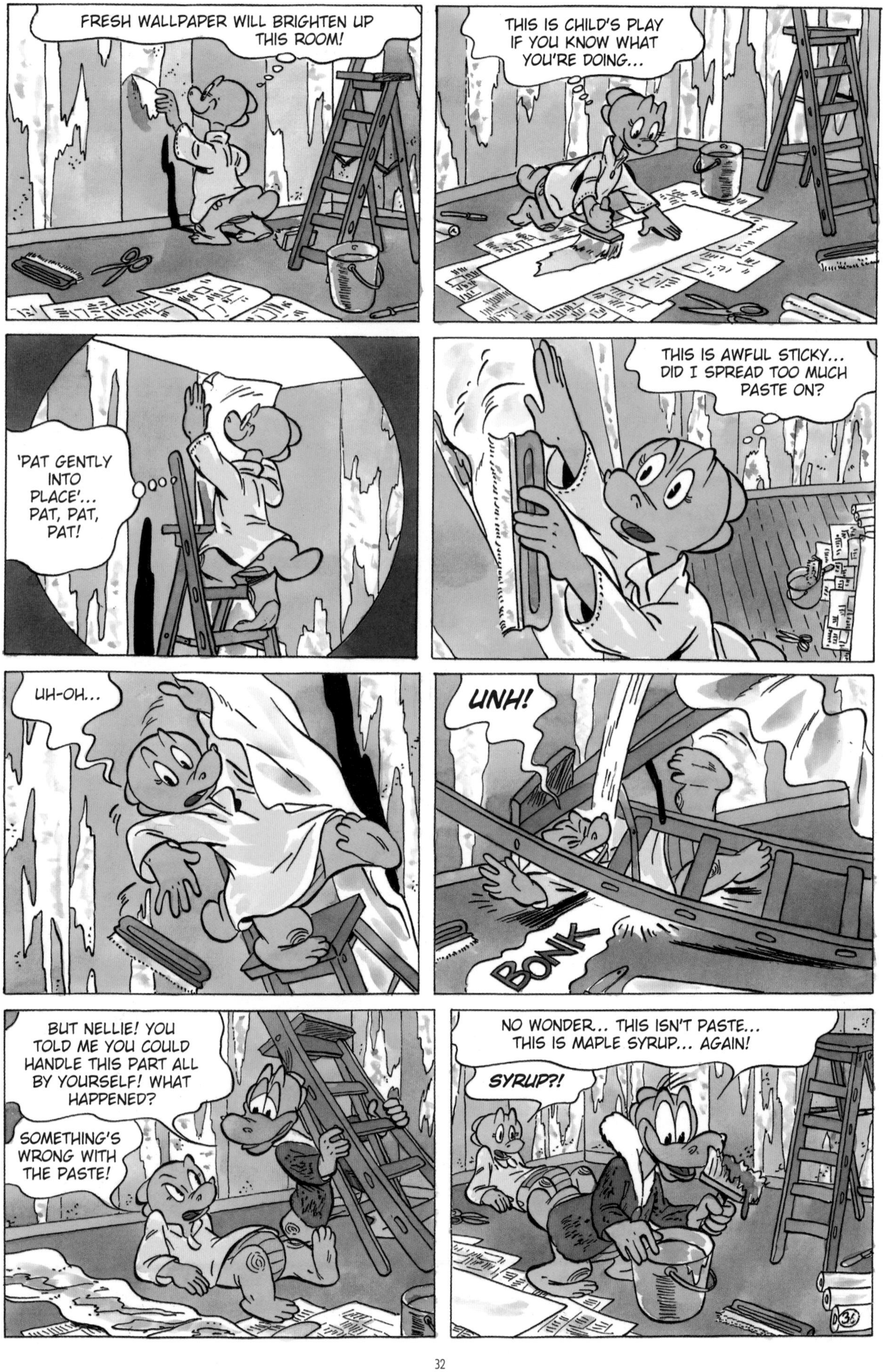
FRESH WALLPAPER WILL BRIGHTEN UP THIS ROOM!
THIS IS CHILD'S PLAY IF YOU KNOW WHAT YOU'RE DOING...
'PAT GENTLY INTO PLACE'... PAT, PAT, PAT!
THIS IS AWFUL STICKY... DID I SPREAD TOO MUCH PASTE ON?
UH-OH...
UNH!
BONK
BUT NELLIE! YOU TOLD ME YOU COULD HANDLE THIS PART ALL BY YOURSELF! WHAT HAPPENED?
SOMETHING'S WRONG WITH THE PASTE!
NO WONDER... THIS ISN'T PASTE... THIS IS MAPLE SYRUP... AGAIN!
SYRUP?!

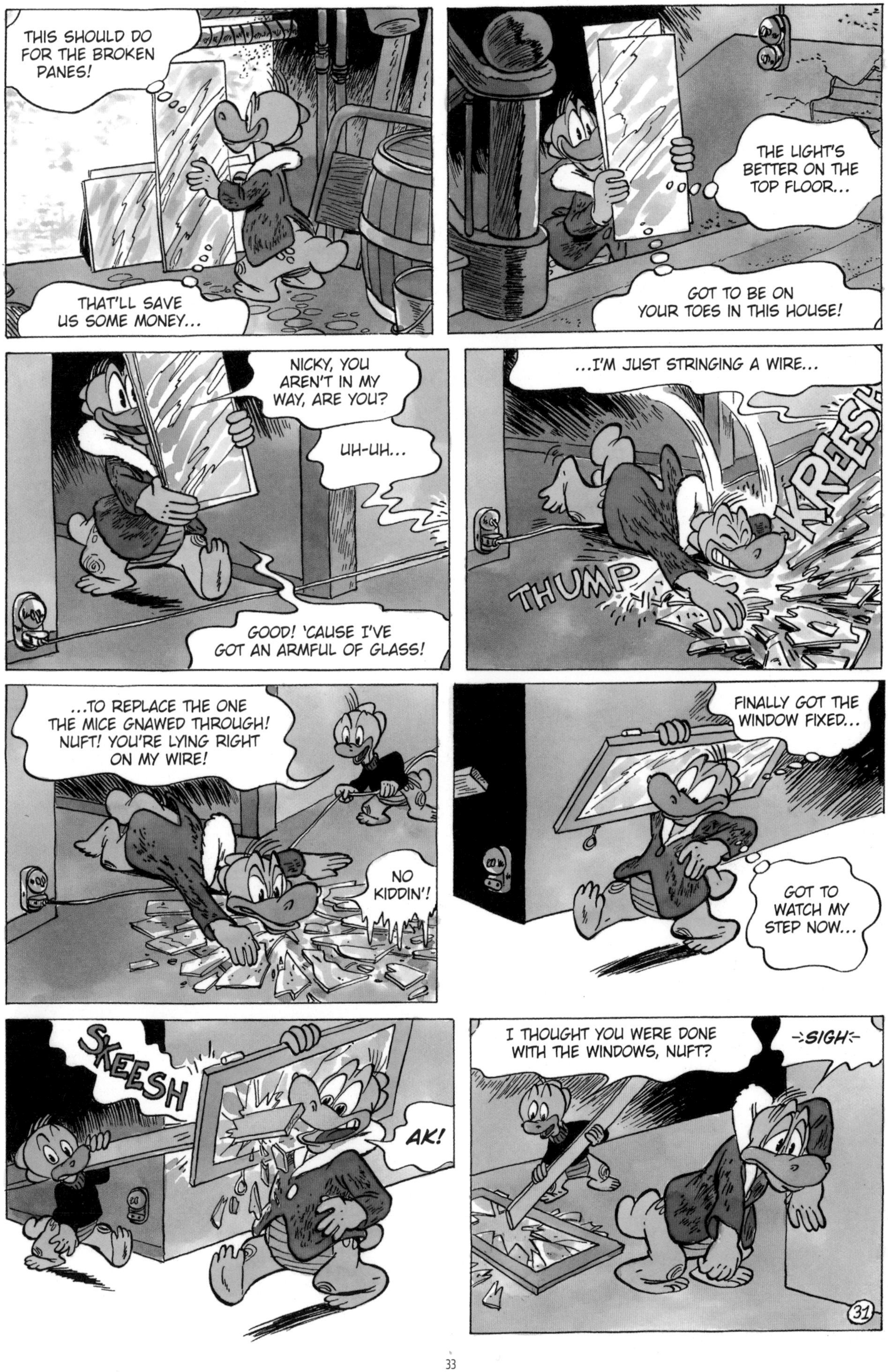
THIS SHOULD DO FOR THE BROKEN PANES!
THAT'LL SAVE US SOME MONEY...
THE LIGHT'S BETTER ON THE TOP FLOOR...
GOT TO BE ON YOUR TOES IN THIS HOUSE!
NICKY, YOU AREN'T IN MY WAY, ARE YOU?
UH-UH...
GOOD! 'CAUSE I'VE GOT AN ARMFUL OF GLASS!
...I'M JUST STRINGING A WIRE...
KREESH
THUMP
...TO REPLACE THE ONE THE MICE GNAWED THROUGH! NUFT! YOU'RE LYING RIGHT ON MY WIRE!
NO KIDDIN'!
FINALLY GOT THE WINDOW FIXED...
GOT TO WATCH MY STEP NOW...
SKEESH
AK!
I THOUGHT YOU WERE DONE WITH THE WINDOWS, NUFT?
SIGH
31

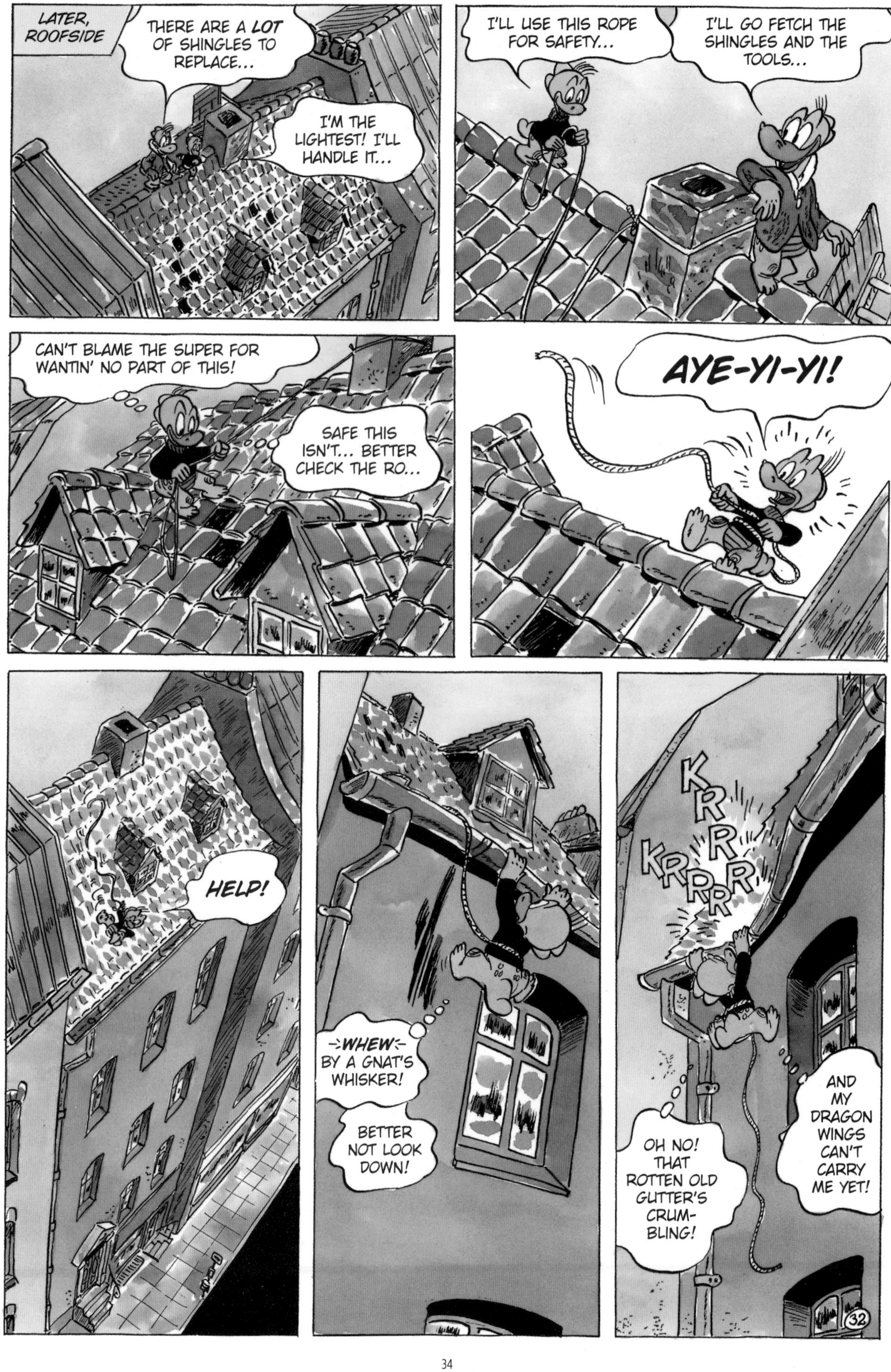
LATER, ROOFSIDE
THERE ARE A LOT OF SHINGLES TO REPLACE...
I'M THE LIGHTEST! I'LL HANDLE IT...
I'LL USE THIS ROPE FOR SAFETY...
I'LL GO FETCH THE SHINGLES AND THE TOOLS...
CAN'T BLAME THE SUPER FOR WANTIN' NO PART OF THIS!
SAFE THIS ISN'T... BETTER CHECK THE RO...
AYE-YI-YI!
HELP!
-WHEW- BY A GNAT'S WHISKER!
BETTER NOT LOOK DOWN!
KRRRR
KRRRR
OH NO! THAT ROTTEN OLD GUTTER'S CRUM-BLING!
AND MY DRAGON WINGS CAN'T CARRY ME YET!
32

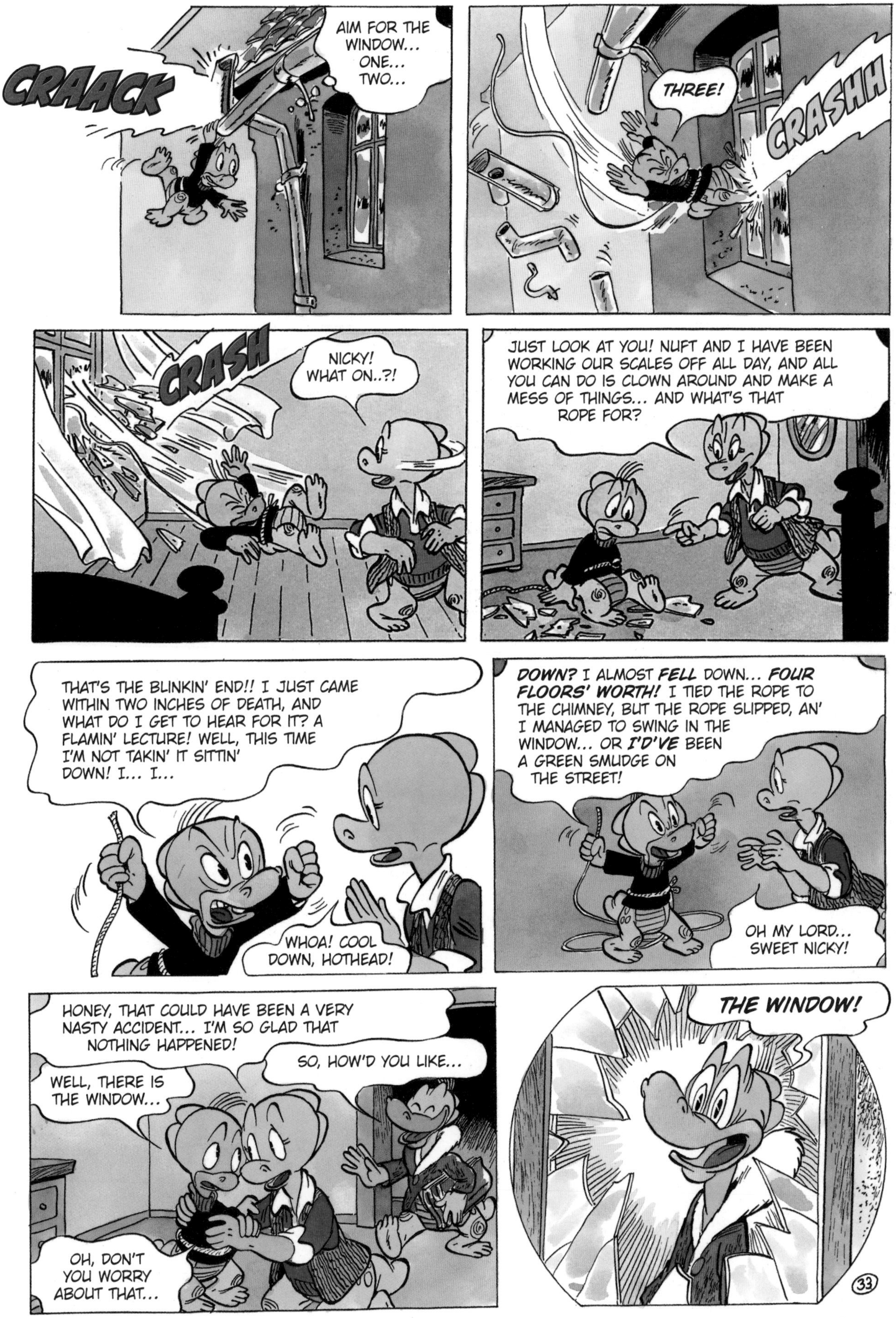
CRAACK
AIM FOR THE WINDOW... ONE... TWO...
THREE!
CRASHH
CRASH
NICKY! WHAT ON..?!
JUST LOOK AT YOU! NUFT AND I HAVE BEEN WORKING OUR SCALES OFF ALL DAY, AND ALL YOU CAN DO IS CLOWN AROUND AND MAKE A MESS OF THINGS... AND WHAT'S THAT ROPE FOR?
THAT'S THE BLINKIN' END!! I JUST CAME WITHIN TWO INCHES OF DEATH, AND WHAT DO I GET TO HEAR FOR IT? A FLAMIN' LECTURE! WELL, THIS TIME I'M NOT TAKIN' IT SITTIN' DOWN! I... I...
WHOA! COOL DOWN, HOTHEAD!
DOWN? I ALMOST FELL DOWN... FOUR FLOORS' WORTH! I TIED THE ROPE TO THE CHIMNEY, BUT THE ROPE SLIPPED, AN' I MANAGED TO SWING IN THE WINDOW... OR I'D'VE BEEN A GREEN SMUDGE ON THE STREET!
OH MY LORD... SWEET NICKY!
HONEY, THAT COULD HAVE BEEN A VERY NASTY ACCIDENT... I'M SO GLAD THAT NOTHING HAPPENED!
WELL, THERE IS THE WINDOW...
SO, HOW'D YOU LIKE...
OH, DON'T YOU WORRY ABOUT THAT...
THE WINDOW!
33

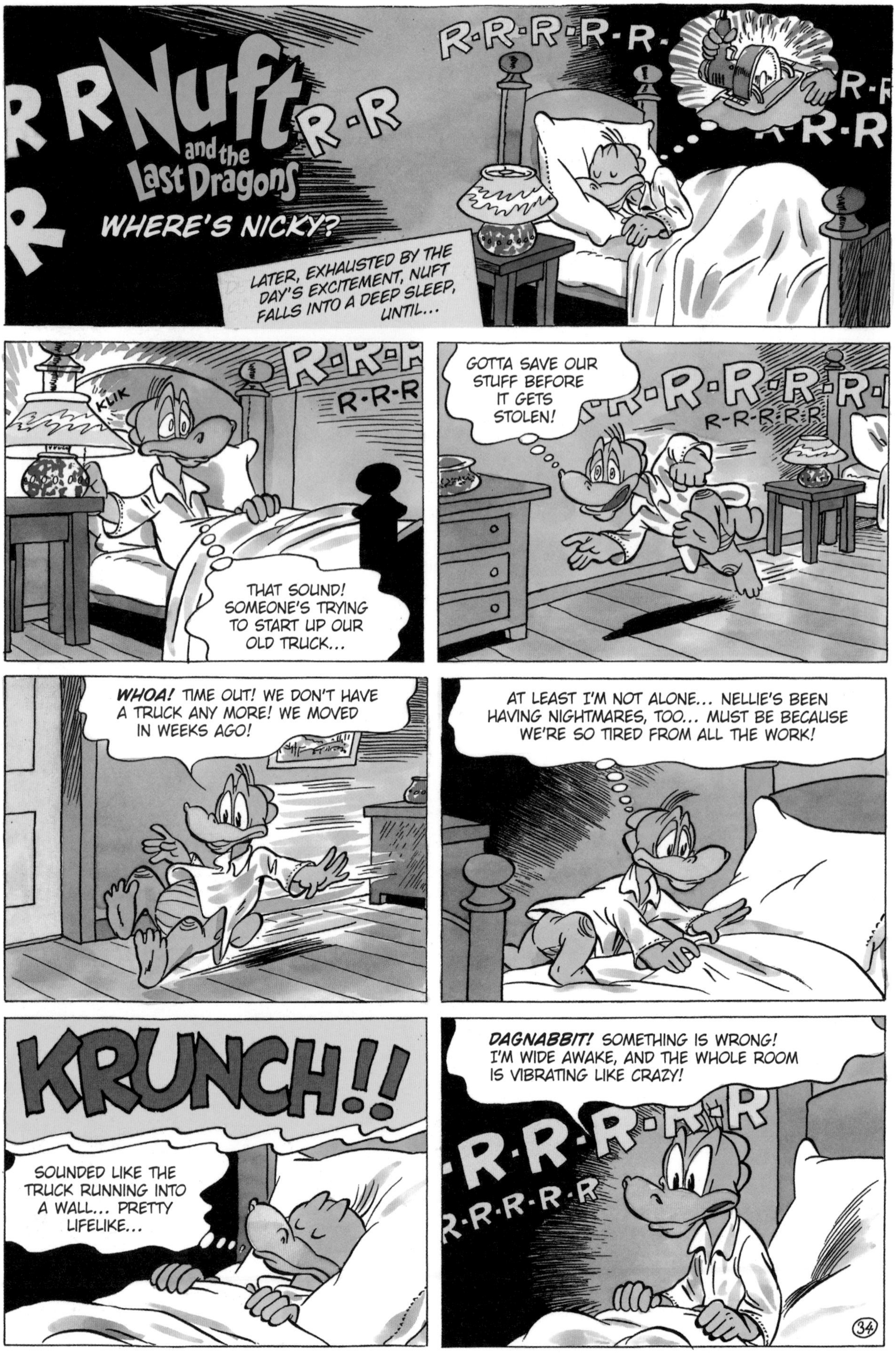

Nuft and the Last Dragons
WHERE'S NICKY?
R-R-R-R-R-
R-R
LATER, EXHAUSTED BY THE DAY'S EXCITEMENT, NUFT FALLS INTO A DEEP SLEEP, UNTIL...
KLIK
R-R-R
THAT SOUND! SOMEONE'S TRYING TO START UP OUR OLD TRUCK...
GOTTA SAVE OUR STUFF BEFORE IT GETS STOLEN!
R-R-R-R-R-R
WHOA! TIME OUT! WE DON'T HAVE A TRUCK ANY MORE! WE MOVED IN WEEKS AGO!
AT LEAST I'M NOT ALONE... NELLIE'S BEEN HAVING NIGHTMARES, TOO... MUST BE BECAUSE WE'RE SO TIRED FROM ALL THE WORK!
KRUNCH!!
SOUNDED LIKE THE TRUCK RUNNING INTO A WALL... PRETTY LIFELIKE...
DAGNABBIT! SOMETHING IS WRONG! I'M WIDE AWAKE, AND THE WHOLE ROOM IS VIBRATING LIKE CRAZY!
R-R-R-R-R-R
R-R-R-R-R
34

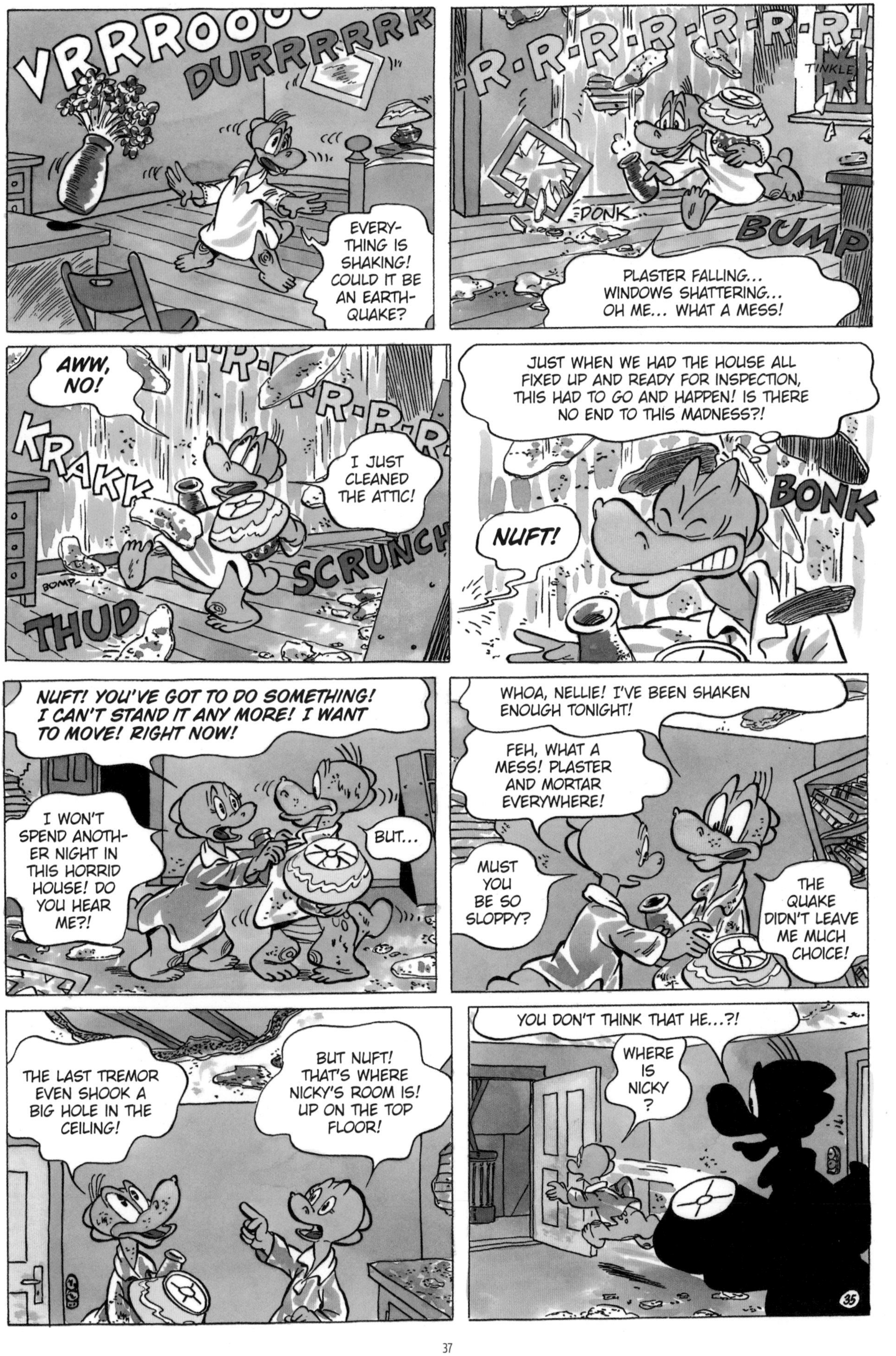
VRRROOOO
DURRRRRRK
EVERY-THING IS SHAKING! COULD IT BE AN EARTH-QUAKE?
-R-R-R-R-R-R-R-R-
TINKLE
DONK
BUMP
PLASTER FALLING... WINDOWS SHATTERING... OH ME... WHAT A MESS!
AWW, NO!
KRAKK
I JUST CLEANED THE ATTIC!
BOMP
THUD
SCRUNCH
JUST WHEN WE HAD THE HOUSE ALL FIXED UP AND READY FOR INSPECTION, THIS HAD TO GO AND HAPPEN! IS THERE NO END TO THIS MADNESS?!
BONK
NUFT!
NUFT! YOU'VE GOT TO DO SOMETHING! I CAN'T STAND IT ANY MORE! I WANT TO MOVE! RIGHT NOW!
I WON'T SPEND ANOTH-ER NIGHT IN THIS HORRID HOUSE! DO YOU HEAR ME?!
BUT...
WHOA, NELLIE! I'VE BEEN SHAKEN ENOUGH TONIGHT!
FEH, WHAT A MESS! PLASTER AND MORTAR EVERYWHERE!
MUST YOU BE SO SLOPPY?
THE QUAKE DIDN'T LEAVE ME MUCH CHOICE!
THE LAST TREMOR EVEN SHOOK A BIG HOLE IN THE CEILING!
BUT NUFT! THAT'S WHERE NICKY'S ROOM IS! UP ON THE TOP FLOOR!
YOU DON'T THINK THAT HE...?!
WHERE IS NICKY ?
35

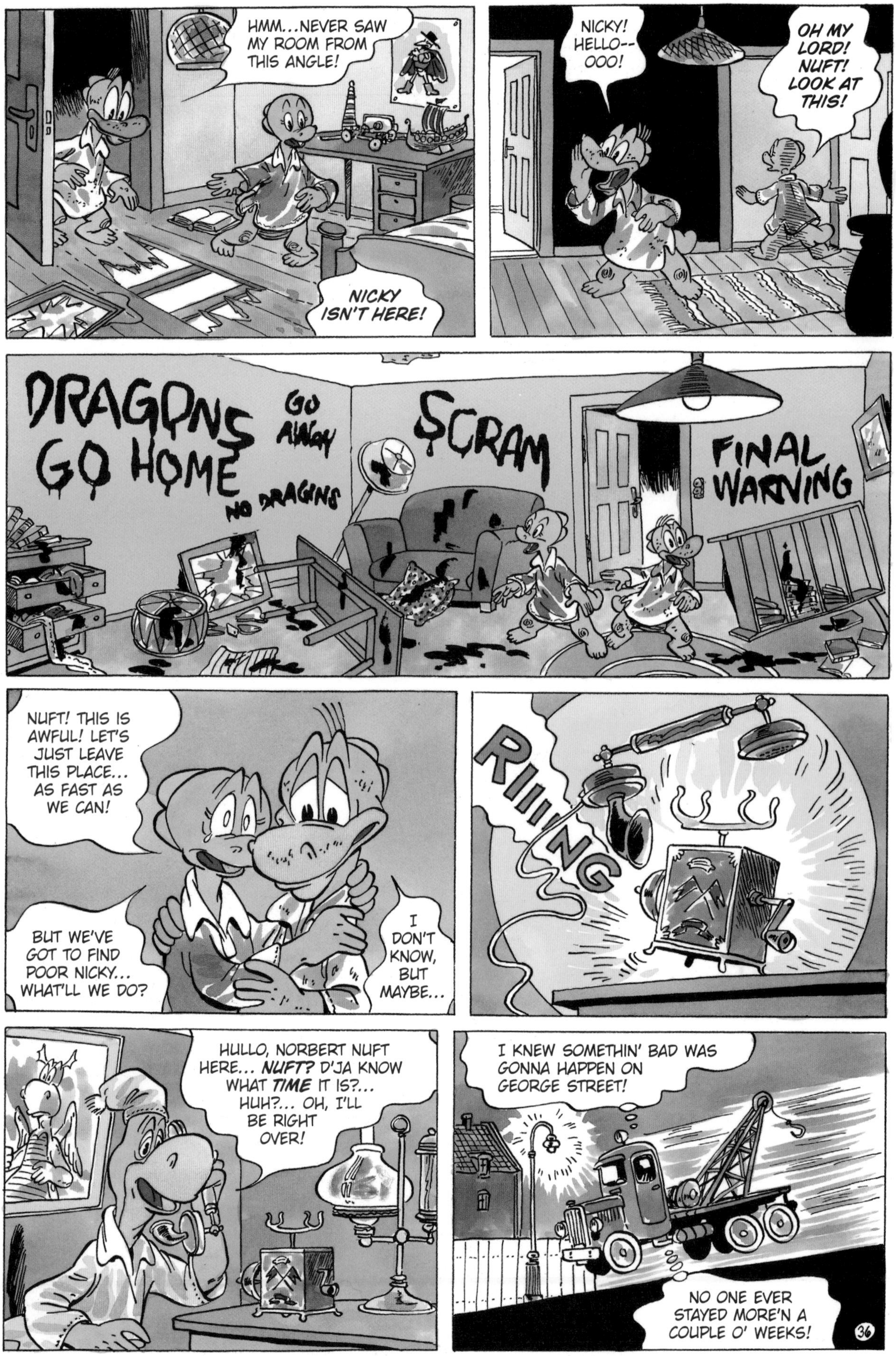
HMM... NEVER SAW MY ROOM FROM THIS ANGLE!
NICKY ISN'T HERE!
NICKY! HELLO--OOO!
OH MY LORD! NUFT! LOOK AT THIS!
DRAGONS GO HOME
GO AWAY
NO DRAGINS
SCRAM
FINAL WARNING
NUFT! THIS IS AWFUL! LET'S JUST LEAVE THIS PLACE... AS FAST AS WE CAN!
BUT WE'VE GOT TO FIND POOR NICKY... WHAT'LL WE DO?
I DON'T KNOW, BUT MAYBE...
RIIIING
HULLO, NORBERT NUFT HERE... NUFT? D'JA KNOW WHAT TIME IT IS?... HUH?... OH, I'LL BE RIGHT OVER!
I KNEW SOMETHIN' BAD WAS GONNA HAPPEN ON GEORGE STREET!
NO ONE EVER STAYED MORE'N A COUPLE O' WEEKS!
36

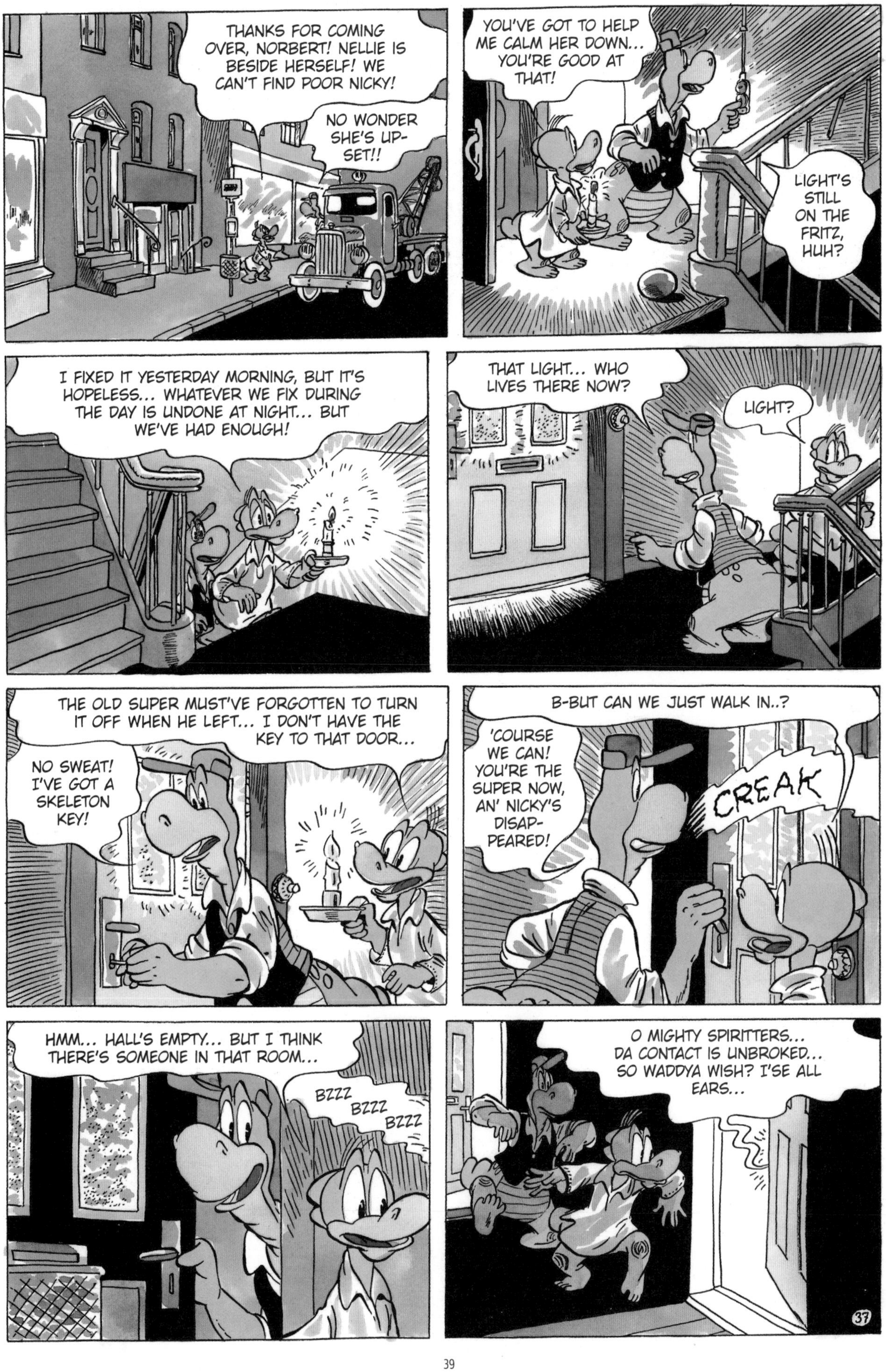
THANKS FOR COMING OVER, NORBERT! NELLIE IS BESIDE HERSELF! WE CAN'T FIND POOR NICKY!
NO WONDER SHE'S UP-SET!!
YOU'VE GOT TO HELP ME CALM HER DOWN... YOU'RE GOOD AT THAT!
LIGHT'S STILL ON THE FRITZ, HUH?
I FIXED IT YESTERDAY MORNING, BUT IT'S HOPELESS... WHATEVER WE FIX DURING THE DAY IS UNDONE AT NIGHT... BUT WE'VE HAD ENOUGH!
THAT LIGHT... WHO LIVES THERE NOW?
LIGHT?
THE OLD SUPER MUST'VE FORGOTTEN TO TURN IT OFF WHEN HE LEFT... I DON'T HAVE THE KEY TO THAT DOOR...
NO SWEAT! I'VE GOT A SKELETON KEY!
B-BUT CAN WE JUST WALK IN..?
'COURSE WE CAN! YOU'RE THE SUPER NOW, AN' NICKY'S DISAP-PEARED!
CREAK
HMM... HALL'S EMPTY... BUT I THINK THERE'S SOMEONE IN THAT ROOM...
BZZZ BZZZ BZZZ
O MIGHTY SPIRITTERS... DA CONTACT IS UNBROKED... SO WADDYA WISH? I'SE ALL EARS...
37

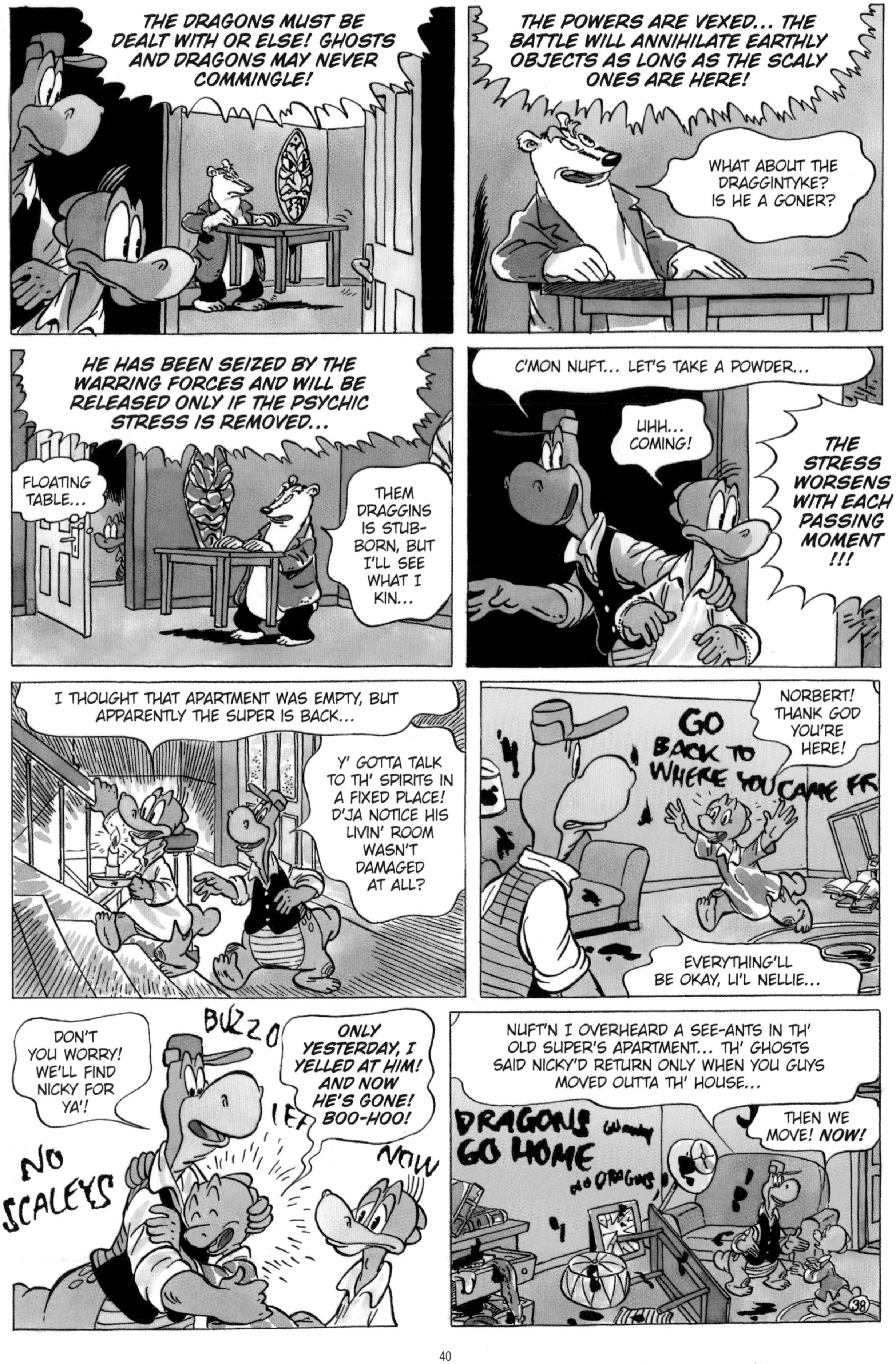
THE DRAGONS MUST BE DEALT WITH OR ELSE! GHOSTS AND DRAGONS MAY NEVER COMMINGLE!
THE POWERS ARE VEXED... THE BATTLE WILL ANNIHILATE EARTHLY OBJECTS AS LONG AS THE SCALY ONES ARE HERE!
WHAT ABOUT THE DRAGGINTYKE? IS HE A GONER?
HE HAS BEEN SEIZED BY THE WARRING FORCES AND WILL BE RELEASED ONLY IF THE PSYCHIC STRESS IS REMOVED...
FLOATING TABLE...
THEM DRAGGINS IS STUB-BORN, BUT I'LL SEE WHAT I KIN...
C'MON NUFT... LET'S TAKE A POWDER...
UHH... COMING!
THE STRESS WORSENS WITH EACH PASSING MOMENT !!!
I THOUGHT THAT APARTMENT WAS EMPTY, BUT APPARENTLY THE SUPER IS BACK...
Y' GOTTA TALK TO TH' SPIRITS IN A FIXED PLACE! D'JA NOTICE HIS LIVIN' ROOM WASN'T DAMAGED AT ALL?
GO BACK TO WHERE YOU CAME FR
NORBERT! THANK GOD YOU'RE HERE!
EVERYTHING'LL BE OKAY, LI'L NELLIE...
DON'T YOU WORRY! WE'LL FIND NICKY FOR YA'!
BUZZO
ONLY YESTERDAY, I YELLED AT HIM! AND NOW HE'S GONE! BOO-HOO!
NO SCALEYS
NOW
NUFT'N I OVERHEARD A SEE-ANTS IN TH' OLD SUPER'S APARTMENT... TH' GHOSTS SAID NICKY'D RETURN ONLY WHEN YOU GUYS MOVED OUTTA TH' HOUSE...
DRAGONS GO HOME
THEN WE MOVE! NOW!
38

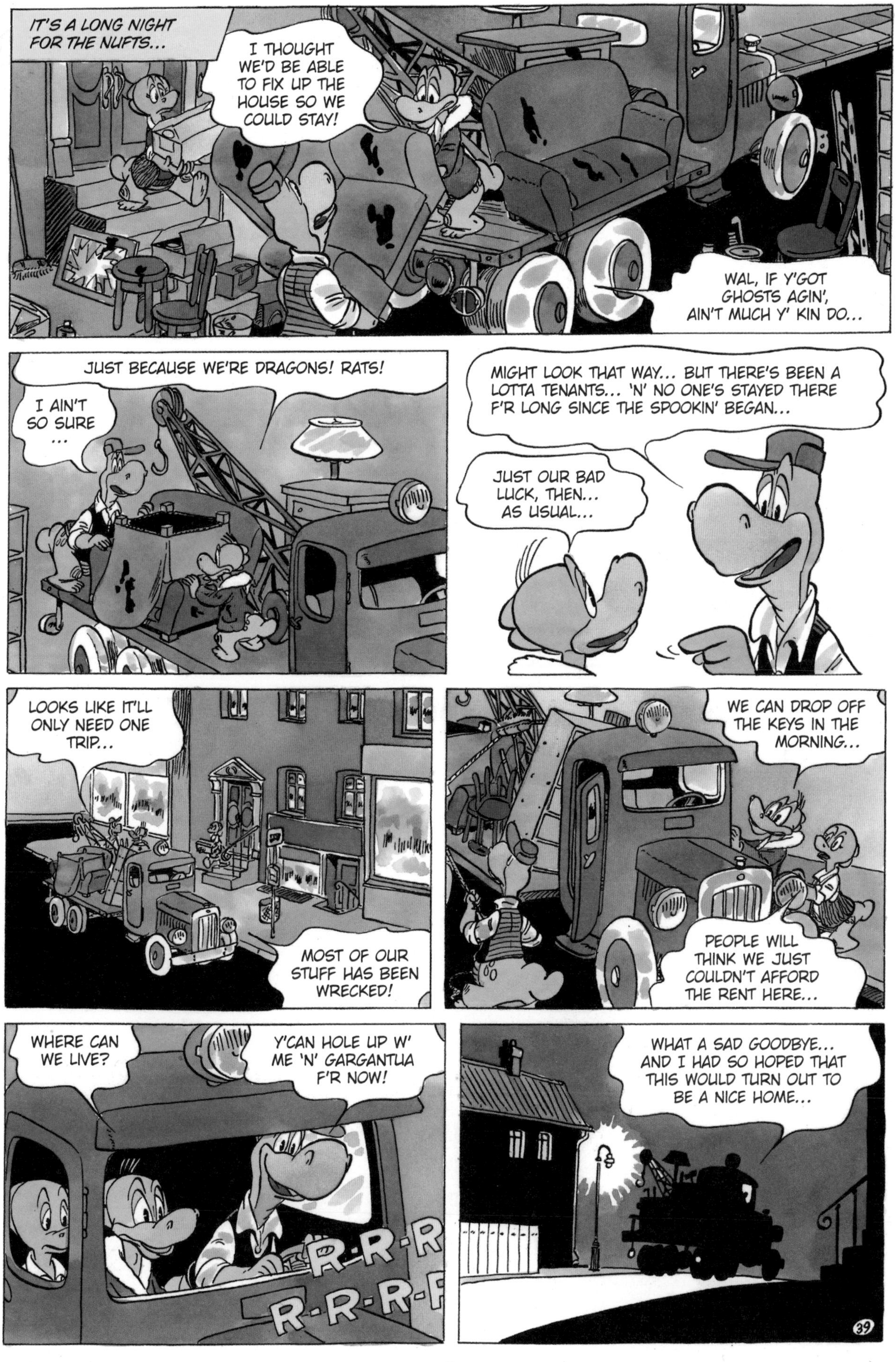
IT'S A LONG NIGHT FOR THE NUFTS...
I THOUGHT WE'D BE ABLE TO FIX UP THE HOUSE SO WE COULD STAY!
WAL, IF Y'GOT GHOSTS AGIN', AIN'T MUCH Y' KIN DO...
JUST BECAUSE WE'RE DRAGONS! RATS!
I AIN'T SO SURE ...
MIGHT LOOK THAT WAY... BUT THERE'S BEEN A LOTTA TENANTS... 'N' NO ONE'S STAYED THERE F'R LONG SINCE THE SPOOKIN' BEGAN...
JUST OUR BAD LUCK, THEN... AS USUAL...
LOOKS LIKE IT'LL ONLY NEED ONE TRIP...
MOST OF OUR STUFF HAS BEEN WRECKED!
WE CAN DROP OFF THE KEYS IN THE MORNING...
PEOPLE WILL THINK WE JUST COULDN'T AFFORD THE RENT HERE...
WHERE CAN WE LIVE?
Y'CAN HOLE UP W' ME 'N' GARGANTUA F'R NOW!
R-R-R
R-R-R-R
WHAT A SAD GOODBYE... AND I HAD SO HOPED THAT THIS WOULD TURN OUT TO BE A NICE HOME...
39

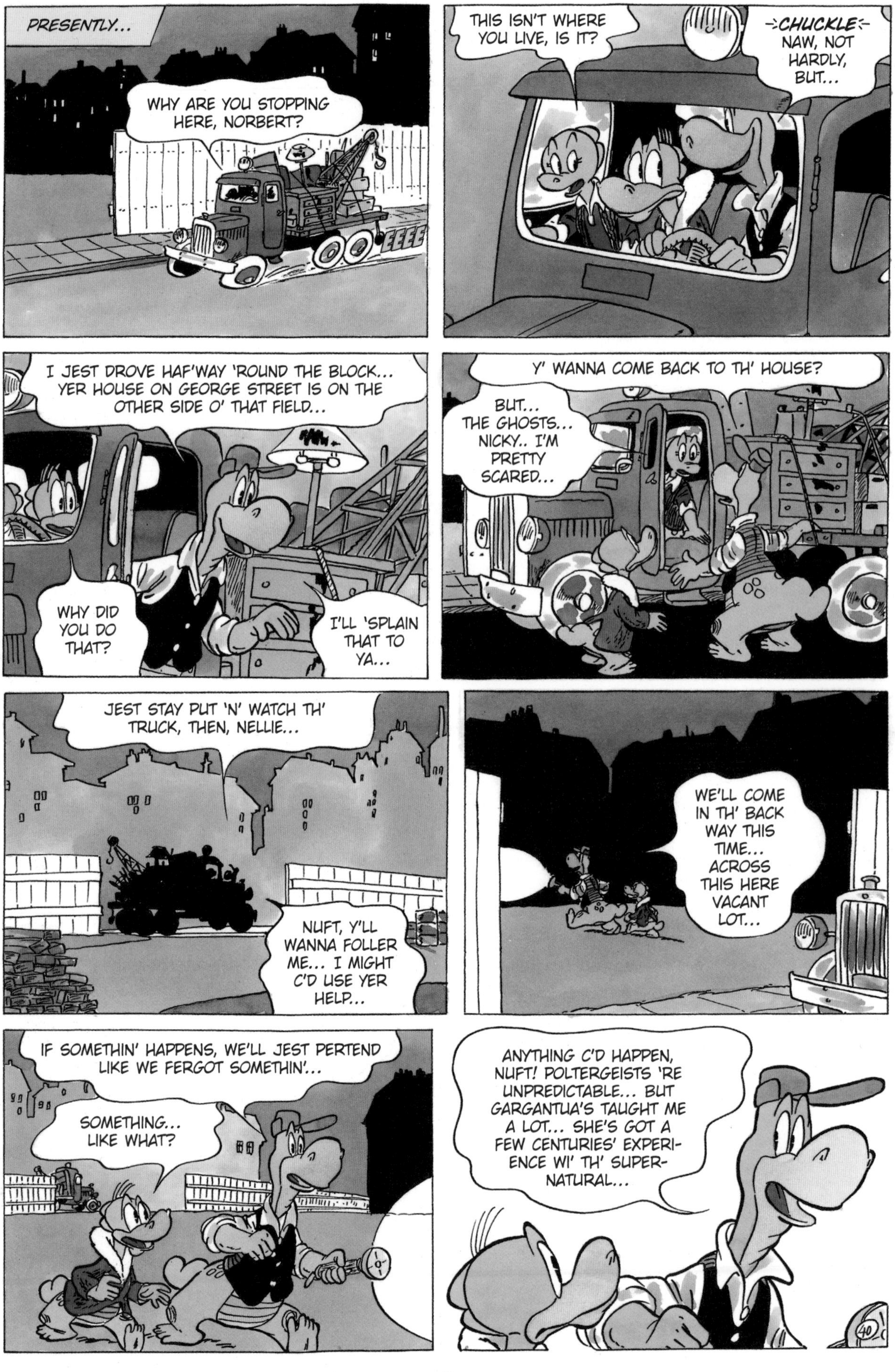
PRESENTLY...
WHY ARE YOU STOPPING HERE, NORBERT?
EEEE
THIS ISN'T WHERE YOU LIVE, IS IT?
CHUCKLE NAW, NOT HARDLY, BUT...
I JEST DROVE HAF'WAY 'ROUND THE BLOCK... YER HOUSE ON GEORGE STREET IS ON THE OTHER SIDE O' THAT FIELD...
WHY DID YOU DO THAT?
I'LL 'SPLAIN THAT TO YA...
Y' WANNA COME BACK TO TH' HOUSE?
BUT... THE GHOSTS... NICKY.. I'M PRETTY SCARED...
JEST STAY PUT 'N' WATCH TH' TRUCK, THEN, NELLIE...
NUFT, Y'LL WANNA FOLLER ME... I MIGHT C'D USE YER HELP...
WE'LL COME IN TH' BACK WAY THIS TIME... ACROSS THIS HERE VACANT LOT...
IF SOMETHIN' HAPPENS, WE'LL JEST PERTEND LIKE WE FERGOT SOMETHIN'...
SOMETHING... LIKE WHAT?
ANYTHING C'D HAPPEN, NUFT! POLTERGEISTS 'RE UNPREDICTABLE... BUT GARGANTUA'S TAUGHT ME A LOT... SHE'S GOT A FEW CENTURIES' EXPERI-ENCE WI' TH' SUPER-NATURAL...
40

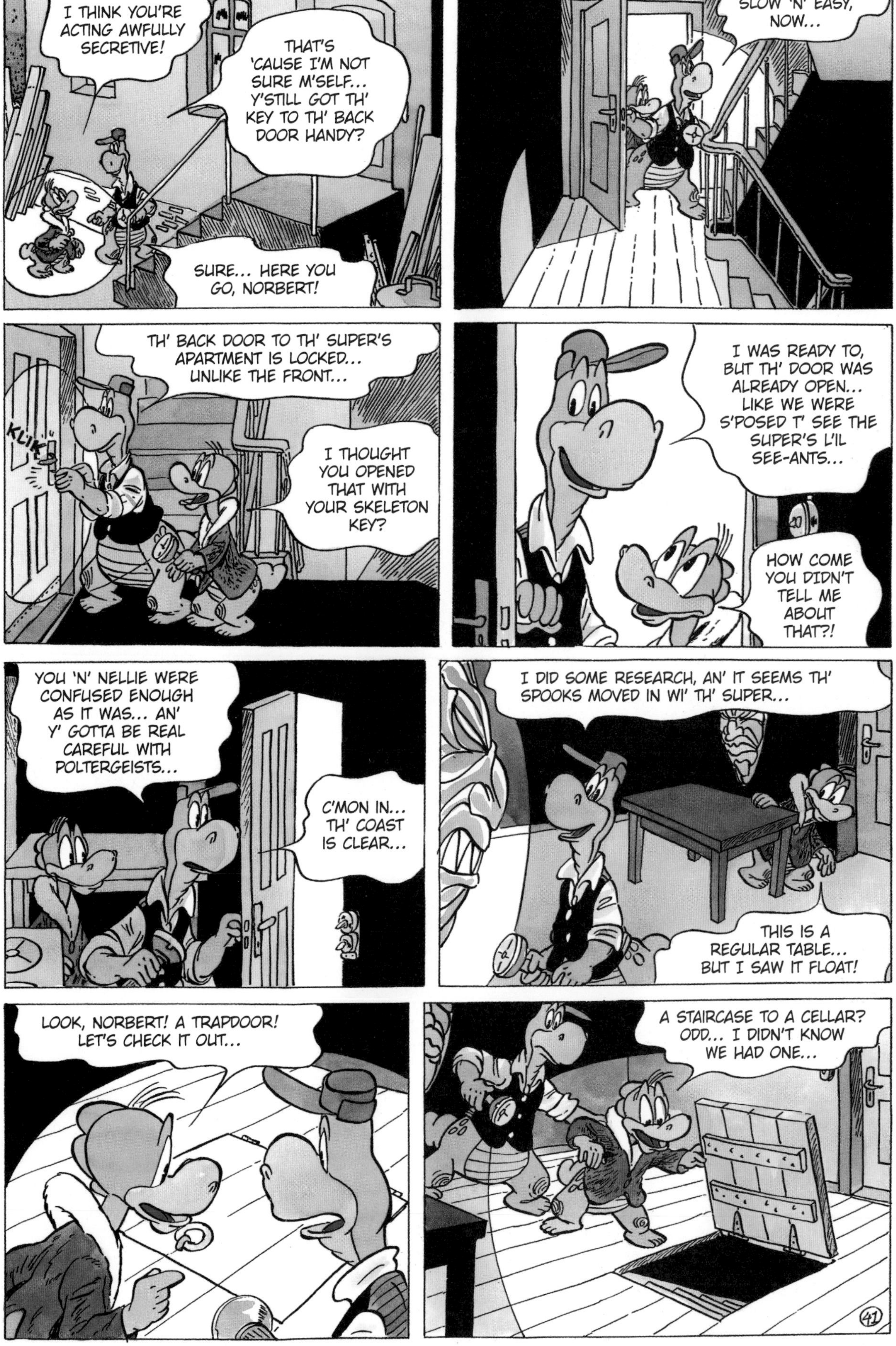
I THINK YOU'RE ACTING AWFULLY SECRETIVE!
THAT'S 'CAUSE I'M NOT SURE M'SELF... Y'STILL GOT TH' KEY TO TH' BACK DOOR HANDY?
SURE... HERE YOU GO, NORBERT!
SLOW 'N' EASY, NOW...
TH' BACK DOOR TO TH' SUPER'S APARTMENT IS LOCKED... UNLIKE THE FRONT...
KLIK
I THOUGHT YOU OPENED THAT WITH YOUR SKELETON KEY?
I WAS READY TO, BUT TH' DOOR WAS ALREADY OPEN... LIKE WE WERE S'POSED T' SEE THE SUPER'S L'IL SEE-ANTS...
HOW COME YOU DIDN'T TELL ME ABOUT THAT?!
YOU 'N' NELLIE WERE CONFUSED ENOUGH AS IT WAS... AN' Y' GOTTA BE REAL CAREFUL WITH POLTERGEISTS...
C'MON IN... TH' COAST IS CLEAR...
I DID SOME RESEARCH, AN' IT SEEMS TH' SPOOKS MOVED IN WI' TH' SUPER...
THIS IS A REGULAR TABLE... BUT I SAW IT FLOAT!
LOOK, NORBERT! A TRAPDOOR! LET'S CHECK IT OUT...
A STAIRCASE TO A CELLAR? ODD... I DIDN'T KNOW WE HAD ONE...
41

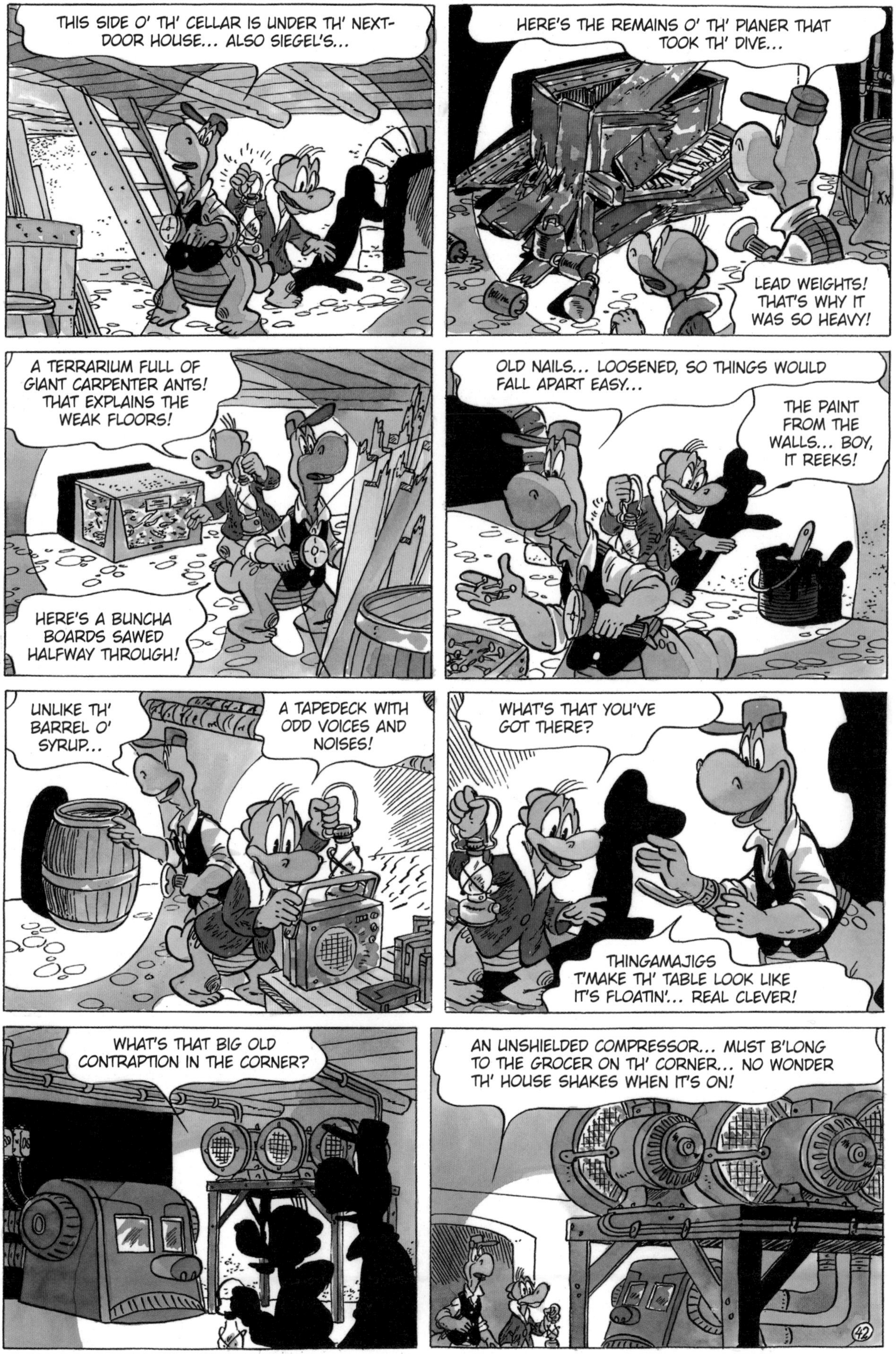

THIS SIDE O' TH' CELLAR IS UNDER TH' NEXT-DOOR HOUSE... ALSO SIEGEL'S...
HERE'S THE REMAINS O' TH' PIANER THAT TOOK TH' DIVE...
LEAD WEIGHTS! THAT'S WHY IT WAS SO HEAVY!
A TERRARIUM FULL OF GIANT CARPENTER ANTS! THAT EXPLAINS THE WEAK FLOORS!
HERE'S A BUNCHA BOARDS SAWED HALFWAY THROUGH!
OLD NAILS... LOOSENED, SO THINGS WOULD FALL APART EASY...
THE PAINT FROM THE WALLS... BOY, IT REEKS!
UNLIKE TH' BARREL O' SYRUP...
A TAPEDECK WITH ODD VOICES AND NOISES!
WHAT'S THAT YOU'VE GOT THERE?
THINGAMAJIGS T'MAKE TH' TABLE LOOK LIKE IT'S FLOATIN'... REAL CLEVER!
WHAT'S THAT BIG OLD CONTRAPTION IN THE CORNER?
AN UNSHIELDED COMPRESSOR... MUST B'LONG TO THE GROCER ON TH' CORNER... NO WONDER TH' HOUSE SHAKES WHEN IT'S ON!
42

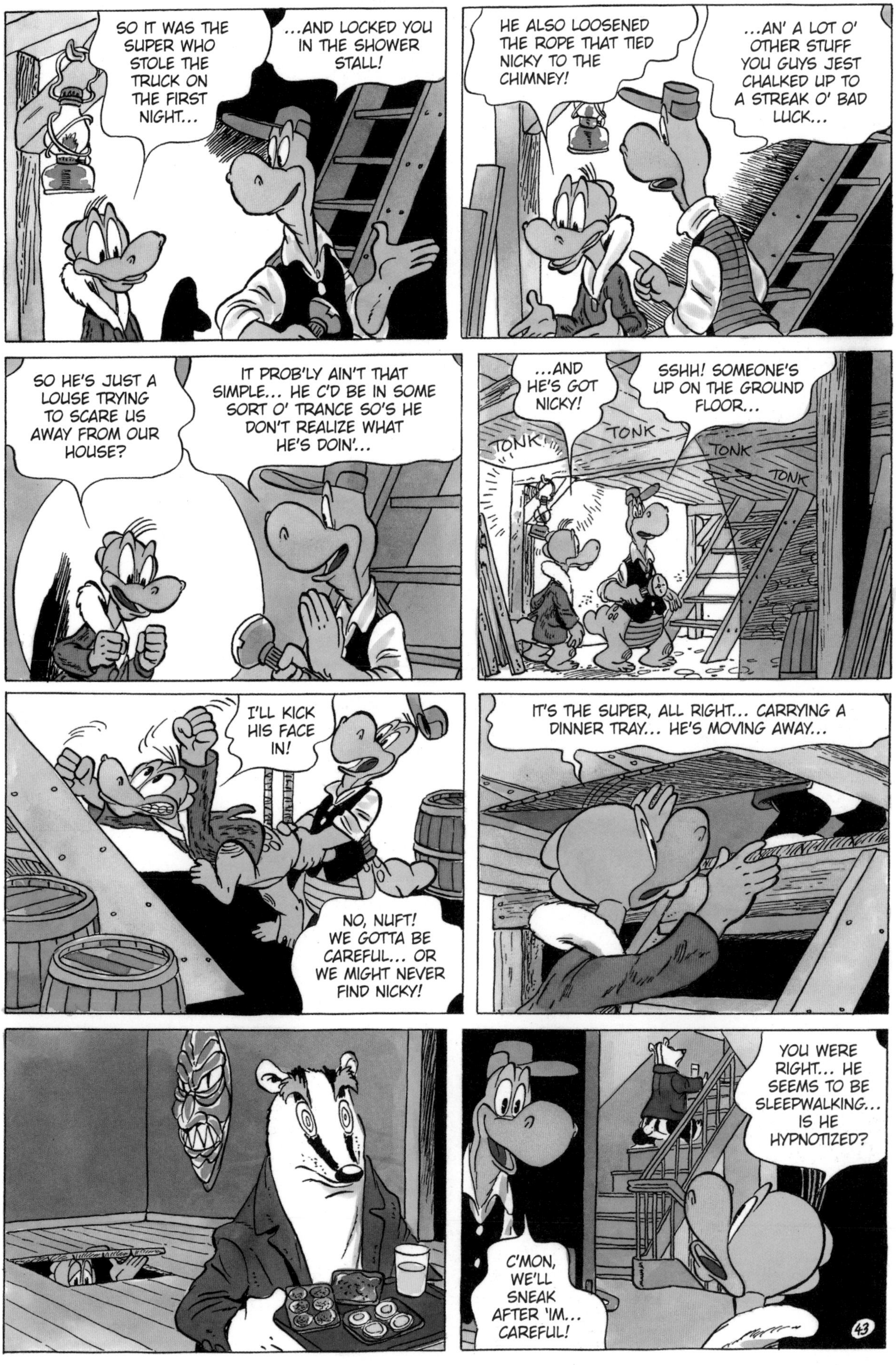
SO IT WAS THE SUPER WHO STOLE THE TRUCK ON THE FIRST NIGHT...
...AND LOCKED YOU IN THE SHOWER STALL!
HE ALSO LOOSENED THE ROPE THAT TIED NICKY TO THE CHIMNEY!
...AN' A LOT O' OTHER STUFF YOU GUYS JEST CHALKED UP TO A STREAK O' BAD LUCK...
SO HE'S JUST A LOUSE TRYING TO SCARE US AWAY FROM OUR HOUSE?
IT PROB'LY AIN'T THAT SIMPLE... HE C'D BE IN SOME SORT O' TRANCE SO'S HE DON'T REALIZE WHAT HE'S DOIN'...
...AND HE'S GOT NICKY!
SSHH! SOMEONE'S UP ON THE GROUND FLOOR...
TONK
TONK
TONK
TONK
I'LL KICK HIS FACE IN!
NO, NUFT! WE GOTTA BE CAREFUL... OR WE MIGHT NEVER FIND NICKY!
IT'S THE SUPER, ALL RIGHT... CARRYING A DINNER TRAY... HE'S MOVING AWAY...
YOU WERE RIGHT... HE SEEMS TO BE SLEEPWALKING... IS HE HYPNOTIZED?
C'MON, WE'LL SNEAK AFTER 'IM... CAREFUL!
43

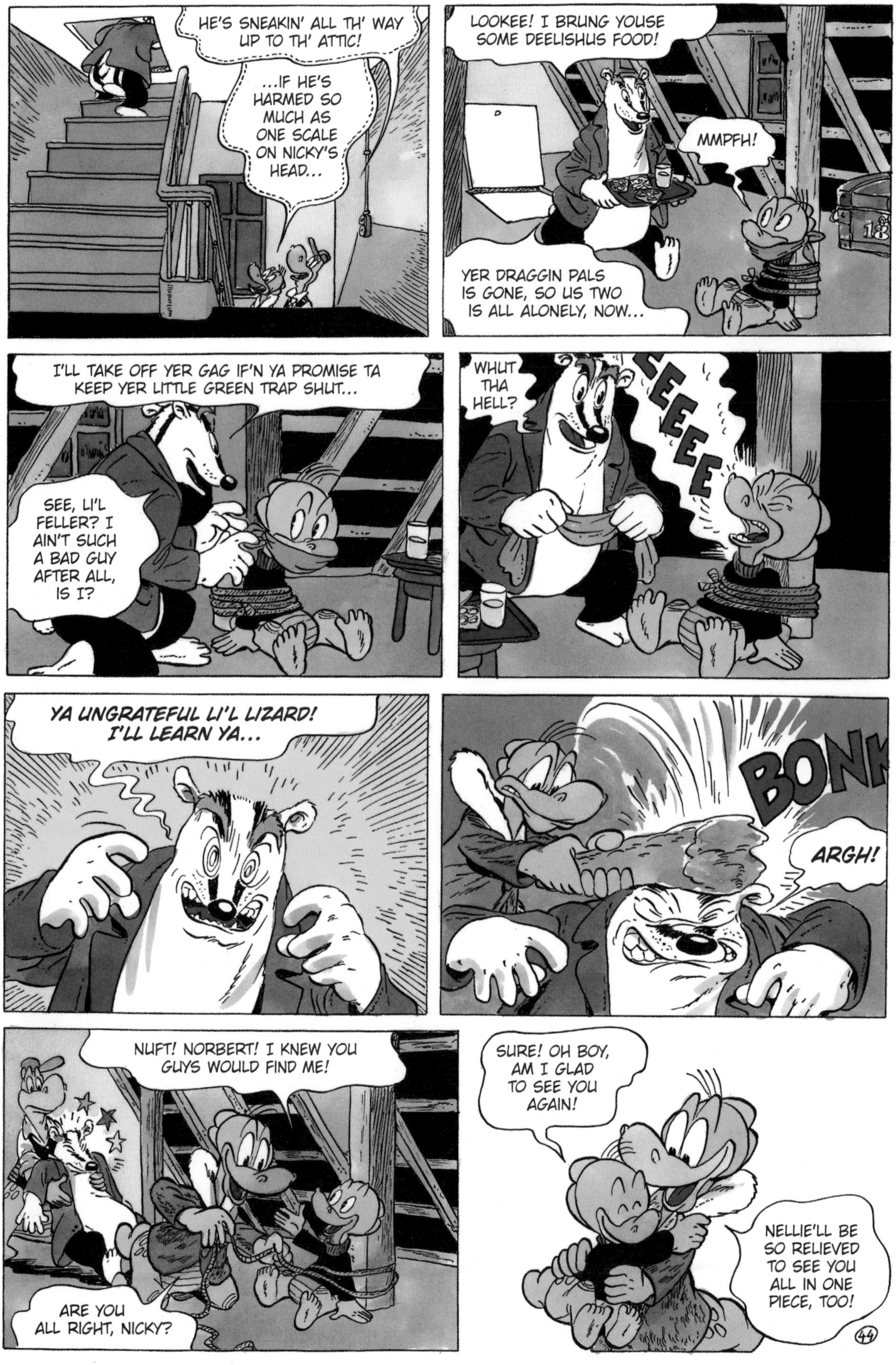
HE'S SNEAKIN' ALL TH' WAY UP TO TH' ATTIC!
...IF HE'S HARMED SO MUCH AS ONE SCALE ON NICKY'S HEAD...
LOOKEE! I BRUNG YOUSE SOME DEELISHUS FOOD!
MMPFH!
YER DRAGGIN PALS IS GONE, SO US TWO IS ALL ALONELY, NOW...
I'LL TAKE OFF YER GAG IF'N YA PROMISE TA KEEP YER LITTLE GREEN TRAP SHUT...
SEE, LI'L FELLER? I AIN'T SUCH A BAD GUY AFTER ALL, IS I?
WHUT THA HELL?
EEEEE
YA UNGRATEFUL LI'L LIZARD! I'LL LEARN YA...
BONK
ARGH!
NUFT! NORBERT! I KNEW YOU GUYS WOULD FIND ME!
ARE YOU ALL RIGHT, NICKY?
SURE! OH BOY, AM I GLAD TO SEE YOU AGAIN!
NELLIE'LL BE SO RELIEVED TO SEE YOU ALL IN ONE PIECE, TOO!
44

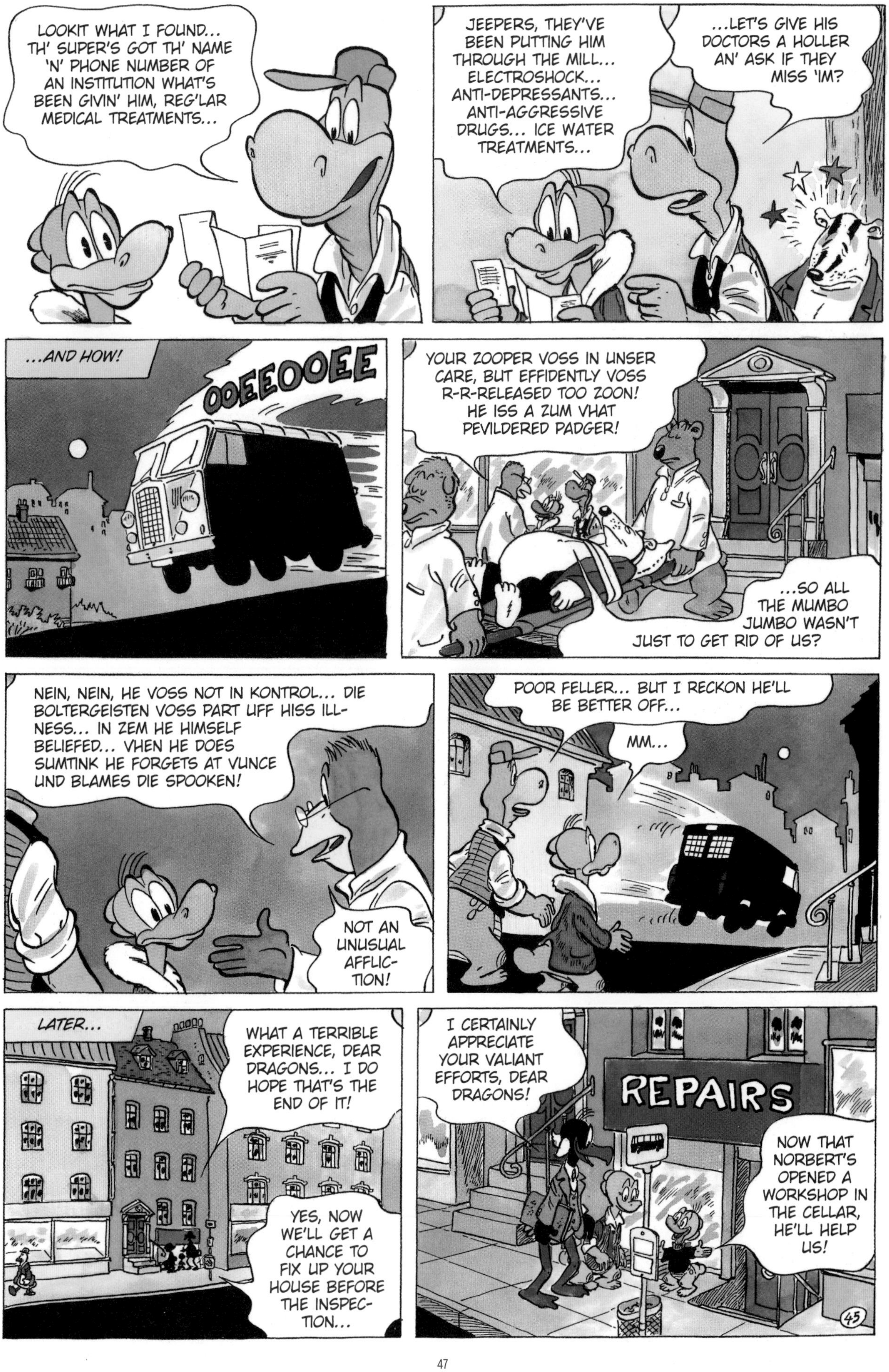
LOOKIT WHAT I FOUND... TH' SUPER'S GOT TH' NAME 'N' PHONE NUMBER OF AN INSTITUTION WHAT'S BEEN GIVIN' HIM, REG'LAR MEDICAL TREATMENTS...
JEEPERS, THEY'VE BEEN PUTTING HIM THROUGH THE MILL... ELECTROSHOCK... ANTI-DEPRESSANTS... ANTI-AGGRESSIVE DRUGS... ICE WATER TREATMENTS...
...LET'S GIVE HIS DOCTORS A HOLLER AN' ASK IF THEY MISS 'IM?
...AND HOW!
OOEEOOEE
YOUR ZOOPER VOSS IN UNSER CARE, BUT EFFIDENTLY VOSS R-R-RELEASED TOO ZOON! HE ISS A ZUM VHAT PEVILDERED PADGER!
...SO ALL THE MUMBO JUMBO WASN'T JUST TO GET RID OF US?
NEIN, NEIN, HE VOSS NOT IN KONTROL... DIE BOLTERGEISTEN VOSS PART UFF HISS ILL-NESS... IN ZEM HE HIMSELF BELIEFED... VHEN HE DOES SUMTINK HE FORGETS AT VUNCE UND BLAMES DIE SPOOKEN!
NOT AN UNUSUAL AFFLIC-TION!
POOR FELLER... BUT I RECKON HE'LL BE BETTER OFF...
MM...
LATER...
WHAT A TERRIBLE EXPERIENCE, DEAR DRAGONS... I DO HOPE THAT'S THE END OF IT!
YES, NOW WE'LL GET A CHANCE TO FIX UP YOUR HOUSE BEFORE THE INSPEC-TION...
I CERTAINLY APPRECIATE YOUR VALIANT EFFORTS, DEAR DRAGONS!
REPAIRS
NOW THAT NORBERT'S OPENED A WORKSHOP IN THE CELLAR, HE'LL HELP US!
45

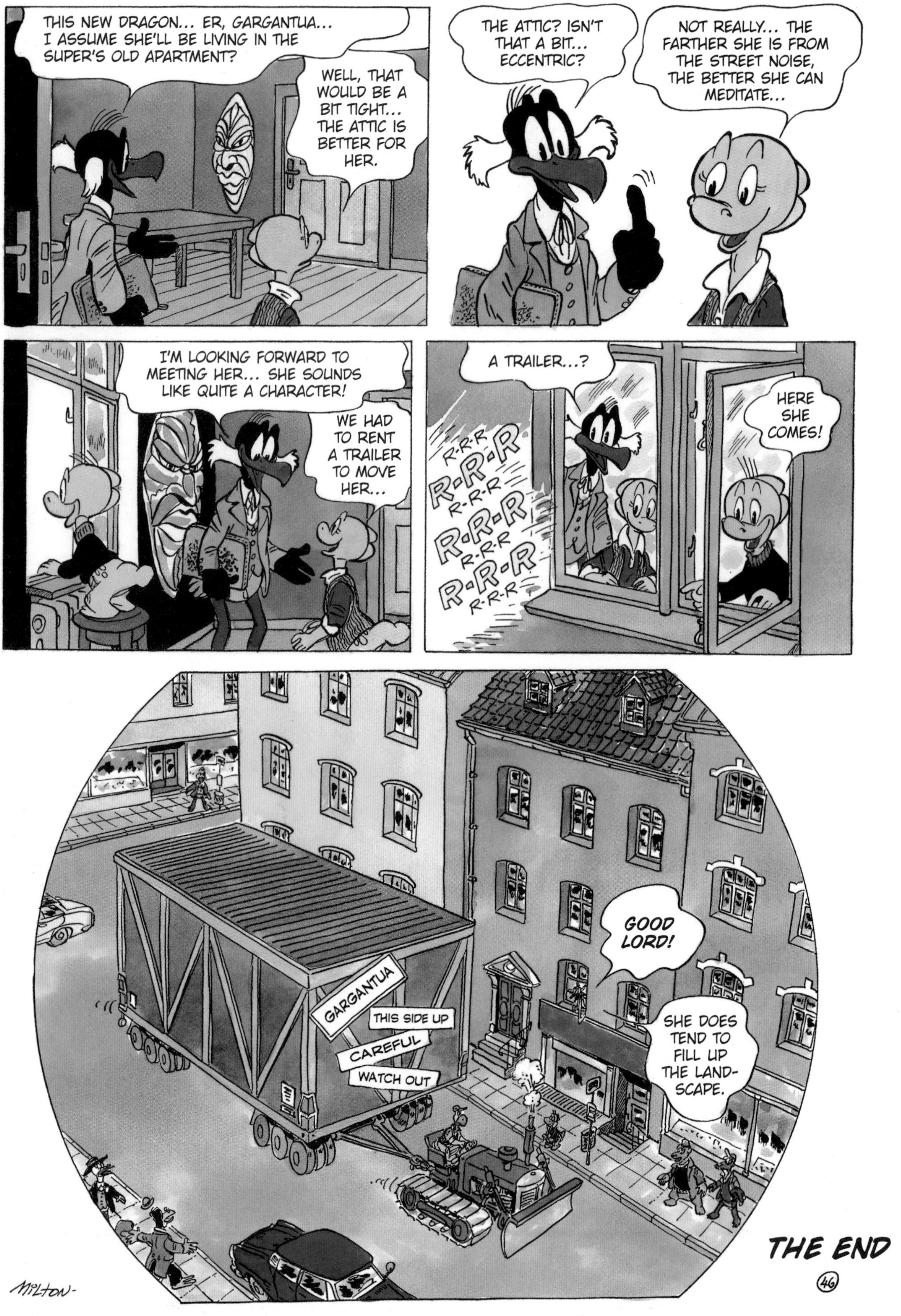
THIS NEW DRAGON... ER, GARGANTUA... I ASSUME SHE'LL BE LIVING IN THE SUPER'S OLD APARTMENT?
WELL, THAT WOULD BE A BIT TIGHT... THE ATTIC IS BETTER FOR HER.
THE ATTIC? ISN'T THAT A BIT... ECCENTRIC?
NOT REALLY... THE FARTHER SHE IS FROM THE STREET NOISE, THE BETTER SHE CAN MEDITATE...
I'M LOOKING FORWARD TO MEETING HER... SHE SOUNDS LIKE QUITE A CHARACTER!
WE HAD TO RENT A TRAILER TO MOVE HER...
A TRAILER...?
HERE SHE COMES!
R-R-R R-R-R R-R-R R-R-R R-R-R R-R-R R-R-R R-R-R R-R-R
GARGANTUA
THIS SIDE UP
CAREFUL
WATCH OUT
GOOD LORD!
SHE DOES TEND TO FILL UP THE LAND-SCAPE.
THE END
46
MILTON-

Trouble on George Street

by Freddy Milton
Translation: Dwight R. Decker
Colors: Freddy Milton

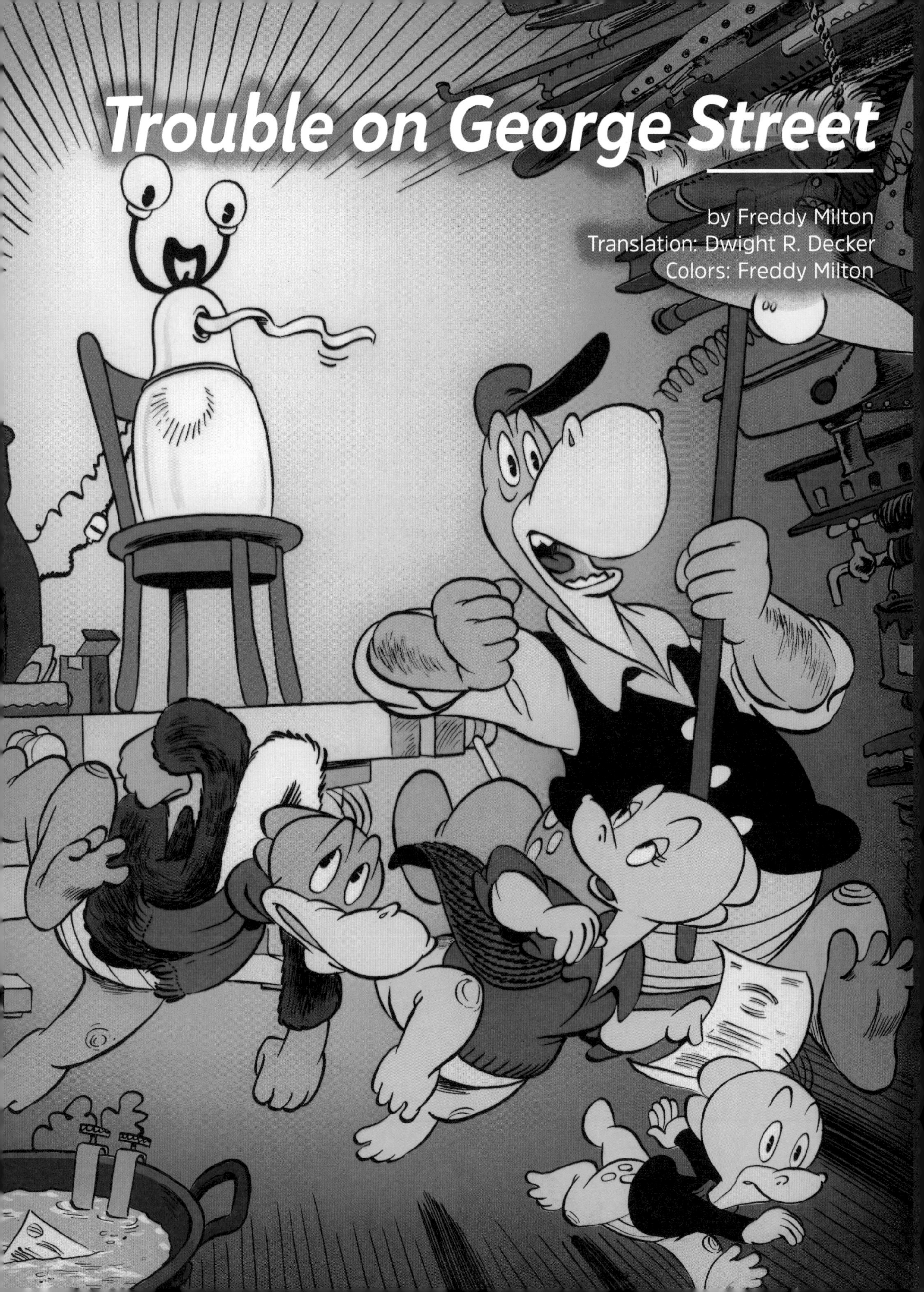

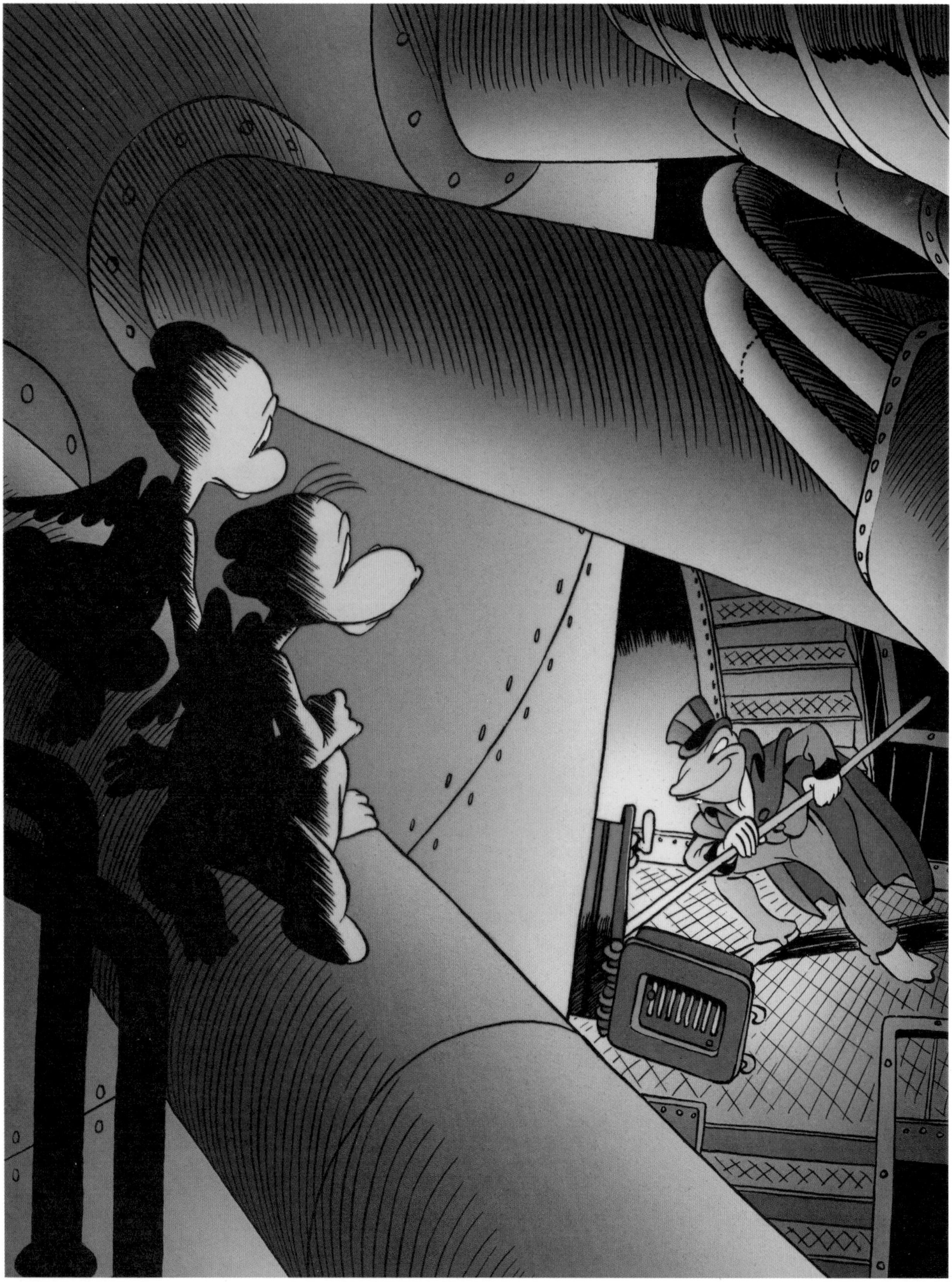

ABOVE: Freddy Milton's back cover art for the Danish edition of *Trouble on George Street*.

PREVIOUS PAGE: Freddy Milton's front cover art for the Danish edition of *Trouble on George Street*.

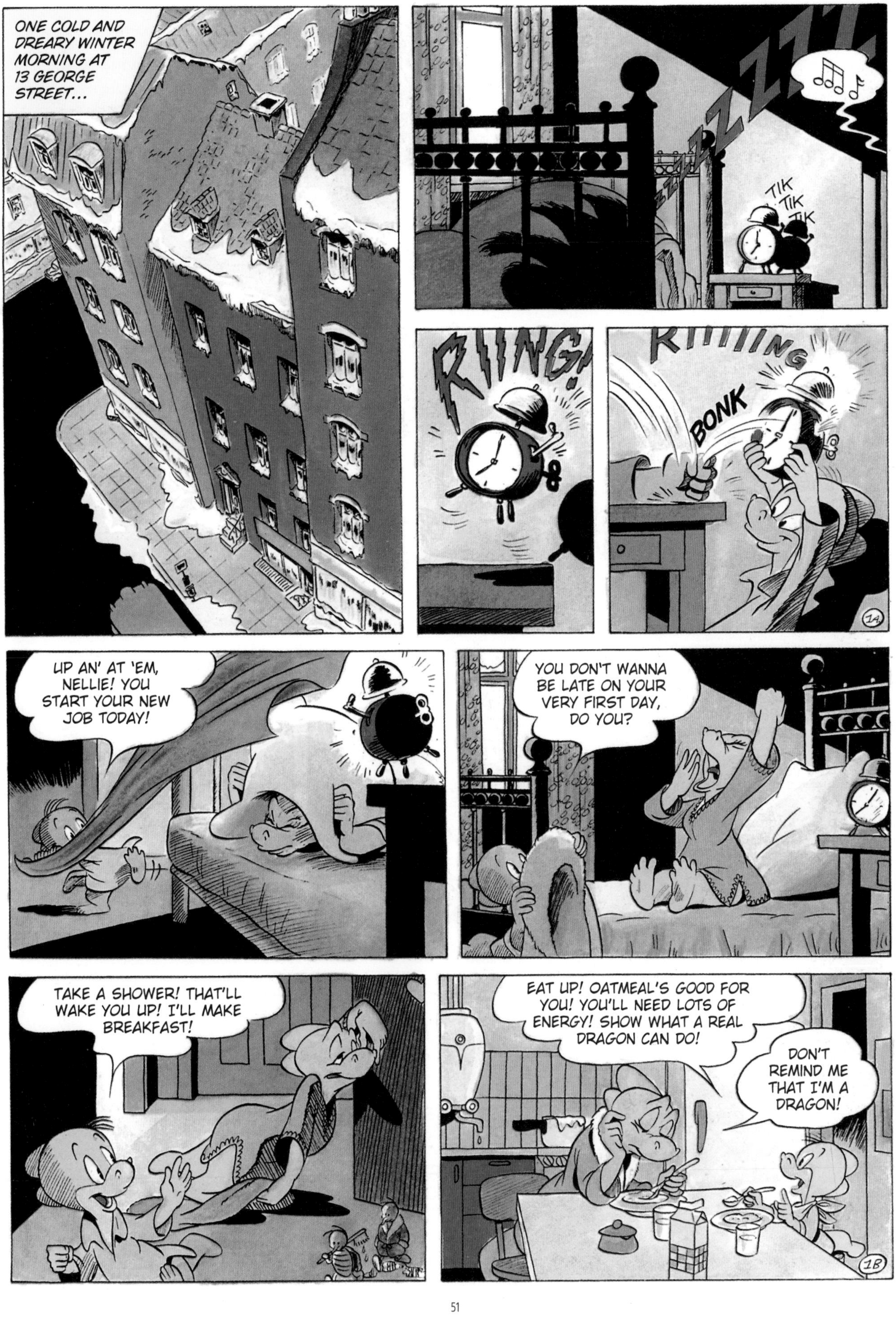
ONE COLD AND DREARY WINTER MORNING AT 13 GEORGE STREET...
ZZZZZZZZZ!
TIK TIK TIK
RIING!
RIIIIING
BONK
1A
UP AN' AT 'EM, NELLIE! YOU START YOUR NEW JOB TODAY!
YOU DON'T WANNA BE LATE ON YOUR VERY FIRST DAY, DO YOU?
TAKE A SHOWER! THAT'LL WAKE YOU UP! I'LL MAKE BREAKFAST!
EAT UP! OATMEAL'S GOOD FOR YOU! YOU'LL NEED LOTS OF ENERGY! SHOW WHAT A REAL DRAGON CAN DO!
DON'T REMIND ME THAT I'M A DRAGON!
1B

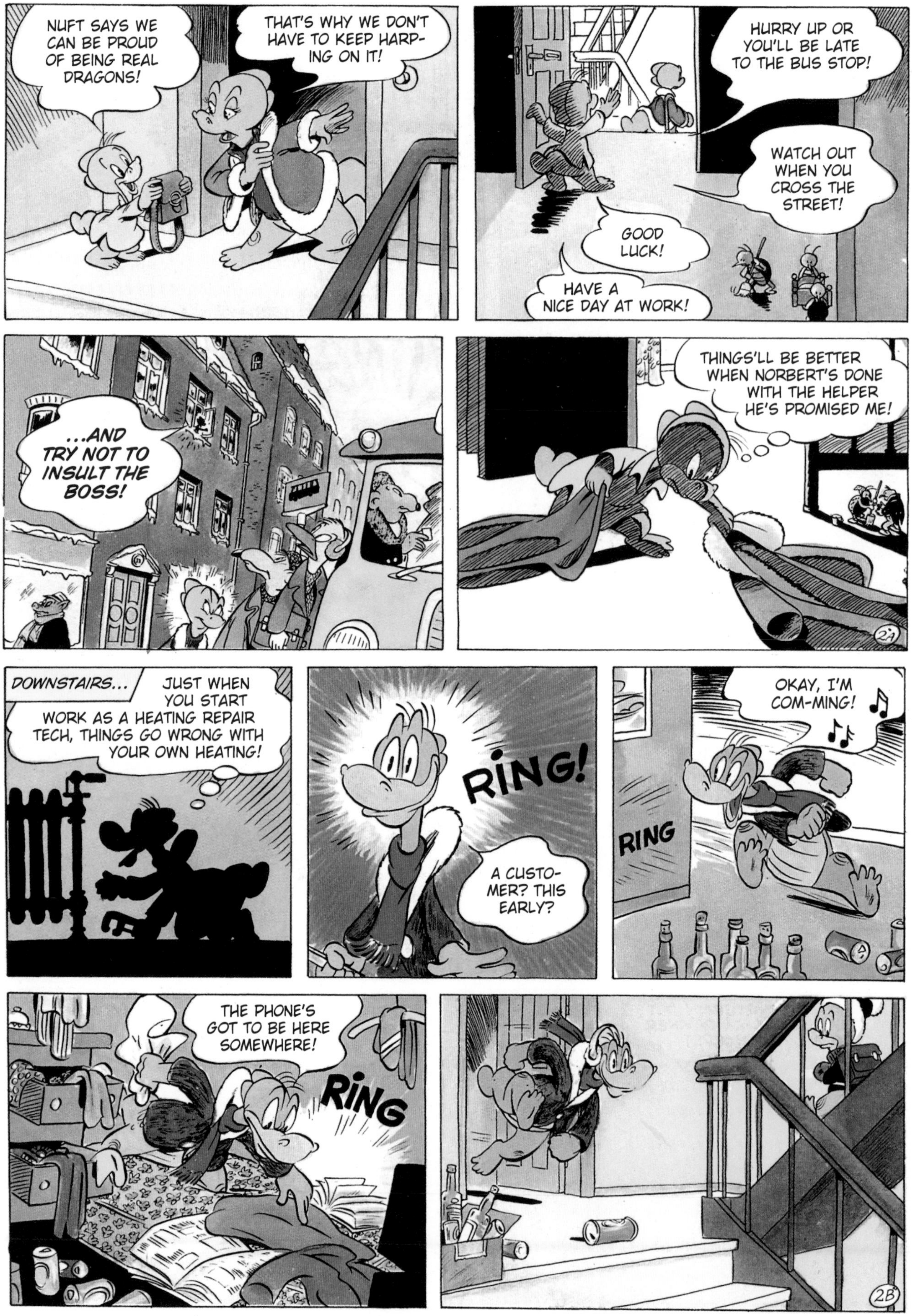
NUFT SAYS WE CAN BE PROUD OF BEING REAL DRAGONS!
THAT'S WHY WE DON'T HAVE TO KEEP HARP-ING ON IT!
HURRY UP OR YOU'LL BE LATE TO THE BUS STOP!
WATCH OUT WHEN YOU CROSS THE STREET!
GOOD LUCK!
HAVE A NICE DAY AT WORK!
...AND TRY NOT TO INSULT THE BOSS!
THINGS'LL BE BETTER WHEN NORBERT'S DONE WITH THE HELPER HE'S PROMISED ME!
2A
DOWNSTAIRS...
JUST WHEN YOU START WORK AS A HEATING REPAIR TECH, THINGS GO WRONG WITH YOUR OWN HEATING!
RING!
A CUSTO-MER? THIS EARLY?
OKAY, I'M COM-MING!
RING
THE PHONE'S GOT TO BE HERE SOMEWHERE!
RING
2B

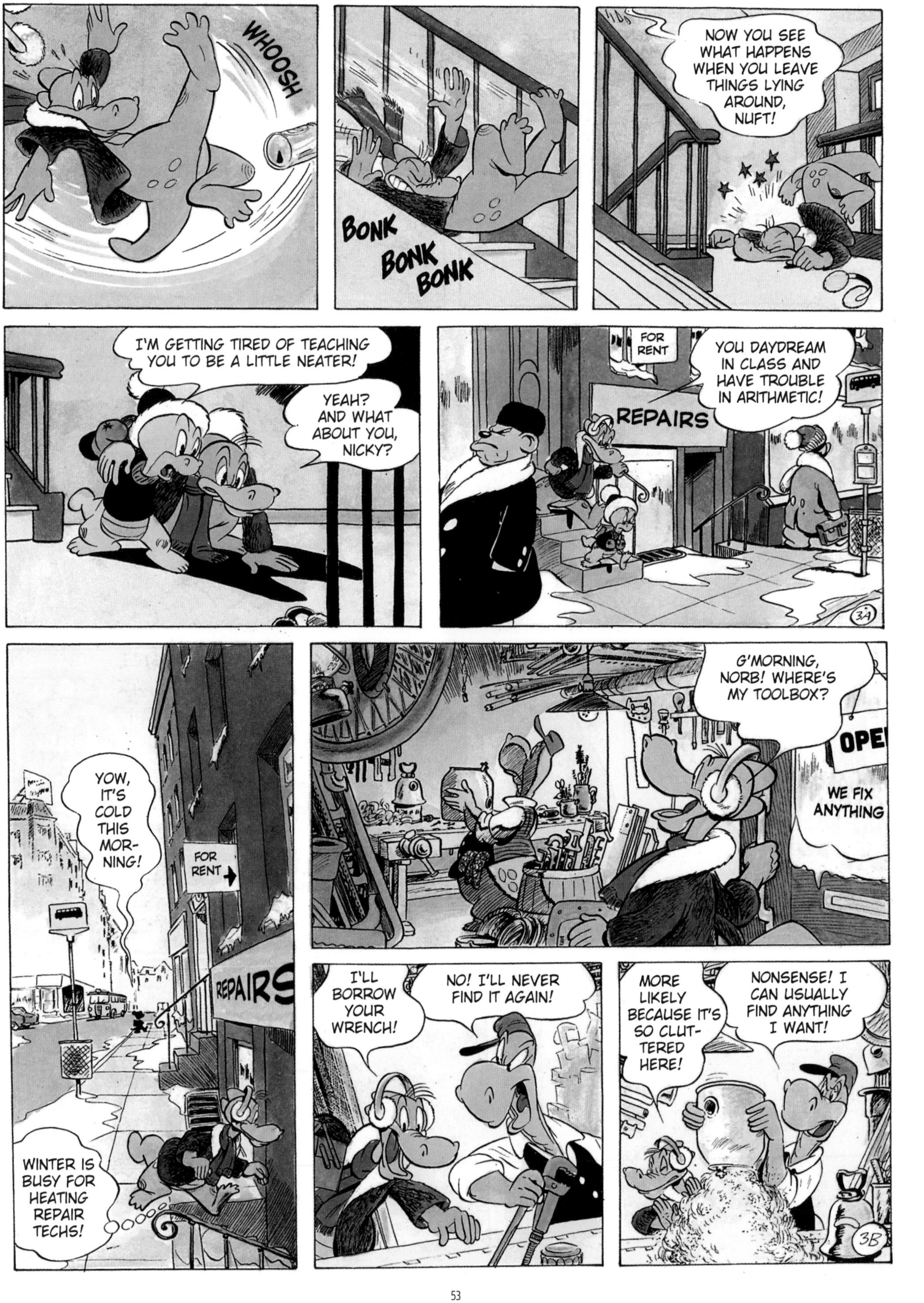
WHOOSH
BONK
BONK
BONK
NOW YOU SEE WHAT HAPPENS WHEN YOU LEAVE THINGS LYING AROUND, NUFT!
I'M GETTING TIRED OF TEACHING YOU TO BE A LITTLE NEATER!
YEAH? AND WHAT ABOUT YOU, NICKY?
FOR RENT
REPAIRS
YOU DAYDREAM IN CLASS AND HAVE TROUBLE IN ARITHMETIC!
3A
YOW, IT'S COLD THIS MOR-NING!
FOR RENT
REPAIRS
WINTER IS BUSY FOR HEATING REPAIR TECHS!
G'MORNING, NORB! WHERE'S MY TOOLBOX?
OPE
WE FIX ANYTHING
I'LL BORROW YOUR WRENCH!
NO! I'LL NEVER FIND IT AGAIN!
MORE LIKELY BECAUSE IT'S SO CLUT-TERED HERE!
NONSENSE! I CAN USUALLY FIND ANYTHING I WANT!
3B

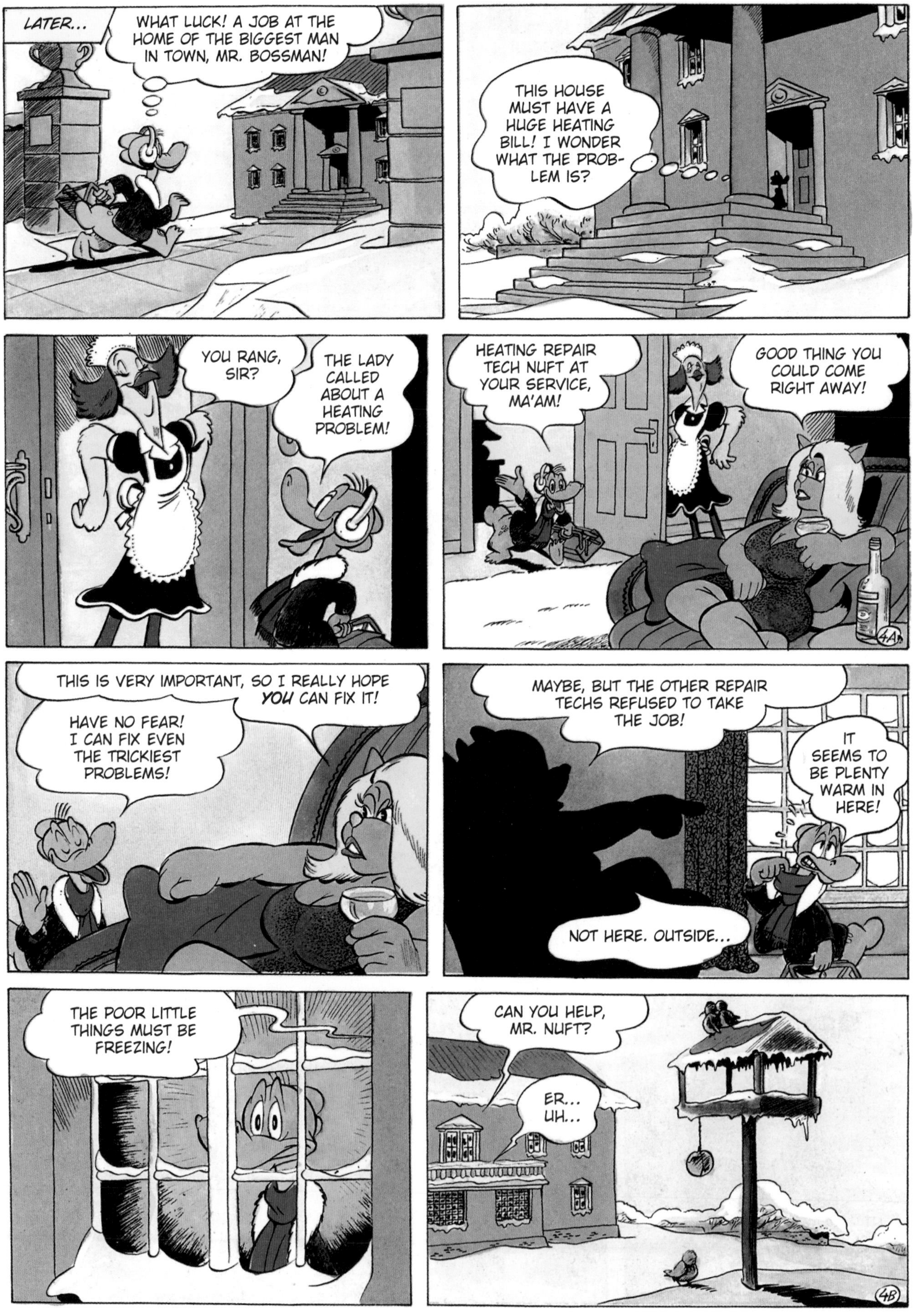
LATER...
WHAT LUCK! A JOB AT THE HOME OF THE BIGGEST MAN IN TOWN, MR. BOSSMAN!
THIS HOUSE MUST HAVE A HUGE HEATING BILL! I WONDER WHAT THE PROB-LEM IS?
YOU RANG, SIR?
THE LADY CALLED ABOUT A HEATING PROBLEM!
HEATING REPAIR TECH NUFT AT YOUR SERVICE, MA'AM!
GOOD THING YOU COULD COME RIGHT AWAY!
4A
THIS IS VERY IMPORTANT, SO I REALLY HOPE *YOU* CAN FIX IT!
HAVE NO FEAR! I CAN FIX EVEN THE TRICKIEST PROBLEMS!
MAYBE, BUT THE OTHER REPAIR TECHS REFUSED TO TAKE THE JOB!
IT SEEMS TO BE PLENTY WARM IN HERE!
NOT HERE. OUTSIDE...
THE POOR LITTLE THINGS MUST BE FREEZING!
CAN YOU HELP, MR. NUFT?
ER... UH...
4B

HMM... NOT EXACTLY AN EASY JOB!

THE FLOOR'S COLD AND COVERED WITH SNOW! SOMETHING HAS TO BE DONE!

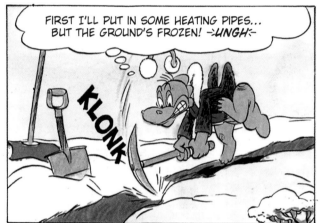

FIRST I'LL PUT IN SOME HEATING PIPES... BUT THE GROUND'S FROZEN! ~UNGH~

KLONK

AND THE PIPES HAVE TO BE INSULATED TO CUT DOWN ON HEAT LOSS!

PIP ?

ZIV ZIV ZIV ZIV ZIV

BONK BONK BONK BONK

FZZZZ FZZZZ FZZZ

ZZ ZZ ZZ ZZ

A LITTLE MASTERPIECE OF A RADIATOR, IF I DO SAY SO MYSELF!

AND IT JUST HAS TO BE CONNECTED...

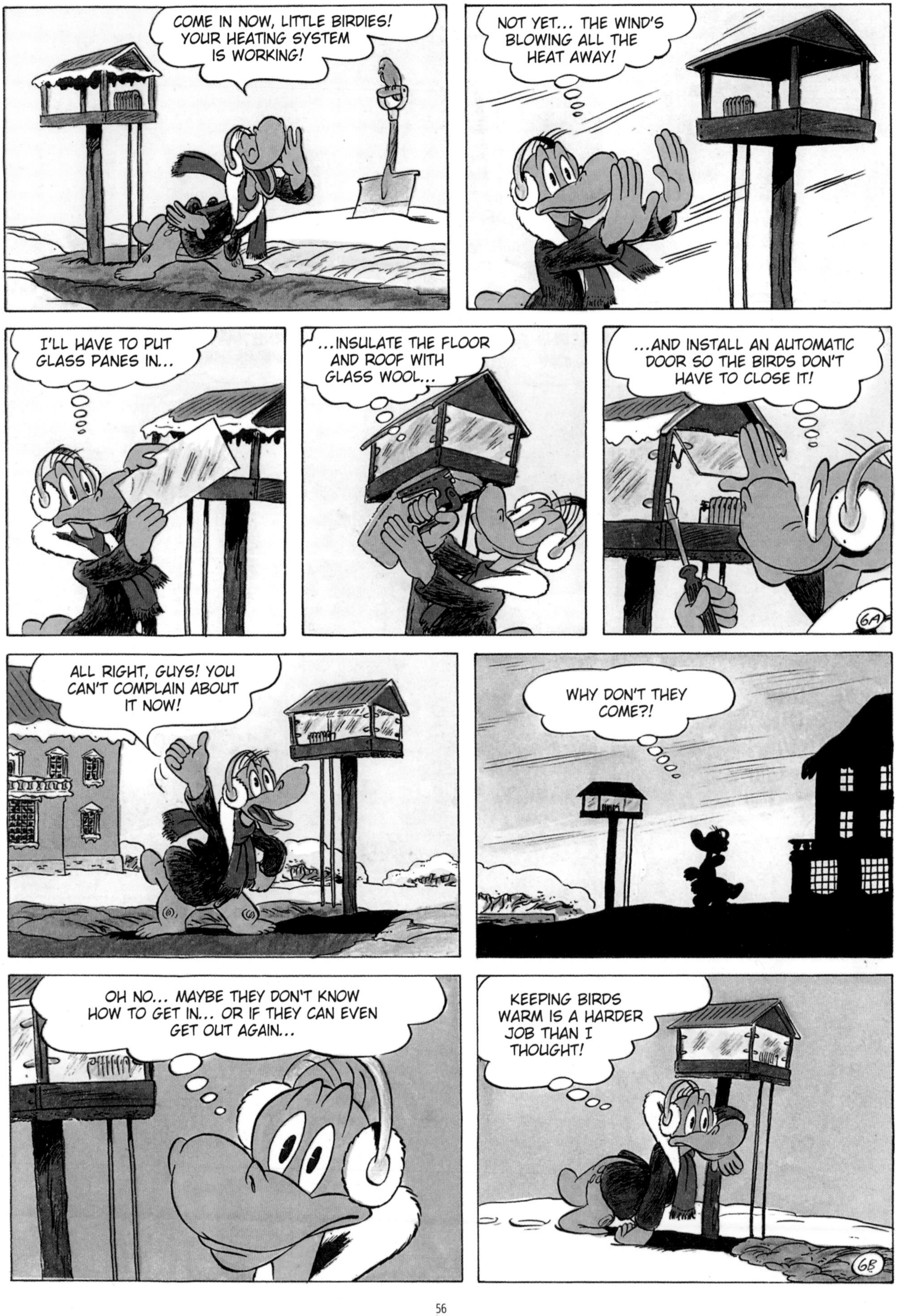
COME IN NOW, LITTLE BIRDIES! YOUR HEATING SYSTEM IS WORKING!
NOT YET... THE WIND'S BLOWING ALL THE HEAT AWAY!
I'LL HAVE TO PUT GLASS PANES IN...
...INSULATE THE FLOOR AND ROOF WITH GLASS WOOL...
...AND INSTALL AN AUTOMATIC DOOR SO THE BIRDS DON'T HAVE TO CLOSE IT!
6A
ALL RIGHT, GUYS! YOU CAN'T COMPLAIN ABOUT IT NOW!
WHY DON'T THEY COME?!
OH NO... MAYBE THEY DON'T KNOW HOW TO GET IN... OR IF THEY CAN EVEN GET OUT AGAIN...
KEEPING BIRDS WARM IS A HARDER JOB THAN I THOUGHT!
6B

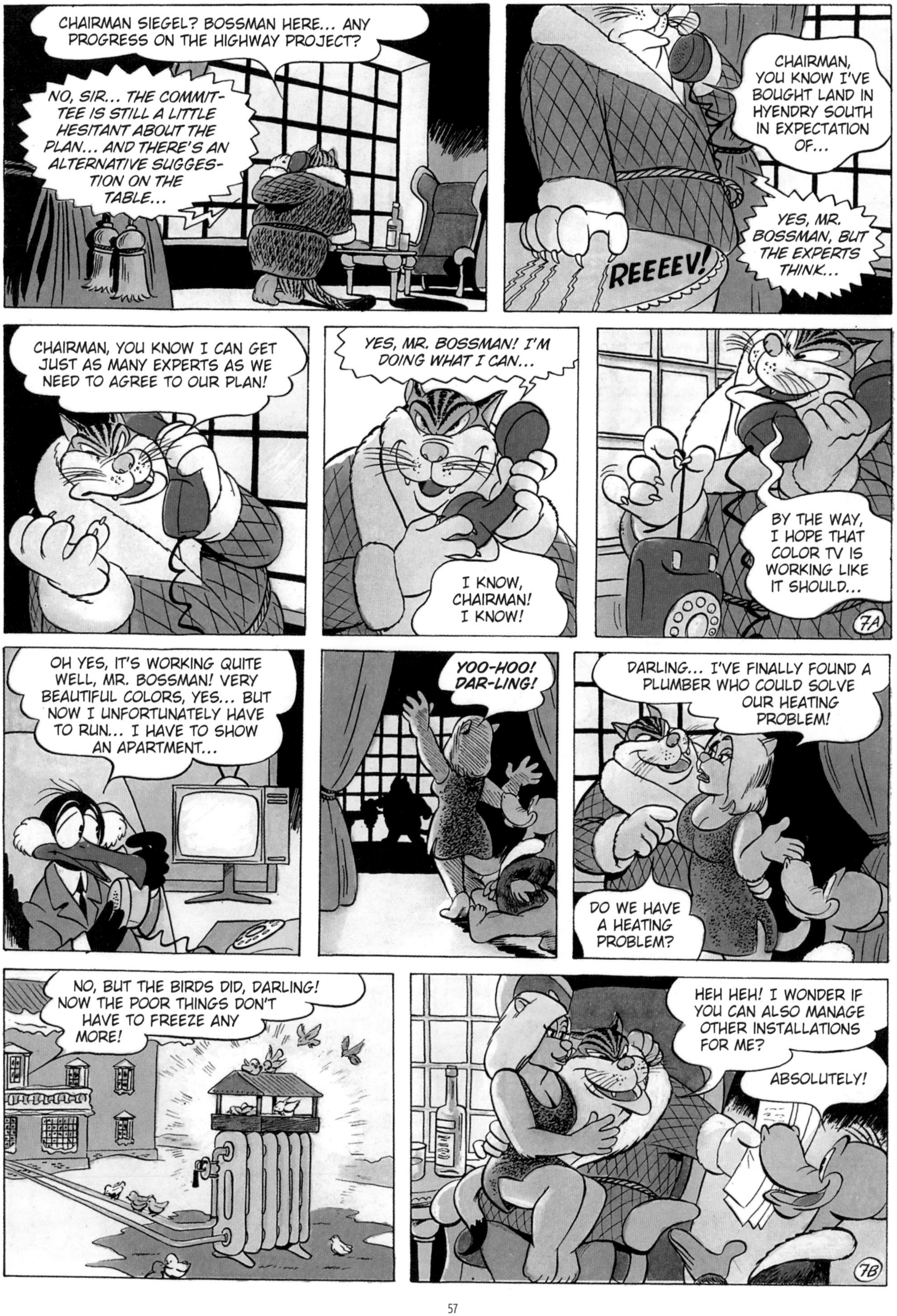
CHAIRMAN SIEGEL? BOSSMAN HERE... ANY PROGRESS ON THE HIGHWAY PROJECT?
NO, SIR... THE COMMITTEE IS STILL A LITTLE HESITANT ABOUT THE PLAN... AND THERE'S AN ALTERNATIVE SUGGESTION ON THE TABLE...
CHAIRMAN, YOU KNOW I'VE BOUGHT LAND IN HYENDRY SOUTH IN EXPECTATION OF...
REEEEV!
YES, MR. BOSSMAN, BUT THE EXPERTS THINK...
CHAIRMAN, YOU KNOW I CAN GET JUST AS MANY EXPERTS AS WE NEED TO AGREE TO OUR PLAN!
YES, MR. BOSSMAN! I'M DOING WHAT I CAN...
I KNOW, CHAIRMAN! I KNOW!
BY THE WAY, I HOPE THAT COLOR TV IS WORKING LIKE IT SHOULD...
7A
OH YES, IT'S WORKING QUITE WELL, MR. BOSSMAN! VERY BEAUTIFUL COLORS, YES... BUT NOW I UNFORTUNATELY HAVE TO RUN... I HAVE TO SHOW AN APARTMENT...
YOO-HOO! DAR-LING!
DARLING... I'VE FINALLY FOUND A PLUMBER WHO COULD SOLVE OUR HEATING PROBLEM!
DO WE HAVE A HEATING PROBLEM?
NO, BUT THE BIRDS DID, DARLING! NOW THE POOR THINGS DON'T HAVE TO FREEZE ANY MORE!
HEH HEH! I WONDER IF YOU CAN ALSO MANAGE OTHER INSTALLATIONS FOR ME?
ABSOLUTELY!
7B

MEANWHILE, NELLIE IS STARTING HER NEW JOB AT CITY HALL IN THE OFFICE OF MR. MYOPICK...

EXCELLENT, MS. NELLIE! BUT WHERE ARE THE FIVE COPIES?

FIVE COPIES?

YES, A COPY FOR EACH STEP OF THE PROCESS, AND ONE FOR THE CENTRAL ARCHIVE!

RIGHT AWAY, SIR!

OH, CAN YOU TAKE THIS SUPER-URGENT DELIVERY FORM TO DEPARTMENT 37?

YOU WANT IT DELIVERED FAST?

WELL, SENDING IT AS A REGULAR URGENT MESSAGE WOULD TAKE FOREVER!

BUT AT THE COUNTER IN DEPARTMENT 37...

COLD IN HERE, ISN'T IT?

COLDER 'N A DOG'S NOSE!

OH NO!

8A

BUT MAYBE I CAN STILL SPEED THINGS UP A LITTLE...

SHOWING INITIATIVE AND EFFICIENCY FROM THE START MAKES A GOOD IMPRESSION!

SUPER-IMPORTANT EXPRESS MESSAGE FOR THE CHIEF ADMINISTRATOR!

I'LL TAKE IT FOR HIM!

SORRY, CAN'T!

THIS HAS TO BE DELIVERED PERSONALLY!

8B

58

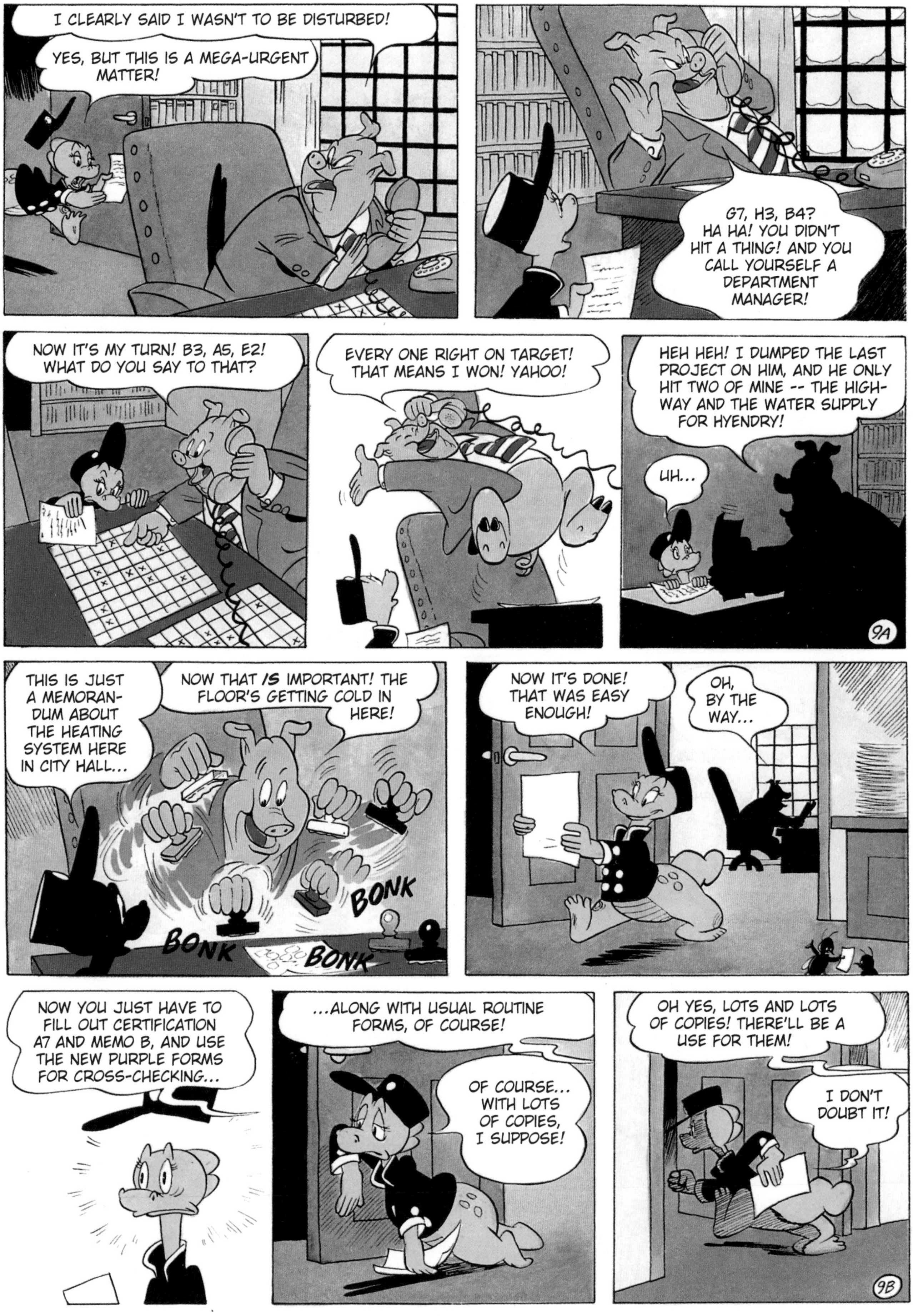
I CLEARLY SAID I WASN'T TO BE DISTURBED!
YES, BUT THIS IS A MEGA-URGENT MATTER!
G7, H3, B4? HA HA! YOU DIDN'T HIT A THING! AND YOU CALL YOURSELF A DEPARTMENT MANAGER!
NOW IT'S MY TURN! B3, A5, E2! WHAT DO YOU SAY TO THAT?
EVERY ONE RIGHT ON TARGET! THAT MEANS I WON! YAHOO!
HEH HEH! I DUMPED THE LAST PROJECT ON HIM, AND HE ONLY HIT TWO OF MINE -- THE HIGH-WAY AND THE WATER SUPPLY FOR HYENDRY!
UH...
9A
THIS IS JUST A MEMORAN-DUM ABOUT THE HEATING SYSTEM HERE IN CITY HALL...
NOW THAT IS IMPORTANT! THE FLOOR'S GETTING COLD IN HERE!
BONK
BONK
BONK
NOW IT'S DONE! THAT WAS EASY ENOUGH!
OH, BY THE WAY...
NOW YOU JUST HAVE TO FILL OUT CERTIFICATION A7 AND MEMO B, AND USE THE NEW PURPLE FORMS FOR CROSS-CHECKING...
...ALONG WITH USUAL ROUTINE FORMS, OF COURSE!
OF COURSE... WITH LOTS OF COPIES, I SUPPOSE!
OH YES, LOTS AND LOTS OF COPIES! THERE'LL BE A USE FOR THEM!
I DON'T DOUBT IT!
9B

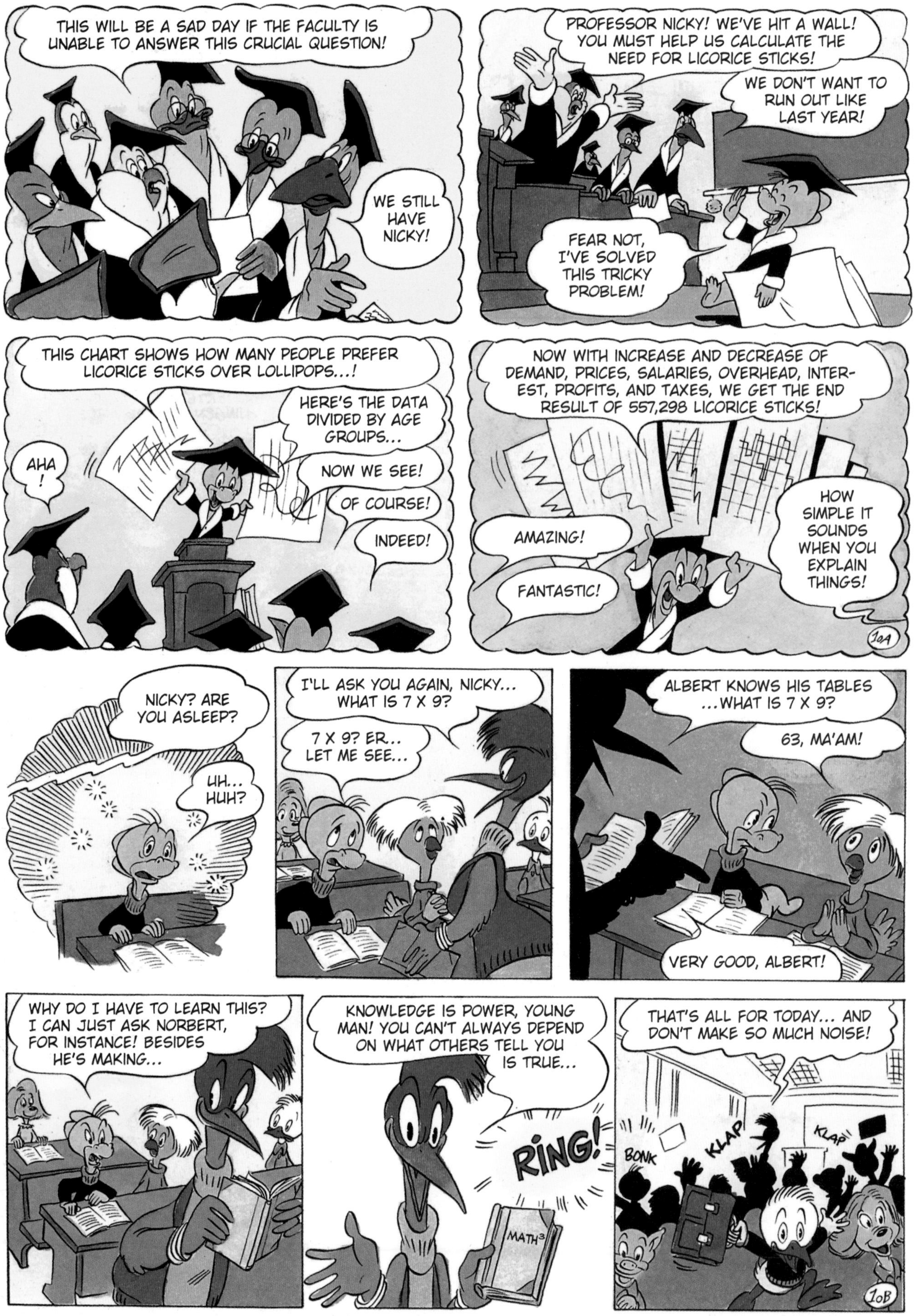

THIS WILL BE A SAD DAY IF THE FACULTY IS UNABLE TO ANSWER THIS CRUCIAL QUESTION!
WE STILL HAVE NICKY!
PROFESSOR NICKY! WE'VE HIT A WALL! YOU MUST HELP US CALCULATE THE NEED FOR LICORICE STICKS!
WE DON'T WANT TO RUN OUT LIKE LAST YEAR!
FEAR NOT, I'VE SOLVED THIS TRICKY PROBLEM!
THIS CHART SHOWS HOW MANY PEOPLE PREFER LICORICE STICKS OVER LOLLIPOPS...!
AHA!
HERE'S THE DATA DIVIDED BY AGE GROUPS...
NOW WE SEE!
OF COURSE!
INDEED!
NOW WITH INCREASE AND DECREASE OF DEMAND, PRICES, SALARIES, OVERHEAD, INTER-EST, PROFITS, AND TAXES, WE GET THE END RESULT OF 557,298 LICORICE STICKS!
AMAZING!
FANTASTIC!
HOW SIMPLE IT SOUNDS WHEN YOU EXPLAIN THINGS!
10A
NICKY? ARE YOU ASLEEP?
UH... HUH?
I'LL ASK YOU AGAIN, NICKY... WHAT IS 7 X 9?
7 X 9? ER.. LET ME SEE...
ALBERT KNOWS HIS TABLES ...WHAT IS 7 X 9?
63, MA'AM!
VERY GOOD, ALBERT!
WHY DO I HAVE TO LEARN THIS? I CAN JUST ASK NORBERT, FOR INSTANCE! BESIDES HE'S MAKING...
KNOWLEDGE IS POWER, YOUNG MAN! YOU CAN'T ALWAYS DEPEND ON WHAT OTHERS TELL YOU IS TRUE...
RING!
MATH3
THAT'S ALL FOR TODAY... AND DON'T MAKE SO MUCH NOISE!
BONK
KLAP
KLAP
10B

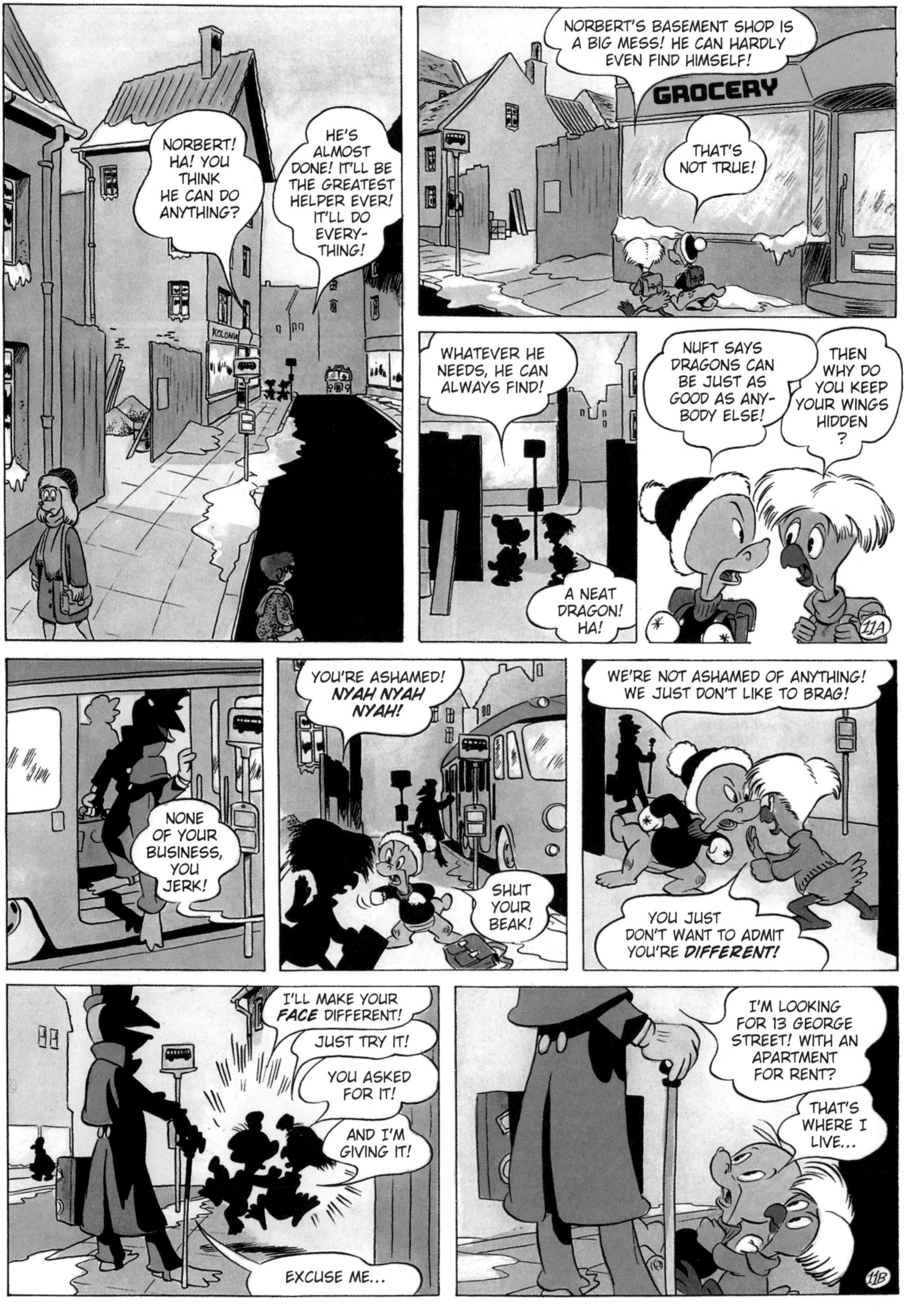
NORBERT! HA! YOU THINK HE CAN DO ANYTHING?
HE'S ALMOST DONE! IT'LL BE THE GREATEST HELPER EVER! IT'LL DO EVERY-THING!
NORBERT'S BASEMENT SHOP IS A BIG MESS! HE CAN HARDLY EVEN FIND HIMSELF!
GROCERY
THAT'S NOT TRUE!
WHATEVER HE NEEDS, HE CAN ALWAYS FIND!
A NEAT DRAGON! HA!
NUFT SAYS DRAGONS CAN BE JUST AS GOOD AS ANY-BODY ELSE!
THEN WHY DO YOU KEEP YOUR WINGS HIDDEN ?
11A
NONE OF YOUR BUSINESS, YOU JERK!
YOU'RE ASHAMED! NYAH NYAH NYAH!
SHUT YOUR BEAK!
WE'RE NOT ASHAMED OF ANYTHING! WE JUST DON'T LIKE TO BRAG!
YOU JUST DON'T WANT TO ADMIT YOU'RE DIFFERENT!
I'LL MAKE YOUR FACE DIFFERENT!
JUST TRY IT!
YOU ASKED FOR IT!
AND I'M GIVING IT!
EXCUSE ME...
I'M LOOKING FOR 13 GEORGE STREET! WITH AN APARTMENT FOR RENT?
THAT'S WHERE I LIVE...
11B

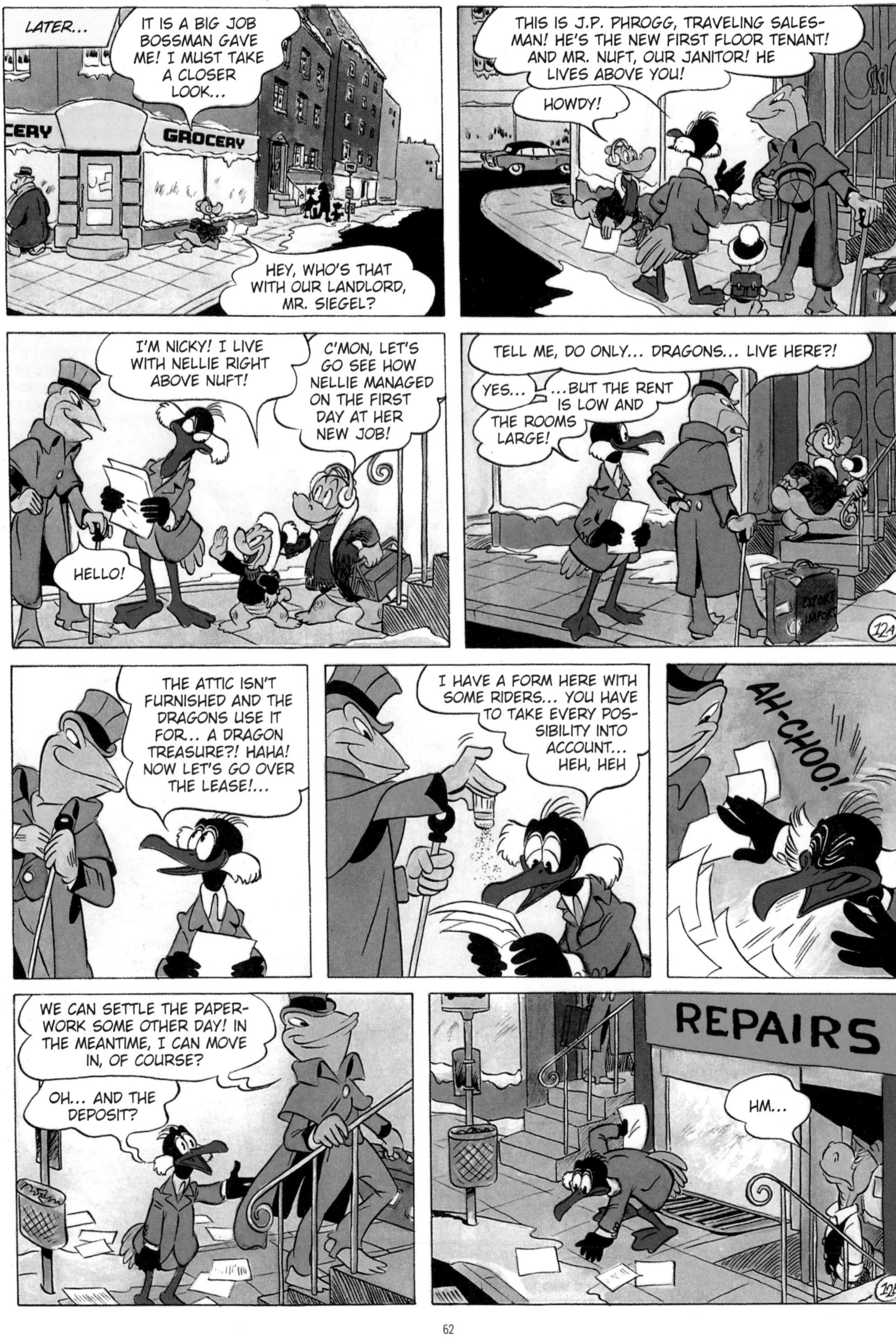
LATER...
IT IS A BIG JOB BOSSMAN GAVE ME! I MUST TAKE A CLOSER LOOK...
CERY
GROCERY
HEY, WHO'S THAT WITH OUR LANDLORD, MR. SIEGEL?
THIS IS J.P. PHROGG, TRAVELING SALESMAN! HE'S THE NEW FIRST FLOOR TENANT! AND MR. NUFT, OUR JANITOR! HE LIVES ABOVE YOU!
HOWDY!
I'M NICKY! I LIVE WITH NELLIE RIGHT ABOVE NUFT!
C'MON, LET'S GO SEE HOW NELLIE MANAGED ON THE FIRST DAY AT HER NEW JOB!
HELLO!
TELL ME, DO ONLY... DRAGONS... LIVE HERE?!
YES...
...BUT THE RENT IS LOW AND
THE ROOMS LARGE!
EXPORT IMPORT
12A
THE ATTIC ISN'T FURNISHED AND THE DRAGONS USE IT FOR... A DRAGON TREASURE?! HAHA! NOW LET'S GO OVER THE LEASE!...
I HAVE A FORM HERE WITH SOME RIDERS... YOU HAVE TO TAKE EVERY POSSIBILITY INTO ACCOUNT... HEH, HEH
AH-CHOO!
WE CAN SETTLE THE PAPERWORK SOME OTHER DAY! IN THE MEANTIME, I CAN MOVE IN, OF COURSE?
OH... AND THE DEPOSIT?
REPAIRS
HM...
12B

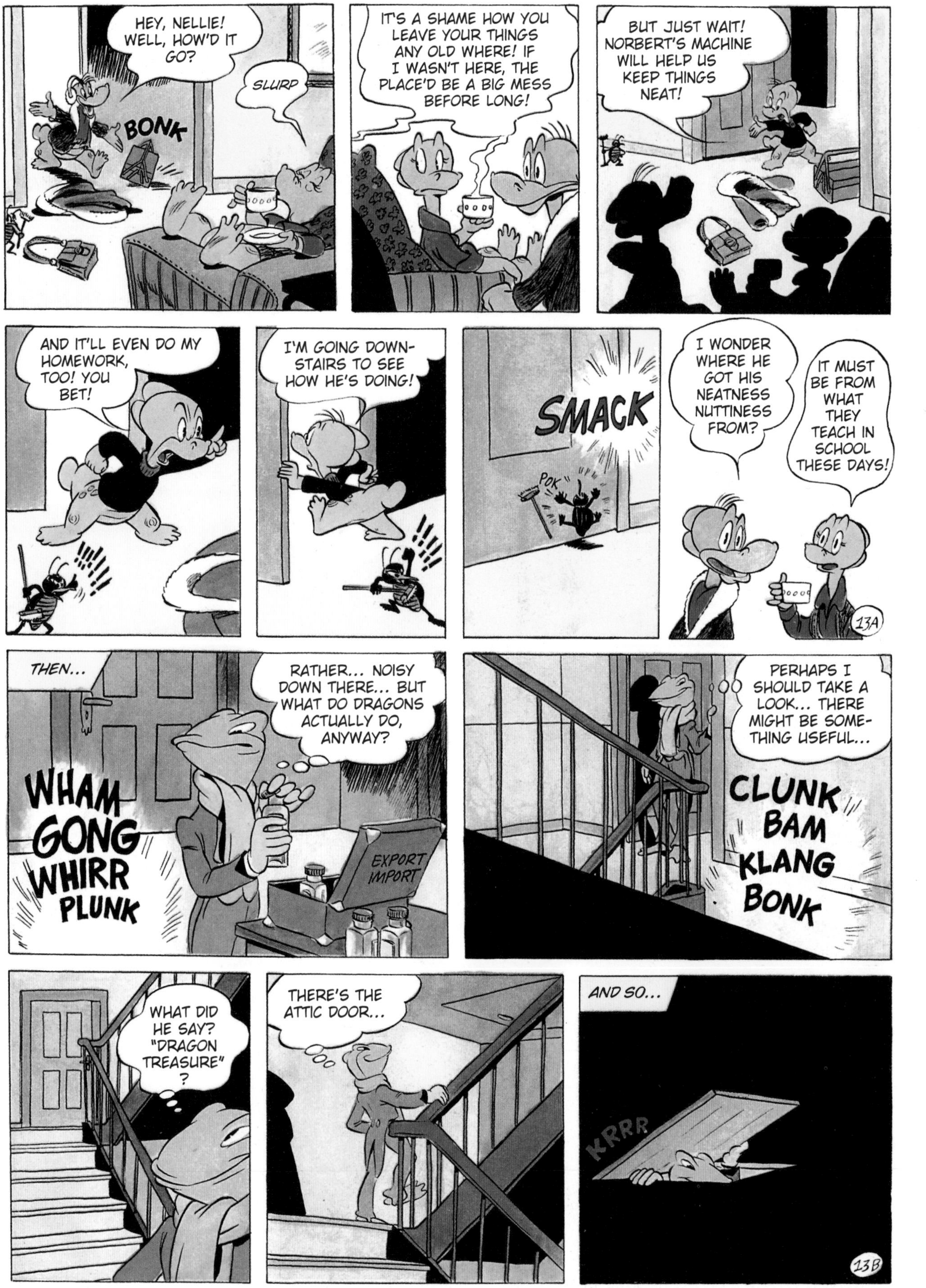
HEY, NELLIE! WELL, HOW'D IT GO?
SLURP
BONK
IT'S A SHAME HOW YOU LEAVE YOUR THINGS ANY OLD WHERE! IF I WASN'T HERE, THE PLACE'D BE A BIG MESS BEFORE LONG!
BUT JUST WAIT! NORBERT'S MACHINE WILL HELP US KEEP THINGS NEAT!
AND IT'LL EVEN DO MY HOMEWORK, TOO! YOU BET!
I'M GOING DOWN-STAIRS TO SEE HOW HE'S DOING!
SMACK
POK
I WONDER WHERE HE GOT HIS NEATNESS NUTTINESS FROM?
IT MUST BE FROM WHAT THEY TEACH IN SCHOOL THESE DAYS!
13A
THEN...
RATHER... NOISY DOWN THERE... BUT WHAT DO DRAGONS ACTUALLY DO, ANYWAY?
WHAM
GONG
WHIRR
PLUNK
EXPORT IMPORT
PERHAPS I SHOULD TAKE A LOOK... THERE MIGHT BE SOME-THING USEFUL...
CLUNK
BAM
KLANG
BONK
WHAT DID HE SAY? "DRAGON TREASURE"?
THERE'S THE ATTIC DOOR...
AND SO...
KRRR
13B

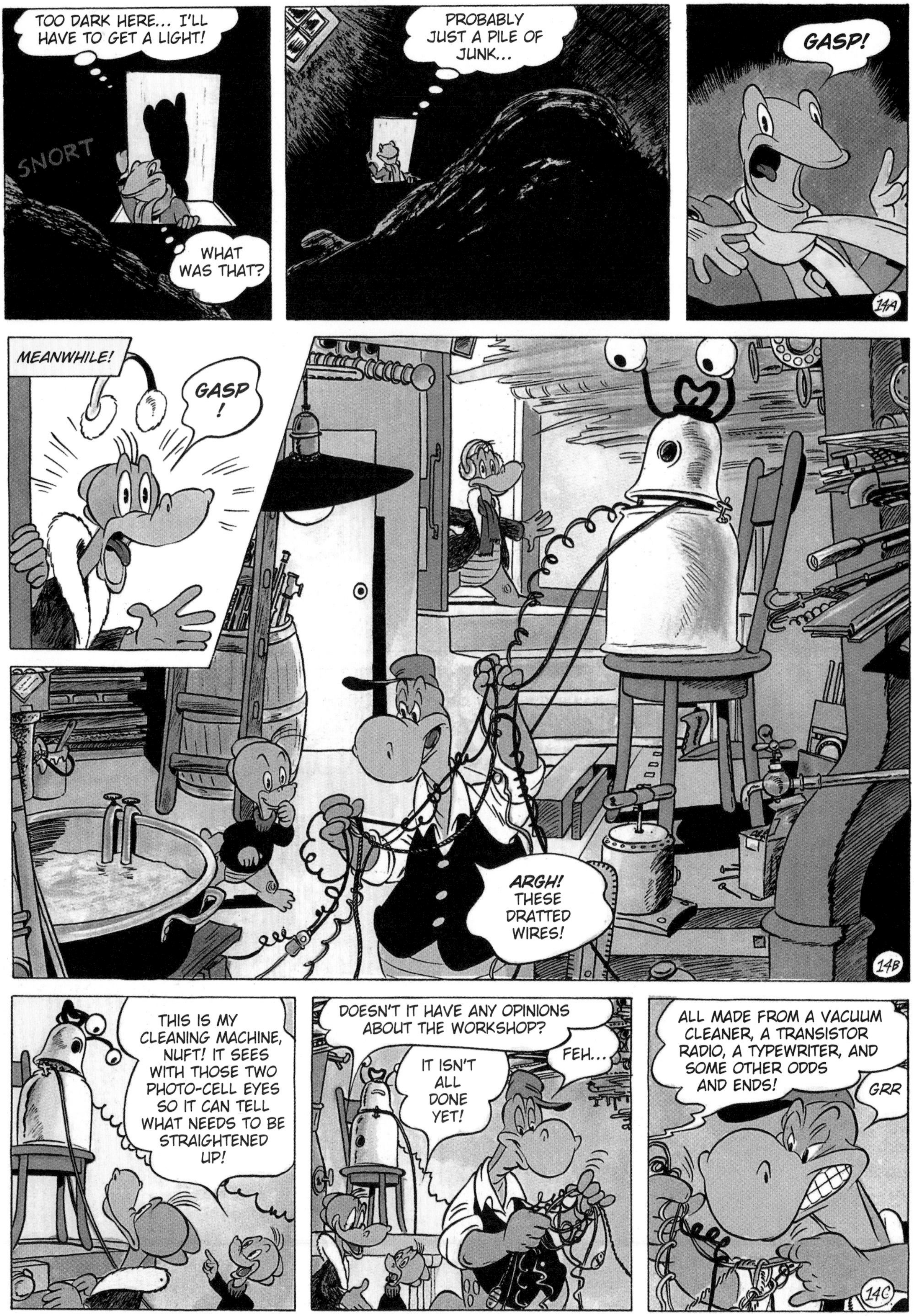
TOO DARK HERE... I'LL HAVE TO GET A LIGHT!
SNORT
WHAT WAS THAT?
PROBABLY JUST A PILE OF JUNK...
GASP!
14A
MEANWHILE!
GASP !
ARGH! THESE DRATTED WIRES!
14B
THIS IS MY CLEANING MACHINE, NUFT! IT SEES WITH THOSE TWO PHOTO-CELL EYES SO IT CAN TELL WHAT NEEDS TO BE STRAIGHTENED UP!
DOESN'T IT HAVE ANY OPINIONS ABOUT THE WORKSHOP?
IT ISN'T ALL DONE YET!
FEH...
ALL MADE FROM A VACUUM CLEANER, A TRANSISTOR RADIO, A TYPEWRITER, AND SOME OTHER ODDS AND ENDS!
GRR
14C

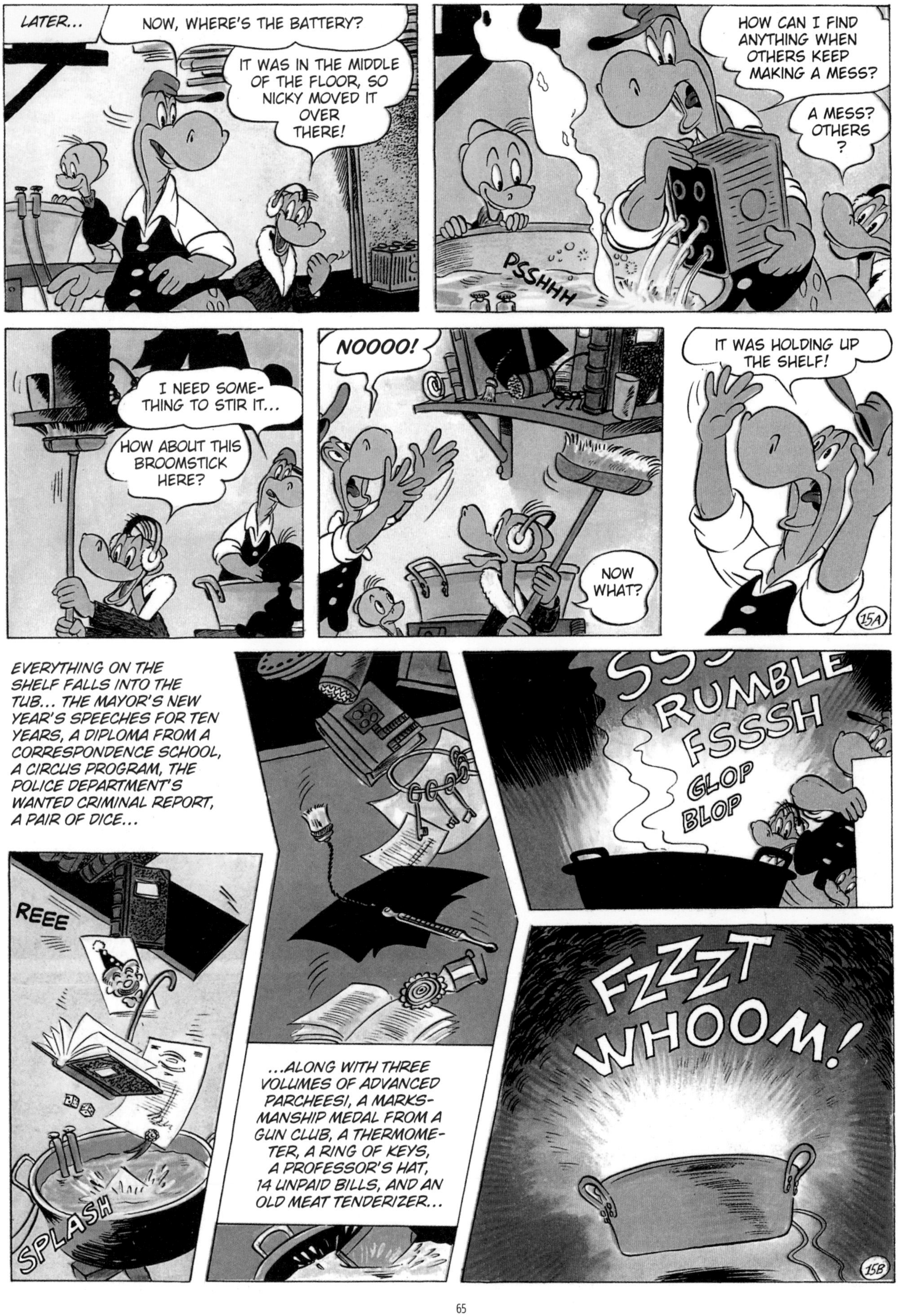
LATER...
NOW, WHERE'S THE BATTERY?
IT WAS IN THE MIDDLE OF THE FLOOR, SO NICKY MOVED IT OVER THERE!
HOW CAN I FIND ANYTHING WHEN OTHERS KEEP MAKING A MESS?
A MESS? OTHERS ?
PSSHHH
I NEED SOMETHING TO STIR IT...
HOW ABOUT THIS BROOMSTICK HERE?
NOOOO!
NOW WHAT?
IT WAS HOLDING UP THE SHELF!
15A
EVERYTHING ON THE SHELF FALLS INTO THE TUB... THE MAYOR'S NEW YEAR'S SPEECHES FOR TEN YEARS, A DIPLOMA FROM A CORRESPONDENCE SCHOOL, A CIRCUS PROGRAM, THE POLICE DEPARTMENT'S WANTED CRIMINAL REPORT, A PAIR OF DICE...
REEE
SPLASH
...ALONG WITH THREE VOLUMES OF ADVANCED PARCHEESI, A MARKSMANSHIP MEDAL FROM A GUN CLUB, A THERMOMETER, A RING OF KEYS, A PROFESSOR'S HAT, 14 UNPAID BILLS, AND AN OLD MEAT TENDERIZER...
RUMBLE
FSSSH
GLOP
BLOP
FZZZT
WHOOM!
15B

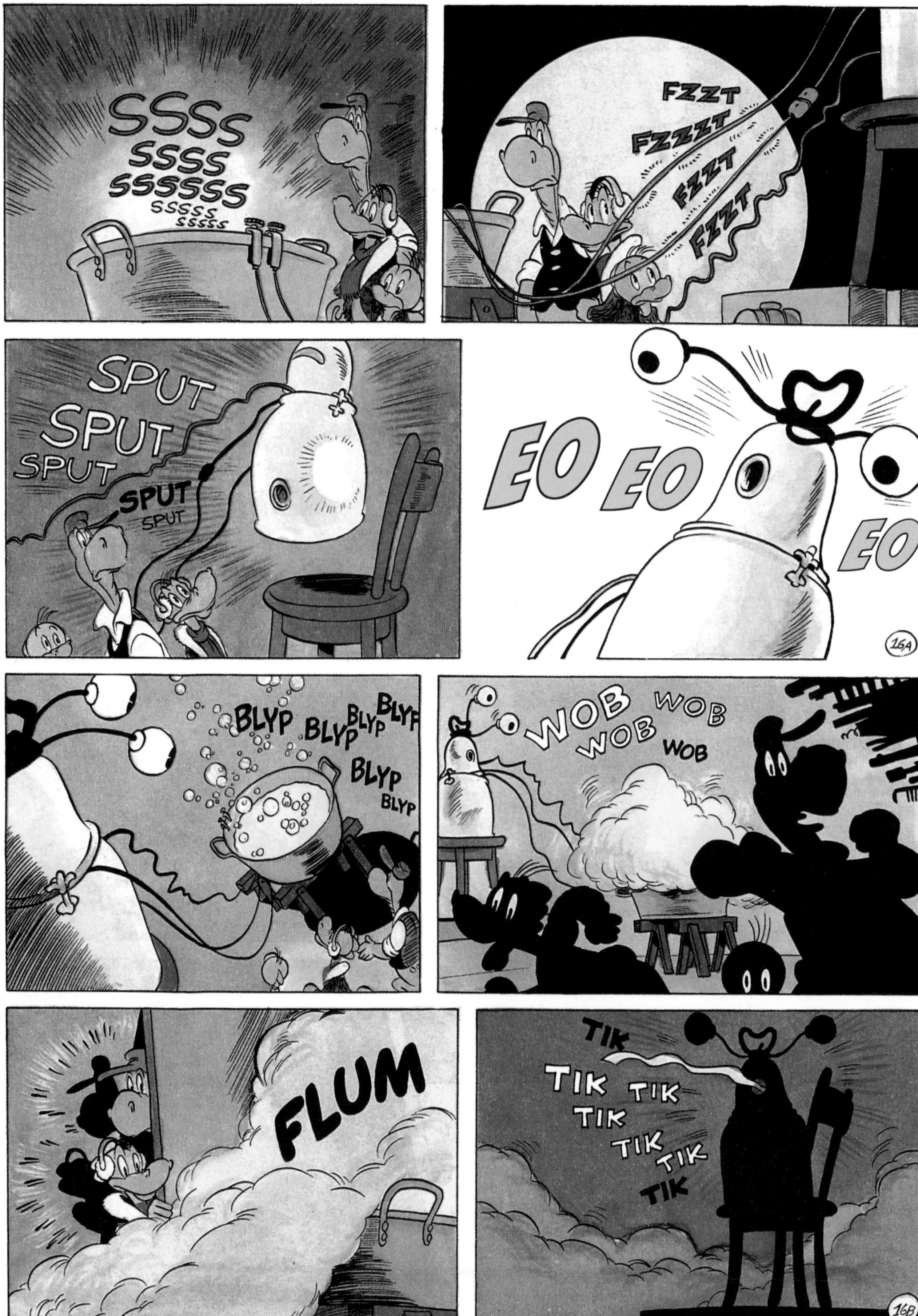
SSSS
SSSS
SSSSSS
SSSSS
SSSSS
FZZT
FZZZT
FZZT
FZZT
SPUT
SPUT
SPUT
SPUT
SPUT
EO
EO
EO
16A
BLYP
BLYP
BLYP
BLYP
BLYP
BLYP
WOB
WOB
WOB
WOB
FLUM
TIK
TIK
TIK
TIK
TIK
TIK
TIK
16B

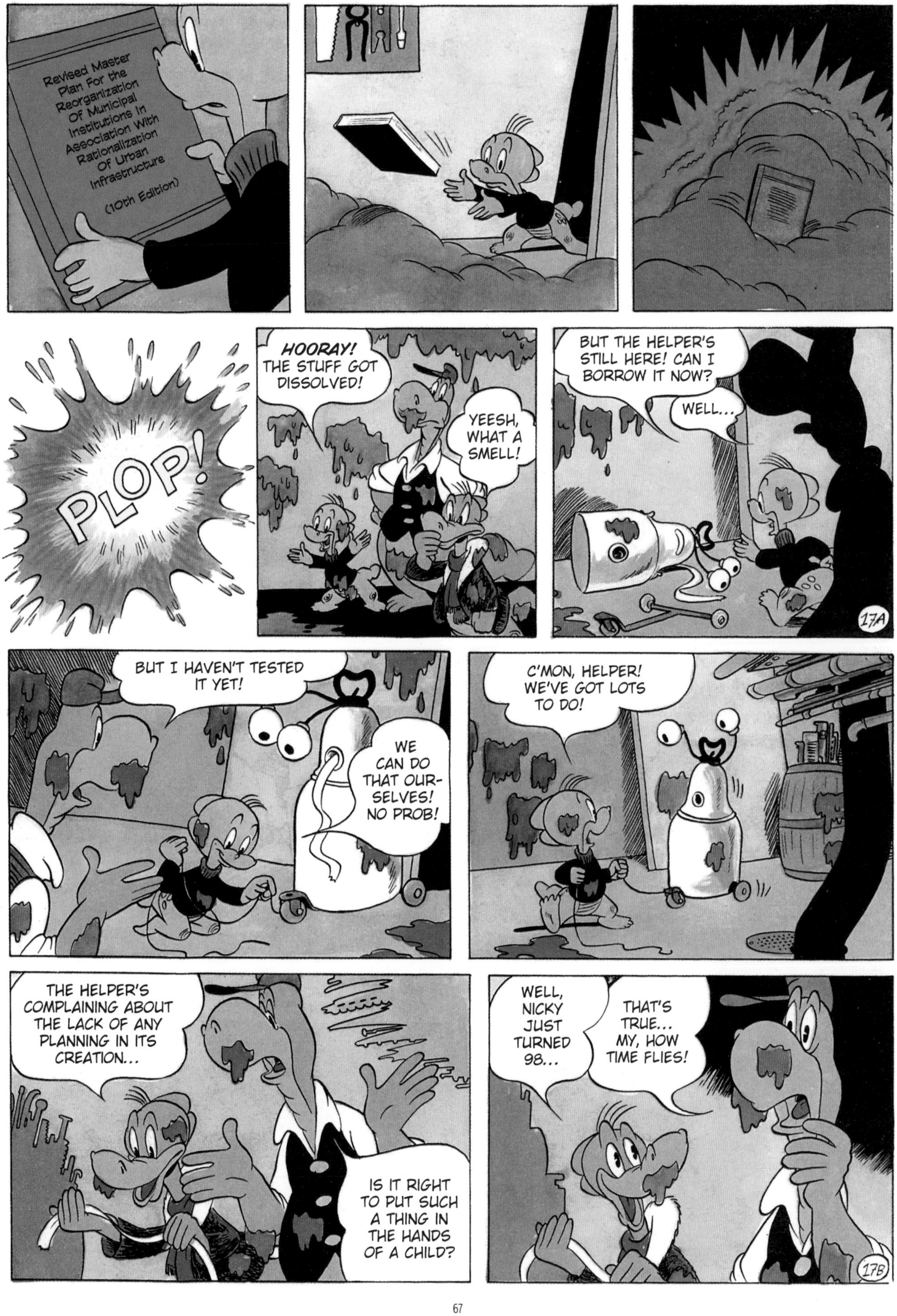

Revised Master Plan For the Reorganization Of Municipal Institutions In Association With Rationalization Of Urban Infrastructure
(10th Edition)
PLOP!
HOORAY! THE STUFF GOT DISSOLVED!
YEESH, WHAT A SMELL!
BUT THE HELPER'S STILL HERE! CAN I BORROW IT NOW?
WELL...
17A
BUT I HAVEN'T TESTED IT YET!
WE CAN DO THAT OUR-SELVES! NO PROB!
C'MON, HELPER! WE'VE GOT LOTS TO DO!
THE HELPER'S COMPLAINING ABOUT THE LACK OF ANY PLANNING IN ITS CREATION...
IS IT RIGHT TO PUT SUCH A THING IN THE HANDS OF A CHILD?
WELL, NICKY JUST TURNED 98...
THAT'S TRUE... MY, HOW TIME FLIES!
17B

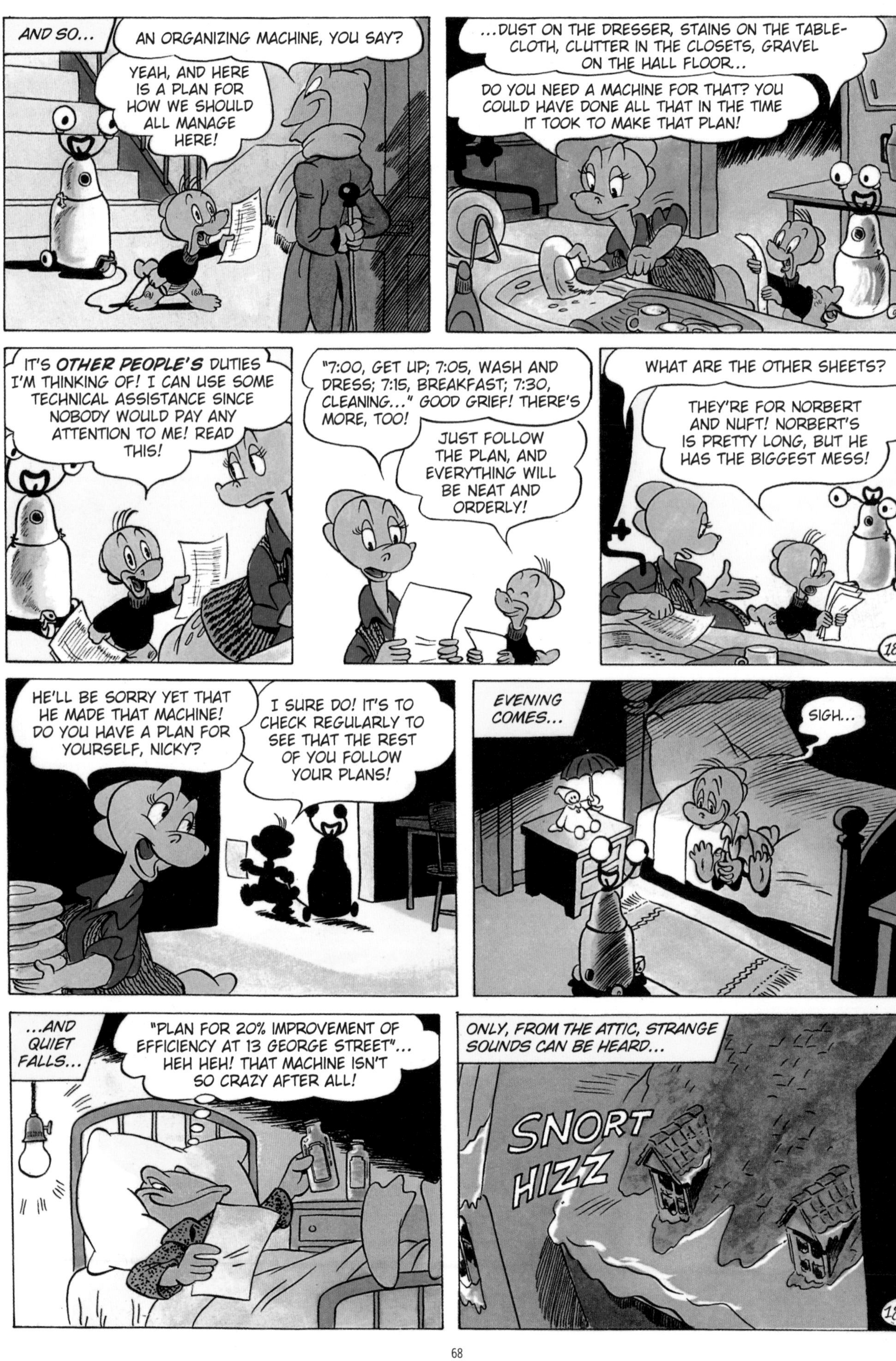
AND SO...
AN ORGANIZING MACHINE, YOU SAY?
YEAH, AND HERE IS A PLAN FOR HOW WE SHOULD ALL MANAGE HERE!
...DUST ON THE DRESSER, STAINS ON THE TABLE-CLOTH, CLUTTER IN THE CLOSETS, GRAVEL ON THE HALL FLOOR...
DO YOU NEED A MACHINE FOR THAT? YOU COULD HAVE DONE ALL THAT IN THE TIME IT TOOK TO MAKE THAT PLAN!
IT'S OTHER PEOPLE'S DUTIES I'M THINKING OF! I CAN USE SOME TECHNICAL ASSISTANCE SINCE NOBODY WOULD PAY ANY ATTENTION TO ME! READ THIS!
"7:00, GET UP; 7:05, WASH AND DRESS; 7:15, BREAKFAST; 7:30, CLEANING..." GOOD GRIEF! THERE'S MORE, TOO!
JUST FOLLOW THE PLAN, AND EVERYTHING WILL BE NEAT AND ORDERLY!
WHAT ARE THE OTHER SHEETS?
THEY'RE FOR NORBERT AND NUFT! NORBERT'S IS PRETTY LONG, BUT HE HAS THE BIGGEST MESS!
18A
HE'LL BE SORRY YET THAT HE MADE THAT MACHINE! DO YOU HAVE A PLAN FOR YOURSELF, NICKY?
I SURE DO! IT'S TO CHECK REGULARLY TO SEE THAT THE REST OF YOU FOLLOW YOUR PLANS!
EVENING COMES...
SIGH...
...AND QUIET FALLS...
"PLAN FOR 20% IMPROVEMENT OF EFFICIENCY AT 13 GEORGE STREET"... HEH HEH! THAT MACHINE ISN'T SO CRAZY AFTER ALL!
ONLY, FROM THE ATTIC, STRANGE SOUNDS CAN BE HEARD...
SNORT
HIZZ
18B

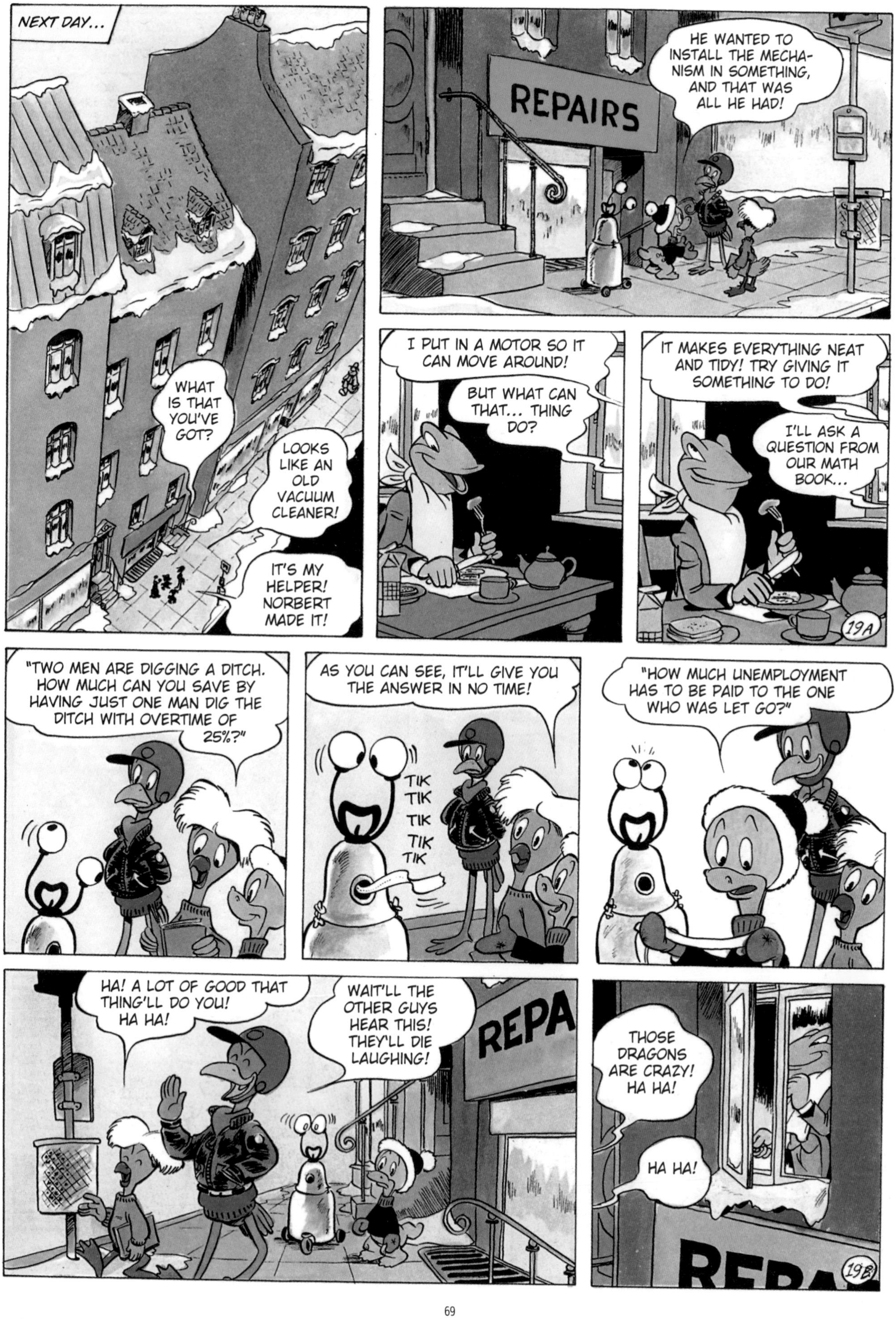
NEXT DAY...
WHAT IS THAT YOU'VE GOT?
LOOKS LIKE AN OLD VACUUM CLEANER!
IT'S MY HELPER! NORBERT MADE IT!
REPAIRS
HE WANTED TO INSTALL THE MECHA-NISM IN SOMETHING, AND THAT WAS ALL HE HAD!
I PUT IN A MOTOR SO IT CAN MOVE AROUND!
BUT WHAT CAN THAT... THING DO?
IT MAKES EVERYTHING NEAT AND TIDY! TRY GIVING IT SOMETHING TO DO!
I'LL ASK A QUESTION FROM OUR MATH BOOK...
19A
"TWO MEN ARE DIGGING A DITCH. HOW MUCH CAN YOU SAVE BY HAVING JUST ONE MAN DIG THE DITCH WITH OVERTIME OF 25%?"
AS YOU CAN SEE, IT'LL GIVE YOU THE ANSWER IN NO TIME!
TIK TIK TIK TIK TIK TIK
"HOW MUCH UNEMPLOYMENT HAS TO BE PAID TO THE ONE WHO WAS LET GO?"
HA! A LOT OF GOOD THAT THING'LL DO YOU! HA HA!
WAIT'LL THE OTHER GUYS HEAR THIS! THEY'LL DIE LAUGHING!
REPA
THOSE DRAGONS ARE CRAZY! HA HA!
HA HA!
19B

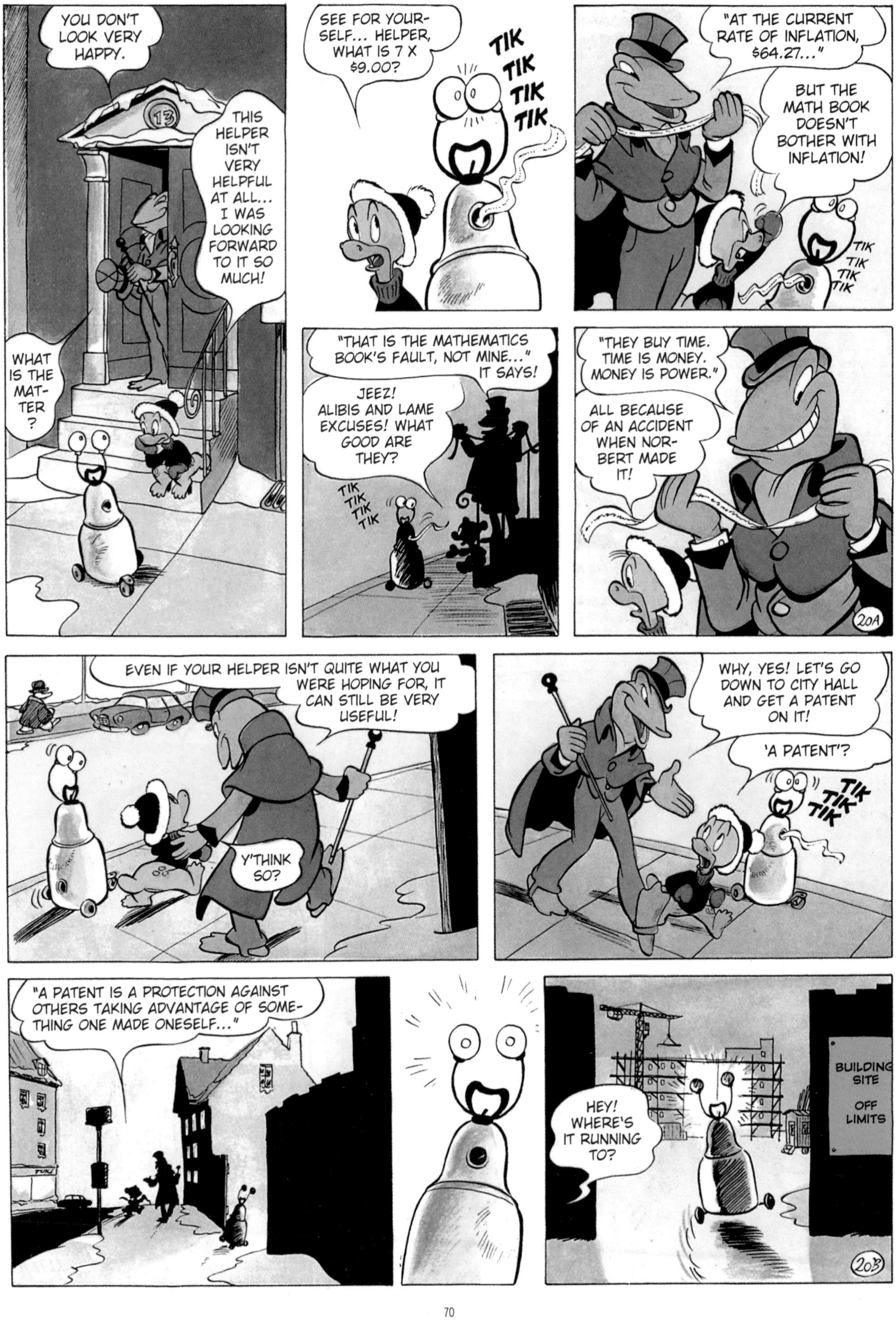
YOU DON'T LOOK VERY HAPPY.
THIS HELPER ISN'T VERY HELPFUL AT ALL... I WAS LOOKING FORWARD TO IT SO MUCH!
WHAT IS THE MAT-TER?
13
SEE FOR YOUR-SELF... HELPER, WHAT IS 7 X $9.00?
TIK TIK TIK TIK
"AT THE CURRENT RATE OF INFLATION, $64.27..."
BUT THE MATH BOOK DOESN'T BOTHER WITH INFLATION!
TIK TIK TIK TIK
"THAT IS THE MATHEMATICS BOOK'S FAULT, NOT MINE..." IT SAYS!
JEEZ! ALIBIS AND LAME EXCUSES! WHAT GOOD ARE THEY?
TIK TIK TIK TIK
"THEY BUY TIME. TIME IS MONEY. MONEY IS POWER."
ALL BECAUSE OF AN ACCIDENT WHEN NOR-BERT MADE IT!
20A
EVEN IF YOUR HELPER ISN'T QUITE WHAT YOU WERE HOPING FOR, IT CAN STILL BE VERY USEFUL!
Y'THINK SO?
WHY, YES! LET'S GO DOWN TO CITY HALL AND GET A PATENT ON IT!
'A PATENT'?
TIK TIK TIK
"A PATENT IS A PROTECTION AGAINST OTHERS TAKING ADVANTAGE OF SOME-THING ONE MADE ONESELF..."
HEY! WHERE'S IT RUNNING TO?
BUILDING SITE OFF LIMITS
20B

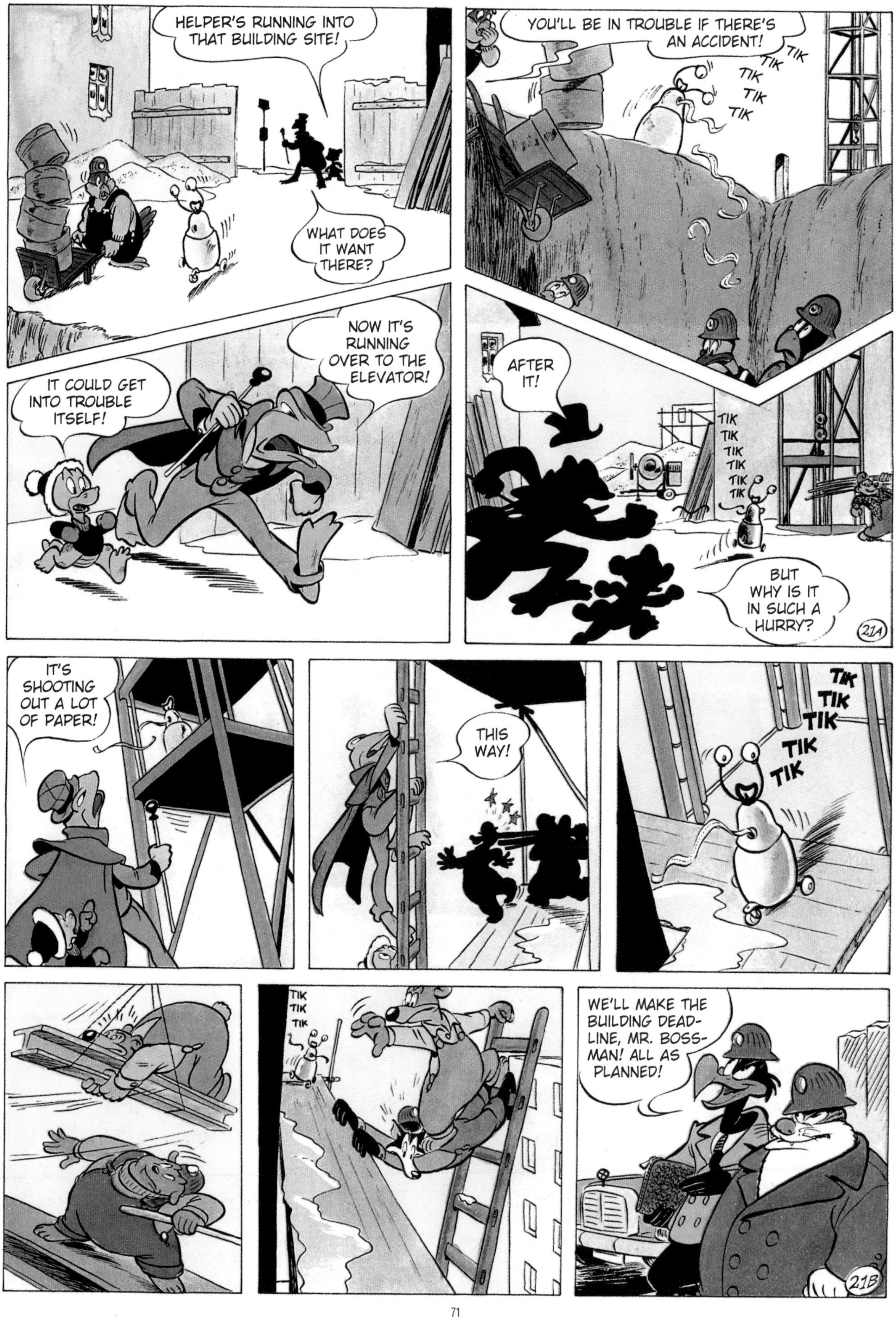
HELPER'S RUNNING INTO THAT BUILDING SITE!
WHAT DOES IT WANT THERE?
YOU'LL BE IN TROUBLE IF THERE'S AN ACCIDENT!
TIK TIK TIK TIK TIK
IT COULD GET INTO TROUBLE ITSELF!
NOW IT'S RUNNING OVER TO THE ELEVATOR!
AFTER IT!
TIK TIK TIK TIK TIK TIK
BUT WHY IS IT IN SUCH A HURRY?
21A
IT'S SHOOTING OUT A LOT OF PAPER!
THIS WAY!
TIK TIK TIK TIK TIK
TIK TIK TIK
WE'LL MAKE THE BUILDING DEAD-LINE, MR. BOSS-MAN! ALL AS PLANNED!
21B

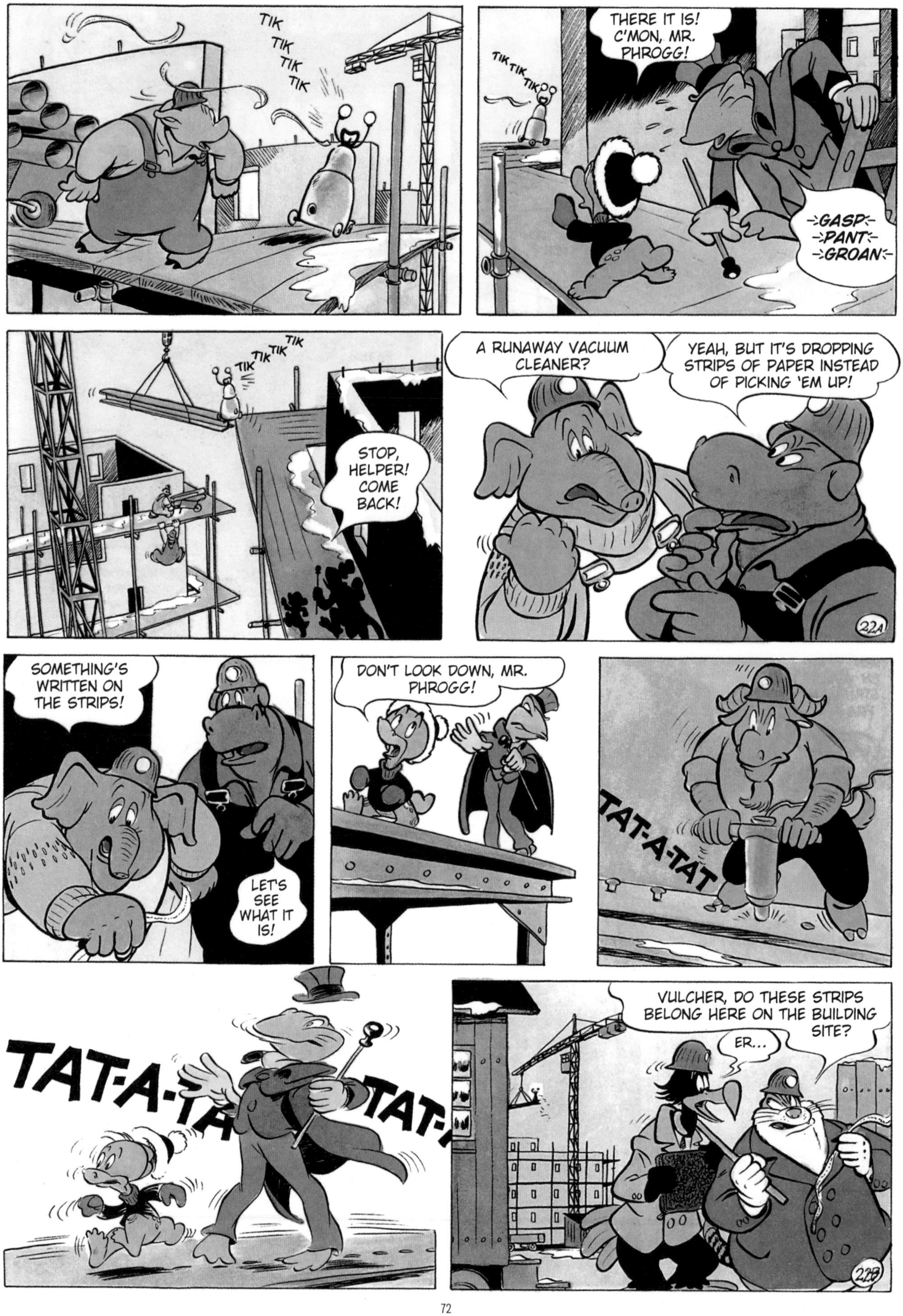
TIK
TIK
TIK
TIK
THERE IT IS! C'MON, MR. PHROGG!
TIK TIK TIK
GASP PANT GROAN
TIK TIK TIK TIK
STOP, HELPER! COME BACK!
A RUNAWAY VACUUM CLEANER?
YEAH, BUT IT'S DROPPING STRIPS OF PAPER INSTEAD OF PICKING 'EM UP!
22A
SOMETHING'S WRITTEN ON THE STRIPS!
LET'S SEE WHAT IT IS!
DON'T LOOK DOWN, MR. PHROGG!
TAT-A-TAT
TAT-A-TA
TAT-A
VULCHER, DO THESE STRIPS BELONG HERE ON THE BUILDING SITE?
ER...
22B

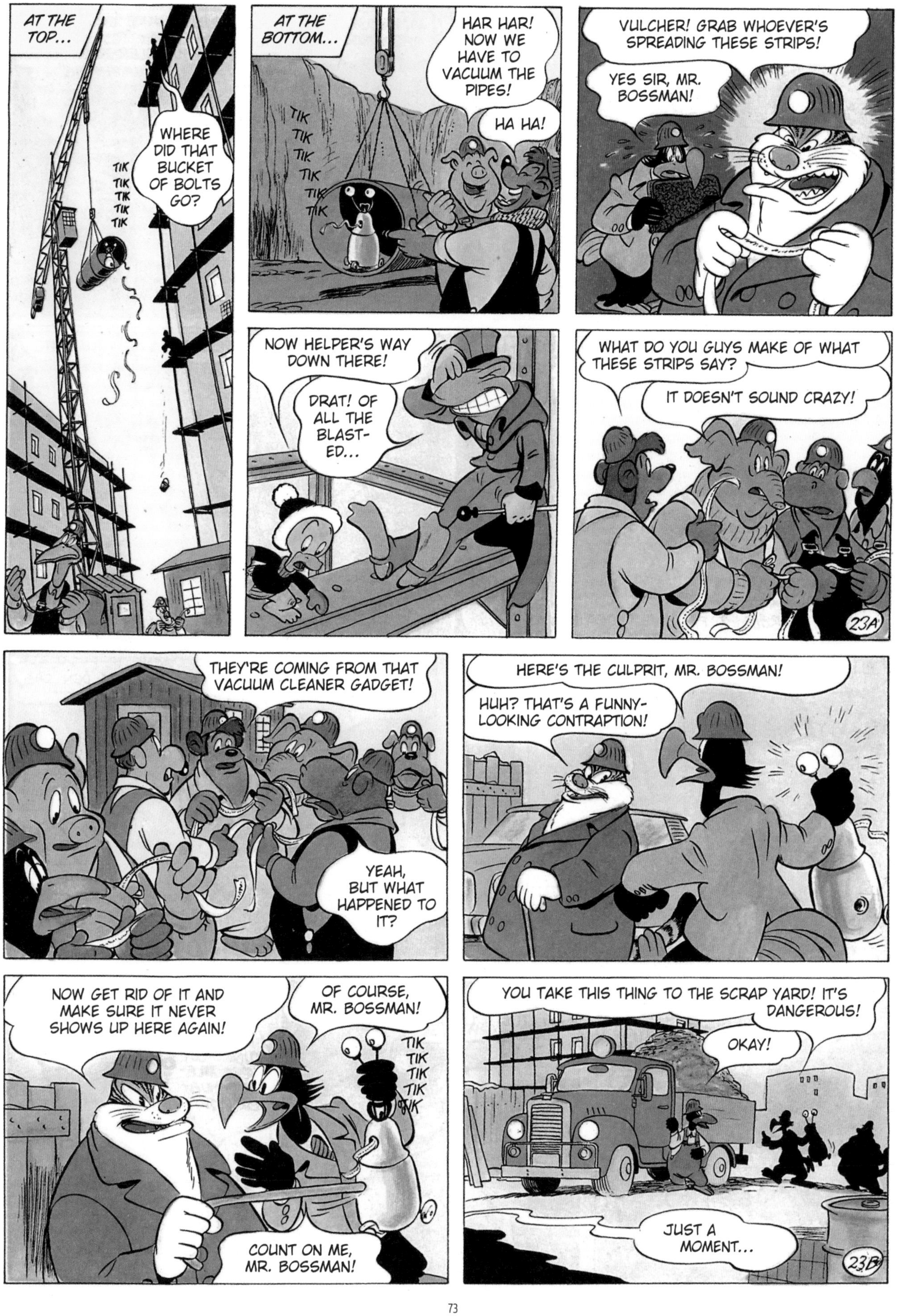

AT THE TOP...
WHERE DID THAT BUCKET OF BOLTS GO?
TIK TIK TIK TIK TIK
AT THE BOTTOM...
HAR HAR! NOW WE HAVE TO VACUUM THE PIPES!
HA HA!
TIK TIK TIK TIK TIK TIK
VULCHER! GRAB WHOEVER'S SPREADING THESE STRIPS!
YES SIR, MR. BOSSMAN!
NOW HELPER'S WAY DOWN THERE!
DRAT! OF ALL THE BLAST-ED...
WHAT DO YOU GUYS MAKE OF WHAT THESE STRIPS SAY?
IT DOESN'T SOUND CRAZY!
23A
THEY'RE COMING FROM THAT VACUUM CLEANER GADGET!
YEAH, BUT WHAT HAPPENED TO IT?
HERE'S THE CULPRIT, MR. BOSSMAN!
HUH? THAT'S A FUNNY-LOOKING CONTRAPTION!
NOW GET RID OF IT AND MAKE SURE IT NEVER SHOWS UP HERE AGAIN!
OF COURSE, MR. BOSSMAN!
TIK TIK TIK TIK TIK
COUNT ON ME, MR. BOSSMAN!
YOU TAKE THIS THING TO THE SCRAP YARD! IT'S DANGEROUS!
OKAY!
JUST A MOMENT...
23B

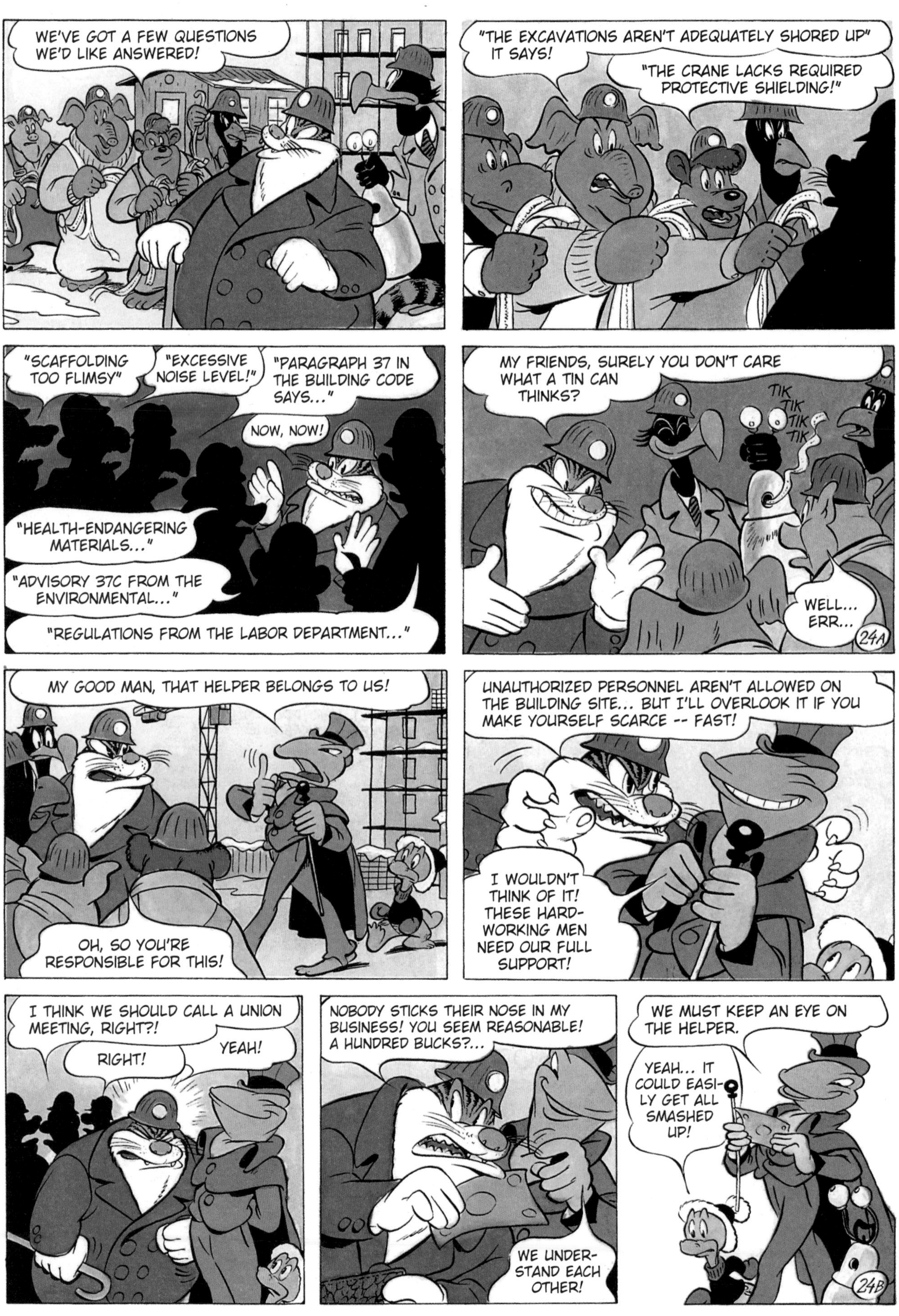

WE'VE GOT A FEW QUESTIONS WE'D LIKE ANSWERED!
"THE EXCAVATIONS AREN'T ADEQUATELY SHORED UP" IT SAYS!
"THE CRANE LACKS REQUIRED PROTECTIVE SHIELDING!"
"SCAFFOLDING TOO FLIMSY"
"EXCESSIVE NOISE LEVEL!"
"PARAGRAPH 37 IN THE BUILDING CODE SAYS..."
NOW, NOW!
"HEALTH-ENDANGERING MATERIALS..."
"ADVISORY 37C FROM THE ENVIRONMENTAL..."
"REGULATIONS FROM THE LABOR DEPARTMENT..."
MY FRIENDS, SURELY YOU DON'T CARE WHAT A TIN CAN THINKS?
TIK TIK TIK TIK
WELL... ERR...
24A
MY GOOD MAN, THAT HELPER BELONGS TO US!
OH, SO YOU'RE RESPONSIBLE FOR THIS!
UNAUTHORIZED PERSONNEL AREN'T ALLOWED ON THE BUILDING SITE... BUT I'LL OVERLOOK IT IF YOU MAKE YOURSELF SCARCE -- FAST!
I WOULDN'T THINK OF IT! THESE HARD-WORKING MEN NEED OUR FULL SUPPORT!
I THINK WE SHOULD CALL A UNION MEETING, RIGHT?!
RIGHT!
YEAH!
NOBODY STICKS THEIR NOSE IN MY BUSINESS! YOU SEEM REASONABLE! A HUNDRED BUCKS?...
WE UNDER-STAND EACH OTHER!
WE MUST KEEP AN EYE ON THE HELPER.
YEAH... IT COULD EASI-LY GET ALL SMASHED UP!
24B

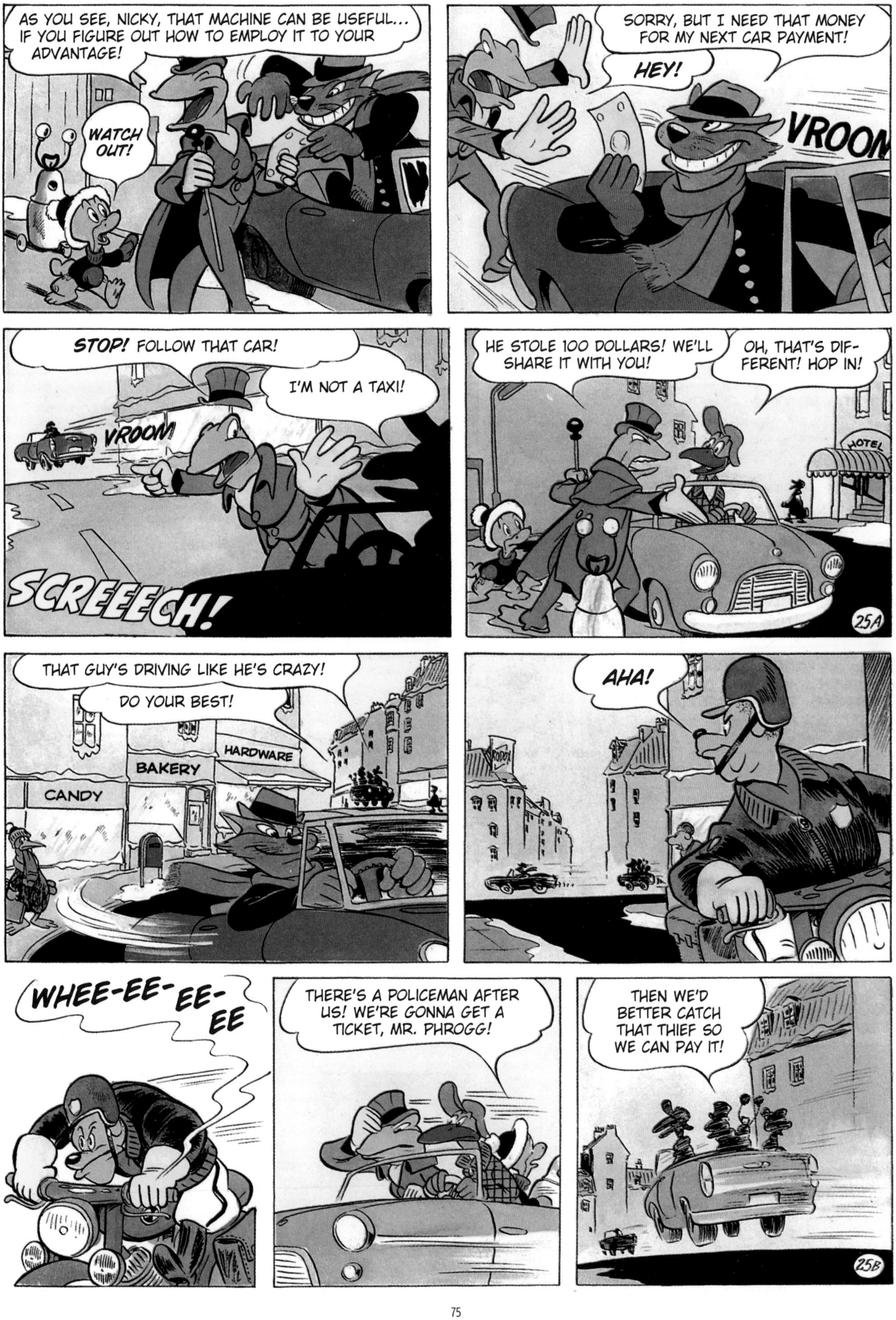
AS YOU SEE, NICKY, THAT MACHINE CAN BE USEFUL... IF YOU FIGURE OUT HOW TO EMPLOY IT TO YOUR ADVANTAGE!
WATCH OUT!
SORRY, BUT I NEED THAT MONEY FOR MY NEXT CAR PAYMENT!
HEY!
VROOM
STOP! FOLLOW THAT CAR!
I'M NOT A TAXI!
VROOM
SCREEECH!
HE STOLE 100 DOLLARS! WE'LL SHARE IT WITH YOU!
OH, THAT'S DIF-FERENT! HOP IN!
HOTEL
25A
THAT GUY'S DRIVING LIKE HE'S CRAZY!
DO YOUR BEST!
HARDWARE
BAKERY
CANDY
AHA!
WHEE-EE-EE-EE
THERE'S A POLICEMAN AFTER US! WE'RE GONNA GET A TICKET, MR. PHROGG!
THEN WE'D BETTER CATCH THAT THIEF SO WE CAN PAY IT!
25B

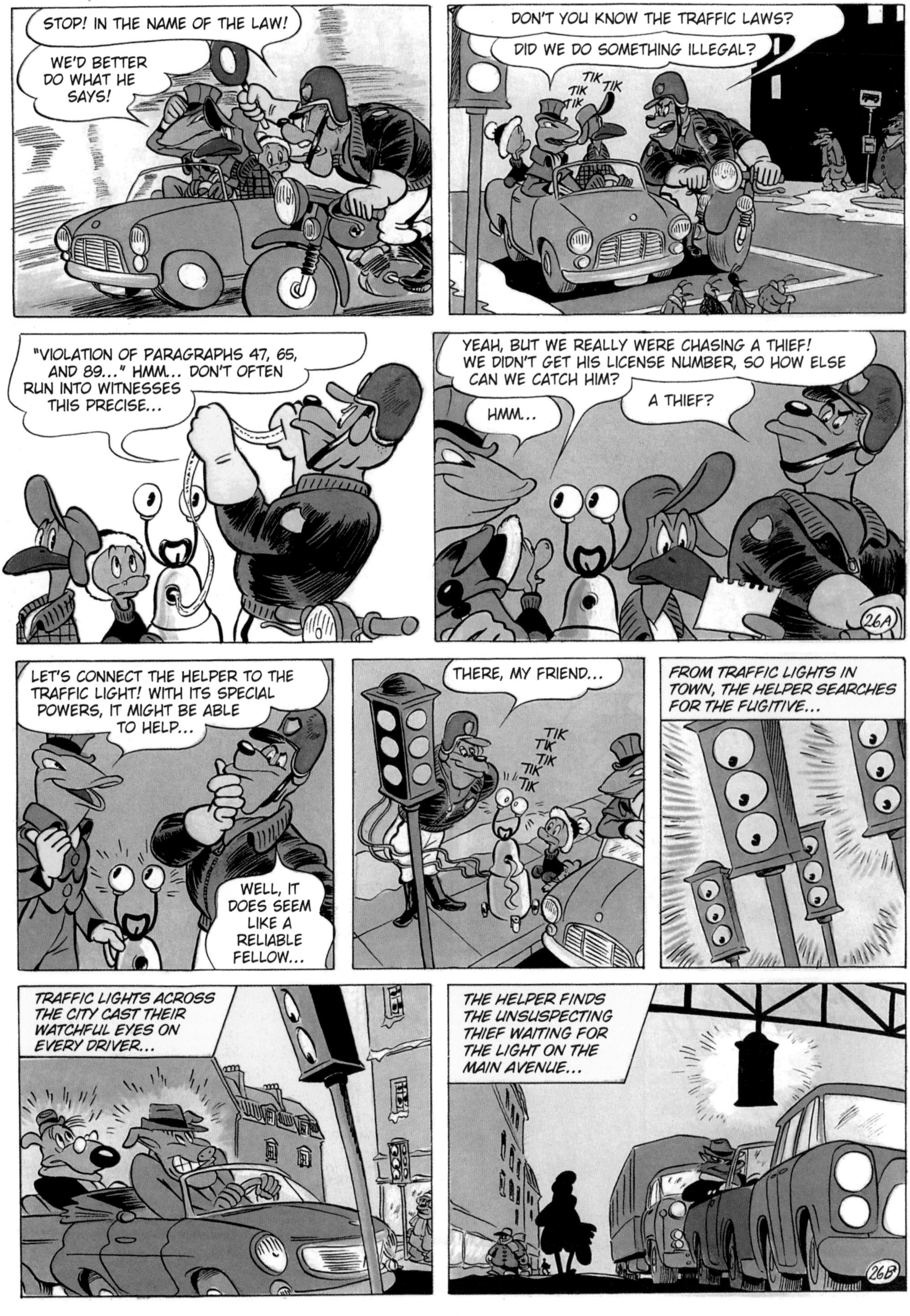
STOP! IN THE NAME OF THE LAW!
WE'D BETTER DO WHAT HE SAYS!
DON'T YOU KNOW THE TRAFFIC LAWS?
DID WE DO SOMETHING ILLEGAL?
TIK TIK TIK TIK
"VIOLATION OF PARAGRAPHS 47, 65, AND 89..." HMM... DON'T OFTEN RUN INTO WITNESSES THIS PRECISE...
YEAH, BUT WE REALLY WERE CHASING A THIEF! WE DIDN'T GET HIS LICENSE NUMBER, SO HOW ELSE CAN WE CATCH HIM?
HMM...
A THIEF?
26A
LET'S CONNECT THE HELPER TO THE TRAFFIC LIGHT! WITH ITS SPECIAL POWERS, IT MIGHT BE ABLE TO HELP...
WELL, IT DOES SEEM LIKE A RELIABLE FELLOW...
THERE, MY FRIEND...
TIK TIK TIK TIK TIK
FROM TRAFFIC LIGHTS IN TOWN, THE HELPER SEARCHES FOR THE FUGITIVE...
TRAFFIC LIGHTS ACROSS THE CITY CAST THEIR WATCHFUL EYES ON EVERY DRIVER...
THE HELPER FINDS THE UNSUSPECTING THIEF WAITING FOR THE LIGHT ON THE MAIN AVENUE...
26B

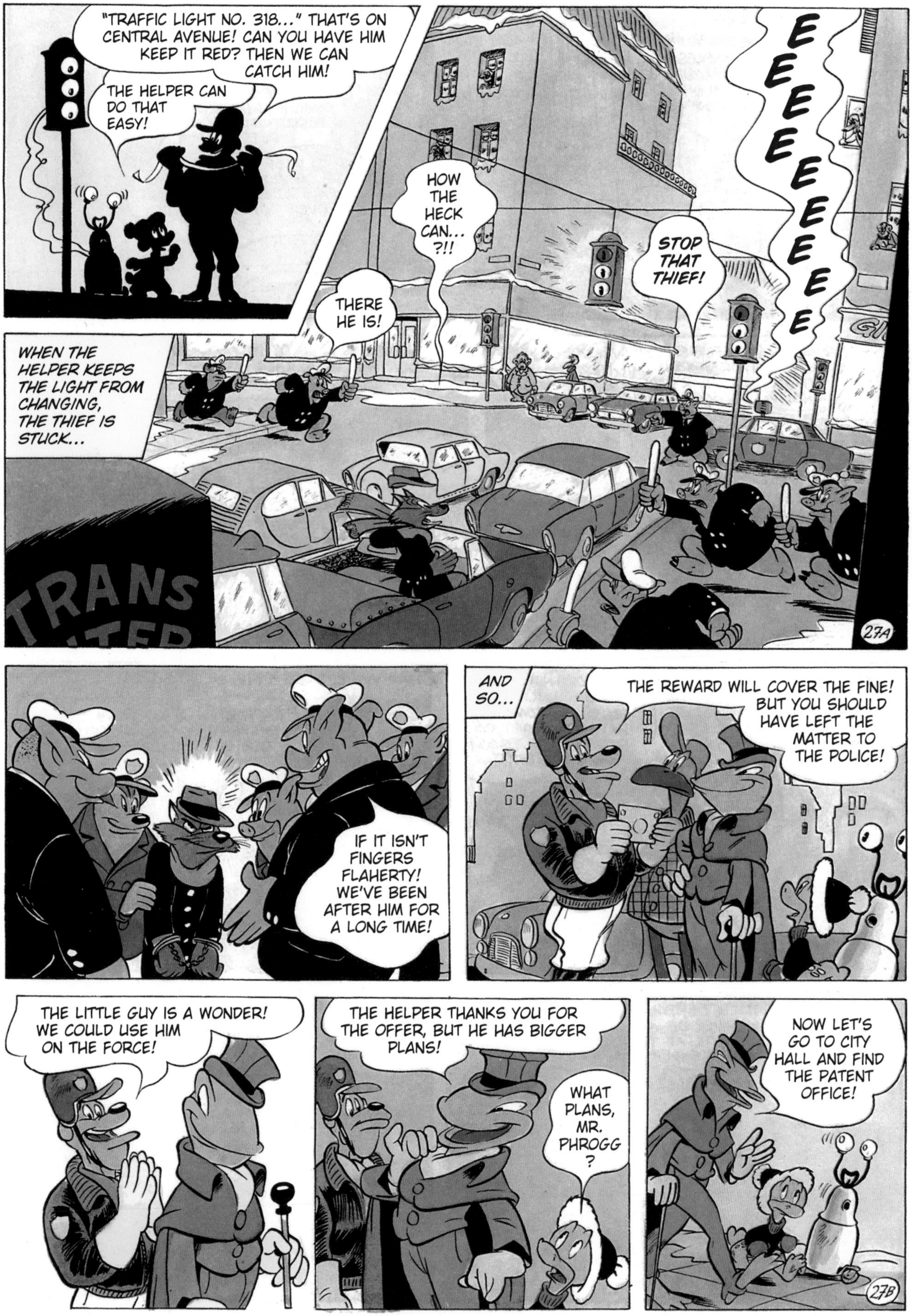
"TRAFFIC LIGHT NO. 318..." THAT'S ON CENTRAL AVENUE! CAN YOU HAVE HIM KEEP IT RED? THEN WE CAN CATCH HIM!
THE HELPER CAN DO THAT EASY!
HOW THE HECK CAN... ?!!
STOP THAT THIEF!
EEEEEEEEEEEE
THERE HE IS!
WHEN THE HELPER KEEPS THE LIGHT FROM CHANGING, THE THIEF IS STUCK...
TRANS
27A
IF IT ISN'T FINGERS FLAHERTY! WE'VE BEEN AFTER HIM FOR A LONG TIME!
AND SO...
THE REWARD WILL COVER THE FINE! BUT YOU SHOULD HAVE LEFT THE MATTER TO THE POLICE!
THE LITTLE GUY IS A WONDER! WE COULD USE HIM ON THE FORCE!
THE HELPER THANKS YOU FOR THE OFFER, BUT HE HAS BIGGER PLANS!
WHAT PLANS, MR. PHROGG ?
NOW LET'S GO TO CITY HALL AND FIND THE PATENT OFFICE!
27B

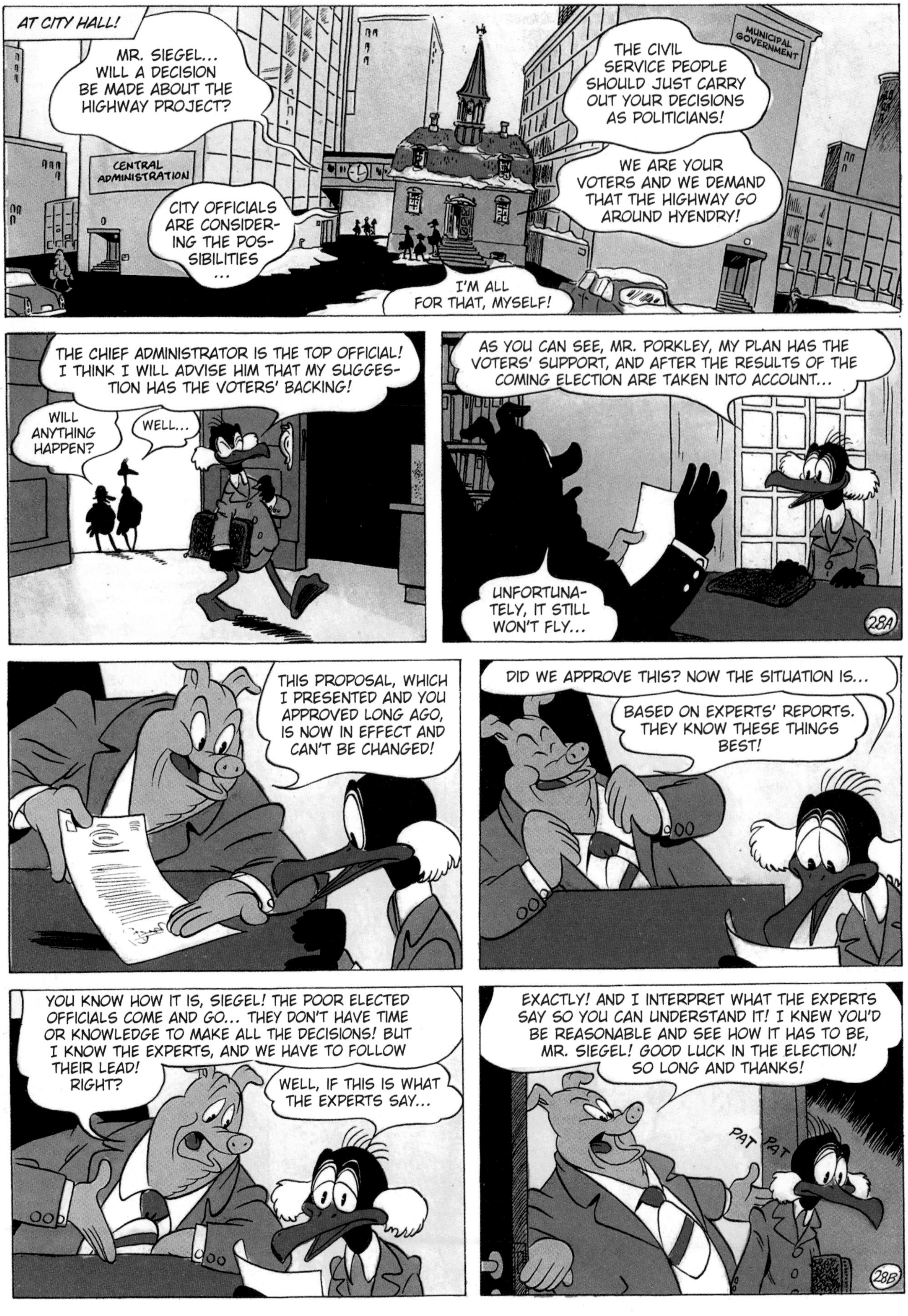
AT CITY HALL!
MR. SIEGEL... WILL A DECISION BE MADE ABOUT THE HIGHWAY PROJECT?
CITY OFFICIALS ARE CONSIDERING THE POSSIBILITIES...
CENTRAL ADMINISTRATION
MUNICIPAL GOVERNMENT
THE CIVIL SERVICE PEOPLE SHOULD JUST CARRY OUT YOUR DECISIONS AS POLITICIANS!
WE ARE YOUR VOTERS AND WE DEMAND THAT THE HIGHWAY GO AROUND HYENDRY!
I'M ALL FOR THAT, MYSELF!
THE CHIEF ADMINISTRATOR IS THE TOP OFFICIAL! I THINK I WILL ADVISE HIM THAT MY SUGGESTION HAS THE VOTERS' BACKING!
WILL ANYTHING HAPPEN?
WELL...
AS YOU CAN SEE, MR. PORKLEY, MY PLAN HAS THE VOTERS' SUPPORT, AND AFTER THE RESULTS OF THE COMING ELECTION ARE TAKEN INTO ACCOUNT...
UNFORTUNATELY, IT STILL WON'T FLY...
28A
THIS PROPOSAL, WHICH I PRESENTED AND YOU APPROVED LONG AGO, IS NOW IN EFFECT AND CAN'T BE CHANGED!
DID WE APPROVE THIS? NOW THE SITUATION IS...
BASED ON EXPERTS' REPORTS. THEY KNOW THESE THINGS BEST!
YOU KNOW HOW IT IS, SIEGEL! THE POOR ELECTED OFFICIALS COME AND GO... THEY DON'T HAVE TIME OR KNOWLEDGE TO MAKE ALL THE DECISIONS! BUT I KNOW THE EXPERTS, AND WE HAVE TO FOLLOW THEIR LEAD! RIGHT?
WELL, IF THIS IS WHAT THE EXPERTS SAY...
EXACTLY! AND I INTERPRET WHAT THE EXPERTS SAY SO YOU CAN UNDERSTAND IT! I KNEW YOU'D BE REASONABLE AND SEE HOW IT HAS TO BE, MR. SIEGEL! GOOD LUCK IN THE ELECTION! SO LONG AND THANKS!
PAT PAT
28B

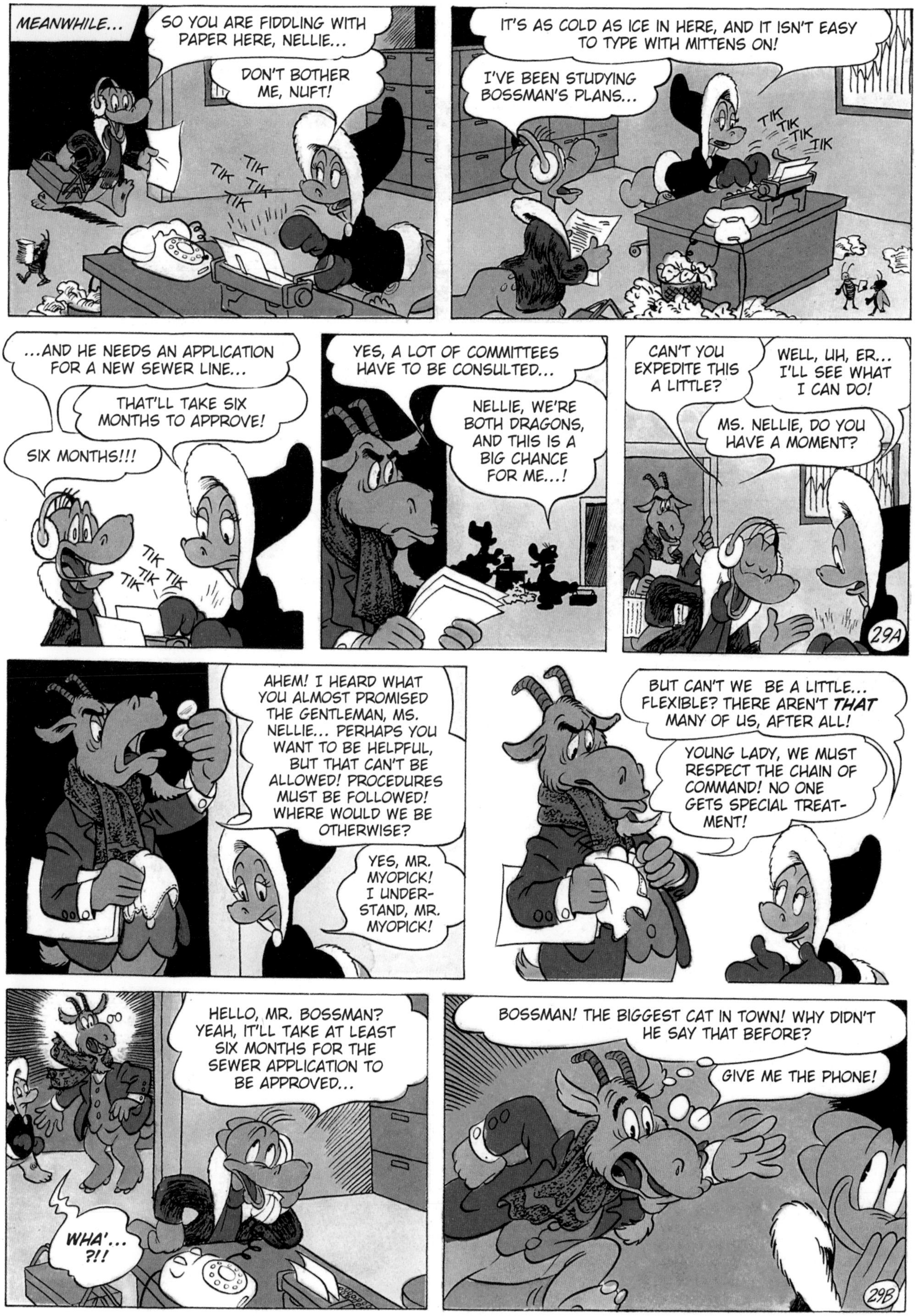
MEANWHILE...
SO YOU ARE FIDDLING WITH PAPER HERE, NELLIE...
DON'T BOTHER ME, NUFT!
TIK TIK TIK TIK
IT'S AS COLD AS ICE IN HERE, AND IT ISN'T EASY TO TYPE WITH MITTENS ON!
I'VE BEEN STUDYING BOSSMAN'S PLANS...
TIK TIK TIK TIK
...AND HE NEEDS AN APPLICATION FOR A NEW SEWER LINE...
THAT'LL TAKE SIX MONTHS TO APPROVE!
SIX MONTHS!!!
TIK TIK TIK TIK
YES, A LOT OF COMMITTEES HAVE TO BE CONSULTED...
NELLIE, WE'RE BOTH DRAGONS, AND THIS IS A BIG CHANCE FOR ME...!
CAN'T YOU EXPEDITE THIS A LITTLE?
WELL, UH, ER... I'LL SEE WHAT I CAN DO!
MS. NELLIE, DO YOU HAVE A MOMENT?
29A
AHEM! I HEARD WHAT YOU ALMOST PROMISED THE GENTLEMAN, MS. NELLIE... PERHAPS YOU WANT TO BE HELPFUL, BUT THAT CAN'T BE ALLOWED! PROCEDURES MUST BE FOLLOWED! WHERE WOULD WE BE OTHERWISE?
YES, MR. MYOPICK! I UNDER-STAND, MR. MYOPICK!
BUT CAN'T WE BE A LITTLE... FLEXIBLE? THERE AREN'T THAT MANY OF US, AFTER ALL!
YOUNG LADY, WE MUST RESPECT THE CHAIN OF COMMAND! NO ONE GETS SPECIAL TREAT-MENT!
HELLO, MR. BOSSMAN? YEAH, IT'LL TAKE AT LEAST SIX MONTHS FOR THE SEWER APPLICATION TO BE APPROVED...
WHA'... ?!!
BOSSMAN! THE BIGGEST CAT IN TOWN! WHY DIDN'T HE SAY THAT BEFORE?
GIVE ME THE PHONE!
29B

HELLO, MR. BOSSMAN? OFFICE MANAGER MYOPICK HERE! YES, IT'S ALL IN ORDER! APPROVED BY TOMORROW!

THANK YOU! NO PROBLEM! I ALWAYS TAKE CARE OF THESE THINGS, AS SURE AS MY NAME IS MYOPICK!

KLIK!

HE HUNG UP? I HOPE HE REMEMBERS MY NAME...

YES, MS. NELLIE, PLEASE BE SO KIND AS TO EXPEDITE THE MATTER TODAY... AND BE SURE TO REMEMBER THE COPIES FOR THE CENTRAL ARCHIVE!

MEANWHILE... THE MOST IMPORTANT THING ON TODAY'S AGENDA IS A DECISION ABOUT THE HIGHWAY PROJECT!

NO! THE WATER SUPPLY FOR HYENDRY COMES FIRST!

EEEEK!

SPROOOSH

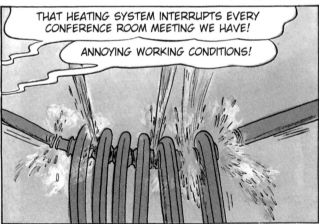

THAT HEATING SYSTEM INTERRUPTS EVERY CONFERENCE ROOM MEETING WE HAVE!

ANNOYING WORKING CONDITIONS!

...MY DEAR COLLEAGUES, SURELY THIS PROBLEM IS THE MOST IMPORTANT?

I SUGGEST CHANGING THE FIRST ITEM ON THE AGENDA TO "CALLING THE JANITOR!"

SECOND!

SECOND!

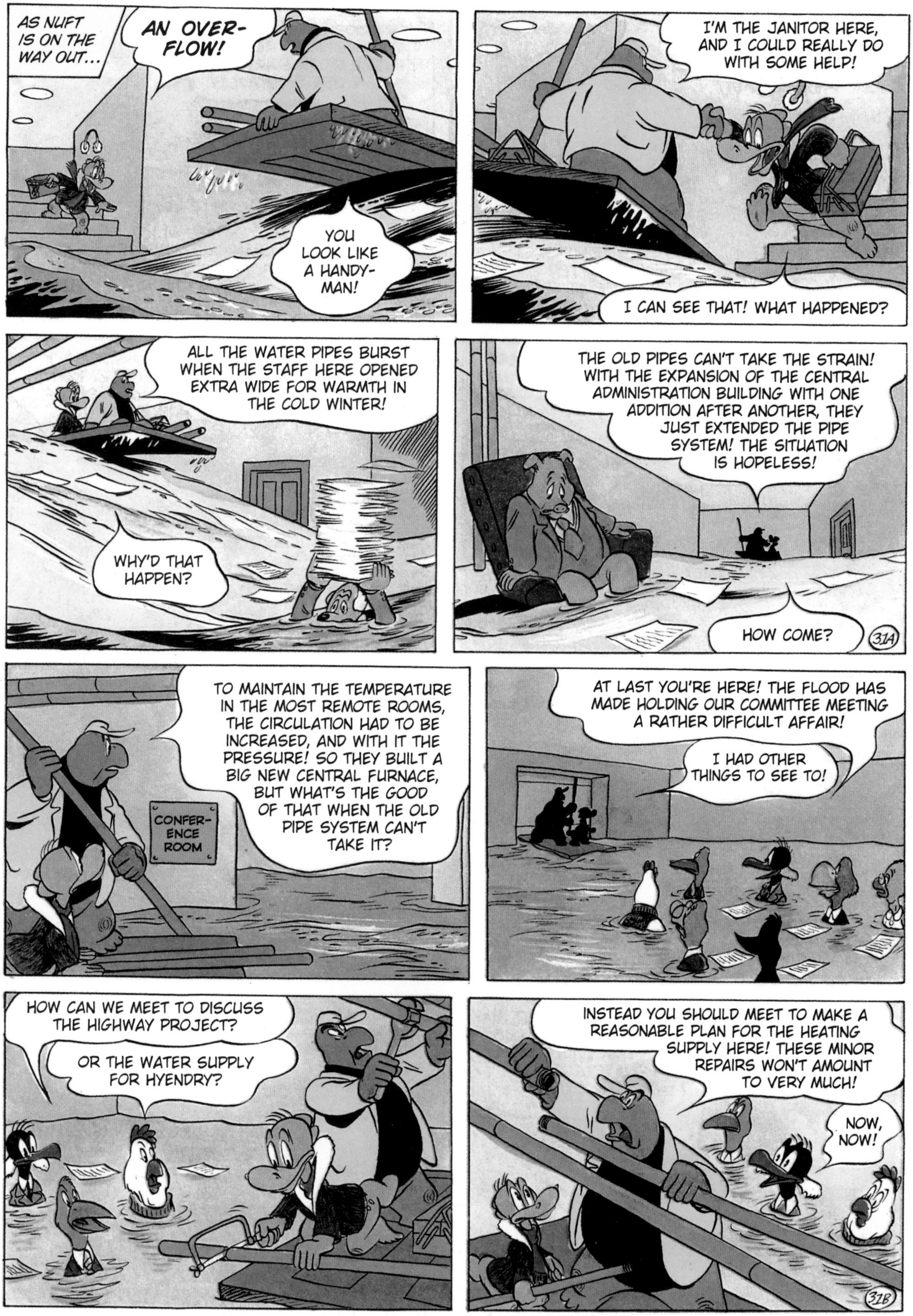
AS NUFT IS ON THE WAY OUT...
AN OVER-FLOW!
YOU LOOK LIKE A HANDY-MAN!
I'M THE JANITOR HERE, AND I COULD REALLY DO WITH SOME HELP!
I CAN SEE THAT! WHAT HAPPENED?
ALL THE WATER PIPES BURST WHEN THE STAFF HERE OPENED EXTRA WIDE FOR WARMTH IN THE COLD WINTER!
WHY'D THAT HAPPEN?
THE OLD PIPES CAN'T TAKE THE STRAIN! WITH THE EXPANSION OF THE CENTRAL ADMINISTRATION BUILDING WITH ONE ADDITION AFTER ANOTHER, THEY JUST EXTENDED THE PIPE SYSTEM! THE SITUATION IS HOPELESS!
HOW COME?
31A
TO MAINTAIN THE TEMPERATURE IN THE MOST REMOTE ROOMS, THE CIRCULATION HAD TO BE INCREASED, AND WITH IT THE PRESSURE! SO THEY BUILT A BIG NEW CENTRAL FURNACE, BUT WHAT'S THE GOOD OF THAT WHEN THE OLD PIPE SYSTEM CAN'T TAKE IT?
CONFER-ENCE ROOM
AT LAST YOU'RE HERE! THE FLOOD HAS MADE HOLDING OUR COMMITTEE MEETING A RATHER DIFFICULT AFFAIR!
I HAD OTHER THINGS TO SEE TO!
HOW CAN WE MEET TO DISCUSS THE HIGHWAY PROJECT?
OR THE WATER SUPPLY FOR HYENDRY?
INSTEAD YOU SHOULD MEET TO MAKE A REASONABLE PLAN FOR THE HEATING SUPPLY HERE! THESE MINOR REPAIRS WON'T AMOUNT TO VERY MUCH!
NOW, NOW!
31B

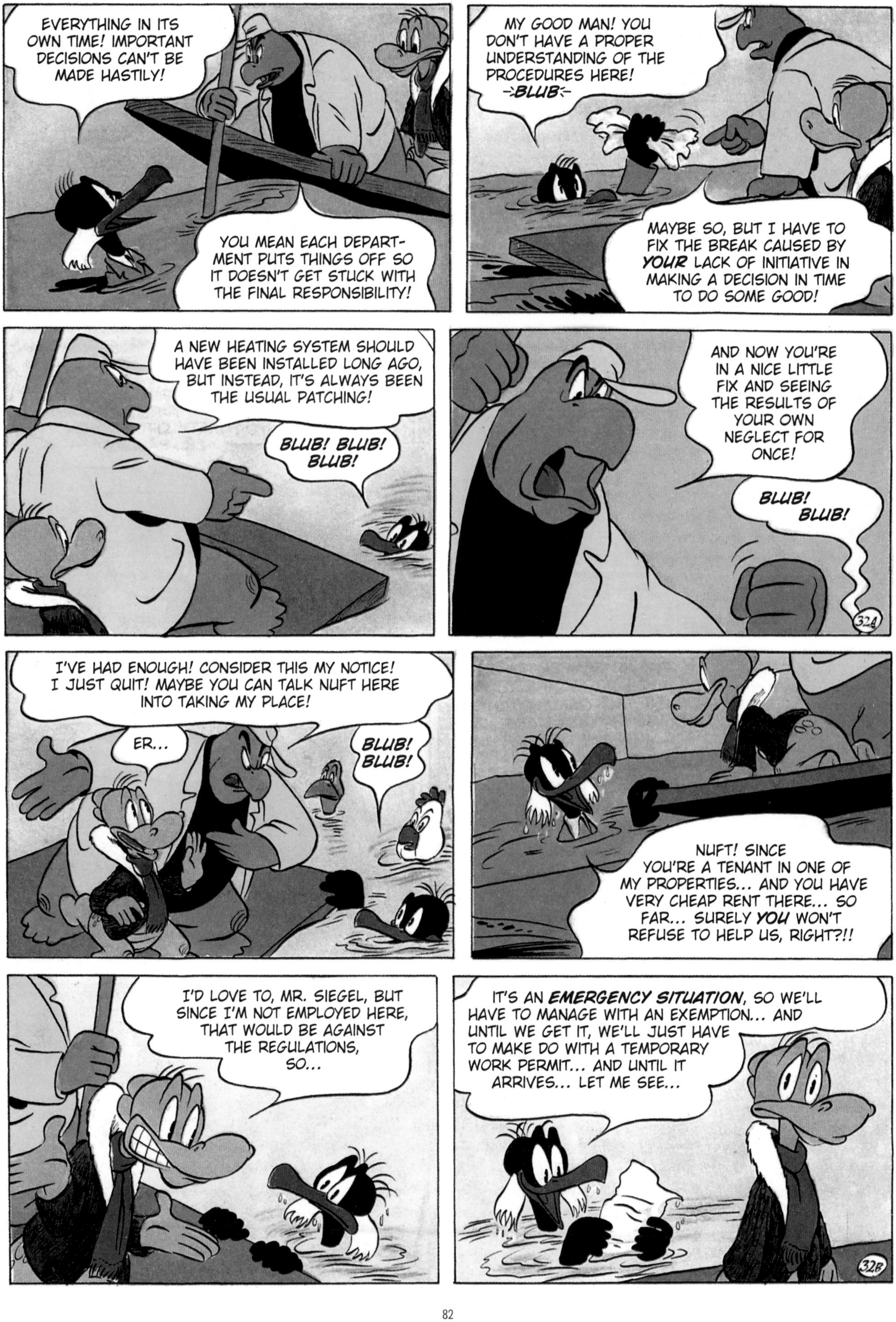
EVERYTHING IN ITS OWN TIME! IMPORTANT DECISIONS CAN'T BE MADE HASTILY!
YOU MEAN EACH DEPARTMENT PUTS THINGS OFF SO IT DOESN'T GET STUCK WITH THE FINAL RESPONSIBILITY!
MY GOOD MAN! YOU DON'T HAVE A PROPER UNDERSTANDING OF THE PROCEDURES HERE!
BLUB
MAYBE SO, BUT I HAVE TO FIX THE BREAK CAUSED BY YOUR LACK OF INITIATIVE IN MAKING A DECISION IN TIME TO DO SOME GOOD!
A NEW HEATING SYSTEM SHOULD HAVE BEEN INSTALLED LONG AGO, BUT INSTEAD, IT'S ALWAYS BEEN THE USUAL PATCHING!
BLUB! BLUB! BLUB!
AND NOW YOU'RE IN A NICE LITTLE FIX AND SEEING THE RESULTS OF YOUR OWN NEGLECT FOR ONCE!
BLUB! BLUB!
32A
I'VE HAD ENOUGH! CONSIDER THIS MY NOTICE! I JUST QUIT! MAYBE YOU CAN TALK NUFT HERE INTO TAKING MY PLACE!
ER...
BLUB! BLUB!
NUFT! SINCE YOU'RE A TENANT IN ONE OF MY PROPERTIES... AND YOU HAVE VERY CHEAP RENT THERE... SO FAR... SURELY YOU WON'T REFUSE TO HELP US, RIGHT?!!
I'D LOVE TO, MR. SIEGEL, BUT SINCE I'M NOT EMPLOYED HERE, THAT WOULD BE AGAINST THE REGULATIONS, SO...
IT'S AN EMERGENCY SITUATION, SO WE'LL HAVE TO MANAGE WITH AN EXEMPTION... AND UNTIL WE GET IT, WE'LL JUST HAVE TO MAKE DO WITH A TEMPORARY WORK PERMIT... AND UNTIL IT ARRIVES... LET ME SEE...
32B

I ALSO HEREBY PROPOSE THAT, FOR ONCE, WE BYPASS THE CIVIL SERVICE AND INVESTIGATE OURSELVES THE MATTER OF OUR HEATING SYSTEM IN THE CENTRAL ARCHIVE...

THAT SOUNDS AS THOUGH THE VOTE IS UNANIMOUS!

BLUB!

BLOB!

BLEB!

BLIB!

NUFT GETS STARTED WITH HIS FORCED LABOR...

FIRST THE WATER HAS TO BE PUMPED OUT!

I'LL TURN THE FURNACE DOWN UNTIL WE'VE GOTTEN THE SITUATION UNDER CONTROL... EVEN IF PEOPLE HAVE TO FREEZE!

33A

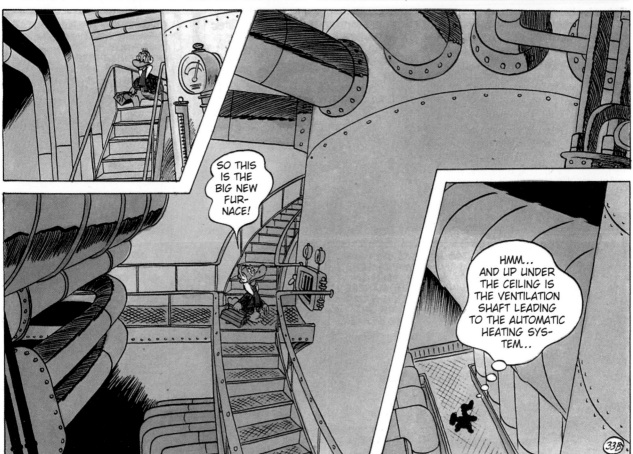

SO THIS IS THE BIG NEW FURNACE!

HMM... AND UP UNDER THE CEILING IS THE VENTILATION SHAFT LEADING TO THE AUTOMATIC HEATING SYSTEM...

33B

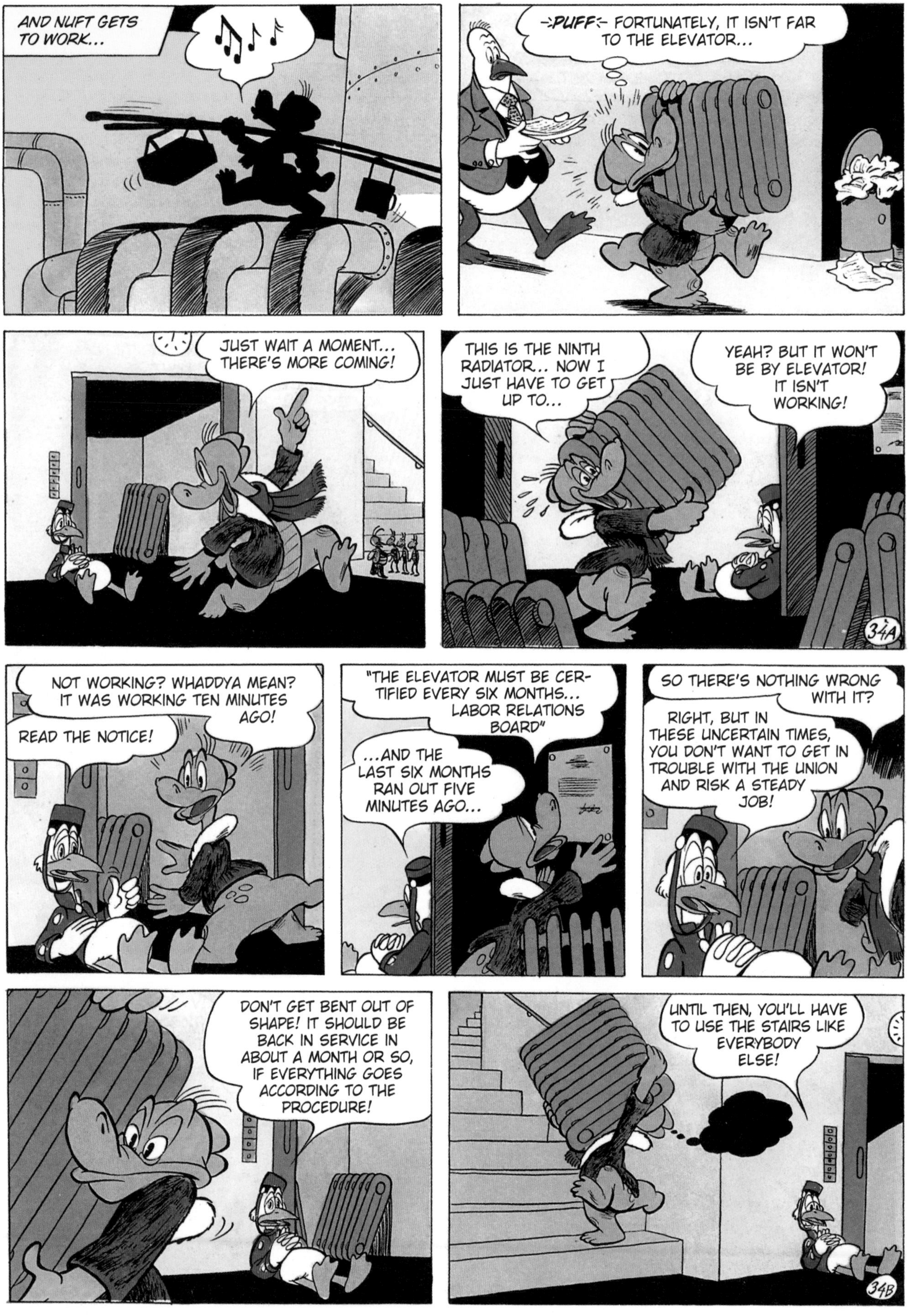
AND NUFT GETS TO WORK...
-PUFF- FORTUNATELY, IT ISN'T FAR TO THE ELEVATOR...
JUST WAIT A MOMENT... THERE'S MORE COMING!
THIS IS THE NINTH RADIATOR... NOW I JUST HAVE TO GET UP TO...
YEAH? BUT IT WON'T BE BY ELEVATOR! IT ISN'T WORKING!
34A
NOT WORKING? WHADDYA MEAN? IT WAS WORKING TEN MINUTES AGO!
READ THE NOTICE!
"THE ELEVATOR MUST BE CERTIFIED EVERY SIX MONTHS... LABOR RELATIONS BOARD"
...AND THE LAST SIX MONTHS RAN OUT FIVE MINUTES AGO...
SO THERE'S NOTHING WRONG WITH IT?
RIGHT, BUT IN THESE UNCERTAIN TIMES, YOU DON'T WANT TO GET IN TROUBLE WITH THE UNION AND RISK A STEADY JOB!
DON'T GET BENT OUT OF SHAPE! IT SHOULD BE BACK IN SERVICE IN ABOUT A MONTH OR SO, IF EVERYTHING GOES ACCORDING TO THE PROCEDURE!
UNTIL THEN, YOU'LL HAVE TO USE THE STAIRS LIKE EVERYBODY ELSE!
34B

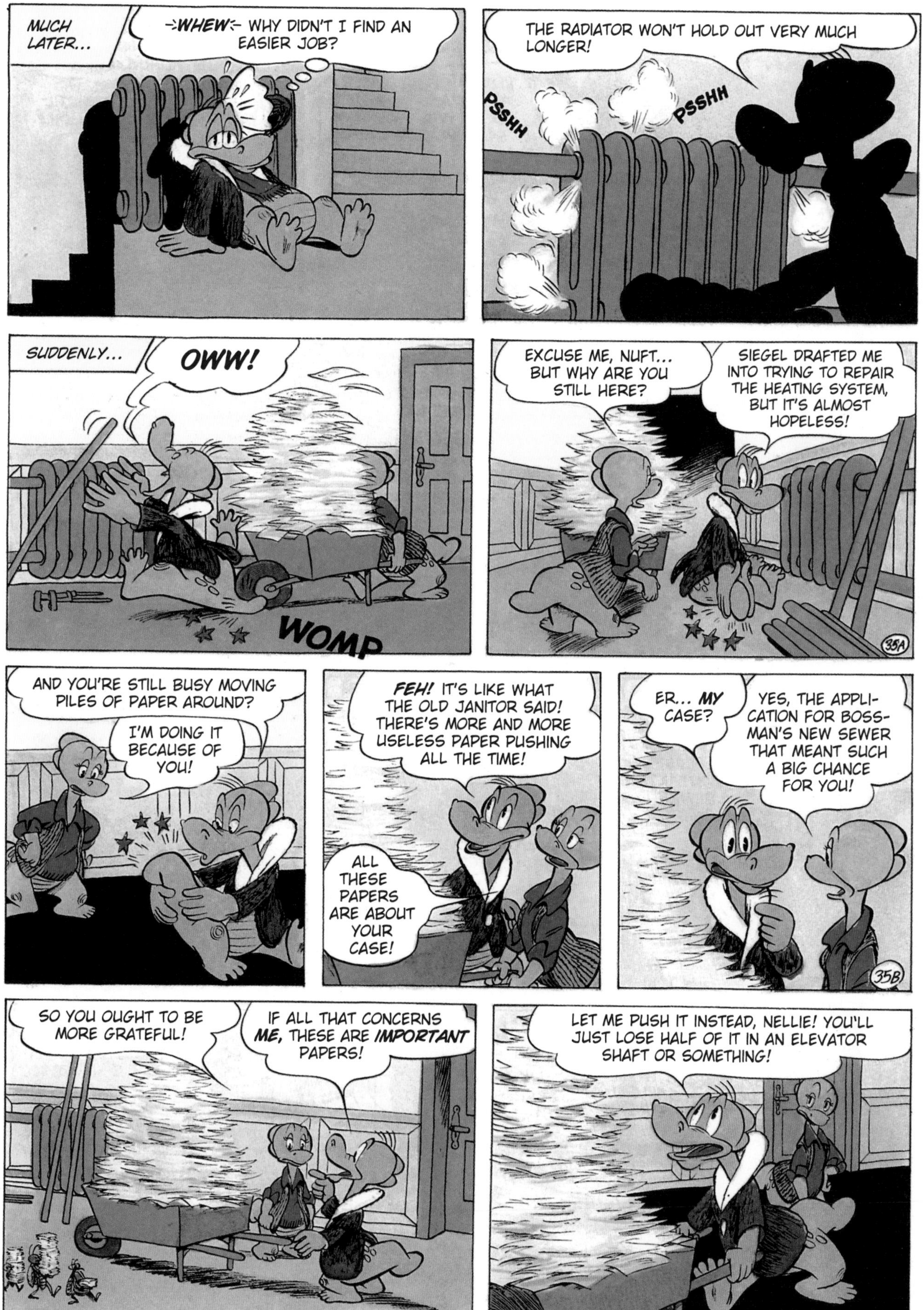
MUCH LATER...
→WHEW← WHY DIDN'T I FIND AN EASIER JOB?
THE RADIATOR WON'T HOLD OUT VERY MUCH LONGER!
PSSHH
PSSHH
SUDDENLY...
OWW!
WOMP
EXCUSE ME, NUFT... BUT WHY ARE YOU STILL HERE?
SIEGEL DRAFTED ME INTO TRYING TO REPAIR THE HEATING SYSTEM, BUT IT'S ALMOST HOPELESS!
35A
AND YOU'RE STILL BUSY MOVING PILES OF PAPER AROUND?
I'M DOING IT BECAUSE OF YOU!
FEH! IT'S LIKE WHAT THE OLD JANITOR SAID! THERE'S MORE AND MORE USELESS PAPER PUSHING ALL THE TIME!
ALL THESE PAPERS ARE ABOUT YOUR CASE!
ER... MY CASE?
YES, THE APPLI-CATION FOR BOSS-MAN'S NEW SEWER THAT MEANT SUCH A BIG CHANCE FOR YOU!
35B
SO YOU OUGHT TO BE MORE GRATEFUL!
IF ALL THAT CONCERNS ME, THESE ARE IMPORTANT PAPERS!
LET ME PUSH IT INSTEAD, NELLIE! YOU'LL JUST LOSE HALF OF IT IN AN ELEVATOR SHAFT OR SOMETHING!

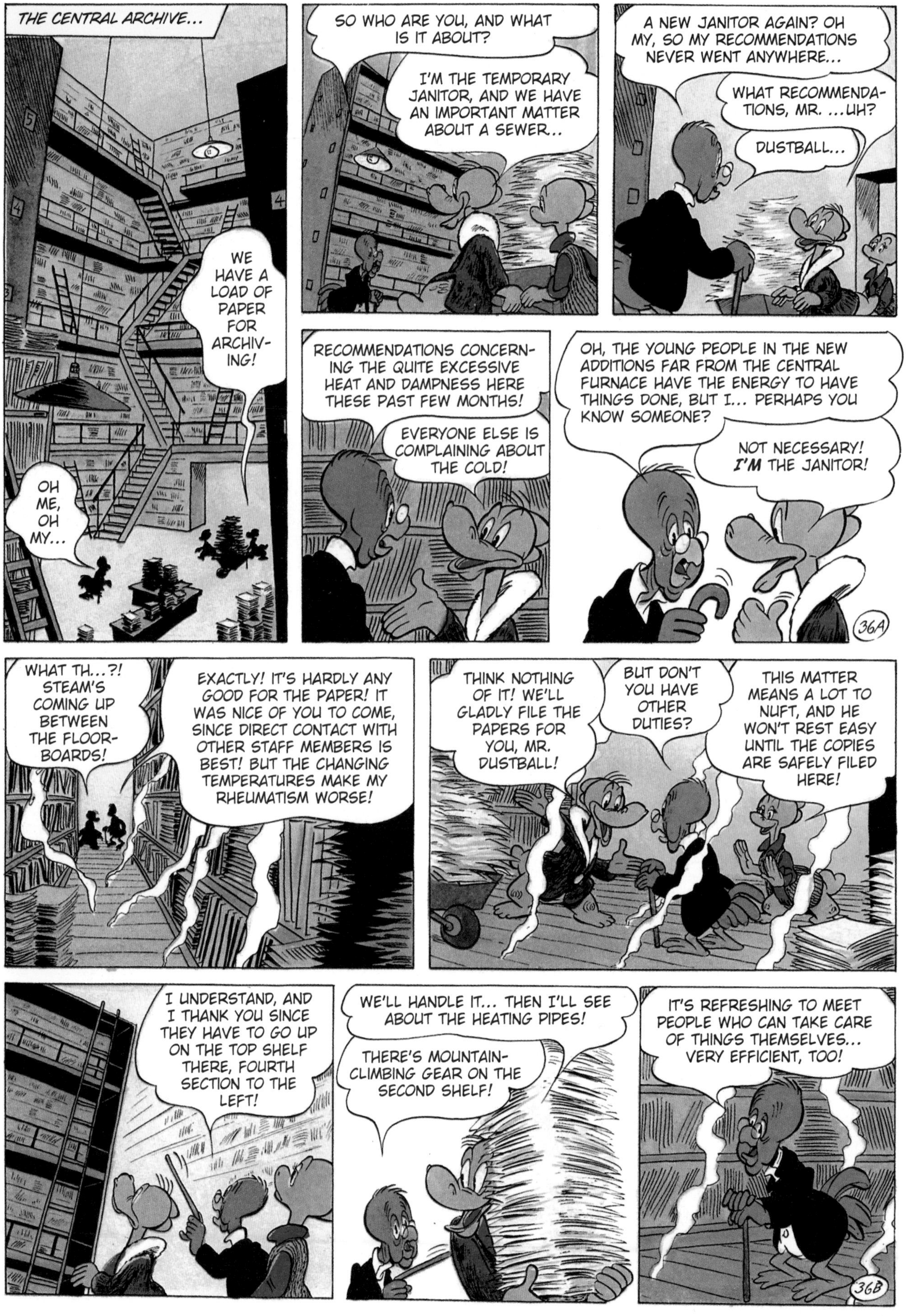
THE CENTRAL ARCHIVE...
WE HAVE A LOAD OF PAPER FOR ARCHIVING!
OH ME, OH MY...
SO WHO ARE YOU, AND WHAT IS IT ABOUT?
I'M THE TEMPORARY JANITOR, AND WE HAVE AN IMPORTANT MATTER ABOUT A SEWER...
A NEW JANITOR AGAIN? OH MY, SO MY RECOMMENDATIONS NEVER WENT ANYWHERE...
WHAT RECOMMENDATIONS, MR. ...UH?
DUSTBALL...
RECOMMENDATIONS CONCERNING THE QUITE EXCESSIVE HEAT AND DAMPNESS HERE THESE PAST FEW MONTHS!
EVERYONE ELSE IS COMPLAINING ABOUT THE COLD!
OH, THE YOUNG PEOPLE IN THE NEW ADDITIONS FAR FROM THE CENTRAL FURNACE HAVE THE ENERGY TO HAVE THINGS DONE, BUT I... PERHAPS YOU KNOW SOMEONE?
NOT NECESSARY! I'M THE JANITOR!
36A
WHAT TH...?! STEAM'S COMING UP BETWEEN THE FLOORBOARDS!
EXACTLY! IT'S HARDLY ANY GOOD FOR THE PAPER! IT WAS NICE OF YOU TO COME, SINCE DIRECT CONTACT WITH OTHER STAFF MEMBERS IS BEST! BUT THE CHANGING TEMPERATURES MAKE MY RHEUMATISM WORSE!
THINK NOTHING OF IT! WE'LL GLADLY FILE THE PAPERS FOR YOU, MR. DUSTBALL!
BUT DON'T YOU HAVE OTHER DUTIES?
THIS MATTER MEANS A LOT TO NUFT, AND HE WON'T REST EASY UNTIL THE COPIES ARE SAFELY FILED HERE!
I UNDERSTAND, AND I THANK YOU SINCE THEY HAVE TO GO UP ON THE TOP SHELF THERE, FOURTH SECTION TO THE LEFT!
WE'LL HANDLE IT... THEN I'LL SEE ABOUT THE HEATING PIPES!
THERE'S MOUNTAIN-CLIMBING GEAR ON THE SECOND SHELF!
IT'S REFRESHING TO MEET PEOPLE WHO CAN TAKE CARE OF THINGS THEMSELVES... VERY EFFICIENT, TOO!
36B

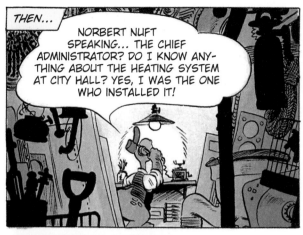

THEN...

NORBERT NUFT SPEAKING... THE CHIEF ADMINISTRATOR? DO I KNOW ANYTHING ABOUT THE HEATING SYSTEM AT CITY HALL? YES, I WAS THE ONE WHO INSTALLED IT!

AHA! SO *YOU'RE* RESPONSIBLE! THE CITY WILL SUE YOU FOR SHODDY WORK!

I DON'T THINK SO, SIR!

OH, WELL... ALL RIGHT... COULD YOU AT LEAST TRY TO SEE WHAT CAN BE DONE?

BECAUSE IT'S THE COUNCIL THAT DECIDED TO OVERLOAD THE SYSTEM BEYOND WHAT IT WAS DESIGNED FOR! YOU CAN FIND THE DOCUMENTS YOURSELF IN THE CENTRAL ARCHIVE...

WHERE ARE YOU GOING, SIR? MAYBE I CAN...?

OVER TO THE CENTRAL ARCHIVE FOR THE HEATING BLUEPRINTS...

AND I HAVE TO DO IT MYSELF IF ANYTHING'S GOING TO HAPPEN RIGHT AWAY!

37A

HMM...

THE PLANS SHOULD BE HERE... FUNNY HOW YOU CAN FORGET THINGS AFTER 20 OR 30 YEARS...

NUFT MIGHT BE RIGHT... THINGS DO NEED CLEANING UP AROUND HERE!

I'LL THINK ABOUT IT IN A YEAR OR TWO...

37B

AH, HERE ARE THE PLANS!

PFFF

SIMPLE ENOUGH... BUT SINCE THEN THEY'VE ADDED NEW ADDITIONS HERE, HERE, HERE, HERE, HERE...

HMM...THAT COULD MEAN THERE MIGHT BE AN OVERLOAD HERE AND HERE...

...AND A VERY CRITICAL POINT HERE...

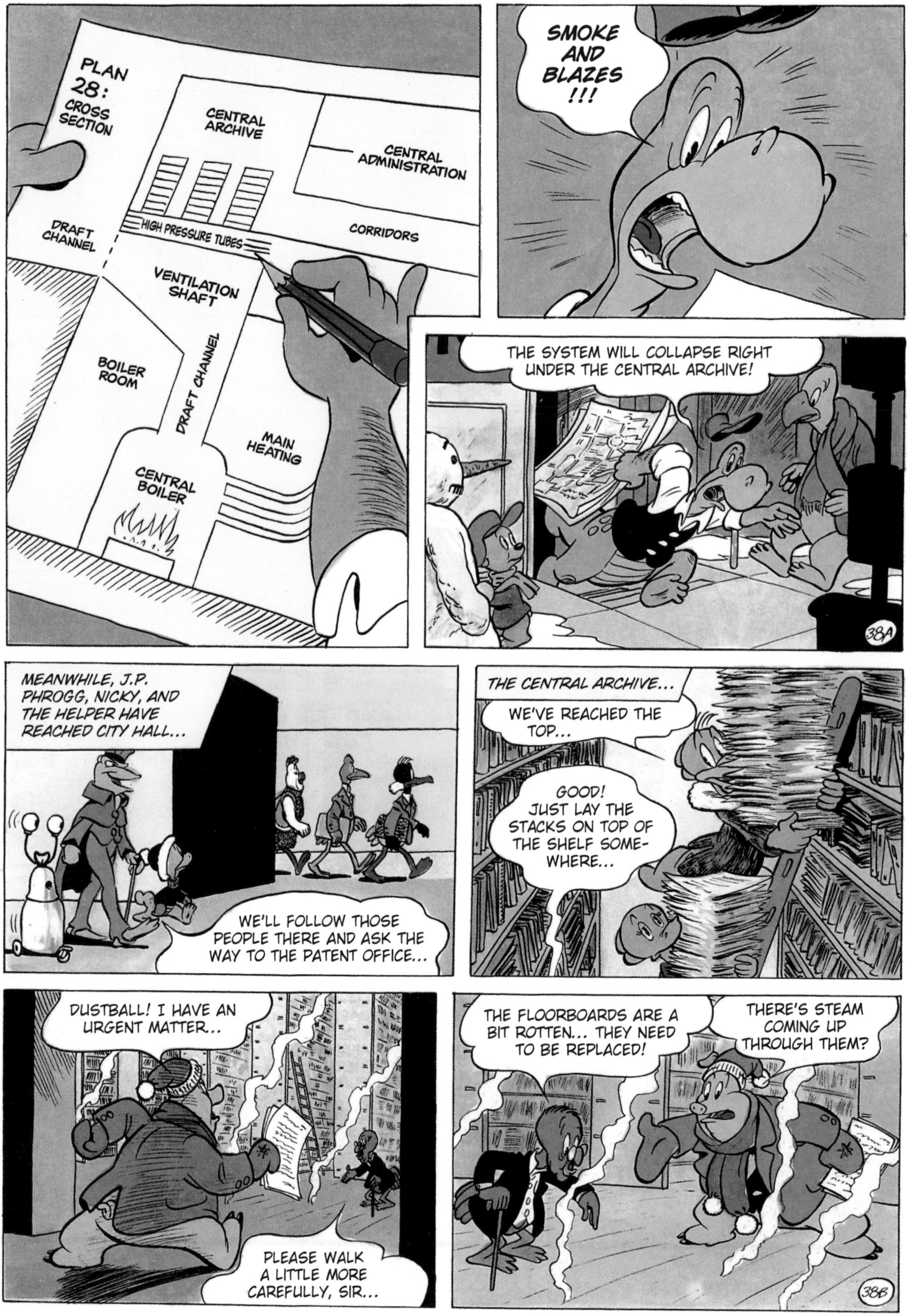
PLAN 28: CROSS SECTION
CENTRAL ARCHIVE
CENTRAL ADMINISTRATION
HIGH PRESSURE TUBES
CORRIDORS
DRAFT CHANNEL
VENTILATION SHAFT
BOILER ROOM
DRAFT CHANNEL
MAIN HEATING
CENTRAL BOILER
SMOKE AND BLAZES !!!
THE SYSTEM WILL COLLAPSE RIGHT UNDER THE CENTRAL ARCHIVE!
38A
MEANWHILE, J.P. PHROGG, NICKY, AND THE HELPER HAVE REACHED CITY HALL...
WE'LL FOLLOW THOSE PEOPLE THERE AND ASK THE WAY TO THE PATENT OFFICE...
THE CENTRAL ARCHIVE...
WE'VE REACHED THE TOP...
GOOD! JUST LAY THE STACKS ON TOP OF THE SHELF SOME-WHERE...
DUSTBALL! I HAVE AN URGENT MATTER...
PLEASE WALK A LITTLE MORE CAREFULLY, SIR...
THE FLOORBOARDS ARE A BIT ROTTEN... THEY NEED TO BE REPLACED!
THERE'S STEAM COMING UP THROUGH THEM?
38B

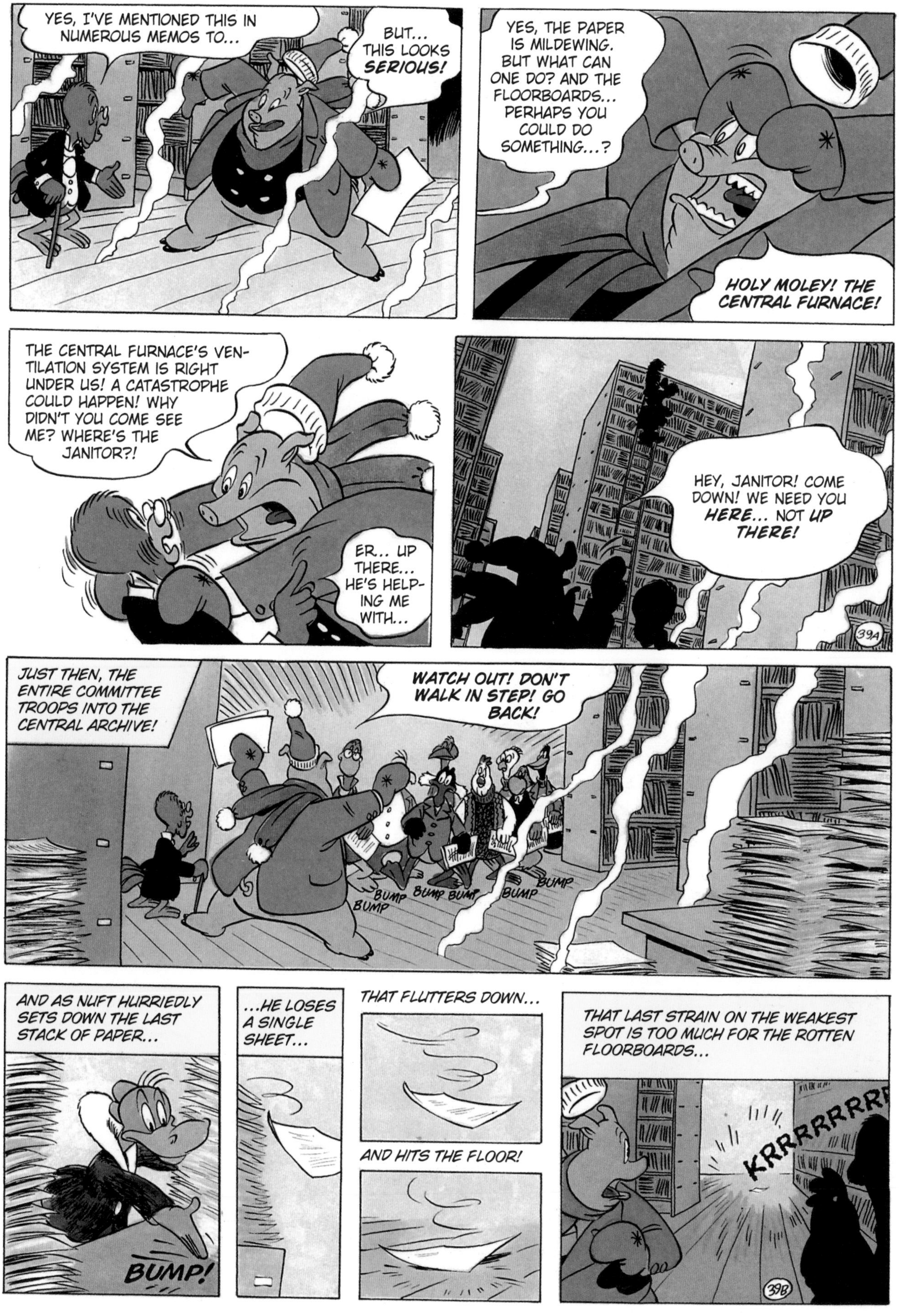

YES, I'VE MENTIONED THIS IN NUMEROUS MEMOS TO...
BUT... THIS LOOKS SERIOUS!
YES, THE PAPER IS MILDEWING. BUT WHAT CAN ONE DO? AND THE FLOORBOARDS... PERHAPS YOU COULD DO SOMETHING...?
HOLY MOLEY! THE CENTRAL FURNACE!
THE CENTRAL FURNACE'S VEN-TILATION SYSTEM IS RIGHT UNDER US! A CATASTROPHE COULD HAPPEN! WHY DIDN'T YOU COME SEE ME? WHERE'S THE JANITOR?!
ER... UP THERE... HE'S HELP-ING ME WITH...
HEY, JANITOR! COME DOWN! WE NEED YOU HERE... NOT UP THERE!
39A
JUST THEN, THE ENTIRE COMMITTEE TROOPS INTO THE CENTRAL ARCHIVE!
WATCH OUT! DON'T WALK IN STEP! GO BACK!
BUMP BUMP
BUMP BUMP
BUMP BUMP
AND AS NUFT HURRIEDLY SETS DOWN THE LAST STACK OF PAPER...
BUMP!
...HE LOSES A SINGLE SHEET...
THAT FLUTTERS DOWN...
AND HITS THE FLOOR!
THAT LAST STRAIN ON THE WEAKEST SPOT IS TOO MUCH FOR THE ROTTEN FLOORBOARDS...
KRRRRRRR
39B

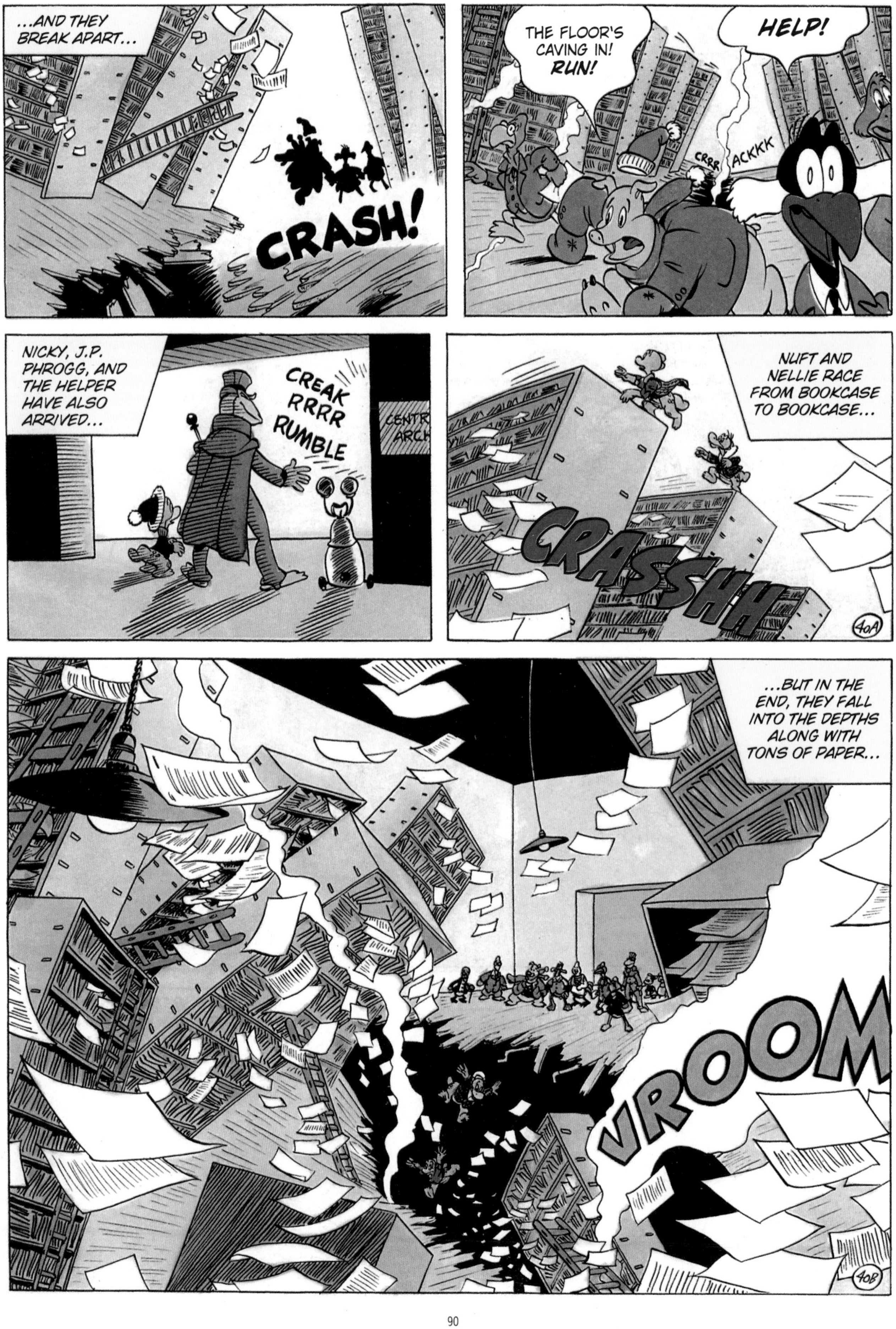
...AND THEY BREAK APART...
CRASH!
THE FLOOR'S CAVING IN! RUN!
HELP!
CRRR ACKKK
NICKY, J.P. PHROGG, AND THE HELPER HAVE ALSO ARRIVED...
CREAK RRRR RUMBLE
NUFT AND NELLIE RACE FROM BOOKCASE TO BOOKCASE...
CRASSHH
40A
...BUT IN THE END, THEY FALL INTO THE DEPTHS ALONG WITH TONS OF PAPER...
VROOM
40B

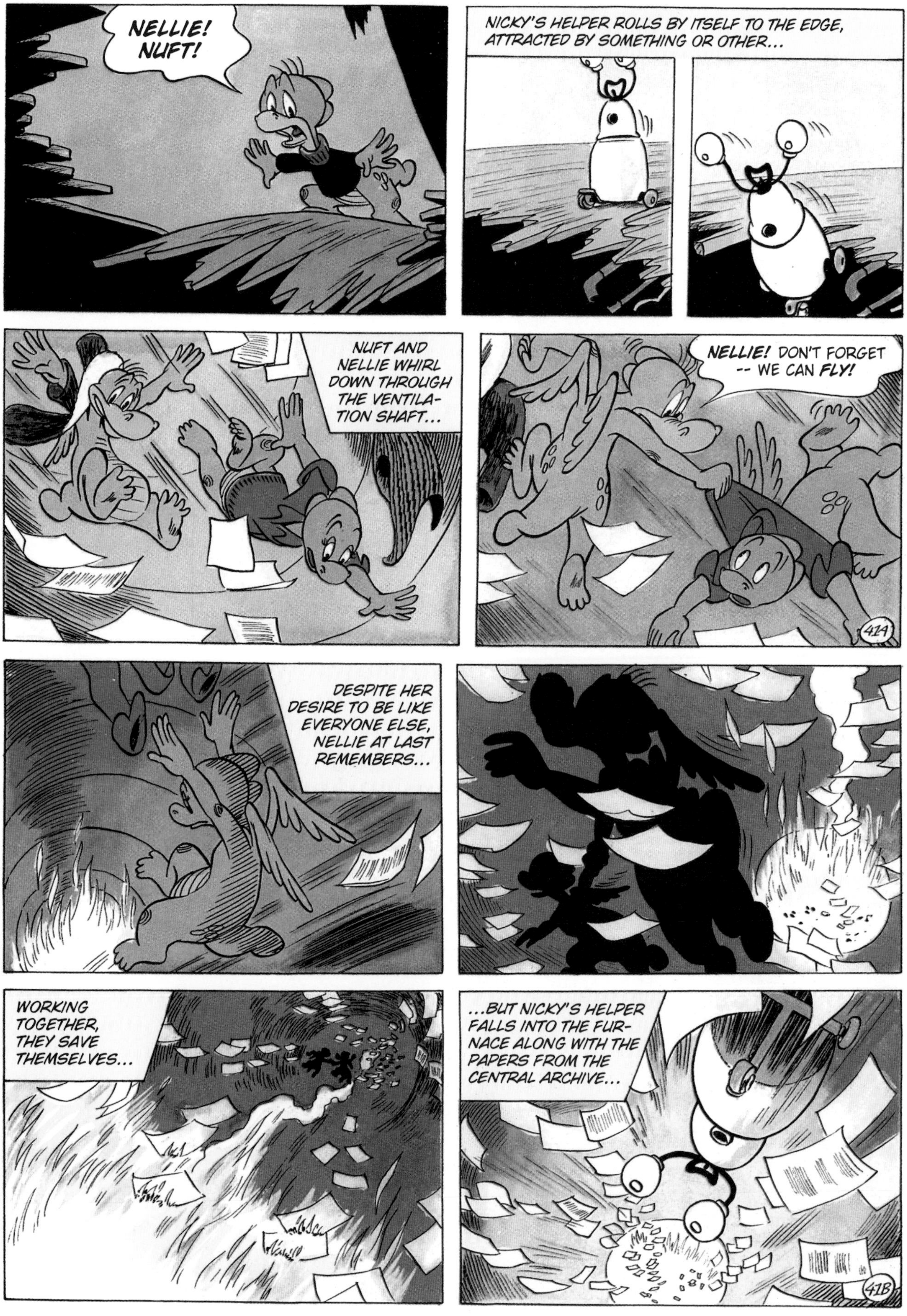

NELLIE! NUFT!
NICKY'S HELPER ROLLS BY ITSELF TO THE EDGE, ATTRACTED BY SOMETHING OR OTHER...
NUFT AND NELLIE WHIRL DOWN THROUGH THE VENTILA-TION SHAFT...
NELLIE! DON'T FORGET -- WE CAN FLY!
41A
DESPITE HER DESIRE TO BE LIKE EVERYONE ELSE, NELLIE AT LAST REMEMBERS...
WORKING TOGETHER, THEY SAVE THEMSELVES...
...BUT NICKY'S HELPER FALLS INTO THE FUR-NACE ALONG WITH THE PAPERS FROM THE CENTRAL ARCHIVE...
41B

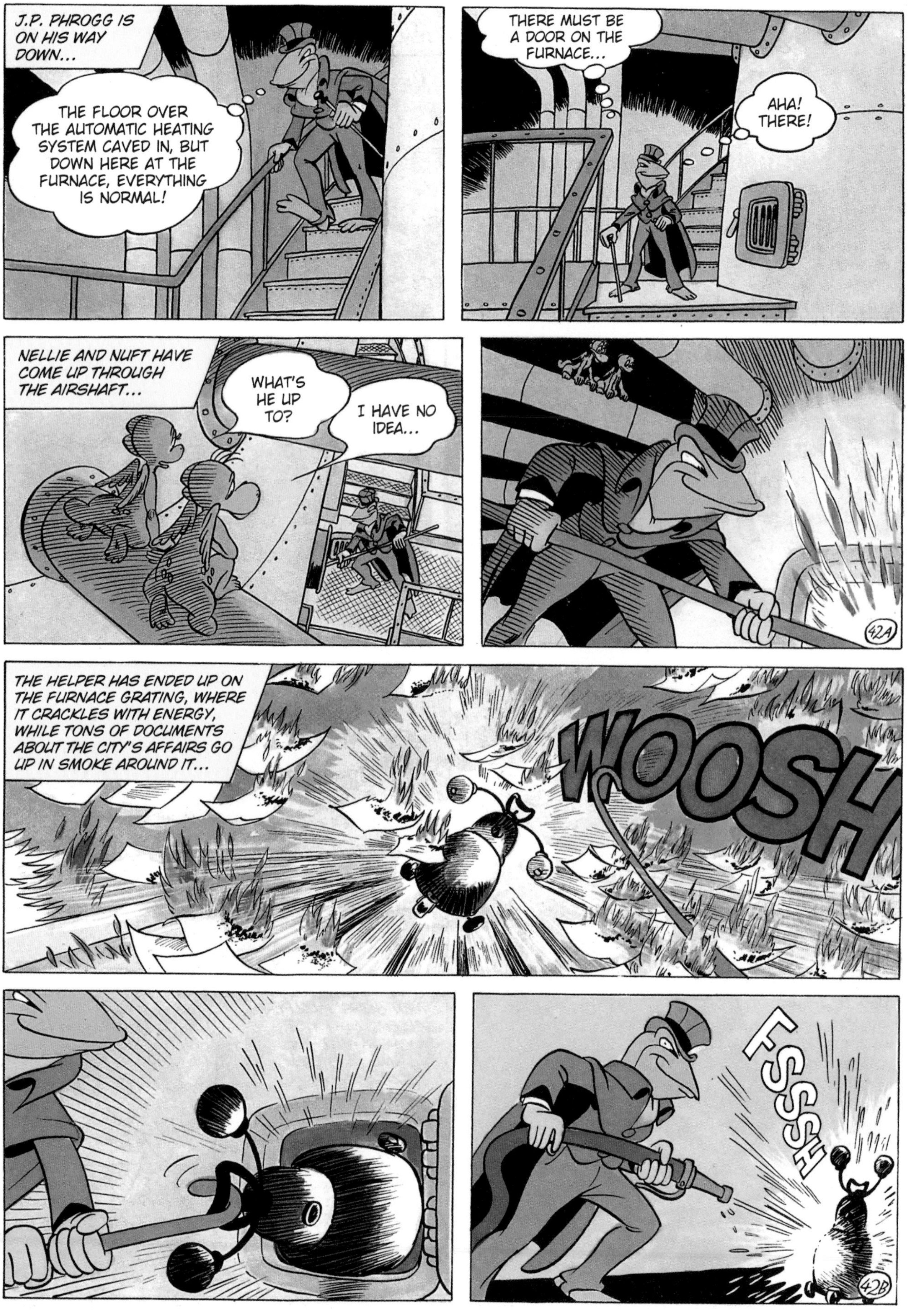
J.P. PHROGG IS ON HIS WAY DOWN...
THE FLOOR OVER THE AUTOMATIC HEATING SYSTEM CAVED IN, BUT DOWN HERE AT THE FURNACE, EVERYTHING IS NORMAL!
THERE MUST BE A DOOR ON THE FURNACE...
AHA! THERE!
NELLIE AND NUFT HAVE COME UP THROUGH THE AIRSHAFT...
WHAT'S HE UP TO?
I HAVE NO IDEA...
42A
THE HELPER HAS ENDED UP ON THE FURNACE GRATING, WHERE IT CRACKLES WITH ENERGY, WHILE TONS OF DOCUMENTS ABOUT THE CITY'S AFFAIRS GO UP IN SMOKE AROUND IT...
WOOSH
FSSSH
42B

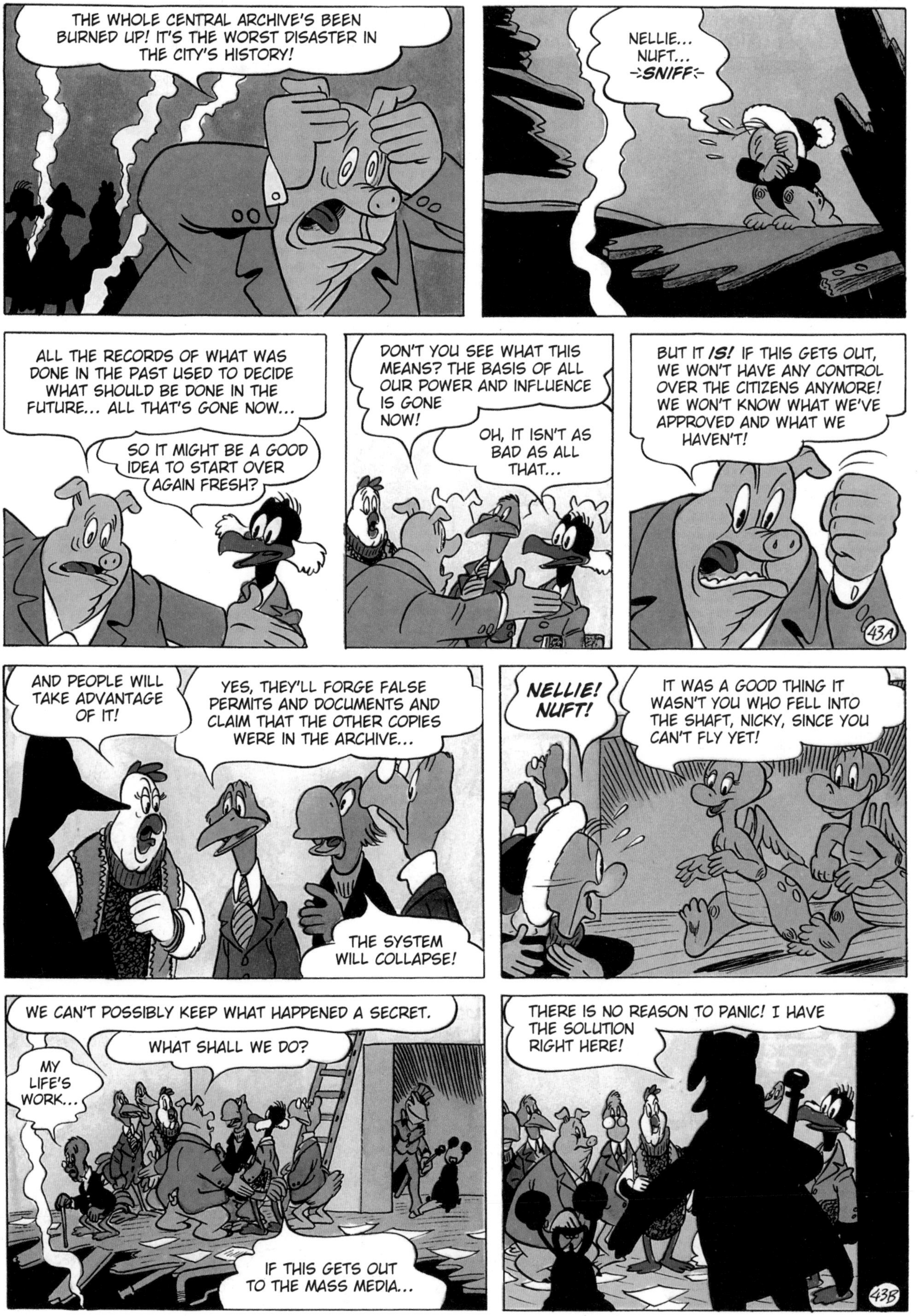
THE WHOLE CENTRAL ARCHIVE'S BEEN BURNED UP! IT'S THE WORST DISASTER IN THE CITY'S HISTORY!
NELLIE... NUFT... -SNIFF-
ALL THE RECORDS OF WHAT WAS DONE IN THE PAST USED TO DECIDE WHAT SHOULD BE DONE IN THE FUTURE... ALL THAT'S GONE NOW...
SO IT MIGHT BE A GOOD IDEA TO START OVER AGAIN FRESH?
DON'T YOU SEE WHAT THIS MEANS? THE BASIS OF ALL OUR POWER AND INFLUENCE IS GONE NOW!
OH, IT ISN'T AS BAD AS ALL THAT...
BUT IT IS! IF THIS GETS OUT, WE WON'T HAVE ANY CONTROL OVER THE CITIZENS ANYMORE! WE WON'T KNOW WHAT WE'VE APPROVED AND WHAT WE HAVEN'T!
43A
AND PEOPLE WILL TAKE ADVANTAGE OF IT!
YES, THEY'LL FORGE FALSE PERMITS AND DOCUMENTS AND CLAIM THAT THE OTHER COPIES WERE IN THE ARCHIVE...
THE SYSTEM WILL COLLAPSE!
NELLIE! NUFT!
IT WAS A GOOD THING IT WASN'T YOU WHO FELL INTO THE SHAFT, NICKY, SINCE YOU CAN'T FLY YET!
WE CAN'T POSSIBLY KEEP WHAT HAPPENED A SECRET.
WHAT SHALL WE DO?
MY LIFE'S WORK...
IF THIS GETS OUT TO THE MASS MEDIA...
THERE IS NO REASON TO PANIC! I HAVE THE SOLUTION RIGHT HERE!
43B

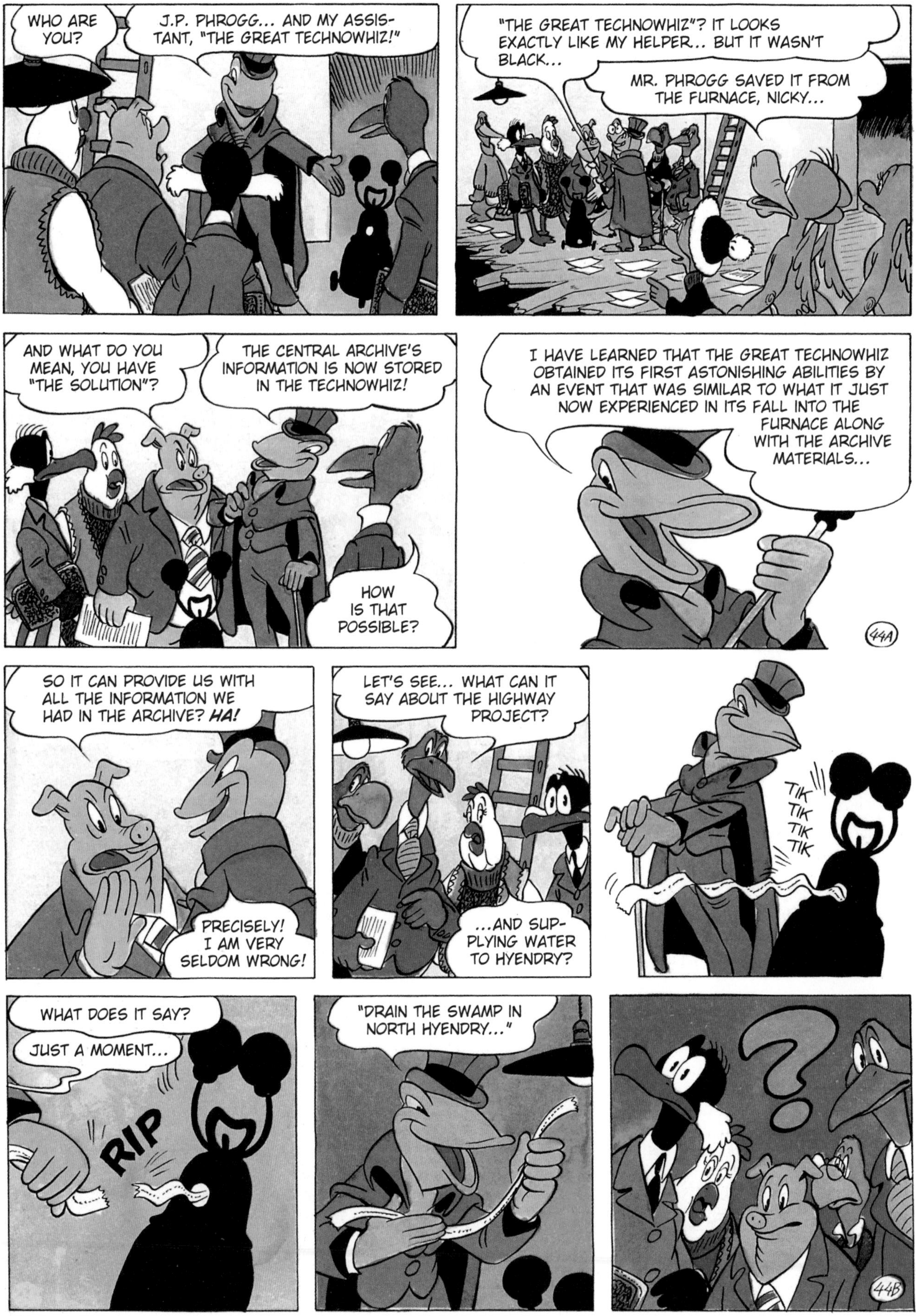
WHO ARE YOU?
J.P. PHROGG... AND MY ASSISTANT, "THE GREAT TECHNOWHIZ!"
"THE GREAT TECHNOWHIZ"? IT LOOKS EXACTLY LIKE MY HELPER... BUT IT WASN'T BLACK...
MR. PHROGG SAVED IT FROM THE FURNACE, NICKY...
AND WHAT DO YOU MEAN, YOU HAVE "THE SOLUTION"?
THE CENTRAL ARCHIVE'S INFORMATION IS NOW STORED IN THE TECHNOWHIZ!
HOW IS THAT POSSIBLE?
I HAVE LEARNED THAT THE GREAT TECHNOWHIZ OBTAINED ITS FIRST ASTONISHING ABILITIES BY AN EVENT THAT WAS SIMILAR TO WHAT IT JUST NOW EXPERIENCED IN ITS FALL INTO THE FURNACE ALONG WITH THE ARCHIVE MATERIALS...
44A
SO IT CAN PROVIDE US WITH ALL THE INFORMATION WE HAD IN THE ARCHIVE? HA!
PRECISELY! I AM VERY SELDOM WRONG!
LET'S SEE... WHAT CAN IT SAY ABOUT THE HIGHWAY PROJECT?
...AND SUPPLYING WATER TO HYENDRY?
TIK TIK TIK TIK
WHAT DOES IT SAY?
JUST A MOMENT...
RIP
"DRAIN THE SWAMP IN NORTH HYENDRY..."
?
44B

ISN'T IT WONDERFUL? THIS WILL SOLVE THE WATER SUPPLY PROBLEM AND MAKE ROOM FOR RELOCATING THE HIGHWAY!

IT SOUNDS GOOD!

A PERFECT SOLUTION FOR BOTH PROBLEMS AT ONCE!

IMPRESSIVE!

AND THERE'S SOMETHING IMPORTANT FOR YOU... YOU WON'T HAVE TO ADMIT TO THE PUBLIC THAT THE CENTRAL ARCHIVE WAS LOST DUE TO ANY NEGLIGENCE IN MAKING YOUR DECISIONS!

45A

YOU CAN JUST ANNOUNCE IT AS A REORGANIZATION AND THAT THE GREAT TECHNOWHIZ IS NOW READY TO SERVE THE CITY!

THAT'S A RELIEF! THE PRESS WOULDN'T BE UNDERSTANDING!...

ONE OTHER QUESTION, BUT IT'S BEYOND EVEN ITS POWERS...

WHAT ABOUT THE HEATING SYSTEM HERE IN CITY HALL AND ALL ITS ADDITIONS?

YES, WHAT ABOUT IT?

TIK TIK TIK TIK TIK TIK

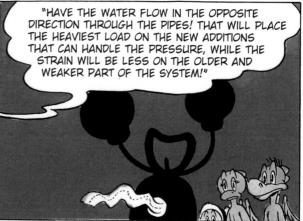

"HAVE THE WATER FLOW IN THE OPPOSITE DIRECTION THROUGH THE PIPES! THAT WILL PLACE THE HEAVIEST LOAD ON THE NEW ADDITIONS THAT CAN HANDLE THE PRESSURE, WHILE THE STRAIN WILL BE LESS ON THE OLDER AND WEAKER PART OF THE SYSTEM!"

HOORAY FOR THE GREAT TECHNOWHIZ!

45B

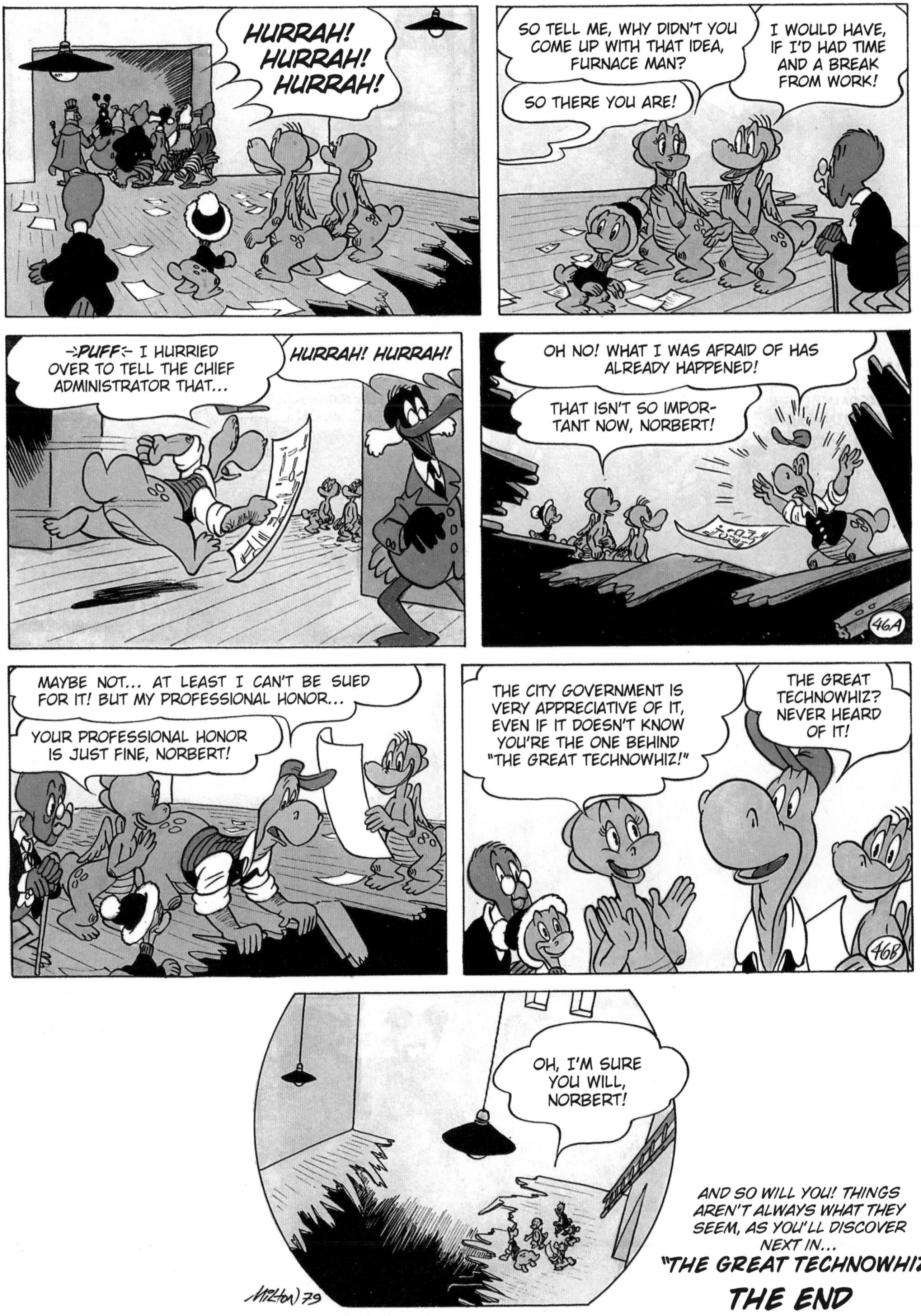
HURRAH! HURRAH! HURRAH!
SO TELL ME, WHY DIDN'T YOU COME UP WITH THAT IDEA, FURNACE MAN?
SO THERE YOU ARE!
I WOULD HAVE, IF I'D HAD TIME AND A BREAK FROM WORK!
-PUFF- I HURRIED OVER TO TELL THE CHIEF ADMINISTRATOR THAT...
HURRAH! HURRAH!
OH NO! WHAT I WAS AFRAID OF HAS ALREADY HAPPENED!
THAT ISN'T SO IMPORTANT NOW, NORBERT!
46A
MAYBE NOT... AT LEAST I CAN'T BE SUED FOR IT! BUT MY PROFESSIONAL HONOR...
YOUR PROFESSIONAL HONOR IS JUST FINE, NORBERT!
THE CITY GOVERNMENT IS VERY APPRECIATIVE OF IT, EVEN IF IT DOESN'T KNOW YOU'RE THE ONE BEHIND "THE GREAT TECHNOWHIZ!"
THE GREAT TECHNOWHIZ? NEVER HEARD OF IT!
46B
OH, I'M SURE YOU WILL, NORBERT!
AND SO WILL YOU! THINGS AREN'T ALWAYS WHAT THEY SEEM, AS YOU'LL DISCOVER NEXT IN...
"THE GREAT TECHNOWHIZ"
THE END

The Great Technowhiz

by Freddy Milton
Translation: Dwight R. Decker
Colors: Freddy Milton

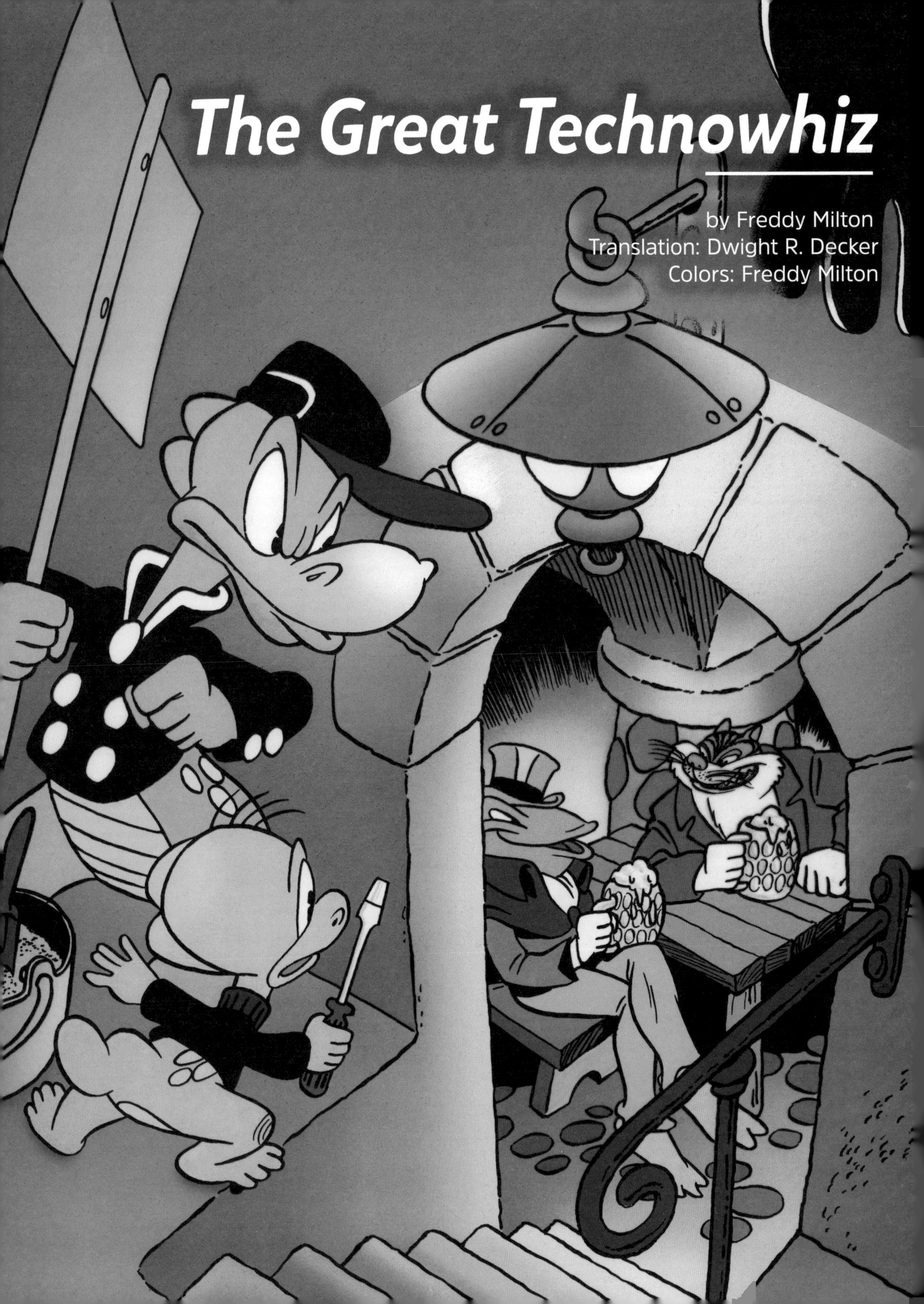

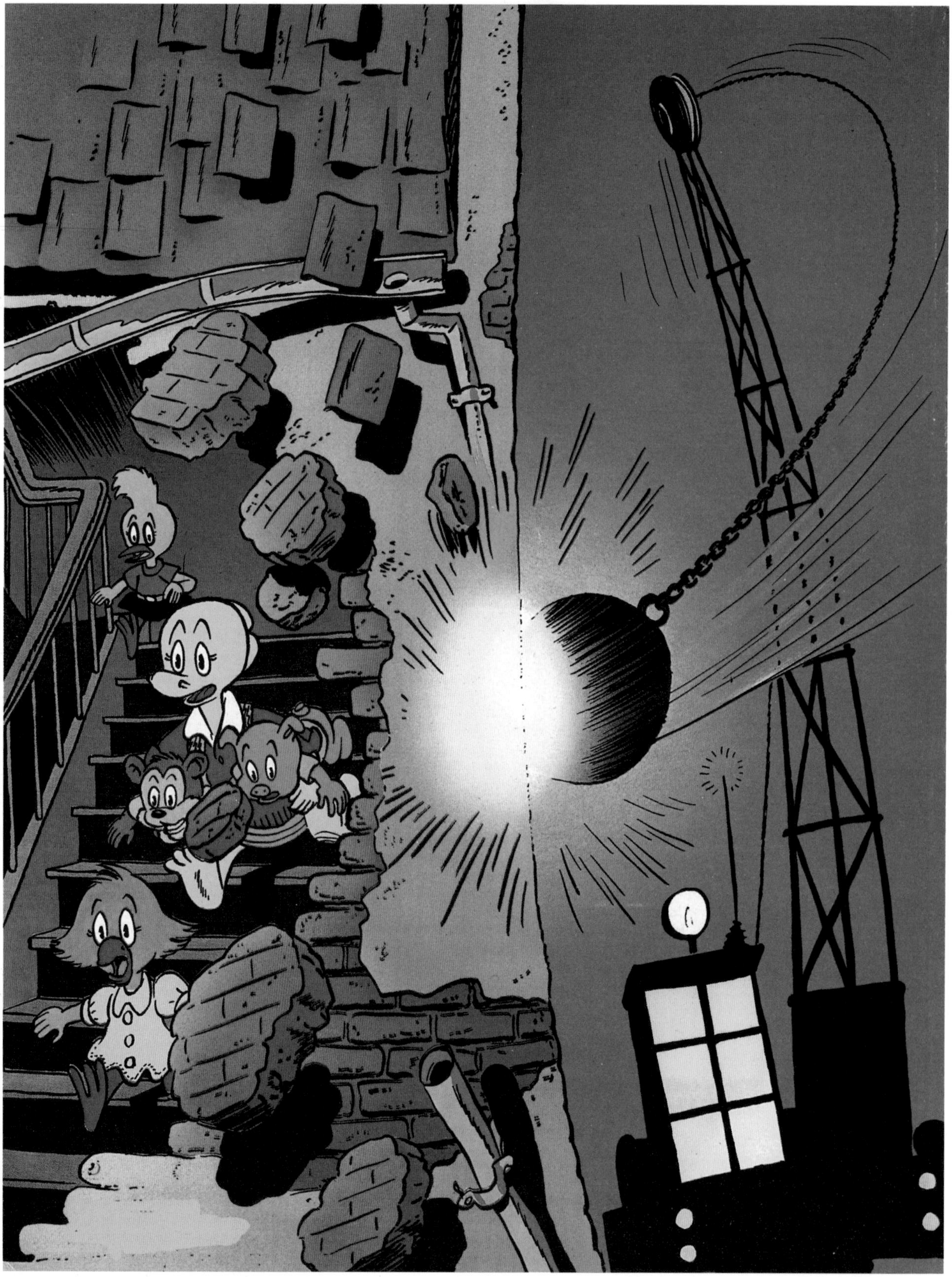

ABOVE: Freddy Milton's back cover art for the Danish edition of *The Great Technowhiz.*

PREVIOUS PAGE: Freddy Milton's front cover art for the Danish edition of *The Great Technowhiz.*

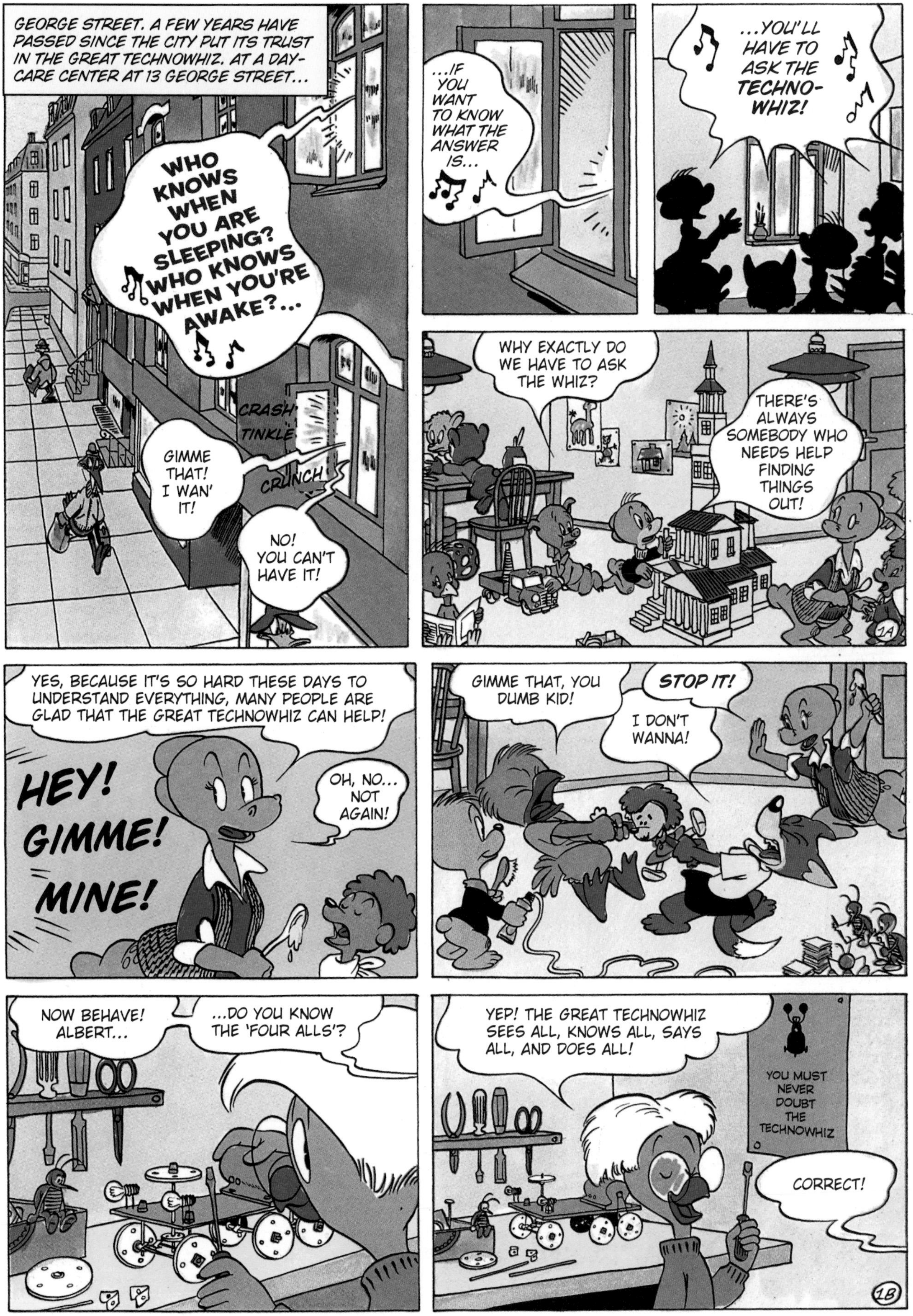
GEORGE STREET. A FEW YEARS HAVE PASSED SINCE THE CITY PUT ITS TRUST IN THE GREAT TECHNOWHIZ. AT A DAY-CARE CENTER AT 13 GEORGE STREET…
WHO KNOWS WHEN YOU ARE SLEEPING? WHO KNOWS WHEN YOU'RE AWAKE?…
CRASH
TINKLE
CRUNCH
GIMME THAT! I WAN' IT!
NO! YOU CAN'T HAVE IT!
…IF YOU WANT TO KNOW WHAT THE ANSWER IS…
…YOU'LL HAVE TO ASK THE TECHNO-WHIZ!
WHY EXACTLY DO WE HAVE TO ASK THE WHIZ?
THERE'S ALWAYS SOMEBODY WHO NEEDS HELP FINDING THINGS OUT!
1A
YES, BECAUSE IT'S SO HARD THESE DAYS TO UNDERSTAND EVERYTHING, MANY PEOPLE ARE GLAD THAT THE GREAT TECHNOWHIZ CAN HELP!
HEY!
GIMME!
MINE!
OH, NO… NOT AGAIN!
GIMME THAT, YOU DUMB KID!
STOP IT!
I DON'T WANNA!
NOW BEHAVE! ALBERT…
…DO YOU KNOW THE 'FOUR ALLS'?
YEP! THE GREAT TECHNOWHIZ SEES ALL, KNOWS ALL, SAYS ALL, AND DOES ALL!
YOU MUST NEVER DOUBT THE TECHNOWHIZ
CORRECT!
1B

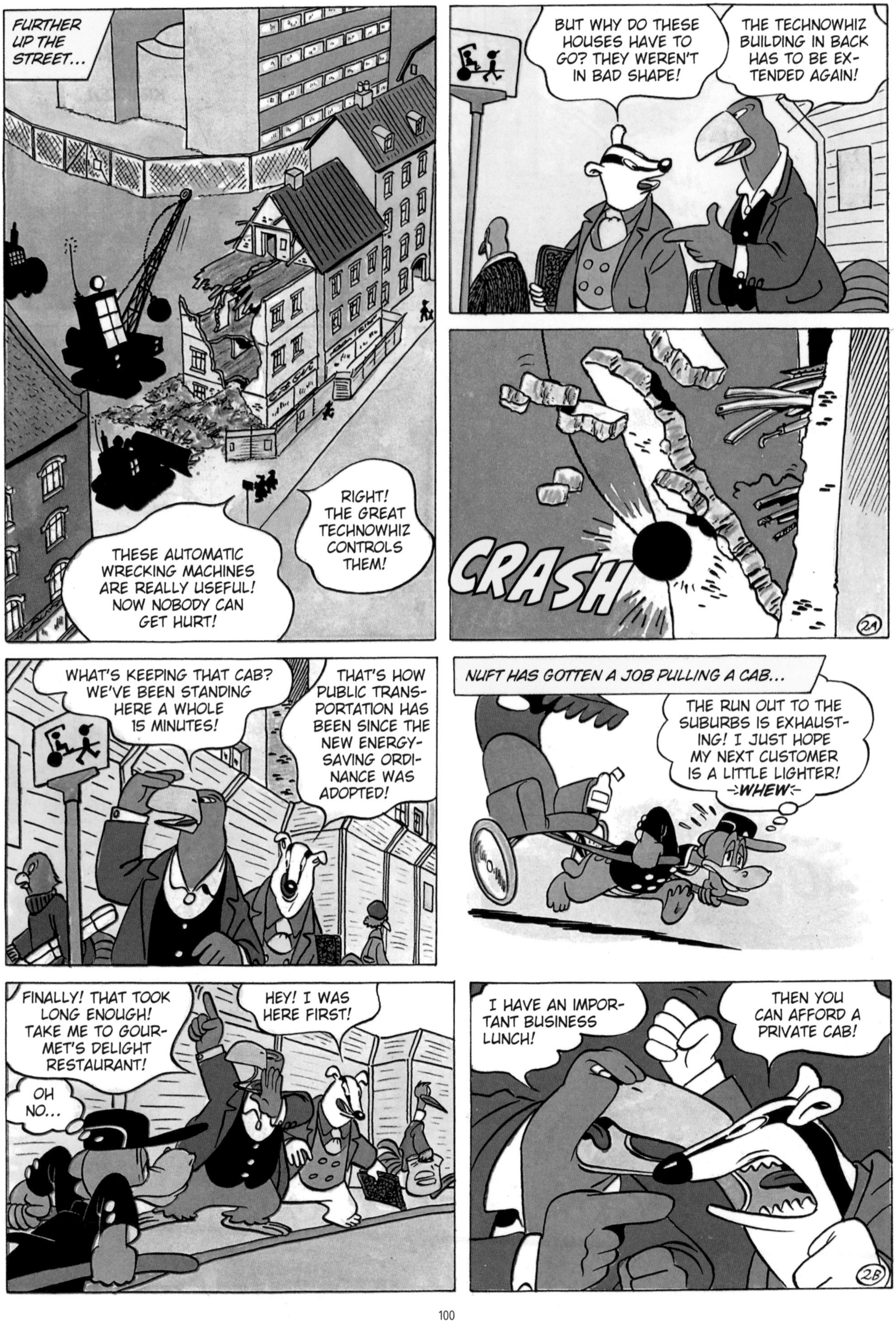
FURTHER UP THE STREET...
THESE AUTOMATIC WRECKING MACHINES ARE REALLY USEFUL! NOW NOBODY CAN GET HURT!
RIGHT! THE GREAT TECHNOWHIZ CONTROLS THEM!
BUT WHY DO THESE HOUSES HAVE TO GO? THEY WEREN'T IN BAD SHAPE!
THE TECHNOWHIZ BUILDING IN BACK HAS TO BE EXTENDED AGAIN!
CRASH
2A
WHAT'S KEEPING THAT CAB? WE'VE BEEN STANDING HERE A WHOLE 15 MINUTES!
THAT'S HOW PUBLIC TRANSPORTATION HAS BEEN SINCE THE NEW ENERGY-SAVING ORDINANCE WAS ADOPTED!
NUFT HAS GOTTEN A JOB PULLING A CAB...
THE RUN OUT TO THE SUBURBS IS EXHAUSTING! I JUST HOPE MY NEXT CUSTOMER IS A LITTLE LIGHTER!
WHEW
FINALLY! THAT TOOK LONG ENOUGH! TAKE ME TO GOURMET'S DELIGHT RESTAURANT!
HEY! I WAS HERE FIRST!
OH NO...
I HAVE AN IMPORTANT BUSINESS LUNCH!
THEN YOU CAN AFFORD A PRIVATE CAB!
2B

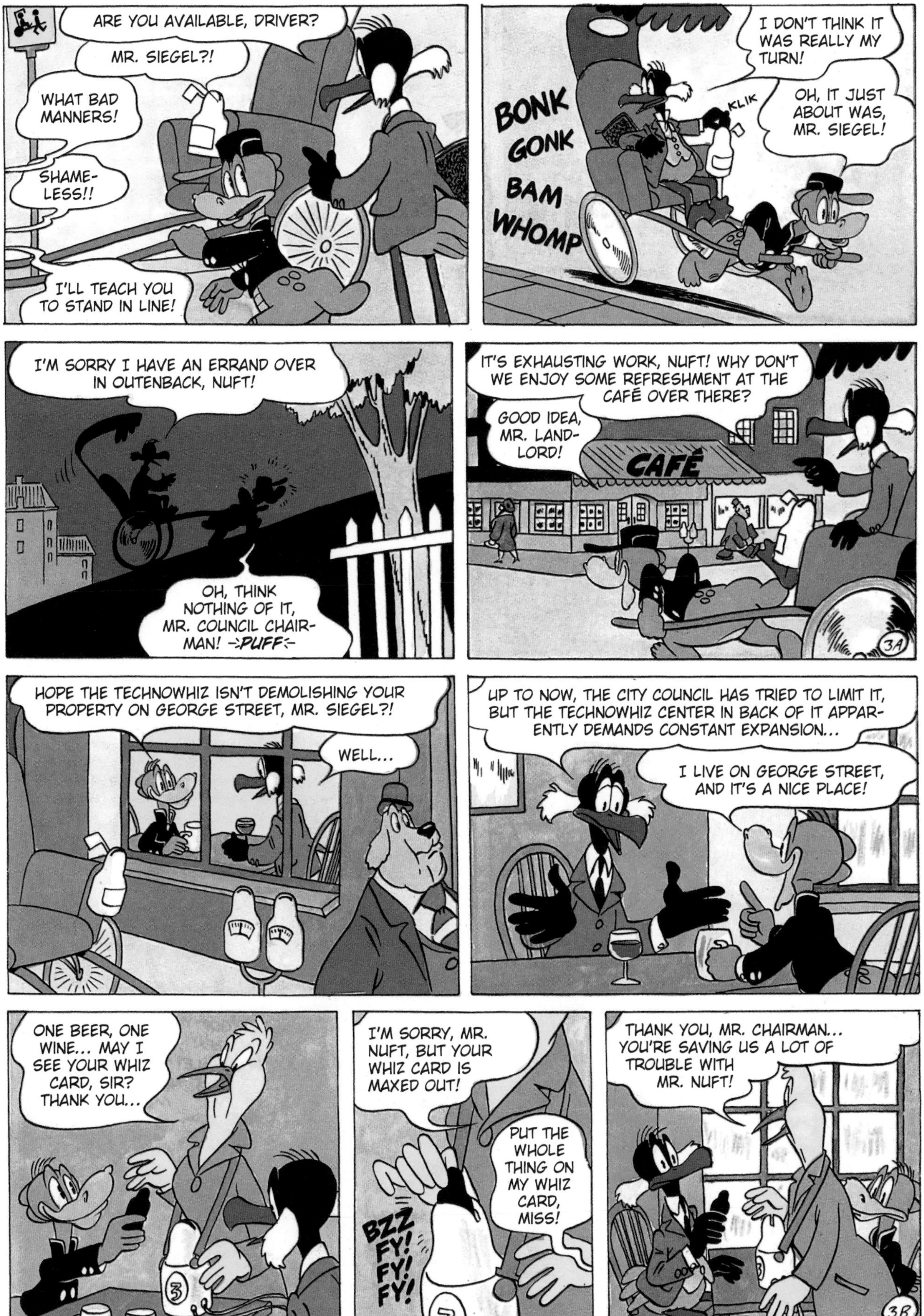
ARE YOU AVAILABLE, DRIVER?
MR. SIEGEL?!
WHAT BAD MANNERS!
SHAME-LESS!!
I'LL TEACH YOU TO STAND IN LINE!
BONK
GONK
BAM
WHOMP
I DON'T THINK IT WAS REALLY MY TURN!
KLIK
OH, IT JUST ABOUT WAS, MR. SIEGEL!
I'M SORRY I HAVE AN ERRAND OVER IN OUTENBACK, NUFT!
OH, THINK NOTHING OF IT, MR. COUNCIL CHAIR-MAN! PUFF
IT'S EXHAUSTING WORK, NUFT! WHY DON'T WE ENJOY SOME REFRESHMENT AT THE CAFÉ OVER THERE?
GOOD IDEA, MR. LAND-LORD!
CAFÉ
3A
HOPE THE TECHNOWHIZ ISN'T DEMOLISHING YOUR PROPERTY ON GEORGE STREET, MR. SIEGEL?!
WELL...
UP TO NOW, THE CITY COUNCIL HAS TRIED TO LIMIT IT, BUT THE TECHNOWHIZ CENTER IN BACK OF IT APPAR-ENTLY DEMANDS CONSTANT EXPANSION...
I LIVE ON GEORGE STREET, AND IT'S A NICE PLACE!
ONE BEER, ONE WINE... MAY I SEE YOUR WHIZ CARD, SIR? THANK YOU...
I'M SORRY, MR. NUFT, BUT YOUR WHIZ CARD IS MAXED OUT!
BZZ FY! FY! FY!
PUT THE WHOLE THING ON MY WHIZ CARD, MISS!
THANK YOU, MR. CHAIRMAN... YOU'RE SAVING US A LOT OF TROUBLE WITH MR. NUFT!
3B

LATER...

LOOKS LIKE A BIG CROWD ON ELM BOULEVARD!

HERE COMES SIEGEL, THE CITY COUNCIL CHAIRMAN!

LET'S HEAR WHAT HE SAYS!

PRESE THE BOULE

ENVIRONMENT

WE DEMAND THE COUNCIL STEP IN!

NATURE

Save the trees

STOP THE TREE CLEARING!

4A

THE TECHNOWHIZ WATCHES OVER THE CITY THROUGH THE TRAFFIC LIGHTS! THE TREES HERE HAVE TO GO... THEY BLOCK ITS VIEW!

BAH!

BOO!

Protect nature!

TREES ARE MORE IMPORTANT THAN SECURITY!

BUT... ER... THE STREET SHOULD BE PRE-SERVED!

HOW CAN YOU CUT DOWN THESE BEAUTIFUL TREES?

SHAME ON YOU!

ER... I'M JUST DOING MY JOB, I...

...VERY WELL! WE'LL POSTPONE ANY CUTTING AND TAKE IT UP AGAIN AT THE NEXT COUNCIL MEETING!

HOORAY!!

VICTO-RY!!!

YAHOO!

4B

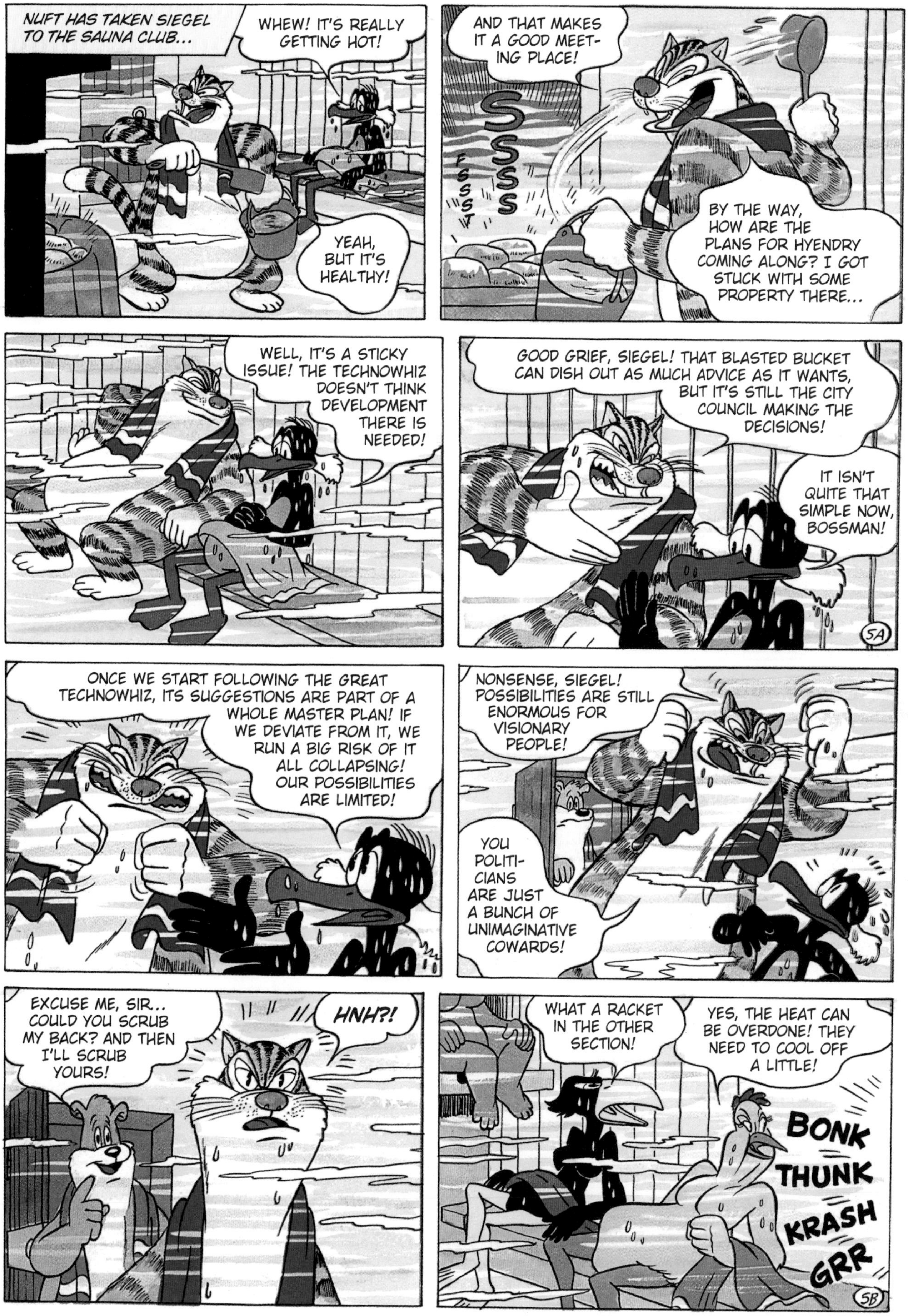
NUFT HAS TAKEN SIEGEL TO THE SAUNA CLUB...
WHEW! IT'S REALLY GETTING HOT!
YEAH, BUT IT'S HEALTHY!
AND THAT MAKES IT A GOOD MEETING PLACE!
SSSS
FSSST
BY THE WAY, HOW ARE THE PLANS FOR HYENDRY COMING ALONG? I GOT STUCK WITH SOME PROPERTY THERE...
WELL, IT'S A STICKY ISSUE! THE TECHNOWHIZ DOESN'T THINK DEVELOPMENT THERE IS NEEDED!
GOOD GRIEF, SIEGEL! THAT BLASTED BUCKET CAN DISH OUT AS MUCH ADVICE AS IT WANTS, BUT IT'S STILL THE CITY COUNCIL MAKING THE DECISIONS!
IT ISN'T QUITE THAT SIMPLE NOW, BOSSMAN!
5A
ONCE WE START FOLLOWING THE GREAT TECHNOWHIZ, ITS SUGGESTIONS ARE PART OF A WHOLE MASTER PLAN! IF WE DEVIATE FROM IT, WE RUN A BIG RISK OF IT ALL COLLAPSING! OUR POSSIBILITIES ARE LIMITED!
NONSENSE, SIEGEL! POSSIBILITIES ARE STILL ENORMOUS FOR VISIONARY PEOPLE!
YOU POLITICIANS ARE JUST A BUNCH OF UNIMAGINATIVE COWARDS!
EXCUSE ME, SIR... COULD YOU SCRUB MY BACK? AND THEN I'LL SCRUB YOURS!
HNH?!
WHAT A RACKET IN THE OTHER SECTION!
YES, THE HEAT CAN BE OVERDONE! THEY NEED TO COOL OFF A LITTLE!
BONK
THUNK
KRASH
GRR
5B

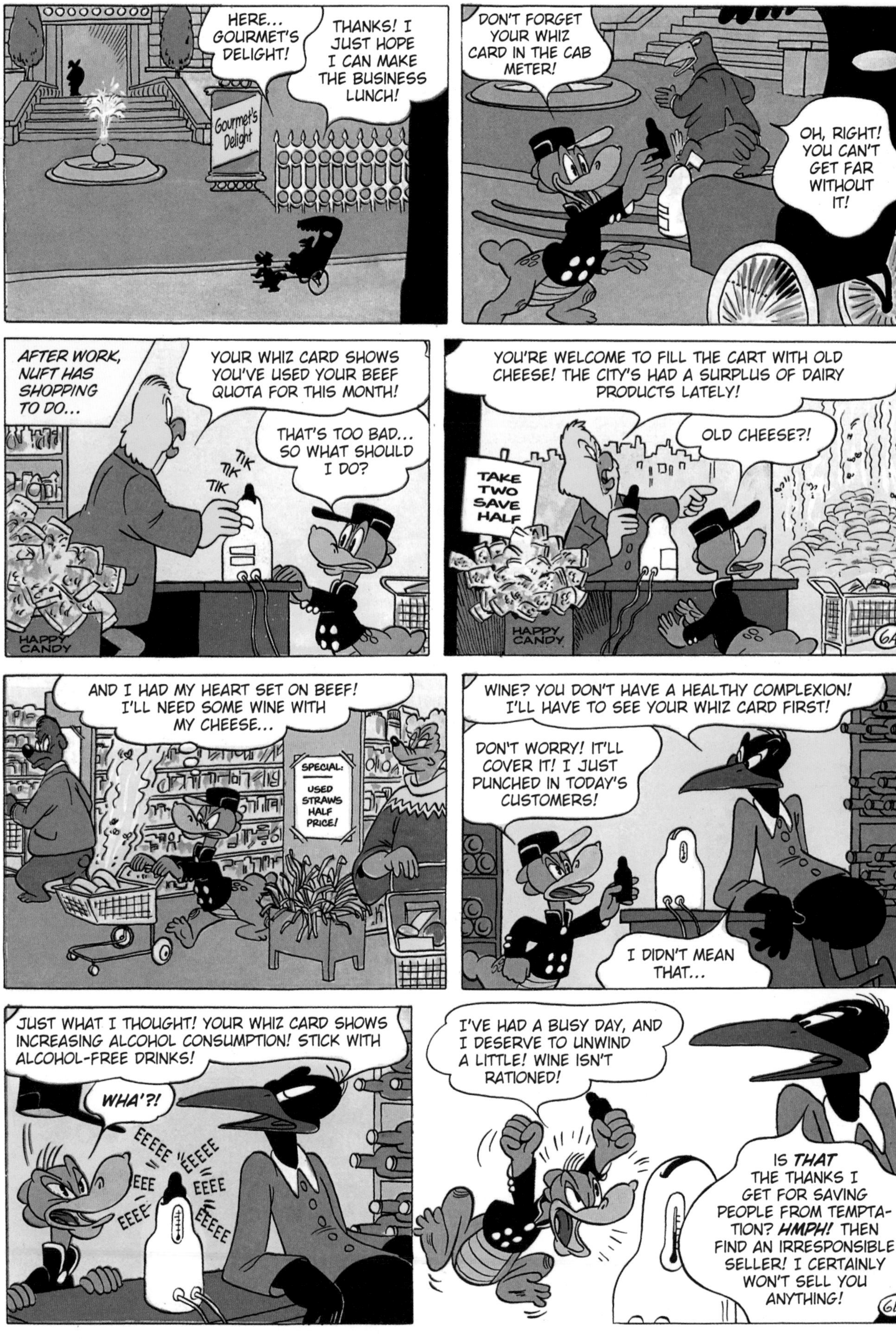
HERE... GOURMET'S DELIGHT!
THANKS! I JUST HOPE I CAN MAKE THE BUSINESS LUNCH!
Gourmet's Delight
DON'T FORGET YOUR WHIZ CARD IN THE CAB METER!
OH, RIGHT! YOU CAN'T GET FAR WITHOUT IT!
AFTER WORK, NUFT HAS SHOPPING TO DO...
YOUR WHIZ CARD SHOWS YOU'VE USED YOUR BEEF QUOTA FOR THIS MONTH!
TIK TIK TIK
THAT'S TOO BAD... SO WHAT SHOULD I DO?
HAPPY CANDY
YOU'RE WELCOME TO FILL THE CART WITH OLD CHEESE! THE CITY'S HAD A SURPLUS OF DAIRY PRODUCTS LATELY!
TAKE TWO SAVE HALF
OLD CHEESE?!
HAPPY CANDY
6A
AND I HAD MY HEART SET ON BEEF! I'LL NEED SOME WINE WITH MY CHEESE...
SPECIAL: USED STRAWS HALF PRICE!
WINE? YOU DON'T HAVE A HEALTHY COMPLEXION! I'LL HAVE TO SEE YOUR WHIZ CARD FIRST!
DON'T WORRY! IT'LL COVER IT! I JUST PUNCHED IN TODAY'S CUSTOMERS!
I DIDN'T MEAN THAT...
JUST WHAT I THOUGHT! YOUR WHIZ CARD SHOWS INCREASING ALCOHOL CONSUMPTION! STICK WITH ALCOHOL-FREE DRINKS!
WHA'?!
EEEEE EEEEE EEE EEEE EEEE EEEEE
I'VE HAD A BUSY DAY, AND I DESERVE TO UNWIND A LITTLE! WINE ISN'T RATIONED!
IS THAT THE THANKS I GET FOR SAVING PEOPLE FROM TEMPTATION? HMPH! THEN FIND AN IRRESPONSIBLE SELLER! I CERTAINLY WON'T SELL YOU ANYTHING!
6B

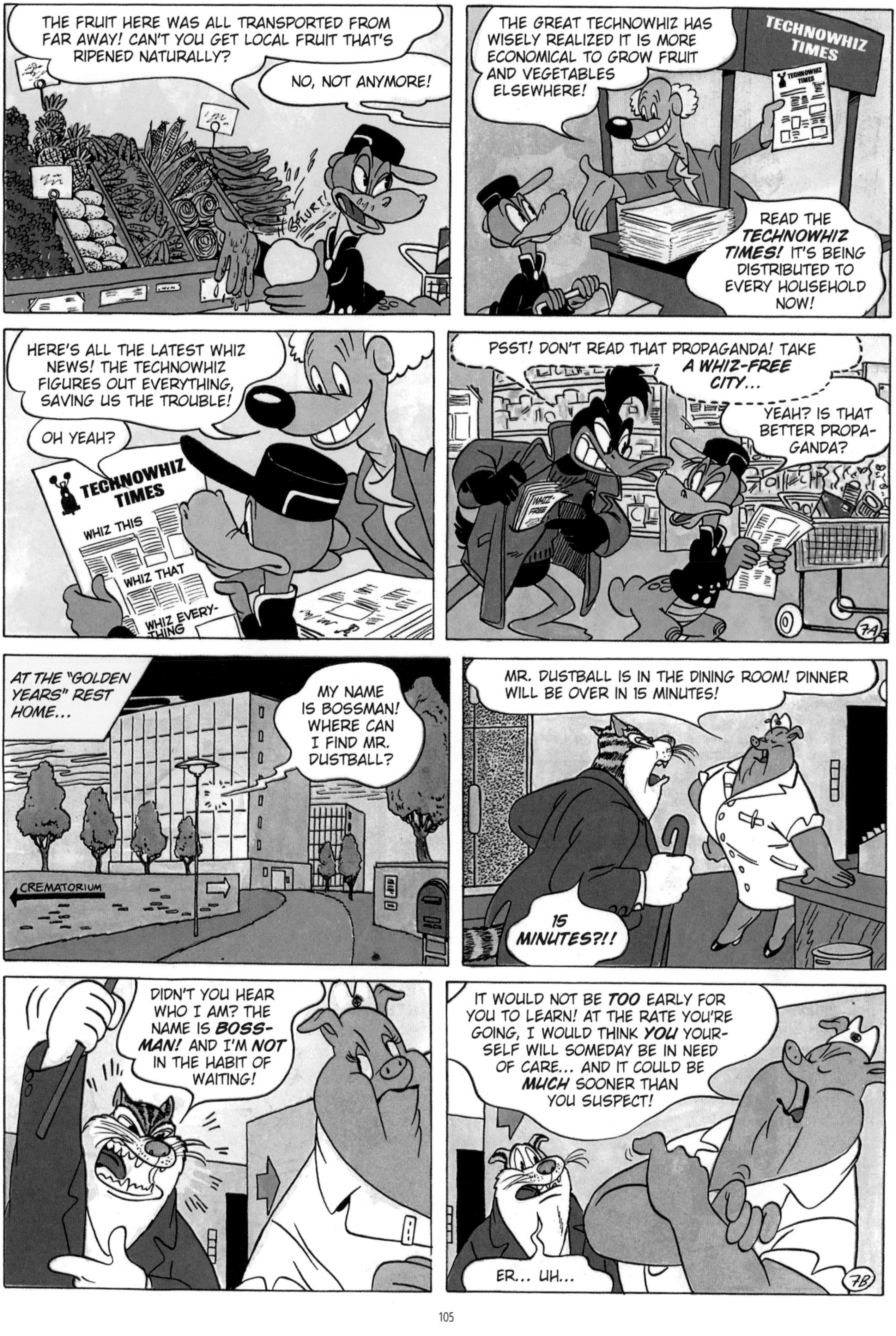
THE FRUIT HERE WAS ALL TRANSPORTED FROM FAR AWAY! CAN'T YOU GET LOCAL FRUIT THAT'S RIPENED NATURALLY?
NO, NOT ANYMORE!
SPLURT!
TECHNOWHIZ TIMES
THE GREAT TECHNOWHIZ HAS WISELY REALIZED IT IS MORE ECONOMICAL TO GROW FRUIT AND VEGETABLES ELSEWHERE!
READ THE *TECHNOWHIZ TIMES!* IT'S BEING DISTRIBUTED TO EVERY HOUSEHOLD NOW!
HERE'S ALL THE LATEST WHIZ NEWS! THE TECHNOWHIZ FIGURES OUT EVERYTHING, SAVING US THE TROUBLE!
OH YEAH?
TECHNOWHIZ TIMES
WHIZ THIS
WHIZ THAT
WHIZ EVERY-THING
PSST! DON'T READ THAT PROPAGANDA! TAKE *A WHIZ-FREE CITY...*
YEAH? IS THAT BETTER PROPA-GANDA?
WHIZ-FREE
AT THE "GOLDEN YEARS" REST HOME...
MY NAME IS BOSSMAN! WHERE CAN I FIND MR. DUSTBALL?
CREMATORIUM
MR. DUSTBALL IS IN THE DINING ROOM! DINNER WILL BE OVER IN 15 MINUTES!
15 MINUTES?!!
DIDN'T YOU HEAR WHO I AM? THE NAME IS *BOSS-MAN!* AND I'M *NOT* IN THE HABIT OF WAITING!
IT WOULD NOT BE *TOO* EARLY FOR YOU TO LEARN! AT THE RATE YOU'RE GOING, I WOULD THINK *YOU* YOUR-SELF WILL SOMEDAY BE IN NEED OF CARE... AND IT COULD BE *MUCH* SOONER THAN YOU SUSPECT!
ER... UH...

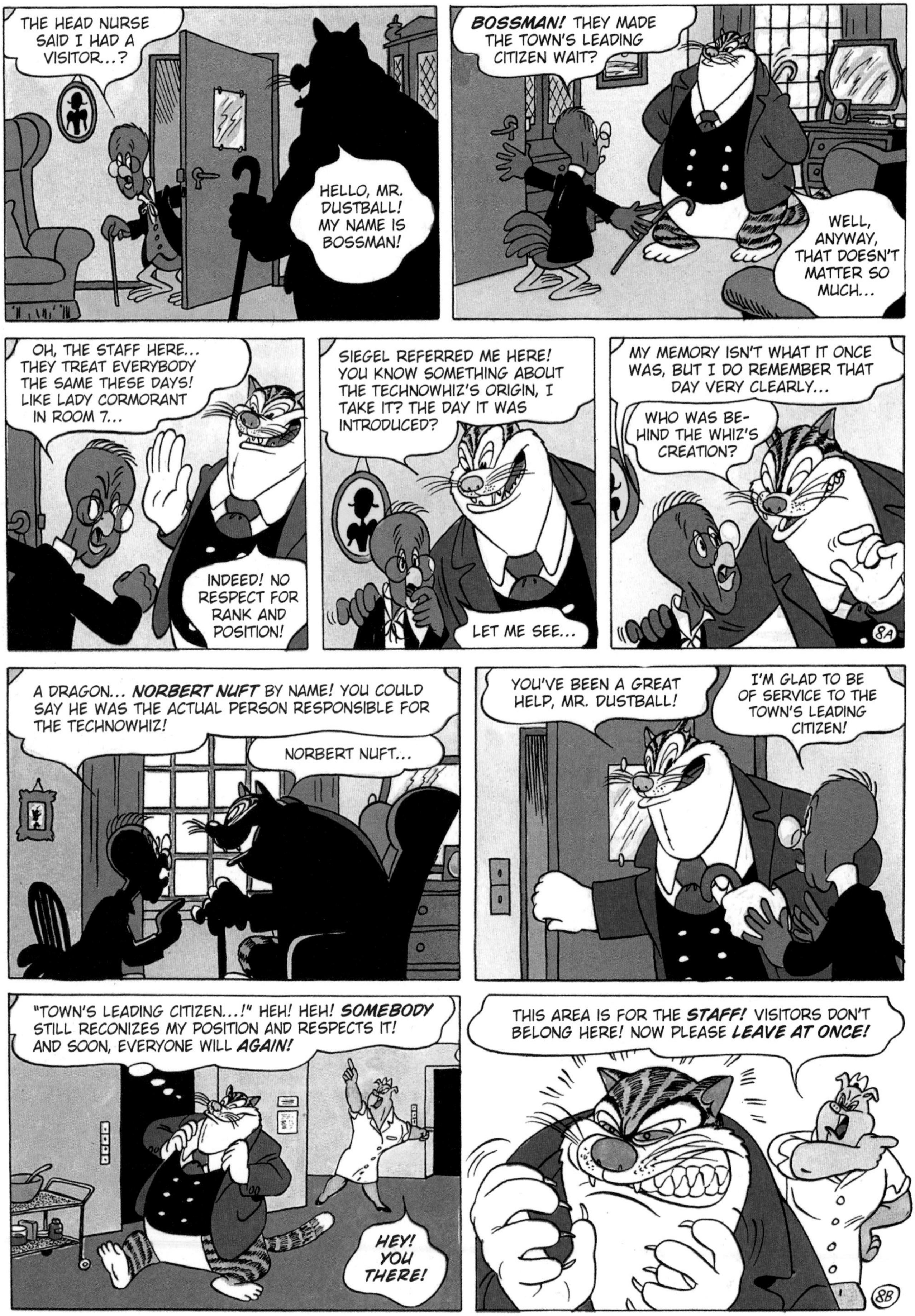

THE HEAD NURSE SAID I HAD A VISITOR...?
HELLO, MR. DUSTBALL! MY NAME IS BOSSMAN!
BOSSMAN! THEY MADE THE TOWN'S LEADING CITIZEN WAIT?
WELL, ANYWAY, THAT DOESN'T MATTER SO MUCH...
OH, THE STAFF HERE... THEY TREAT EVERYBODY THE SAME THESE DAYS! LIKE LADY CORMORANT IN ROOM 7...
INDEED! NO RESPECT FOR RANK AND POSITION!
SIEGEL REFERRED ME HERE! YOU KNOW SOMETHING ABOUT THE TECHNOWHIZ'S ORIGIN, I TAKE IT? THE DAY IT WAS INTRODUCED?
LET ME SEE...
MY MEMORY ISN'T WHAT IT ONCE WAS, BUT I DO REMEMBER THAT DAY VERY CLEARLY...
WHO WAS BEHIND THE WHIZ'S CREATION?
8A
A DRAGON... NORBERT NUFT BY NAME! YOU COULD SAY HE WAS THE ACTUAL PERSON RESPONSIBLE FOR THE TECHNOWHIZ!
NORBERT NUFT...
YOU'VE BEEN A GREAT HELP, MR. DUSTBALL!
I'M GLAD TO BE OF SERVICE TO THE TOWN'S LEADING CITIZEN!
"TOWN'S LEADING CITIZEN...!" HEH! HEH! SOMEBODY STILL RECONIZES MY POSITION AND RESPECTS IT! AND SOON, EVERYONE WILL AGAIN!
HEY! YOU THERE!
THIS AREA IS FOR THE STAFF! VISITORS DON'T BELONG HERE! NOW PLEASE LEAVE AT ONCE!
8B

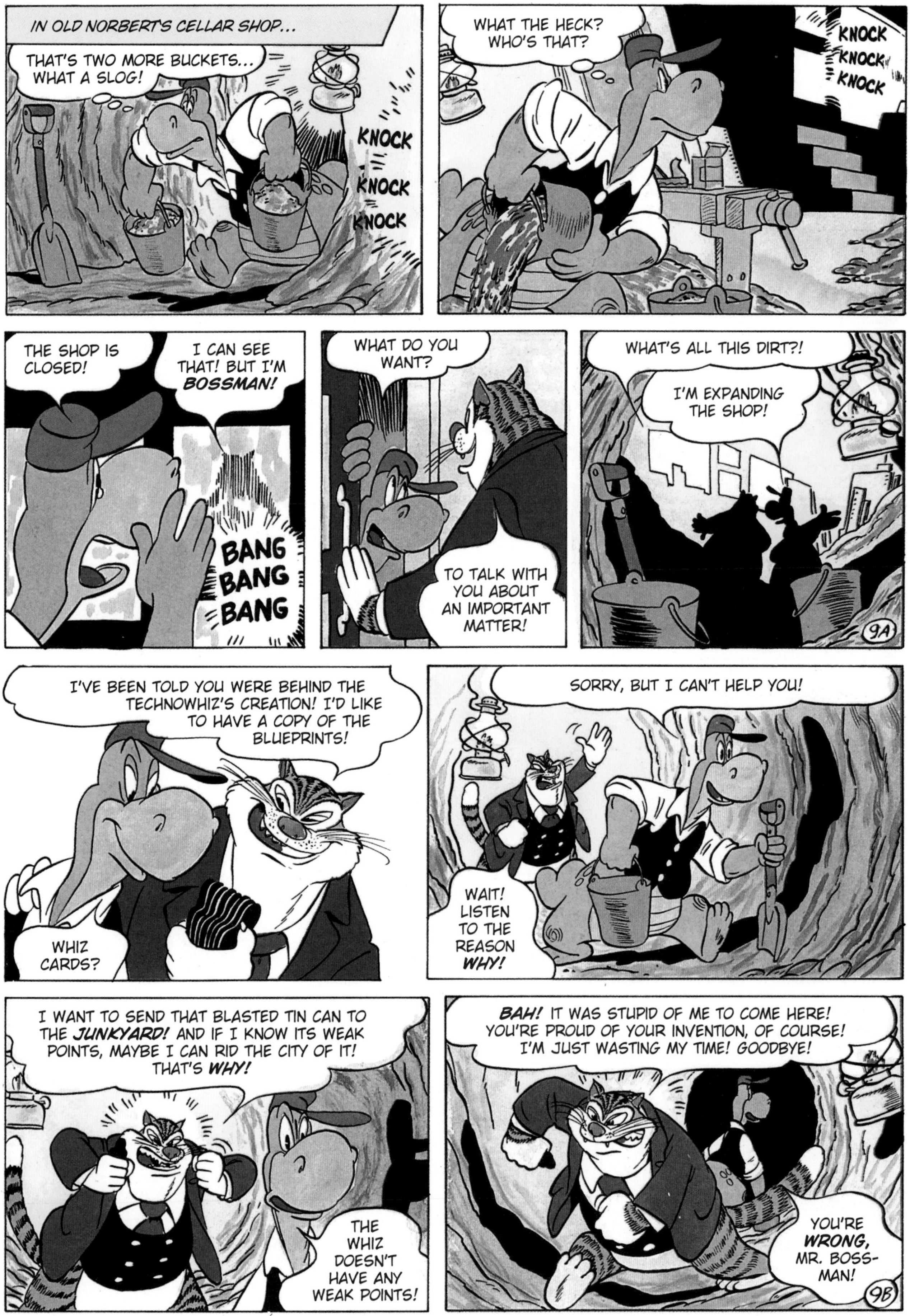

IN OLD NORBERT'S CELLAR SHOP...
THAT'S TWO MORE BUCKETS... WHAT A SLOG!
KNOCK KNOCK KNOCK
WHAT THE HECK? WHO'S THAT?
KNOCK KNOCK KNOCK
THE SHOP IS CLOSED!
I CAN SEE THAT! BUT I'M **BOSSMAN!**
BANG BANG BANG
WHAT DO YOU WANT?
TO TALK WITH YOU ABOUT AN IMPORTANT MATTER!
WHAT'S ALL THIS DIRT?!
I'M EXPANDING THE SHOP!
9A
I'VE BEEN TOLD YOU WERE BEHIND THE TECHNOWHIZ'S CREATION! I'D LIKE TO HAVE A COPY OF THE BLUEPRINTS!
WHIZ CARDS?
SORRY, BUT I CAN'T HELP YOU!
WAIT! LISTEN TO THE REASON **WHY!**
I WANT TO SEND THAT BLASTED TIN CAN TO THE **JUNKYARD!** AND IF I KNOW ITS WEAK POINTS, MAYBE I CAN RID THE CITY OF IT! THAT'S **WHY!**
THE WHIZ DOESN'T HAVE ANY WEAK POINTS!
BAH! IT WAS STUPID OF ME TO COME HERE! YOU'RE PROUD OF YOUR INVENTION, OF COURSE! I'M JUST WASTING MY TIME! GOODBYE!
YOU'RE **WRONG,** MR. BOSS-MAN!
9B

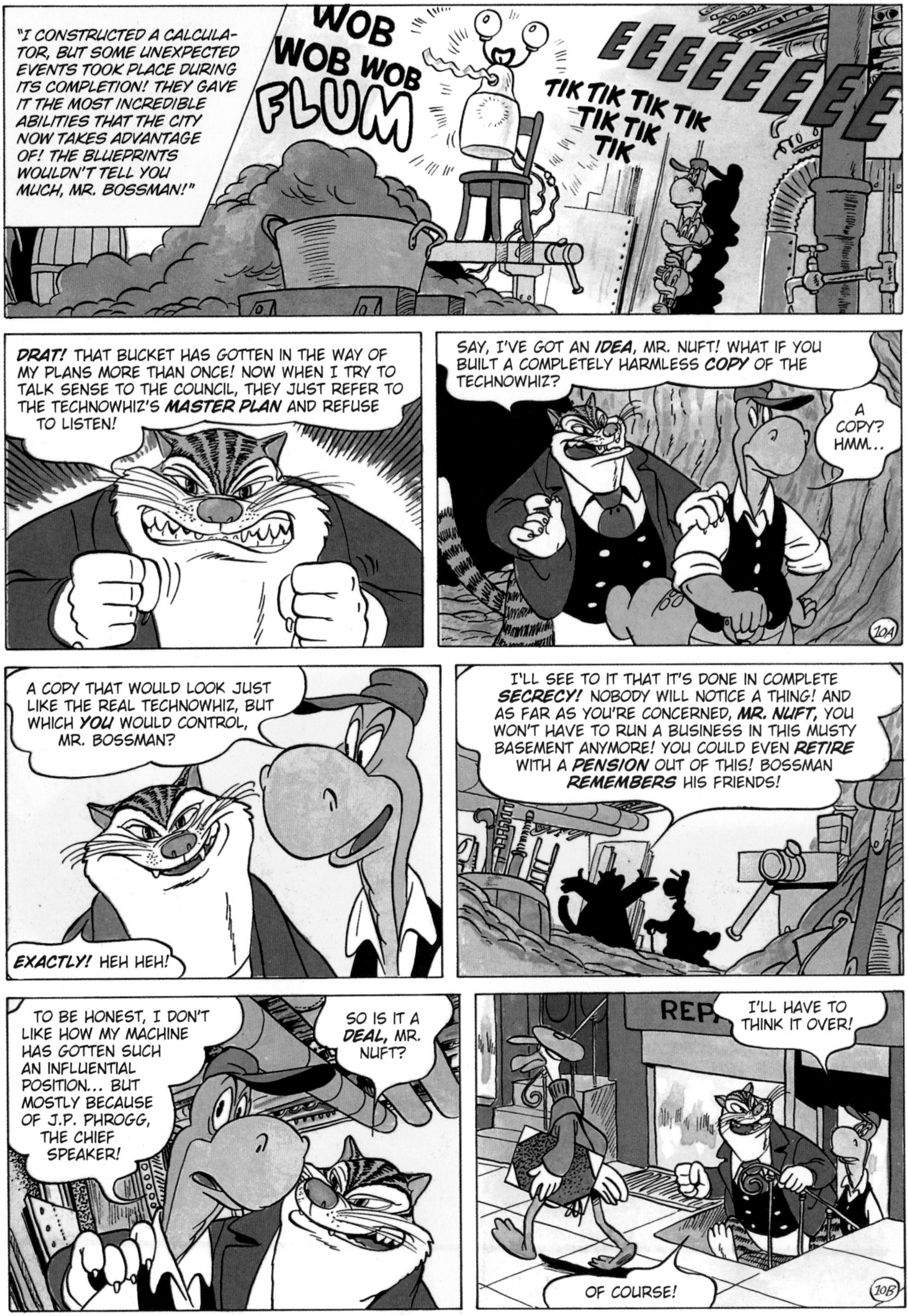
"I CONSTRUCTED A CALCULATOR, BUT SOME UNEXPECTED EVENTS TOOK PLACE DURING ITS COMPLETION! THEY GAVE IT THE MOST INCREDIBLE ABILITIES THAT THE CITY NOW TAKES ADVANTAGE OF! THE BLUEPRINTS WOULDN'T TELL YOU MUCH, MR. BOSSMAN!"
WOB WOB WOB FLUM
TIK TIK TIK TIK TIK TIK TIK
EEEEEEEEE
DRAT! THAT BUCKET HAS GOTTEN IN THE WAY OF MY PLANS MORE THAN ONCE! NOW WHEN I TRY TO TALK SENSE TO THE COUNCIL, THEY JUST REFER TO THE TECHNOWHIZ'S MASTER PLAN AND REFUSE TO LISTEN!
SAY, I'VE GOT AN IDEA, MR. NUFT! WHAT IF YOU BUILT A COMPLETELY HARMLESS COPY OF THE TECHNOWHIZ?
A COPY? HMM...
10A
A COPY THAT WOULD LOOK JUST LIKE THE REAL TECHNOWHIZ, BUT WHICH YOU WOULD CONTROL, MR. BOSSMAN?
EXACTLY! HEH HEH!
I'LL SEE TO IT THAT IT'S DONE IN COMPLETE SECRECY! NOBODY WILL NOTICE A THING! AND AS FAR AS YOU'RE CONCERNED, MR. NUFT, YOU WON'T HAVE TO RUN A BUSINESS IN THIS MUSTY BASEMENT ANYMORE! YOU COULD EVEN RETIRE WITH A PENSION OUT OF THIS! BOSSMAN REMEMBERS HIS FRIENDS!
TO BE HONEST, I DON'T LIKE HOW MY MACHINE HAS GOTTEN SUCH AN INFLUENTIAL POSITION... BUT MOSTLY BECAUSE OF J.P. PHROGG, THE CHIEF SPEAKER!
SO IS IT A DEAL, MR. NUFT?
REP
I'LL HAVE TO THINK IT OVER!
OF COURSE!
10B

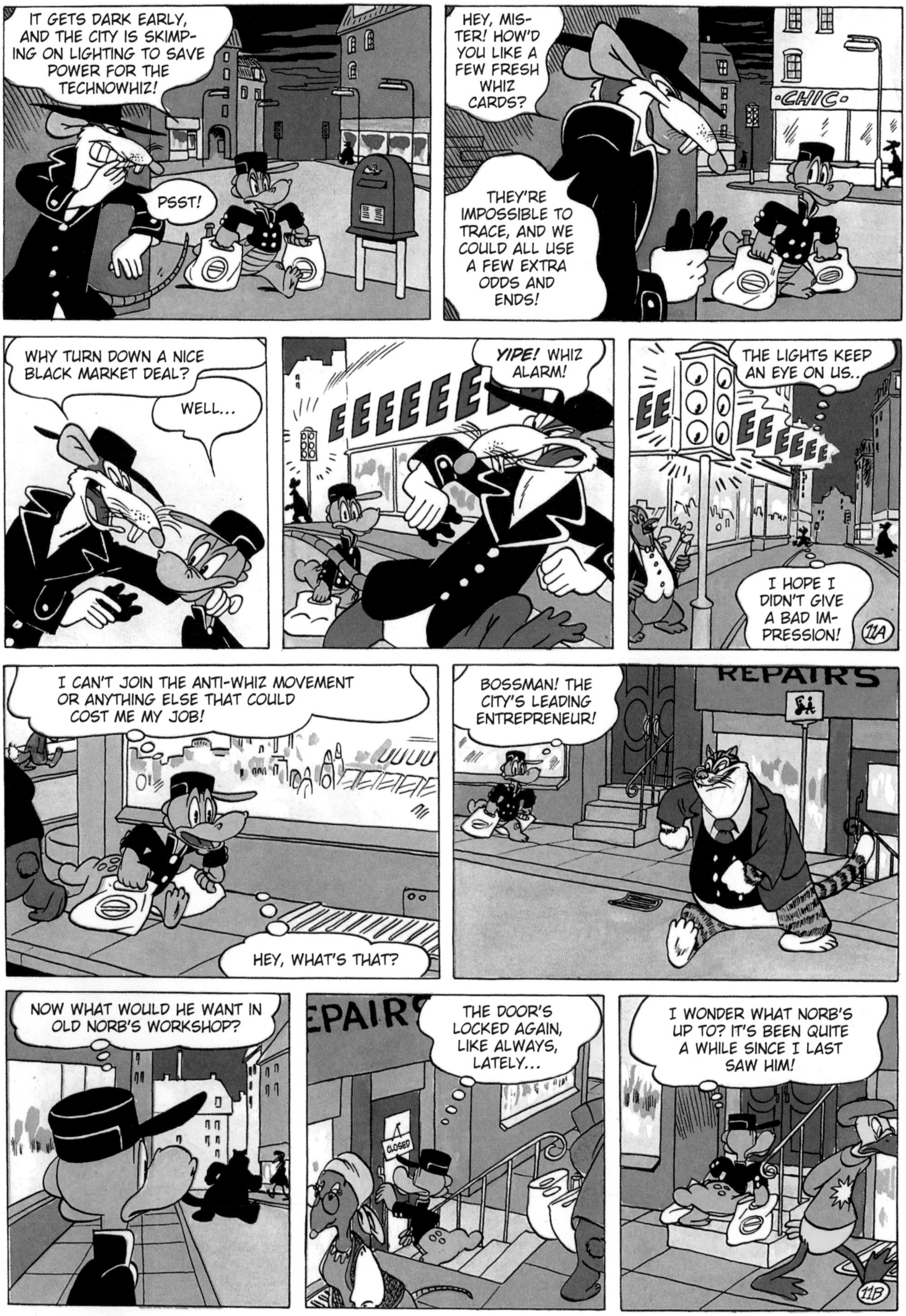
IT GETS DARK EARLY, AND THE CITY IS SKIMP-ING ON LIGHTING TO SAVE POWER FOR THE TECHNOWHIZ!
PSST!
HEY, MIS-TER! HOW'D YOU LIKE A FEW FRESH WHIZ CARDS?
CHIC
THEY'RE IMPOSSIBLE TO TRACE, AND WE COULD ALL USE A FEW EXTRA ODDS AND ENDS!
WHY TURN DOWN A NICE BLACK MARKET DEAL?
WELL...
EEEEEE
YIPE! WHIZ ALARM!
THE LIGHTS KEEP AN EYE ON US..
EE
EEEEEE
I HOPE I DIDN'T GIVE A BAD IM-PRESSION!
11A
I CAN'T JOIN THE ANTI-WHIZ MOVEMENT OR ANYTHING ELSE THAT COULD COST ME MY JOB!
HEY, WHAT'S THAT?
BOSSMAN! THE CITY'S LEADING ENTREPRENEUR!
REPAIRS
NOW WHAT WOULD HE WANT IN OLD NORB'S WORKSHOP?
EPAIRS
THE DOOR'S LOCKED AGAIN, LIKE ALWAYS, LATELY...
CLOSED
I WONDER WHAT NORB'S UP TO? IT'S BEEN QUITE A WHILE SINCE I LAST SAW HIM!
11B

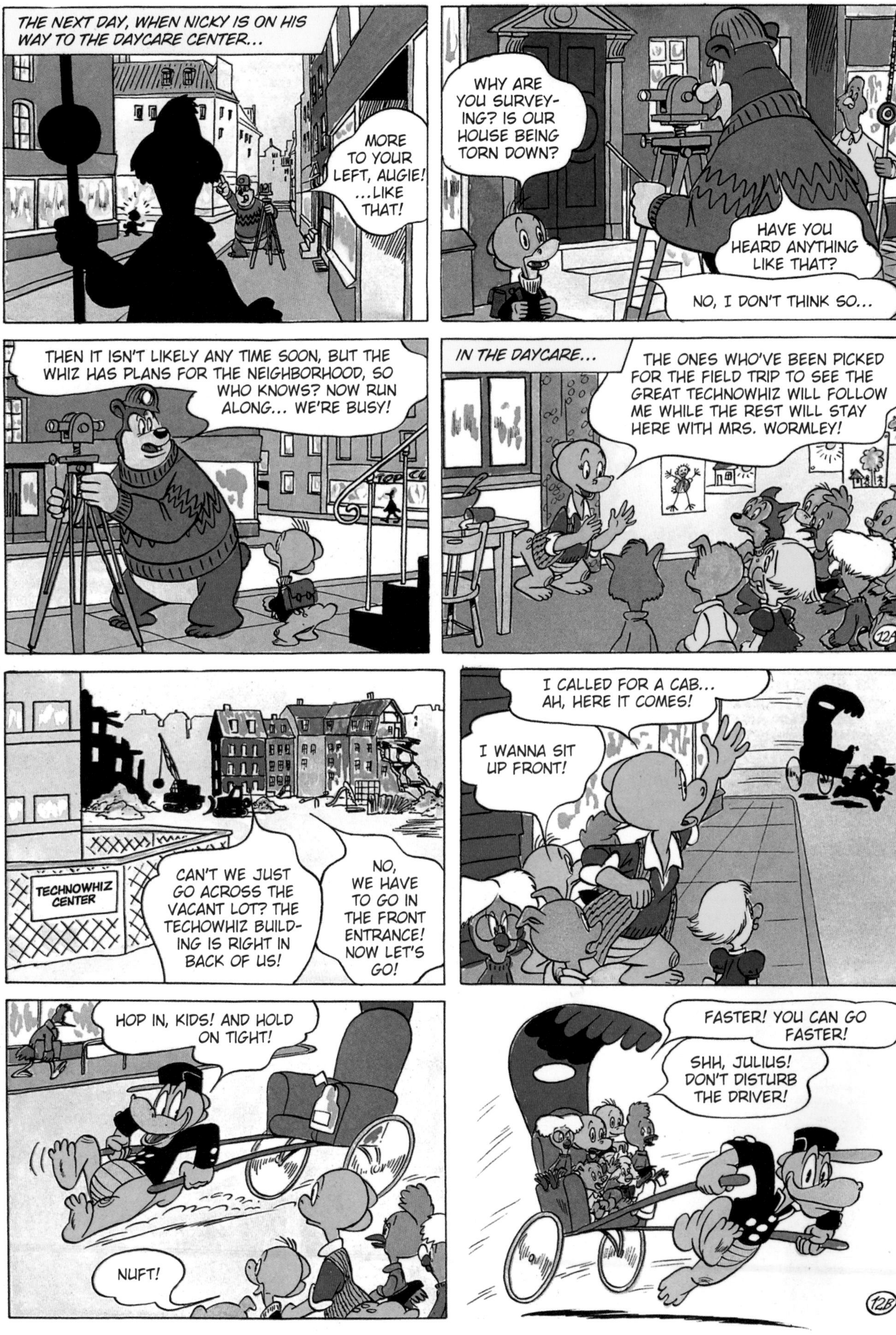
THE NEXT DAY, WHEN NICKY IS ON HIS WAY TO THE DAYCARE CENTER...
MORE TO YOUR LEFT, AUGIE! ...LIKE THAT!
WHY ARE YOU SURVEY-ING? IS OUR HOUSE BEING TORN DOWN?
HAVE YOU HEARD ANYTHING LIKE THAT?
NO, I DON'T THINK SO...
THEN IT ISN'T LIKELY ANY TIME SOON, BUT THE WHIZ HAS PLANS FOR THE NEIGHBORHOOD, SO WHO KNOWS? NOW RUN ALONG... WE'RE BUSY!
IN THE DAYCARE...
THE ONES WHO'VE BEEN PICKED FOR THE FIELD TRIP TO SEE THE GREAT TECHNOWHIZ WILL FOLLOW ME WHILE THE REST WILL STAY HERE WITH MRS. WORMLEY!
12A
TECHNOWHIZ CENTER
CAN'T WE JUST GO ACROSS THE VACANT LOT? THE TECHOWHIZ BUILD-ING IS RIGHT IN BACK OF US!
NO, WE HAVE TO GO IN THE FRONT ENTRANCE! NOW LET'S GO!
I CALLED FOR A CAB... AH, HERE IT COMES!
I WANNA SIT UP FRONT!
HOP IN, KIDS! AND HOLD ON TIGHT!
NUFT!
FASTER! YOU CAN GO FASTER!
SHH, JULIUS! DON'T DISTURB THE DRIVER!
12B

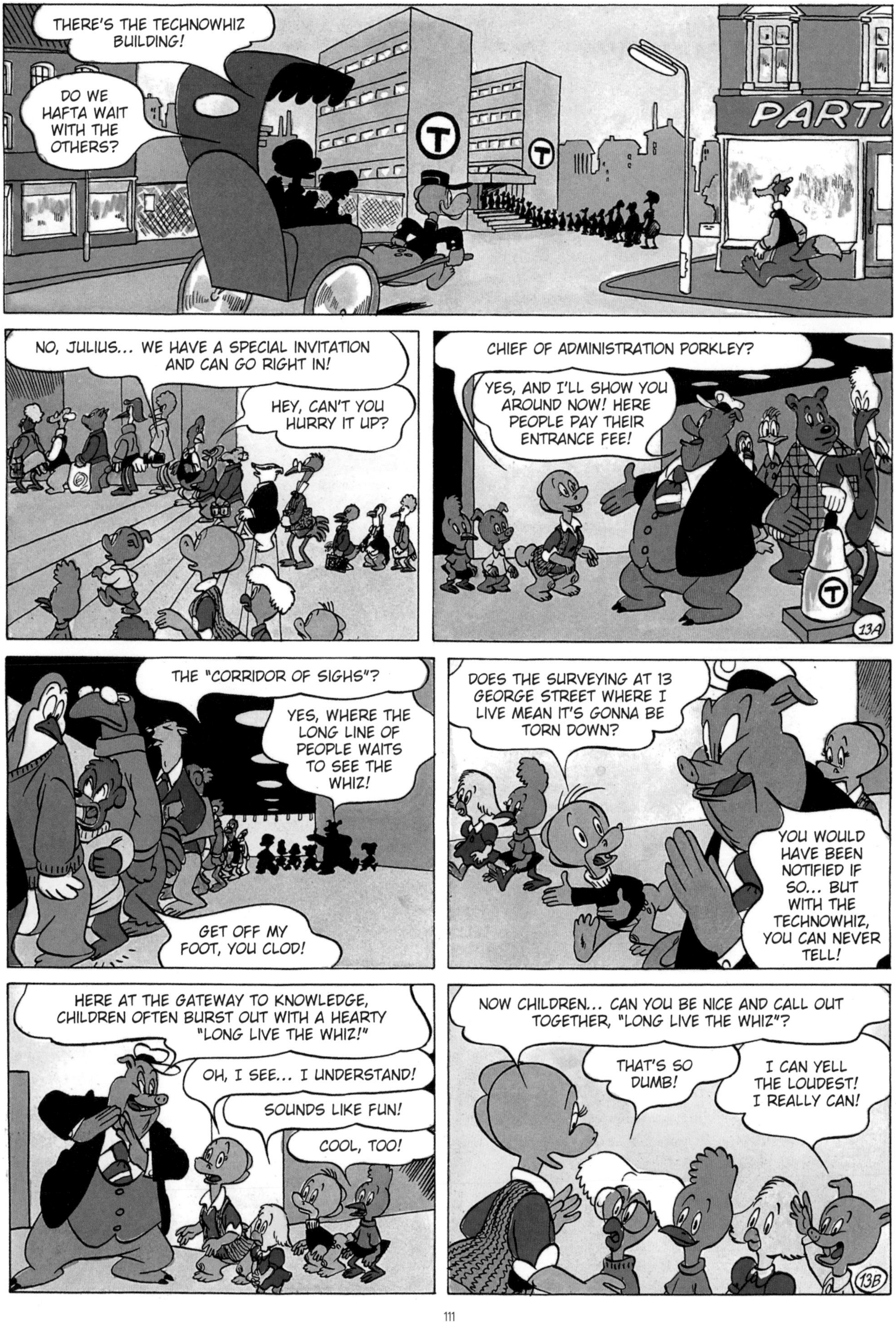
THERE'S THE TECHNOWHIZ BUILDING!
DO WE HAFTA WAIT WITH THE OTHERS?
PARTI
NO, JULIUS... WE HAVE A SPECIAL INVITATION AND CAN GO RIGHT IN!
HEY, CAN'T YOU HURRY IT UP?
CHIEF OF ADMINISTRATION PORKLEY?
YES, AND I'LL SHOW YOU AROUND NOW! HERE PEOPLE PAY THEIR ENTRANCE FEE!
13A
THE "CORRIDOR OF SIGHS"?
YES, WHERE THE LONG LINE OF PEOPLE WAITS TO SEE THE WHIZ!
GET OFF MY FOOT, YOU CLOD!
DOES THE SURVEYING AT 13 GEORGE STREET WHERE I LIVE MEAN IT'S GONNA BE TORN DOWN?
YOU WOULD HAVE BEEN NOTIFIED IF SO... BUT WITH THE TECHNOWHIZ, YOU CAN NEVER TELL!
HERE AT THE GATEWAY TO KNOWLEDGE, CHILDREN OFTEN BURST OUT WITH A HEARTY "LONG LIVE THE WHIZ!"
OH, I SEE... I UNDERSTAND!
SOUNDS LIKE FUN!
COOL, TOO!
NOW CHILDREN... CAN YOU BE NICE AND CALL OUT TOGETHER, "LONG LIVE THE WHIZ"?
THAT'S SO DUMB!
I CAN YELL THE LOUDEST! I REALLY CAN!
13B

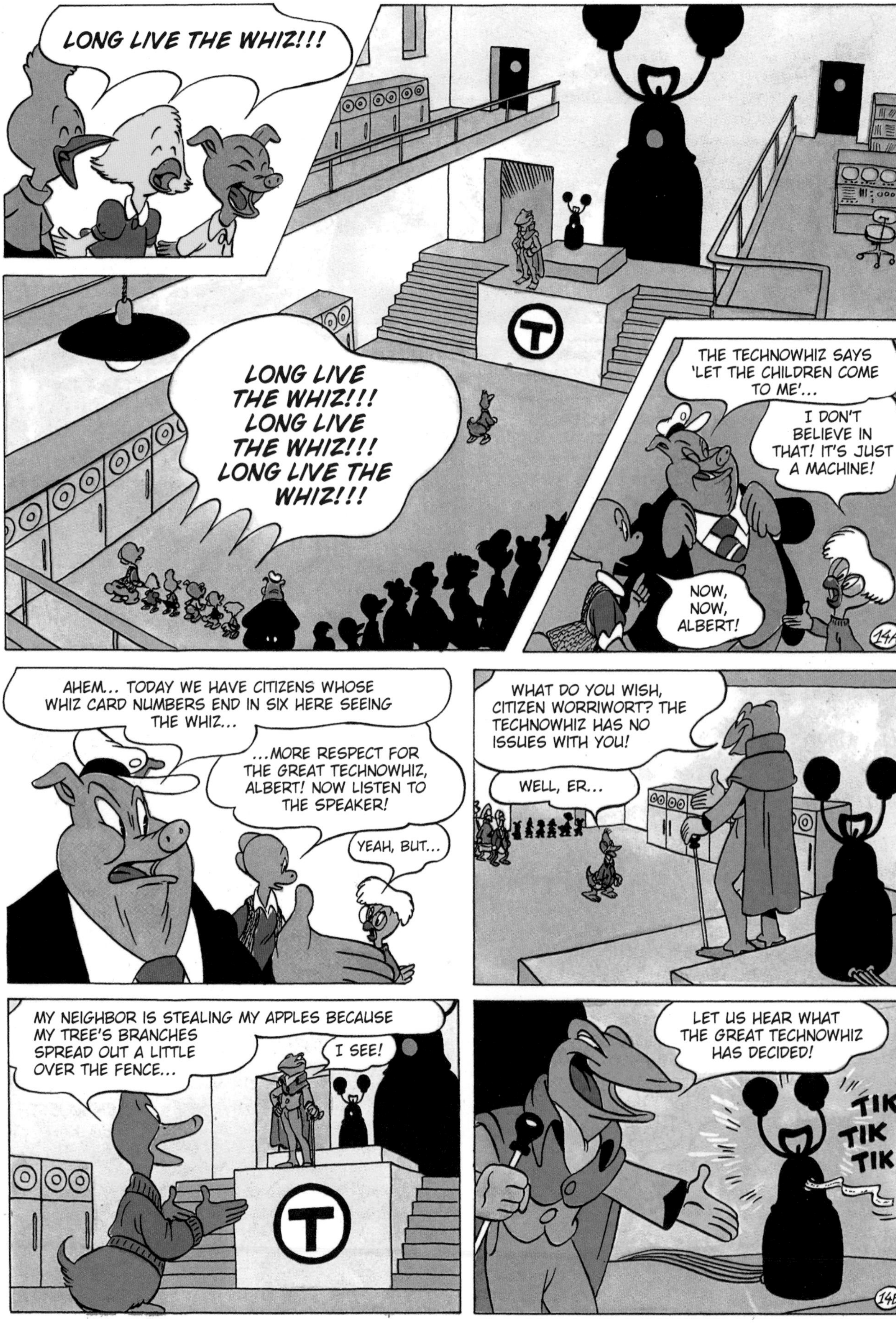
LONG LIVE THE WHIZ!!!
LONG LIVE THE WHIZ!!! LONG LIVE THE WHIZ!!! LONG LIVE THE WHIZ!!!
THE TECHNOWHIZ SAYS 'LET THE CHILDREN COME TO ME'...
I DON'T BELIEVE IN THAT! IT'S JUST A MACHINE!
NOW, NOW, ALBERT!
14A
AHEM... TODAY WE HAVE CITIZENS WHOSE WHIZ CARD NUMBERS END IN SIX HERE SEEING THE WHIZ...
...MORE RESPECT FOR THE GREAT TECHNOWHIZ, ALBERT! NOW LISTEN TO THE SPEAKER!
YEAH, BUT...
WHAT DO YOU WISH, CITIZEN WORRIWORT? THE TECHNOWHIZ HAS NO ISSUES WITH YOU!
WELL, ER...
MY NEIGHBOR IS STEALING MY APPLES BECAUSE MY TREE'S BRANCHES SPREAD OUT A LITTLE OVER THE FENCE...
I SEE!
LET US HEAR WHAT THE GREAT TECHNOWHIZ HAS DECIDED!
TIK TIK TIK
14B

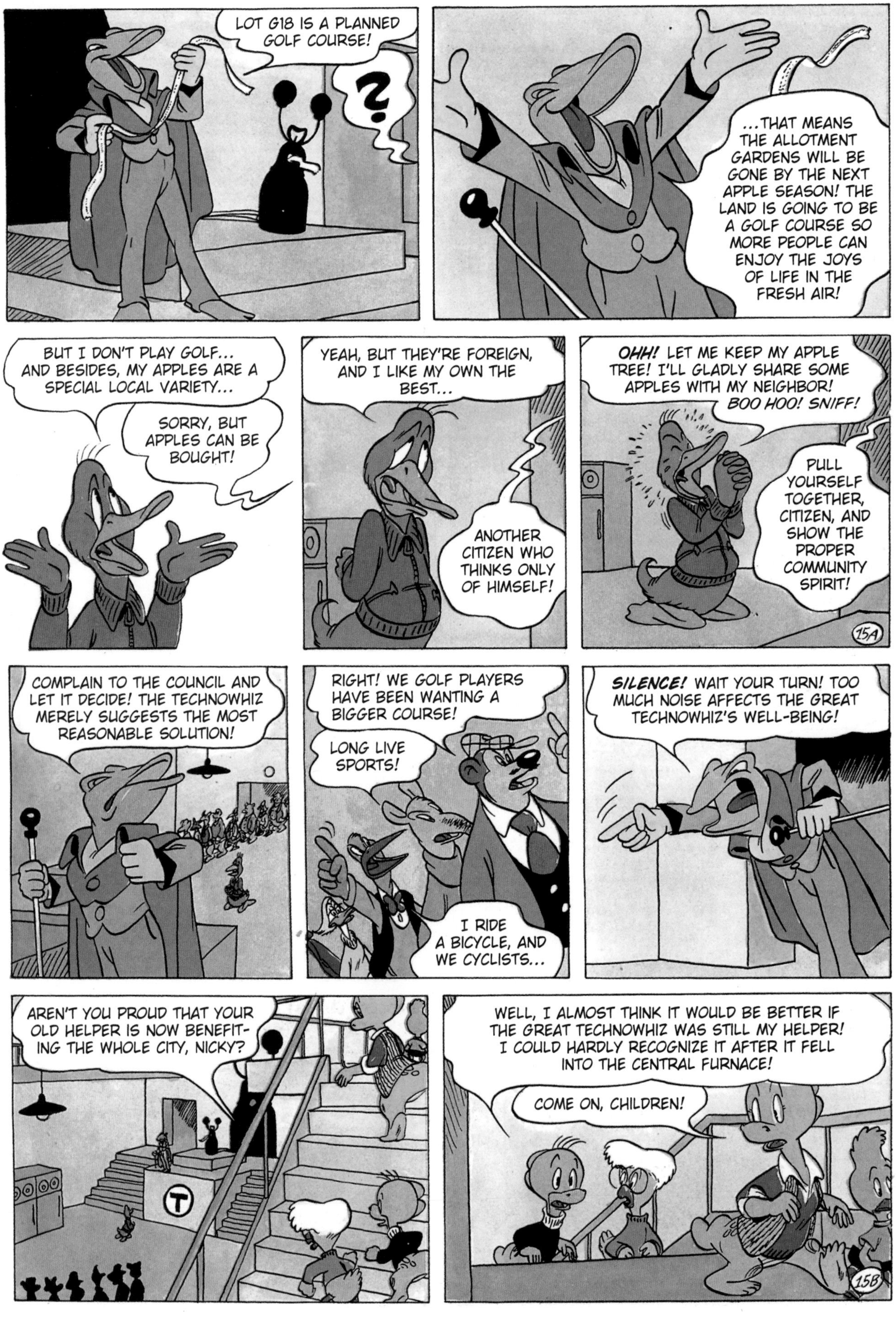
LOT G18 IS A PLANNED GOLF COURSE!
?
...THAT MEANS THE ALLOTMENT GARDENS WILL BE GONE BY THE NEXT APPLE SEASON! THE LAND IS GOING TO BE A GOLF COURSE SO MORE PEOPLE CAN ENJOY THE JOYS OF LIFE IN THE FRESH AIR!
BUT I DON'T PLAY GOLF... AND BESIDES, MY APPLES ARE A SPECIAL LOCAL VARIETY...
SORRY, BUT APPLES CAN BE BOUGHT!
YEAH, BUT THEY'RE FOREIGN, AND I LIKE MY OWN THE BEST...
ANOTHER CITIZEN WHO THINKS ONLY OF HIMSELF!
OHH! LET ME KEEP MY APPLE TREE! I'LL GLADLY SHARE SOME APPLES WITH MY NEIGHBOR! BOO HOO! SNIFF!
PULL YOURSELF TOGETHER, CITIZEN, AND SHOW THE PROPER COMMUNITY SPIRIT!
15A
COMPLAIN TO THE COUNCIL AND LET IT DECIDE! THE TECHNOWHIZ MERELY SUGGESTS THE MOST REASONABLE SOLUTION!
RIGHT! WE GOLF PLAYERS HAVE BEEN WANTING A BIGGER COURSE!
LONG LIVE SPORTS!
I RIDE A BICYCLE, AND WE CYCLISTS...
SILENCE! WAIT YOUR TURN! TOO MUCH NOISE AFFECTS THE GREAT TECHNOWHIZ'S WELL-BEING!
AREN'T YOU PROUD THAT YOUR OLD HELPER IS NOW BENEFITING THE WHOLE CITY, NICKY?
T
WELL, I ALMOST THINK IT WOULD BE BETTER IF THE GREAT TECHNOWHIZ WAS STILL MY HELPER! I COULD HARDLY RECOGNIZE IT AFTER IT FELL INTO THE CENTRAL FURNACE!
COME ON, CHILDREN!
15B

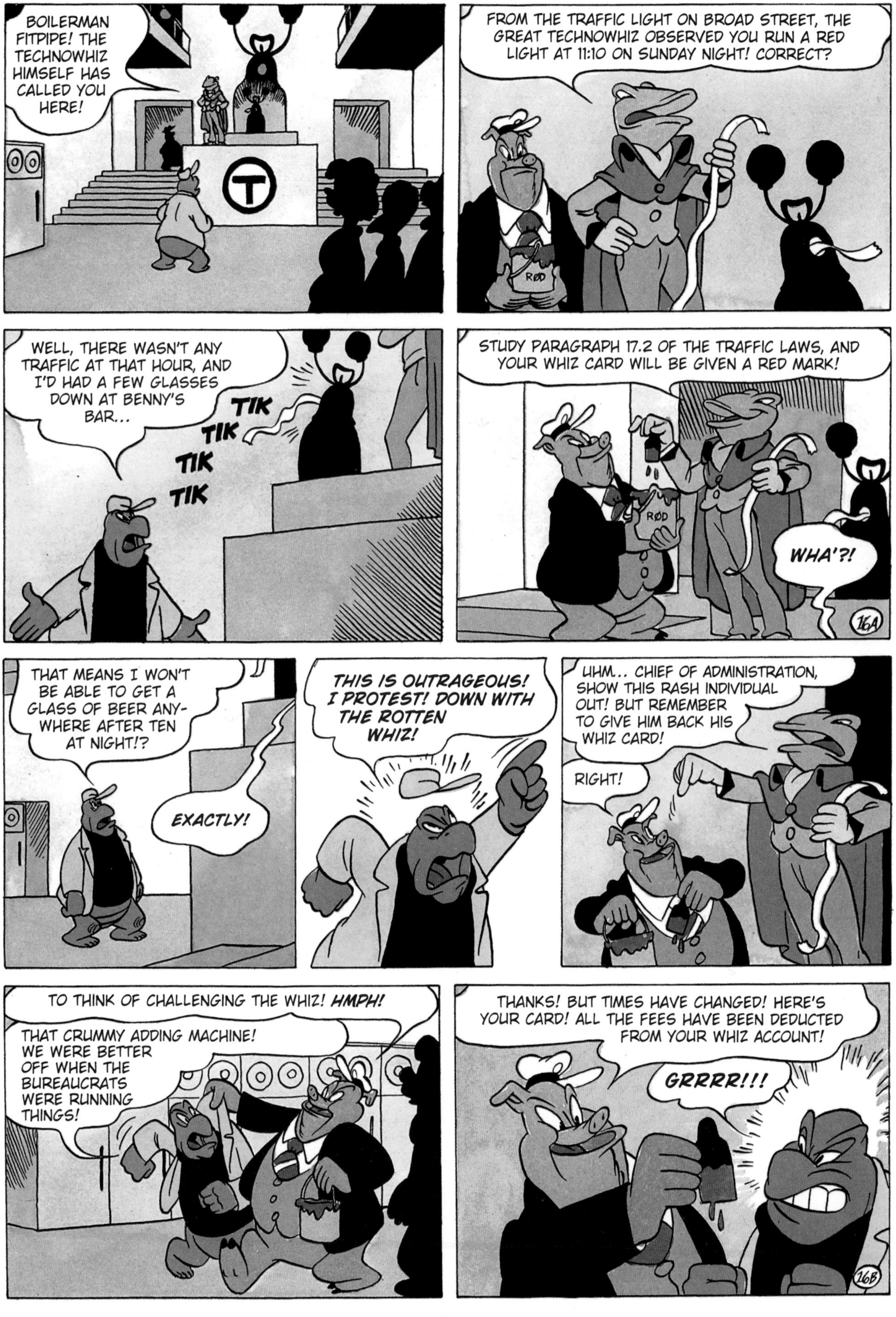
BOILERMAN FITPIPE! THE TECHNOWHIZ HIMSELF HAS CALLED YOU HERE!
FROM THE TRAFFIC LIGHT ON BROAD STREET, THE GREAT TECHNOWHIZ OBSERVED YOU RUN A RED LIGHT AT 11:10 ON SUNDAY NIGHT! CORRECT?
RØD
WELL, THERE WASN'T ANY TRAFFIC AT THAT HOUR, AND I'D HAD A FEW GLASSES DOWN AT BENNY'S BAR...
TIK
TIK
TIK
TIK
STUDY PARAGRAPH 17.2 OF THE TRAFFIC LAWS, AND YOUR WHIZ CARD WILL BE GIVEN A RED MARK!
RØD
WHA'?!
16A
THAT MEANS I WON'T BE ABLE TO GET A GLASS OF BEER ANYWHERE AFTER TEN AT NIGHT!?
EXACTLY!
THIS IS OUTRAGEOUS! I PROTEST! DOWN WITH THE ROTTEN WHIZ!
UHM... CHIEF OF ADMINISTRATION, SHOW THIS RASH INDIVIDUAL OUT! BUT REMEMBER TO GIVE HIM BACK HIS WHIZ CARD!
RIGHT!
TO THINK OF CHALLENGING THE WHIZ! HMPH!
THAT CRUMMY ADDING MACHINE! WE WERE BETTER OFF WHEN THE BUREAUCRATS WERE RUNNING THINGS!
THANKS! BUT TIMES HAVE CHANGED! HERE'S YOUR CARD! ALL THE FEES HAVE BEEN DEDUCTED FROM YOUR WHIZ ACCOUNT!
GRRRR!!!
16B

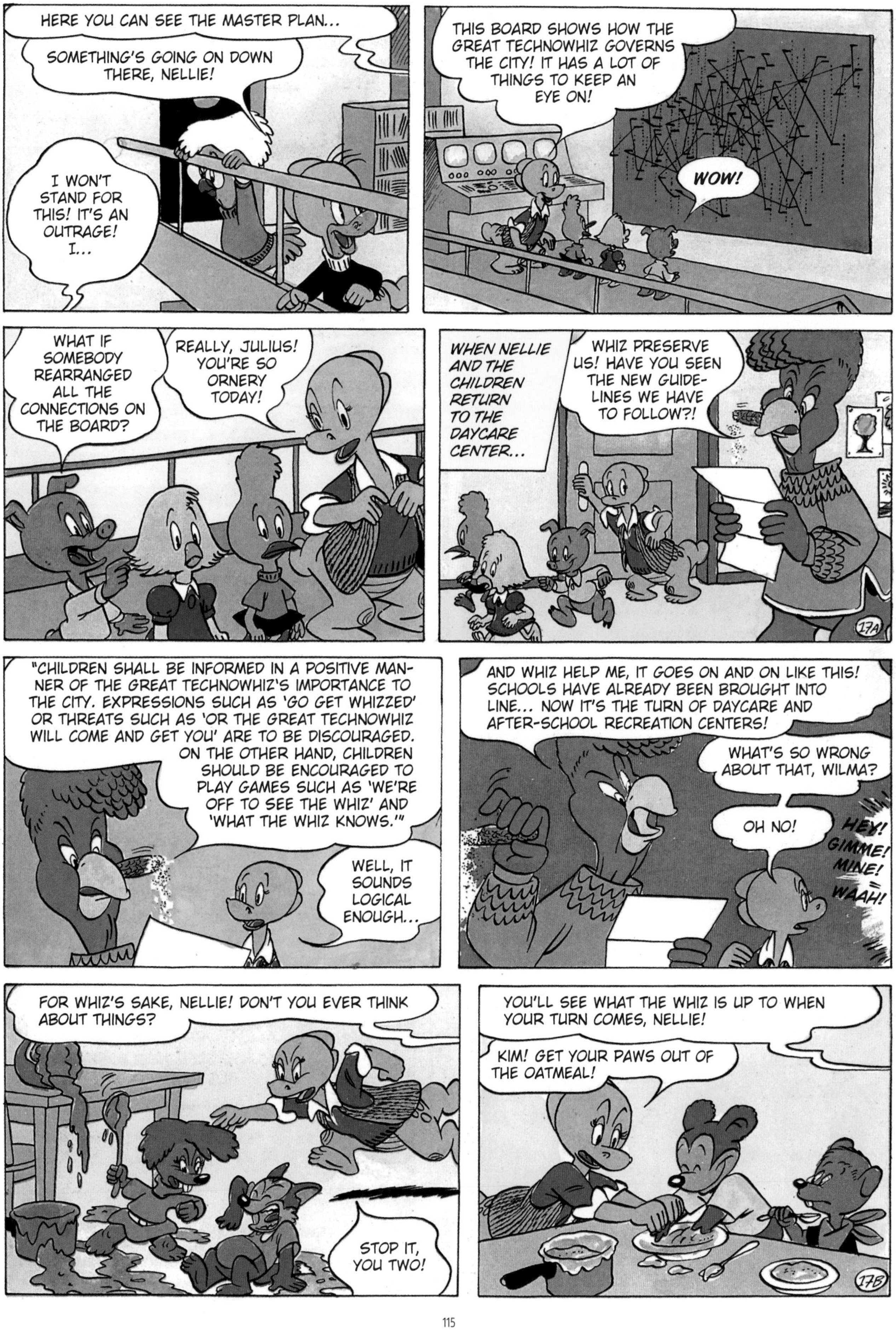
HERE YOU CAN SEE THE MASTER PLAN...
SOMETHING'S GOING ON DOWN THERE, NELLIE!
I WON'T STAND FOR THIS! IT'S AN OUTRAGE! I...
THIS BOARD SHOWS HOW THE GREAT TECHNOWHIZ GOVERNS THE CITY! IT HAS A LOT OF THINGS TO KEEP AN EYE ON!
WOW!
WHAT IF SOMEBODY REARRANGED ALL THE CONNECTIONS ON THE BOARD?
REALLY, JULIUS! YOU'RE SO ORNERY TODAY!
WHEN NELLIE AND THE CHILDREN RETURN TO THE DAYCARE CENTER...
WHIZ PRESERVE US! HAVE YOU SEEN THE NEW GUIDELINES WE HAVE TO FOLLOW?!
17A
"CHILDREN SHALL BE INFORMED IN A POSITIVE MANNER OF THE GREAT TECHNOWHIZ'S IMPORTANCE TO THE CITY. EXPRESSIONS SUCH AS 'GO GET WHIZZED' OR THREATS SUCH AS 'OR THE GREAT TECHNOWHIZ WILL COME AND GET YOU' ARE TO BE DISCOURAGED. ON THE OTHER HAND, CHILDREN SHOULD BE ENCOURAGED TO PLAY GAMES SUCH AS 'WE'RE OFF TO SEE THE WHIZ' AND 'WHAT THE WHIZ KNOWS.'"
WELL, IT SOUNDS LOGICAL ENOUGH...
AND WHIZ HELP ME, IT GOES ON AND ON LIKE THIS! SCHOOLS HAVE ALREADY BEEN BROUGHT INTO LINE... NOW IT'S THE TURN OF DAYCARE AND AFTER-SCHOOL RECREATION CENTERS!
WHAT'S SO WRONG ABOUT THAT, WILMA?
OH NO!
HEY! GIMME! MINE! WAAH!
FOR WHIZ'S SAKE, NELLIE! DON'T YOU EVER THINK ABOUT THINGS?
STOP IT, YOU TWO!
YOU'LL SEE WHAT THE WHIZ IS UP TO WHEN YOUR TURN COMES, NELLIE!
KIM! GET YOUR PAWS OUT OF THE OATMEAL!
17B

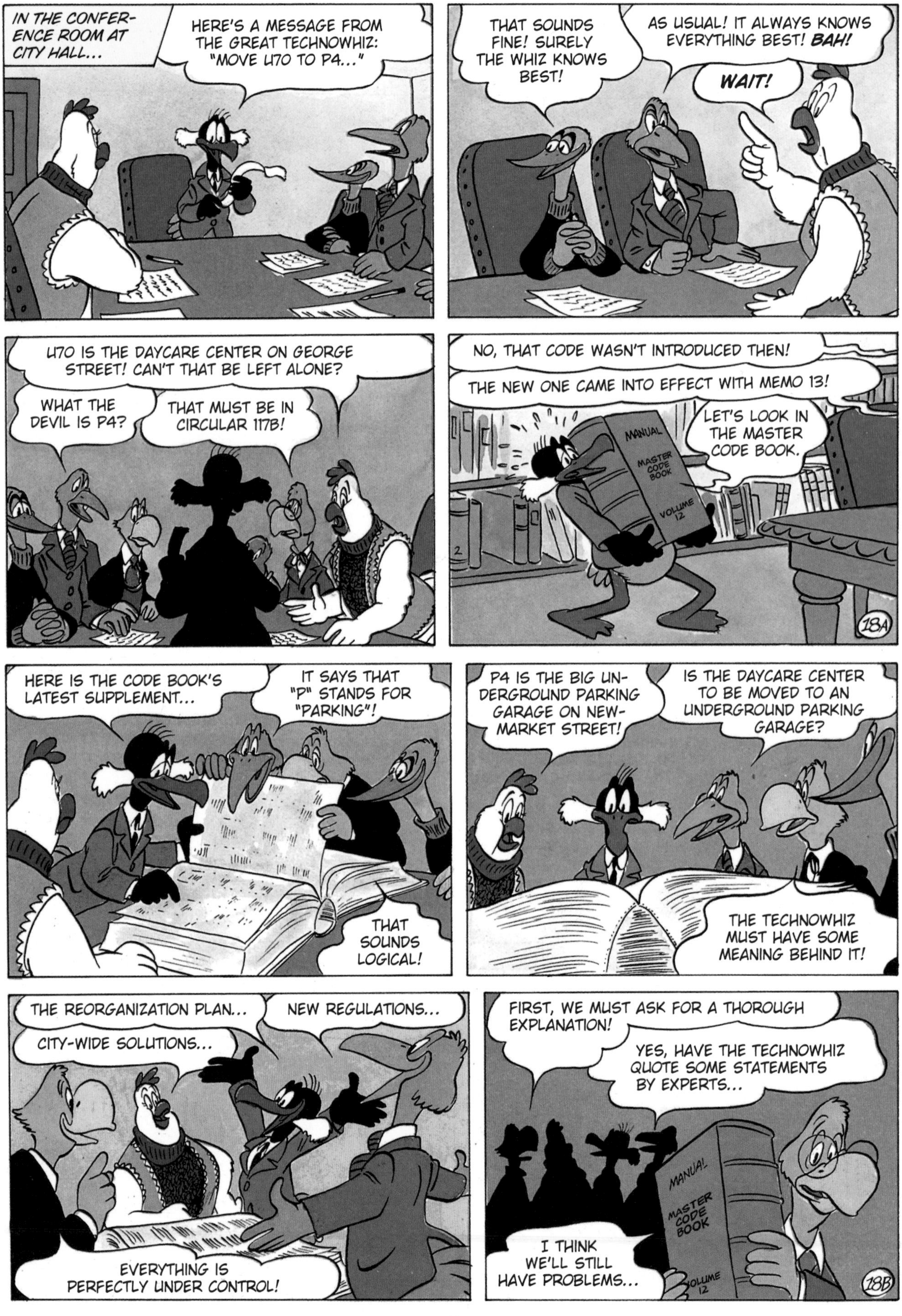
IN THE CONFERENCE ROOM AT CITY HALL...
HERE'S A MESSAGE FROM THE GREAT TECHNOWHIZ: "MOVE U70 TO P4..."
THAT SOUNDS FINE! SURELY THE WHIZ KNOWS BEST!
AS USUAL! IT ALWAYS KNOWS EVERYTHING BEST! BAH!
WAIT!
U70 IS THE DAYCARE CENTER ON GEORGE STREET! CAN'T THAT BE LEFT ALONE?
WHAT THE DEVIL IS P4?
THAT MUST BE IN CIRCULAR 117B!
NO, THAT CODE WASN'T INTRODUCED THEN!
THE NEW ONE CAME INTO EFFECT WITH MEMO 13!
LET'S LOOK IN THE MASTER CODE BOOK.
MANUAL MASTER CODE BOOK VOLUME 12
18A
HERE IS THE CODE BOOK'S LATEST SUPPLEMENT...
IT SAYS THAT "P" STANDS FOR "PARKING"!
THAT SOUNDS LOGICAL!
P4 IS THE BIG UNDERGROUND PARKING GARAGE ON NEWMARKET STREET!
IS THE DAYCARE CENTER TO BE MOVED TO AN UNDERGROUND PARKING GARAGE?
THE TECHNOWHIZ MUST HAVE SOME MEANING BEHIND IT!
THE REORGANIZATION PLAN...
NEW REGULATIONS...
CITY-WIDE SOLUTIONS...
EVERYTHING IS PERFECTLY UNDER CONTROL!
FIRST, WE MUST ASK FOR A THOROUGH EXPLANATION!
YES, HAVE THE TECHNOWHIZ QUOTE SOME STATEMENTS BY EXPERTS...
MANUAL MASTER CODE BOOK VOLUME 12
I THINK WE'LL STILL HAVE PROBLEMS...
18B

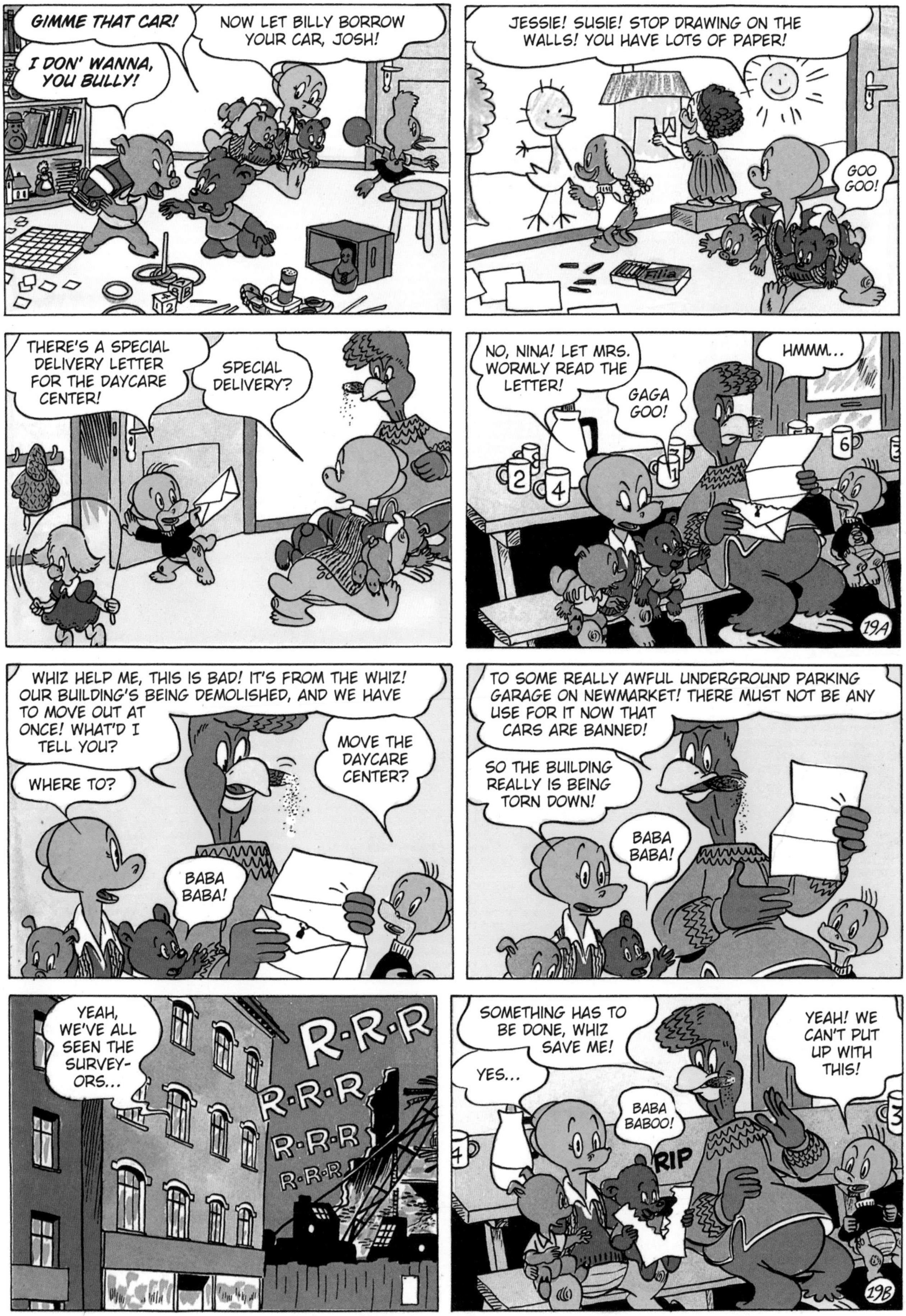
GIMME THAT CAR!
I DON' WANNA, YOU BULLY!
NOW LET BILLY BORROW YOUR CAR, JOSH!
JESSIE! SUSIE! STOP DRAWING ON THE WALLS! YOU HAVE LOTS OF PAPER!
GOO GOO!
THERE'S A SPECIAL DELIVERY LETTER FOR THE DAYCARE CENTER!
SPECIAL DELIVERY?
NO, NINA! LET MRS. WORMLY READ THE LETTER!
GAGA GOO!
HMMM...
19A
WHIZ HELP ME, THIS IS BAD! IT'S FROM THE WHIZ! OUR BUILDING'S BEING DEMOLISHED, AND WE HAVE TO MOVE OUT AT ONCE! WHAT'D I TELL YOU?
WHERE TO?
MOVE THE DAYCARE CENTER?
BABA BABA!
TO SOME REALLY AWFUL UNDERGROUND PARKING GARAGE ON NEWMARKET! THERE MUST NOT BE ANY USE FOR IT NOW THAT CARS ARE BANNED!
SO THE BUILDING REALLY IS BEING TORN DOWN!
BABA BABA!
YEAH, WE'VE ALL SEEN THE SURVEY-ORS...
R-R-R
R-R-R
R-R-R
R-R-R
SOMETHING HAS TO BE DONE, WHIZ SAVE ME!
YES...
YEAH! WE CAN'T PUT UP WITH THIS!
BABA BABOO!
RIP
19B

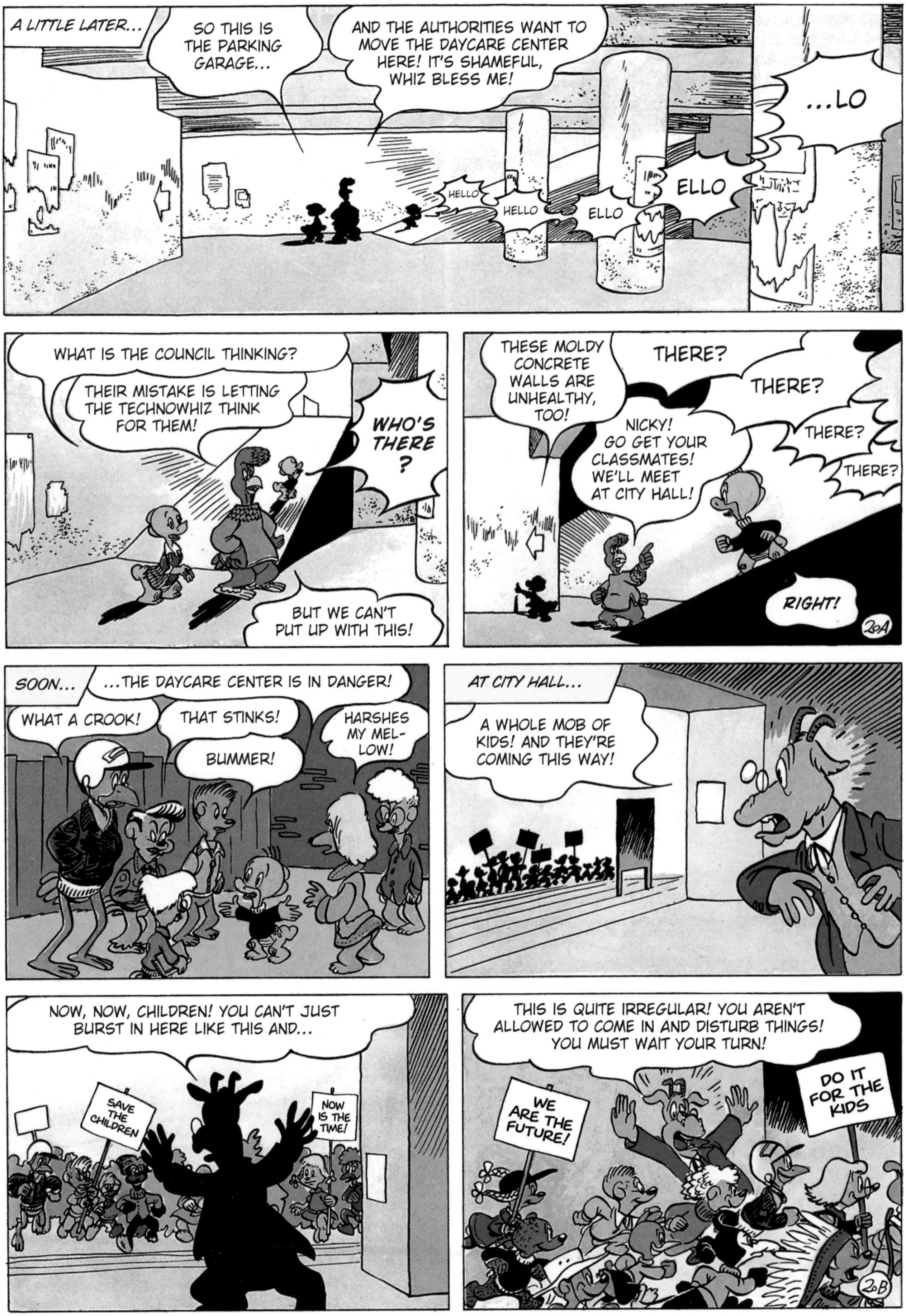

A LITTLE LATER...
SO THIS IS THE PARKING GARAGE...
AND THE AUTHORITIES WANT TO MOVE THE DAYCARE CENTER HERE! IT'S SHAMEFUL, WHIZ BLESS ME!
...LO
HELLO
HELLO
ELLO
ELLO
WHAT IS THE COUNCIL THINKING?
THEIR MISTAKE IS LETTING THE TECHNOWHIZ THINK FOR THEM!
WHO'S THERE ?
BUT WE CAN'T PUT UP WITH THIS!
THESE MOLDY CONCRETE WALLS ARE UNHEALTHY, TOO!
THERE?
THERE?
THERE?
THERE?
NICKY! GO GET YOUR CLASSMATES! WE'LL MEET AT CITY HALL!
RIGHT!
20A
SOON...
...THE DAYCARE CENTER IS IN DANGER!
WHAT A CROOK!
THAT STINKS!
BUMMER!
HARSHES MY MEL-LOW!
AT CITY HALL...
A WHOLE MOB OF KIDS! AND THEY'RE COMING THIS WAY!
NOW, NOW, CHILDREN! YOU CAN'T JUST BURST IN HERE LIKE THIS AND...
SAVE THE CHILDREN
NOW IS THE TIME!
THIS IS QUITE IRREGULAR! YOU AREN'T ALLOWED TO COME IN AND DISTURB THINGS! YOU MUST WAIT YOUR TURN!
WE ARE THE FUTURE!
DO IT FOR THE KIDS
20B

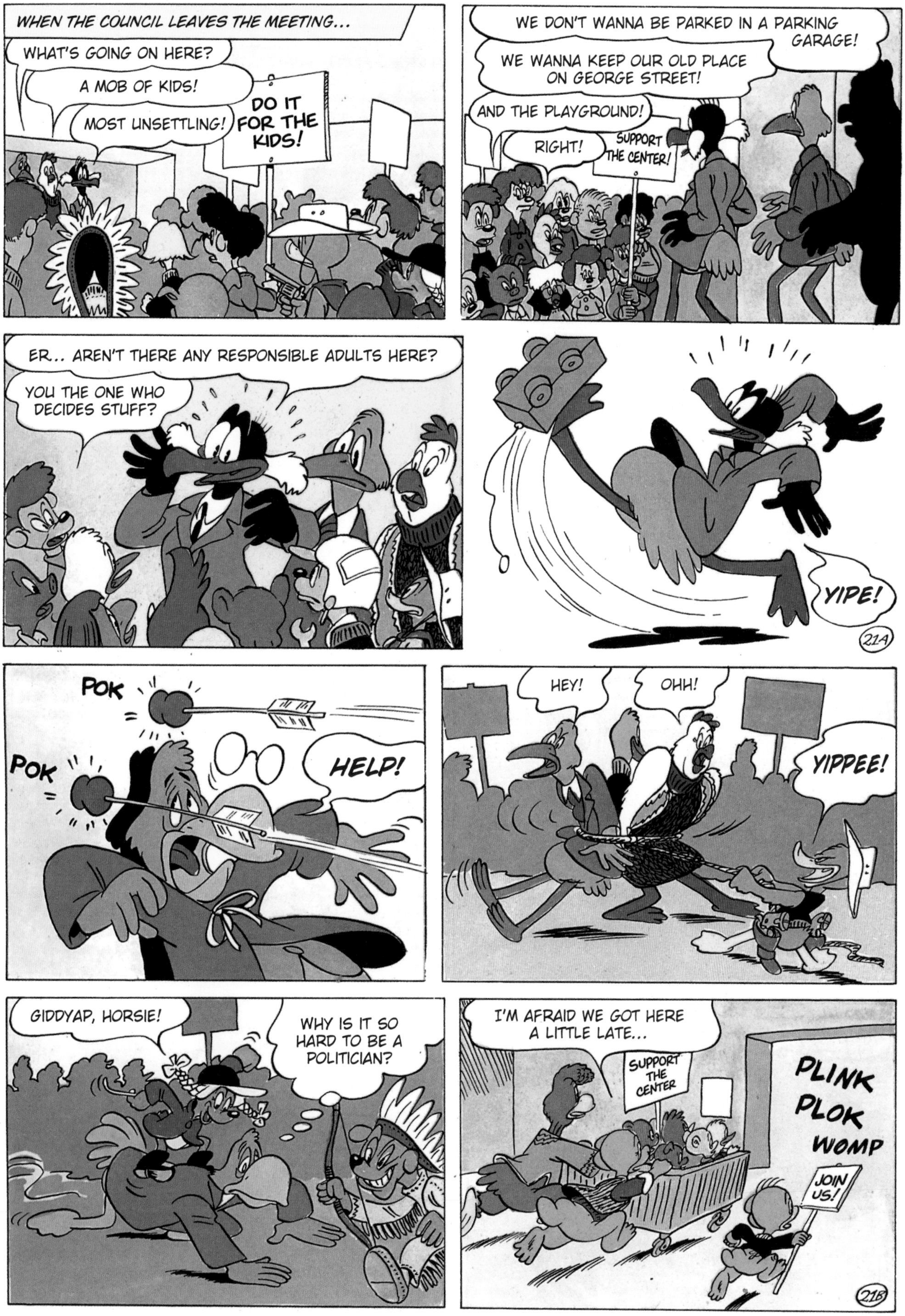
WHEN THE COUNCIL LEAVES THE MEETING...
WHAT'S GOING ON HERE?
A MOB OF KIDS!
MOST UNSETTLING!
DO IT FOR THE KIDS!
WE DON'T WANNA BE PARKED IN A PARKING GARAGE!
WE WANNA KEEP OUR OLD PLACE ON GEORGE STREET!
AND THE PLAYGROUND!
RIGHT!
SUPPORT THE CENTER!
ER... AREN'T THERE ANY RESPONSIBLE ADULTS HERE?
YOU THE ONE WHO DECIDES STUFF?
YIPE!
21A
POK
POK
HELP!
HEY!
OHH!
YIPPEE!
GIDDYAP, HORSIE!
WHY IS IT SO HARD TO BE A POLITICIAN?
I'M AFRAID WE GOT HERE A LITTLE LATE...
SUPPORT THE CENTER
PLINK
PLOK
WOMP
JOIN US!
21B

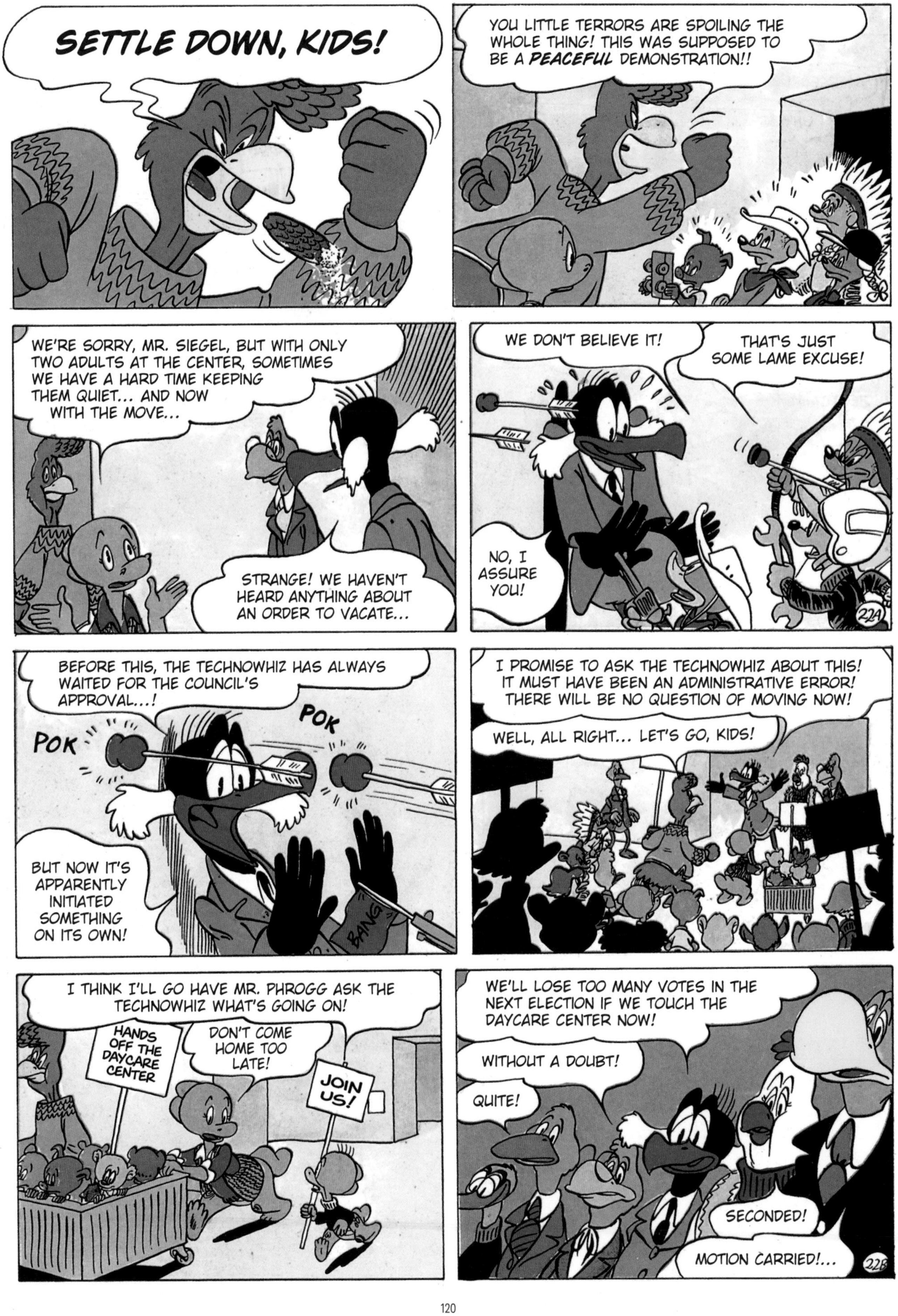
SETTLE DOWN, KIDS!
YOU LITTLE TERRORS ARE SPOILING THE WHOLE THING! THIS WAS SUPPOSED TO BE A PEACEFUL DEMONSTRATION!!
WE'RE SORRY, MR. SIEGEL, BUT WITH ONLY TWO ADULTS AT THE CENTER, SOMETIMES WE HAVE A HARD TIME KEEPING THEM QUIET... AND NOW WITH THE MOVE...
STRANGE! WE HAVEN'T HEARD ANYTHING ABOUT AN ORDER TO VACATE...
WE DON'T BELIEVE IT!
THAT'S JUST SOME LAME EXCUSE!
NO, I ASSURE YOU!
22A
BEFORE THIS, THE TECHNOWHIZ HAS ALWAYS WAITED FOR THE COUNCIL'S APPROVAL...!
POK
POK
BUT NOW IT'S APPARENTLY INITIATED SOMETHING ON ITS OWN!
BANG
I PROMISE TO ASK THE TECHNOWHIZ ABOUT THIS! IT MUST HAVE BEEN AN ADMINISTRATIVE ERROR! THERE WILL BE NO QUESTION OF MOVING NOW!
WELL, ALL RIGHT... LET'S GO, KIDS!
I THINK I'LL GO HAVE MR. PHROGG ASK THE TECHNOWHIZ WHAT'S GOING ON!
HANDS OFF THE DAYCARE CENTER
DON'T COME HOME TOO LATE!
JOIN US!
WE'LL LOSE TOO MANY VOTES IN THE NEXT ELECTION IF WE TOUCH THE DAYCARE CENTER NOW!
WITHOUT A DOUBT!
QUITE!
SECONDED!
MOTION CARRIED!...
22B

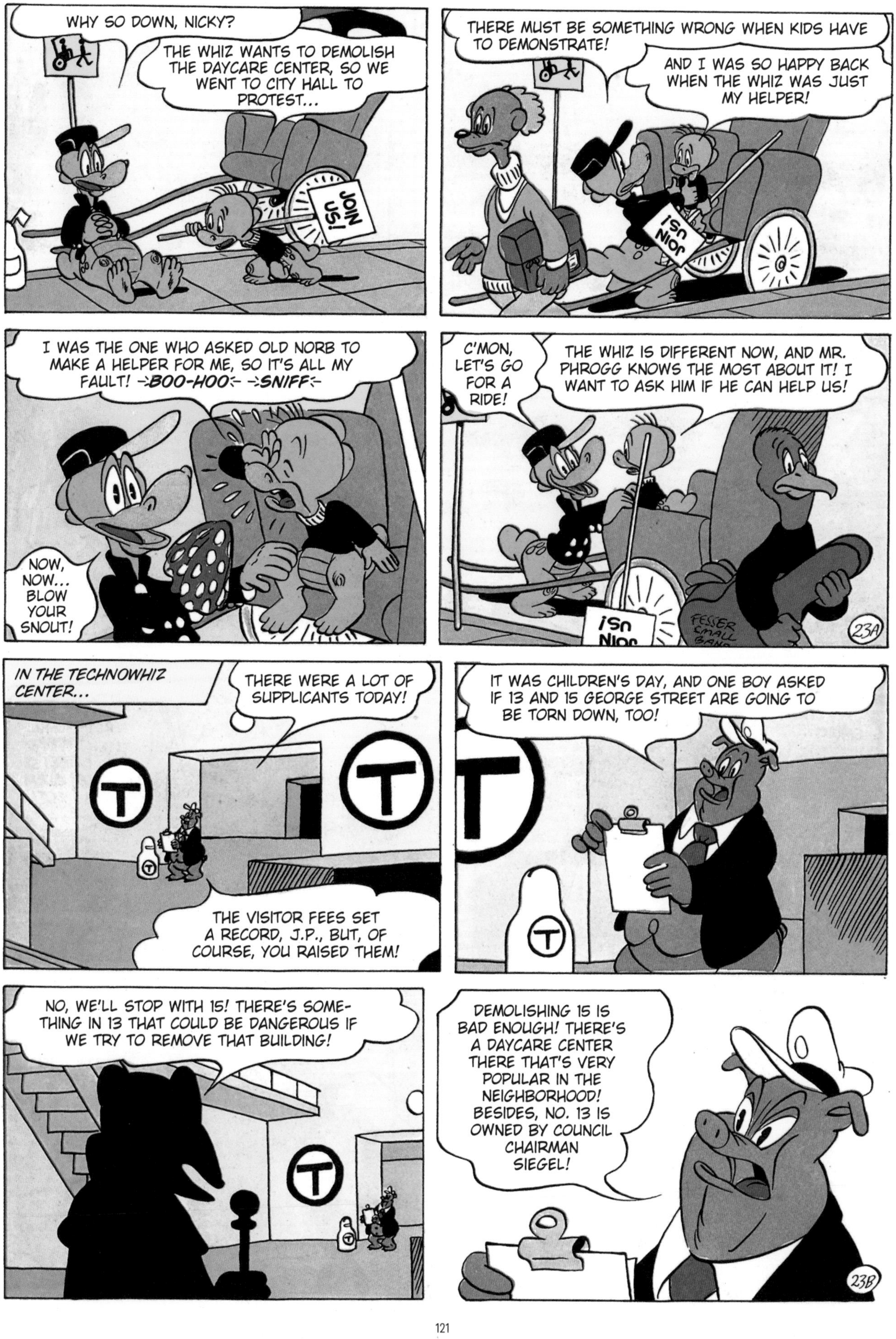
WHY SO DOWN, NICKY?
THE WHIZ WANTS TO DEMOLISH THE DAYCARE CENTER, SO WE WENT TO CITY HALL TO PROTEST...
JOIN US!
THERE MUST BE SOMETHING WRONG WHEN KIDS HAVE TO DEMONSTRATE!
AND I WAS SO HAPPY BACK WHEN THE WHIZ WAS JUST MY HELPER!
I WAS THE ONE WHO ASKED OLD NORB TO MAKE A HELPER FOR ME, SO IT'S ALL MY FAULT! BOO-HOO SNIFF
NOW, NOW... BLOW YOUR SNOUT!
C'MON, LET'S GO FOR A RIDE!
THE WHIZ IS DIFFERENT NOW, AND MR. PHROGG KNOWS THE MOST ABOUT IT! I WANT TO ASK HIM IF HE CAN HELP US!
23A
IN THE TECHNOWHIZ CENTER...
THERE WERE A LOT OF SUPPLICANTS TODAY!
THE VISITOR FEES SET A RECORD, J.P., BUT, OF COURSE, YOU RAISED THEM!
IT WAS CHILDREN'S DAY, AND ONE BOY ASKED IF 13 AND 15 GEORGE STREET ARE GOING TO BE TORN DOWN, TOO!
NO, WE'LL STOP WITH 15! THERE'S SOME-THING IN 13 THAT COULD BE DANGEROUS IF WE TRY TO REMOVE THAT BUILDING!
DEMOLISHING 15 IS BAD ENOUGH! THERE'S A DAYCARE CENTER THERE THAT'S VERY POPULAR IN THE NEIGHBORHOOD! BESIDES, NO. 13 IS OWNED BY COUNCIL CHAIRMAN SIEGEL!
23B

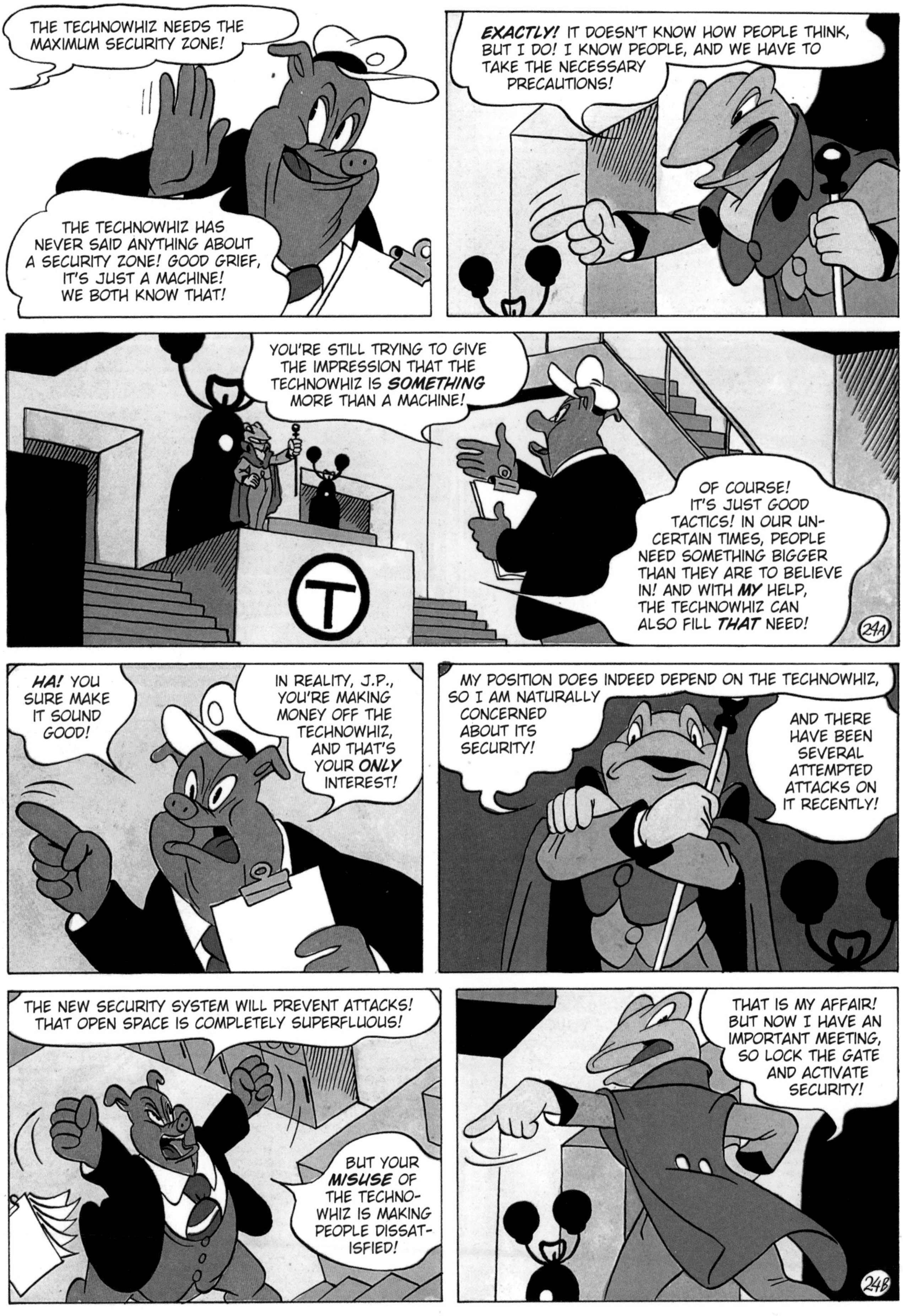
THE TECHNOWHIZ NEEDS THE MAXIMUM SECURITY ZONE!
THE TECHNOWHIZ HAS NEVER SAID ANYTHING ABOUT A SECURITY ZONE! GOOD GRIEF, IT'S JUST A MACHINE! WE BOTH KNOW THAT!
EXACTLY! IT DOESN'T KNOW HOW PEOPLE THINK, BUT I DO! I KNOW PEOPLE, AND WE HAVE TO TAKE THE NECESSARY PRECAUTIONS!
YOU'RE STILL TRYING TO GIVE THE IMPRESSION THAT THE TECHNOWHIZ IS SOMETHING MORE THAN A MACHINE!
OF COURSE! IT'S JUST GOOD TACTICS! IN OUR UNCERTAIN TIMES, PEOPLE NEED SOMETHING BIGGER THAN THEY ARE TO BELIEVE IN! AND WITH MY HELP, THE TECHNOWHIZ CAN ALSO FILL THAT NEED!
T
24A
HA! YOU SURE MAKE IT SOUND GOOD!
IN REALITY, J.P., YOU'RE MAKING MONEY OFF THE TECHNOWHIZ, AND THAT'S YOUR ONLY INTEREST!
MY POSITION DOES INDEED DEPEND ON THE TECHNOWHIZ, SO I AM NATURALLY CONCERNED ABOUT ITS SECURITY!
AND THERE HAVE BEEN SEVERAL ATTEMPTED ATTACKS ON IT RECENTLY!
THE NEW SECURITY SYSTEM WILL PREVENT ATTACKS! THAT OPEN SPACE IS COMPLETELY SUPERFLUOUS!
BUT YOUR MISUSE OF THE TECHNOWHIZ IS MAKING PEOPLE DISSATISFIED!
THAT IS MY AFFAIR! BUT NOW I HAVE AN IMPORTANT MEETING, SO LOCK THE GATE AND ACTIVATE SECURITY!
24B

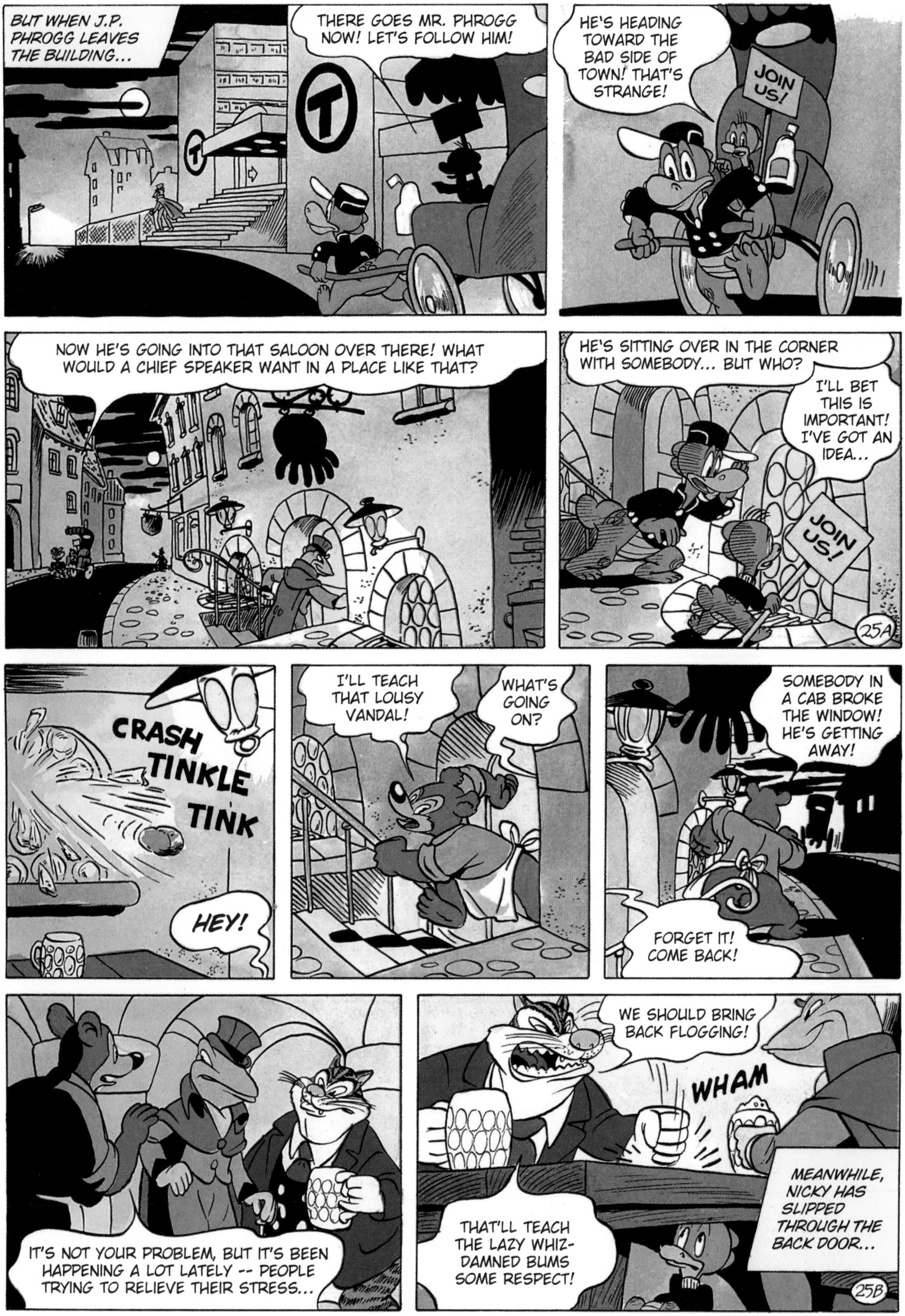
BUT WHEN J.P. PHROGG LEAVES THE BUILDING...
THERE GOES MR. PHROGG NOW! LET'S FOLLOW HIM!
HE'S HEADING TOWARD THE BAD SIDE OF TOWN! THAT'S STRANGE!
JOIN US!
NOW HE'S GOING INTO THAT SALOON OVER THERE! WHAT WOULD A CHIEF SPEAKER WANT IN A PLACE LIKE THAT?
HE'S SITTING OVER IN THE CORNER WITH SOMEBODY... BUT WHO?
I'LL BET THIS IS IMPORTANT! I'VE GOT AN IDEA...
JOIN US!
25A
CRASH
TINKLE
TINK
HEY!
I'LL TEACH THAT LOUSY VANDAL!
WHAT'S GOING ON?
SOMEBODY IN A CAB BROKE THE WINDOW! HE'S GETTING AWAY!
FORGET IT! COME BACK!
IT'S NOT YOUR PROBLEM, BUT IT'S BEEN HAPPENING A LOT LATELY -- PEOPLE TRYING TO RELIEVE THEIR STRESS...
WE SHOULD BRING BACK FLOGGING!
WHAM
THAT'LL TEACH THE LAZY WHIZ-DAMNED BUMS SOME RESPECT!
MEANWHILE, NICKY HAS SLIPPED THROUGH THE BACK DOOR...
25B

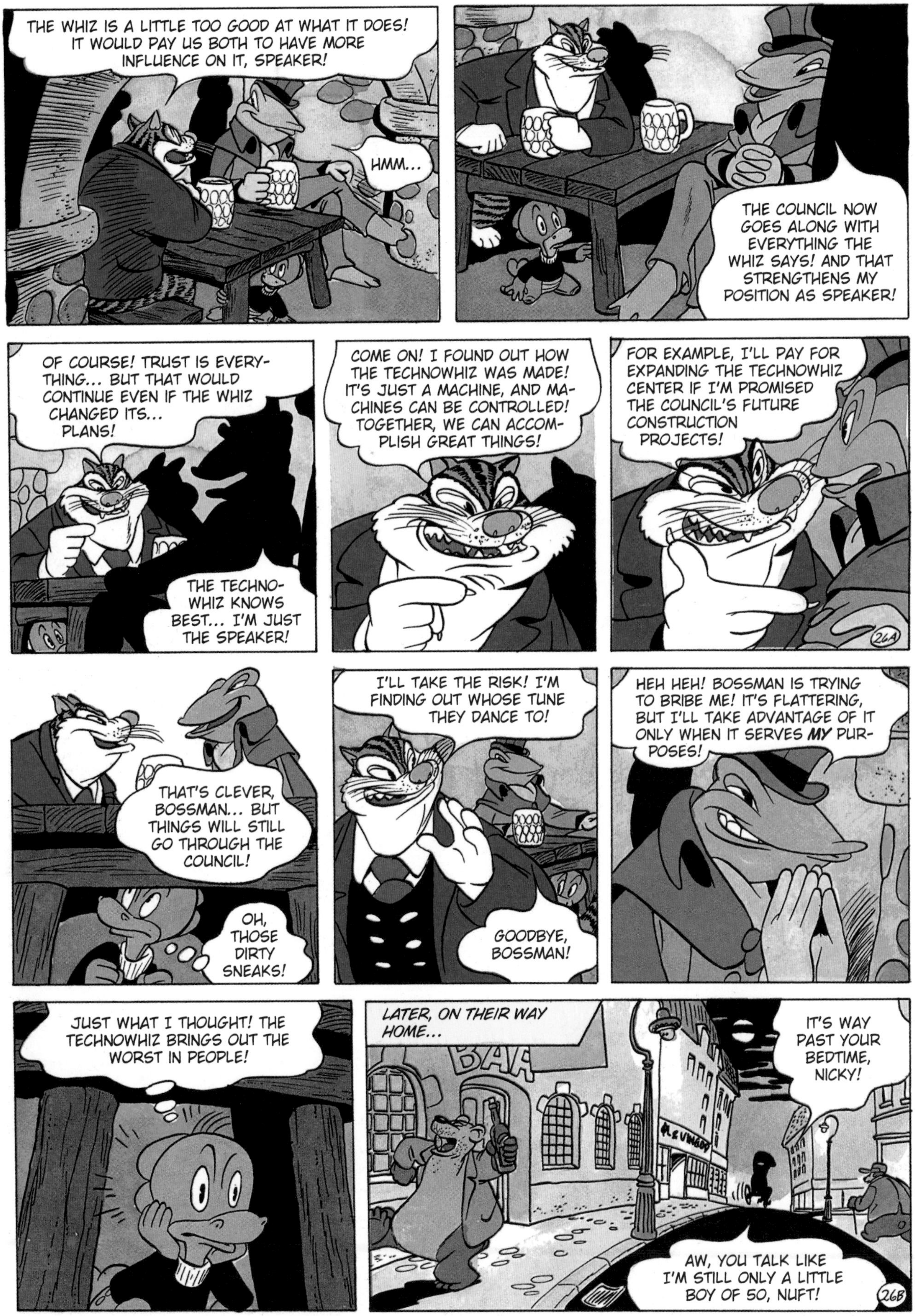
THE WHIZ IS A LITTLE TOO GOOD AT WHAT IT DOES! IT WOULD PAY US BOTH TO HAVE MORE INFLUENCE ON IT, SPEAKER!
HMM...
THE COUNCIL NOW GOES ALONG WITH EVERYTHING THE WHIZ SAYS! AND THAT STRENGTHENS MY POSITION AS SPEAKER!
OF COURSE! TRUST IS EVERY-THING... BUT THAT WOULD CONTINUE EVEN IF THE WHIZ CHANGED ITS... PLANS!
THE TECHNO-WHIZ KNOWS BEST... I'M JUST THE SPEAKER!
COME ON! I FOUND OUT HOW THE TECHNOWHIZ WAS MADE! IT'S JUST A MACHINE, AND MA-CHINES CAN BE CONTROLLED! TOGETHER, WE CAN ACCOM-PLISH GREAT THINGS!
FOR EXAMPLE, I'LL PAY FOR EXPANDING THE TECHNOWHIZ CENTER IF I'M PROMISED THE COUNCIL'S FUTURE CONSTRUCTION PROJECTS!
26A
THAT'S CLEVER, BOSSMAN... BUT THINGS WILL STILL GO THROUGH THE COUNCIL!
OH, THOSE DIRTY SNEAKS!
I'LL TAKE THE RISK! I'M FINDING OUT WHOSE TUNE THEY DANCE TO!
GOODBYE, BOSSMAN!
HEH HEH! BOSSMAN IS TRYING TO BRIBE ME! IT'S FLATTERING, BUT I'LL TAKE ADVANTAGE OF IT ONLY WHEN IT SERVES MY PUR-POSES!
JUST WHAT I THOUGHT! THE TECHNOWHIZ BRINGS OUT THE WORST IN PEOPLE!
LATER, ON THEIR WAY HOME...
IT'S WAY PAST YOUR BEDTIME, NICKY!
AW, YOU TALK LIKE I'M STILL ONLY A LITTLE BOY OF 50, NUFT!
26B

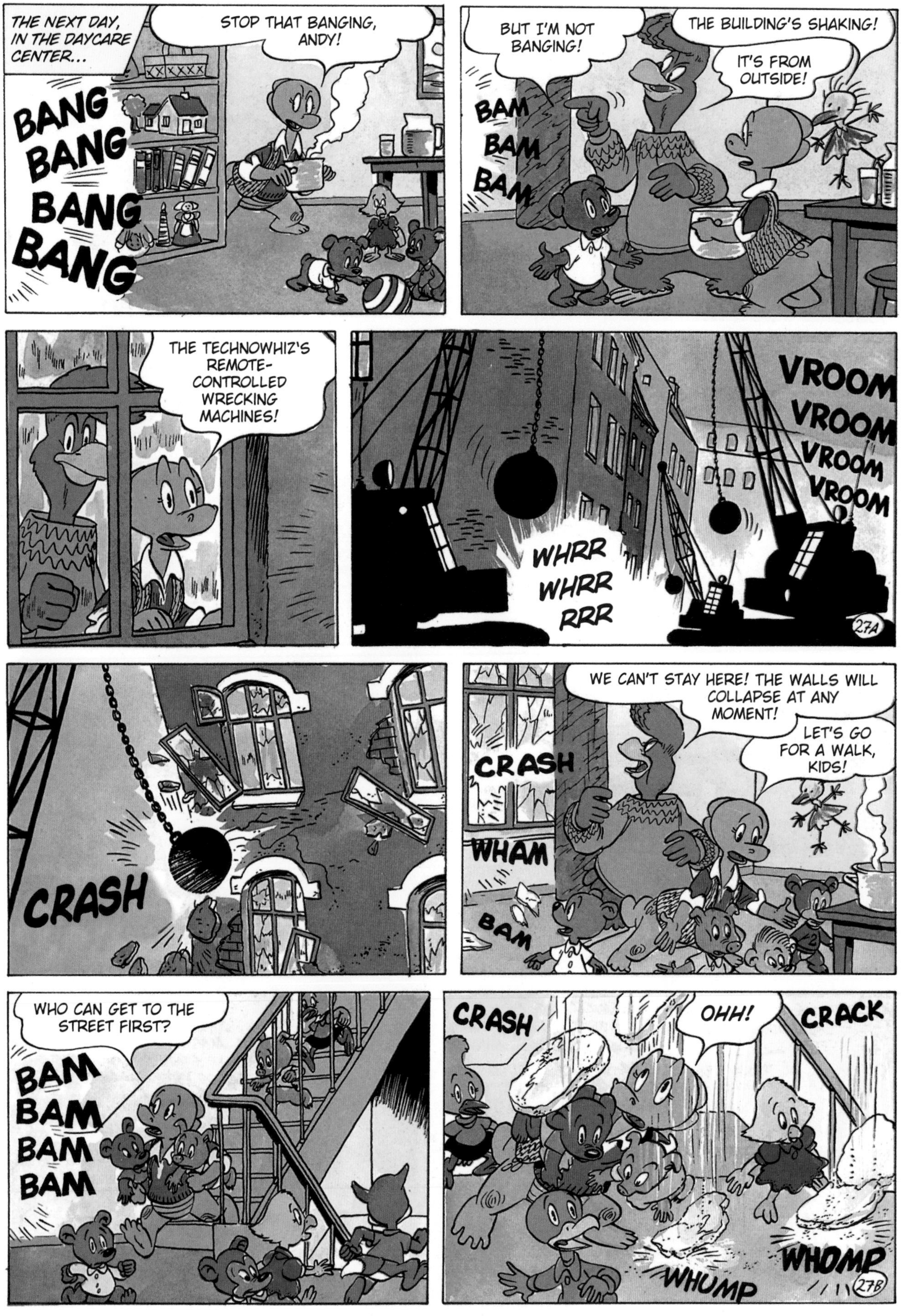
THE NEXT DAY, IN THE DAYCARE CENTER...
STOP THAT BANGING, ANDY!
BANG BANG BANG BANG
BUT I'M NOT BANGING!
THE BUILDING'S SHAKING!
IT'S FROM OUTSIDE!
BAM BAM BAM
THE TECHNOWHIZ'S REMOTE-CONTROLLED WRECKING MACHINES!
VROOM VROOM VROOM VROOM
WHRR WHRR RRR
27A
CRASH
WE CAN'T STAY HERE! THE WALLS WILL COLLAPSE AT ANY MOMENT!
LET'S GO FOR A WALK, KIDS!
CRASH
WHAM
BAM
WHO CAN GET TO THE STREET FIRST?
BAM BAM BAM BAM
CRASH
OHH!
CRACK
WHOMP
WHUMP
27B

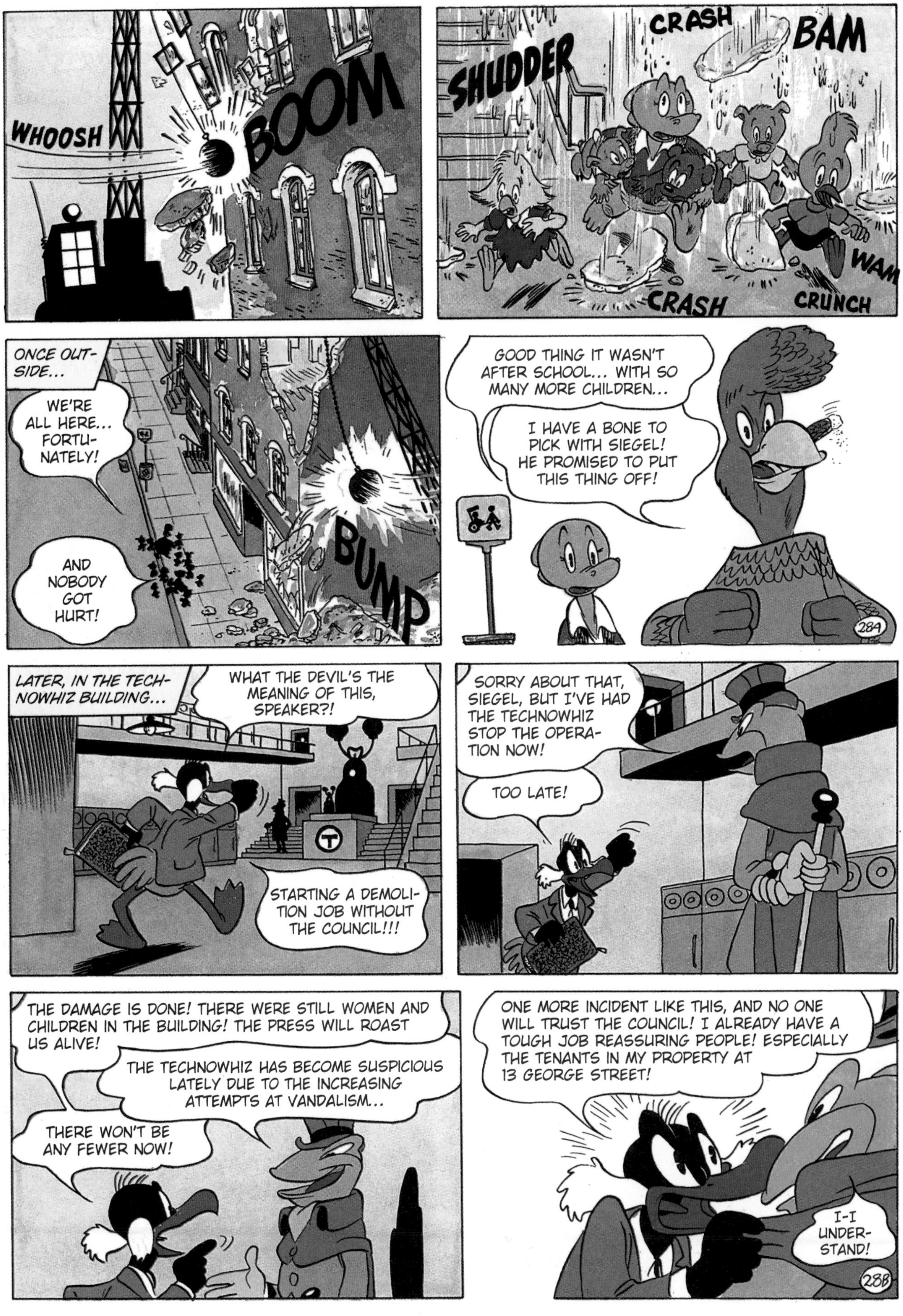
WHOOSH
BOOM
SHUDDER
CRASH
BAM
WAM
CRASH
CRUNCH
ONCE OUTSIDE...
WE'RE ALL HERE... FORTUNATELY!
AND NOBODY GOT HURT!
BUMP
GOOD THING IT WASN'T AFTER SCHOOL... WITH SO MANY MORE CHILDREN...
I HAVE A BONE TO PICK WITH SIEGEL! HE PROMISED TO PUT THIS THING OFF!
284
LATER, IN THE TECHNOWHIZ BUILDING...
WHAT THE DEVIL'S THE MEANING OF THIS, SPEAKER?!
STARTING A DEMOLITION JOB WITHOUT THE COUNCIL!!!
SORRY ABOUT THAT, SIEGEL, BUT I'VE HAD THE TECHNOWHIZ STOP THE OPERATION NOW!
TOO LATE!
THE DAMAGE IS DONE! THERE WERE STILL WOMEN AND CHILDREN IN THE BUILDING! THE PRESS WILL ROAST US ALIVE!
THE TECHNOWHIZ HAS BECOME SUSPICIOUS LATELY DUE TO THE INCREASING ATTEMPTS AT VANDALISM...
THERE WON'T BE ANY FEWER NOW!
ONE MORE INCIDENT LIKE THIS, AND NO ONE WILL TRUST THE COUNCIL! I ALREADY HAVE A TOUGH JOB REASSURING PEOPLE! ESPECIALLY THE TENANTS IN MY PROPERTY AT 13 GEORGE STREET!
I-I UNDERSTAND!
288

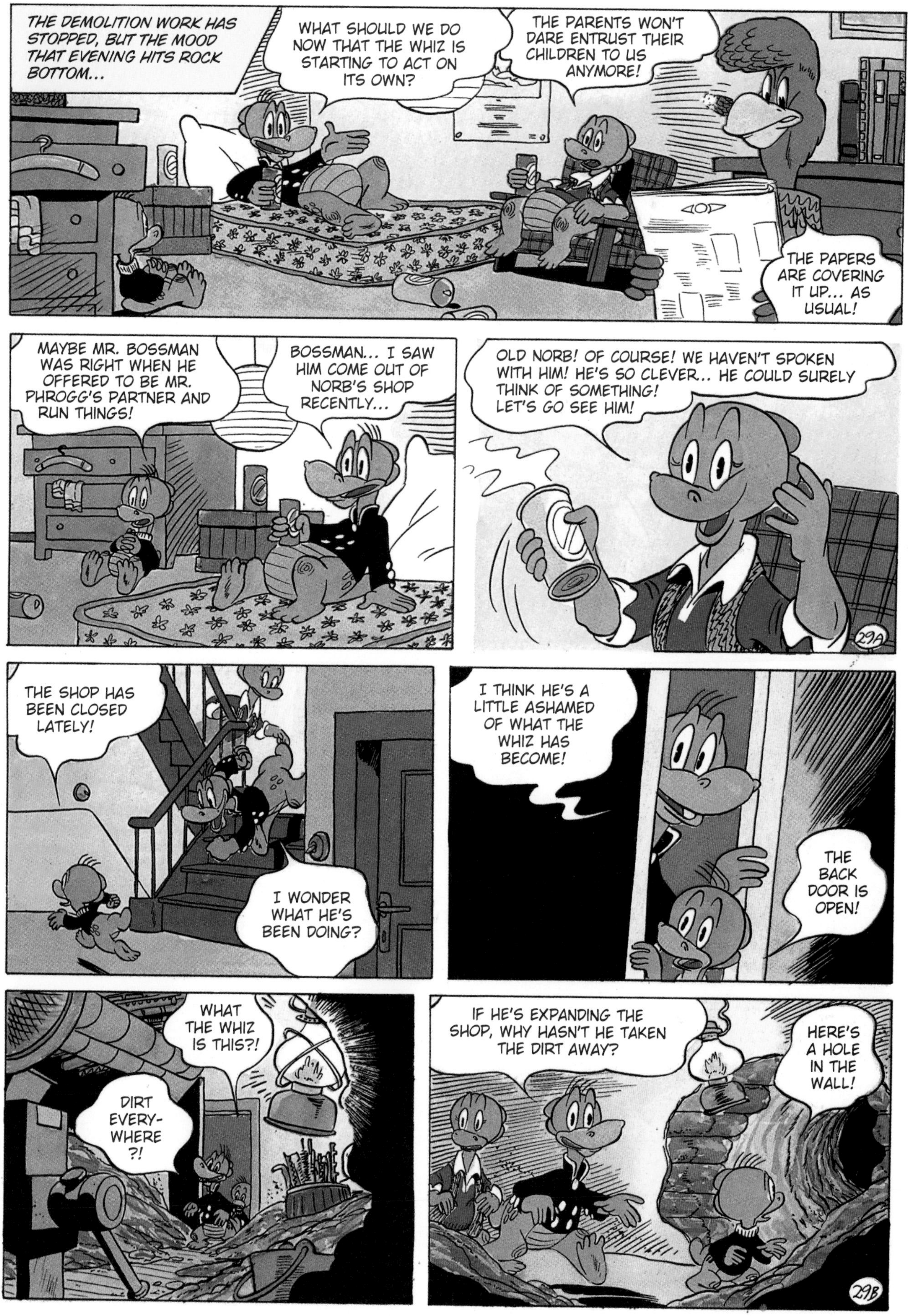
THE DEMOLITION WORK HAS STOPPED, BUT THE MOOD THAT EVENING HITS ROCK BOTTOM...
WHAT SHOULD WE DO NOW THAT THE WHIZ IS STARTING TO ACT ON ITS OWN?
THE PARENTS WON'T DARE ENTRUST THEIR CHILDREN TO US ANYMORE!
THE PAPERS ARE COVERING IT UP... AS USUAL!
MAYBE MR. BOSSMAN WAS RIGHT WHEN HE OFFERED TO BE MR. PHROGG'S PARTNER AND RUN THINGS!
BOSSMAN... I SAW HIM COME OUT OF NORB'S SHOP RECENTLY...
OLD NORB! OF COURSE! WE HAVEN'T SPOKEN WITH HIM! HE'S SO CLEVER... HE COULD SURELY THINK OF SOMETHING! LET'S GO SEE HIM!
29A
THE SHOP HAS BEEN CLOSED LATELY!
I WONDER WHAT HE'S BEEN DOING?
I THINK HE'S A LITTLE ASHAMED OF WHAT THE WHIZ HAS BECOME!
THE BACK DOOR IS OPEN!
WHAT THE WHIZ IS THIS?!
DIRT EVERY-WHERE ?!
IF HE'S EXPANDING THE SHOP, WHY HASN'T HE TAKEN THE DIRT AWAY?
HERE'S A HOLE IN THE WALL!
29B

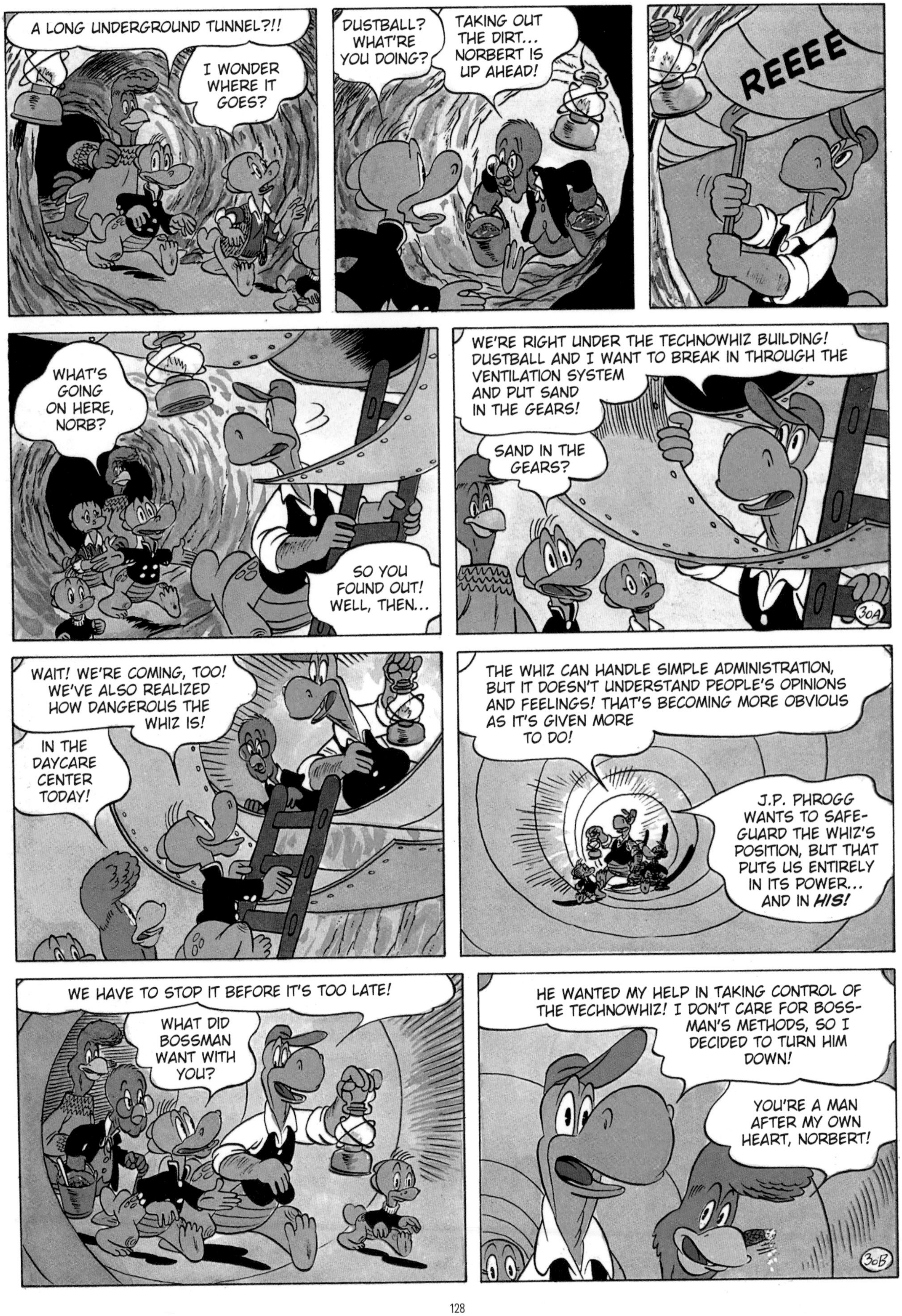
A LONG UNDERGROUND TUNNEL?!!
I WONDER WHERE IT GOES?
DUSTBALL? WHAT'RE YOU DOING?
TAKING OUT THE DIRT... NORBERT IS UP AHEAD!
REEEE
WHAT'S GOING ON HERE, NORB?
SO YOU FOUND OUT! WELL, THEN...
WE'RE RIGHT UNDER THE TECHNOWHIZ BUILDING! DUSTBALL AND I WANT TO BREAK IN THROUGH THE VENTILATION SYSTEM AND PUT SAND IN THE GEARS!
SAND IN THE GEARS?
30A
WAIT! WE'RE COMING, TOO! WE'VE ALSO REALIZED HOW DANGEROUS THE WHIZ IS!
IN THE DAYCARE CENTER TODAY!
THE WHIZ CAN HANDLE SIMPLE ADMINISTRATION, BUT IT DOESN'T UNDERSTAND PEOPLE'S OPINIONS AND FEELINGS! THAT'S BECOMING MORE OBVIOUS AS IT'S GIVEN MORE TO DO!
J.P. PHROGG WANTS TO SAFE-GUARD THE WHIZ'S POSITION, BUT THAT PUTS US ENTIRELY IN ITS POWER... AND IN HIS!
WE HAVE TO STOP IT BEFORE IT'S TOO LATE!
WHAT DID BOSSMAN WANT WITH YOU?
HE WANTED MY HELP IN TAKING CONTROL OF THE TECHNOWHIZ! I DON'T CARE FOR BOSS-MAN'S METHODS, SO I DECIDED TO TURN HIM DOWN!
YOU'RE A MAN AFTER MY OWN HEART, NORBERT!
30B

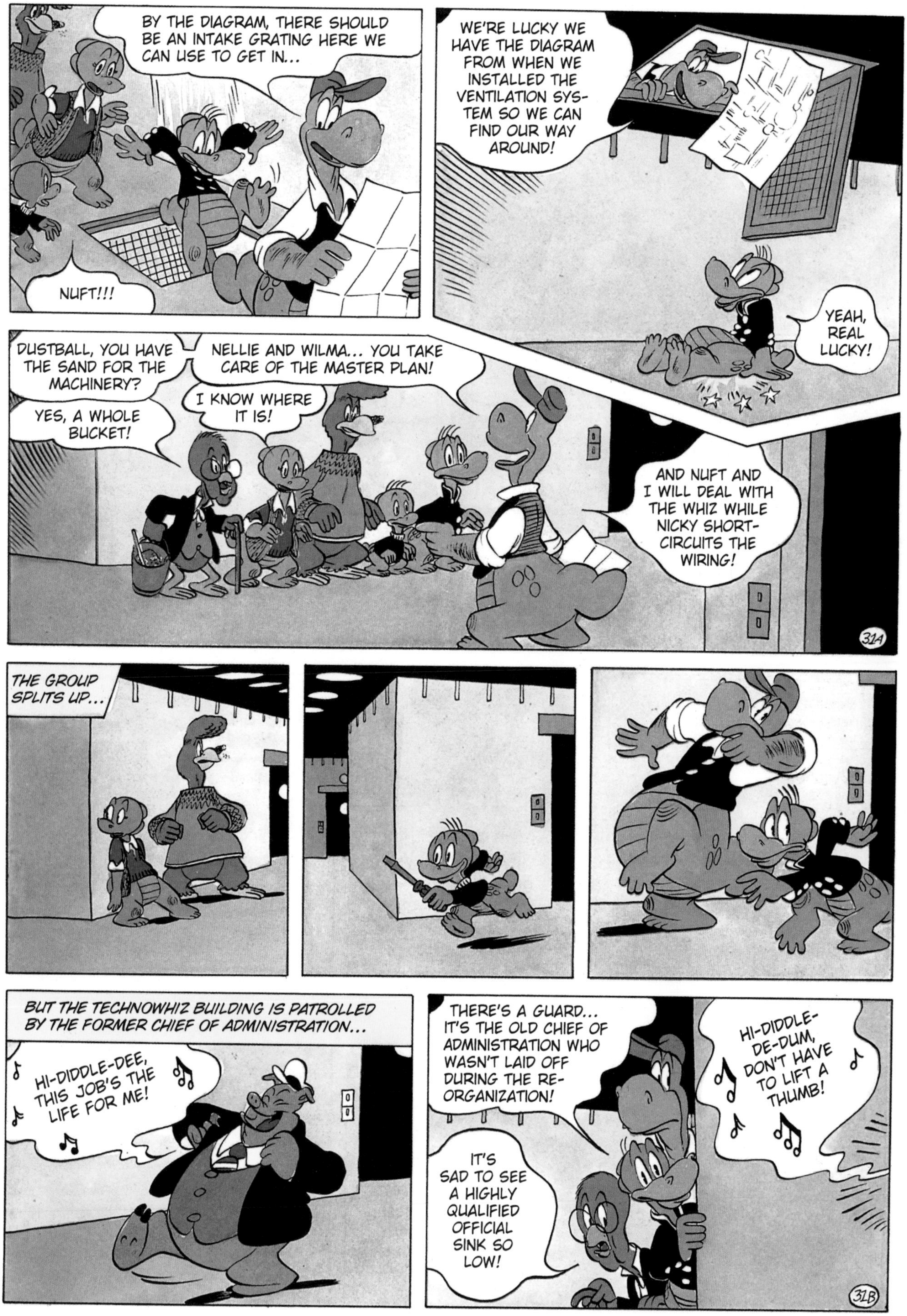

BY THE DIAGRAM, THERE SHOULD BE AN INTAKE GRATING HERE WE CAN USE TO GET IN...
NUFT!!!
WE'RE LUCKY WE HAVE THE DIAGRAM FROM WHEN WE INSTALLED THE VENTILATION SYS-TEM SO WE CAN FIND OUR WAY AROUND!
YEAH, REAL LUCKY!
DUSTBALL, YOU HAVE THE SAND FOR THE MACHINERY?
YES, A WHOLE BUCKET!
NELLIE AND WILMA... YOU TAKE CARE OF THE MASTER PLAN!
I KNOW WHERE IT IS!
AND NUFT AND I WILL DEAL WITH THE WHIZ WHILE NICKY SHORT-CIRCUITS THE WIRING!
31A
THE GROUP SPLITS UP...
BUT THE TECHNOWHIZ BUILDING IS PATROLLED BY THE FORMER CHIEF OF ADMINISTRATION...
HI-DIDDLE-DEE, THIS JOB'S THE LIFE FOR ME!
THERE'S A GUARD... IT'S THE OLD CHIEF OF ADMINISTRATION WHO WASN'T LAID OFF DURING THE RE-ORGANIZATION!
HI-DIDDLE-DE-DUM, DON'T HAVE TO LIFT A THUMB!
IT'S SAD TO SEE A HIGHLY QUALIFIED OFFICIAL SINK SO LOW!
31B

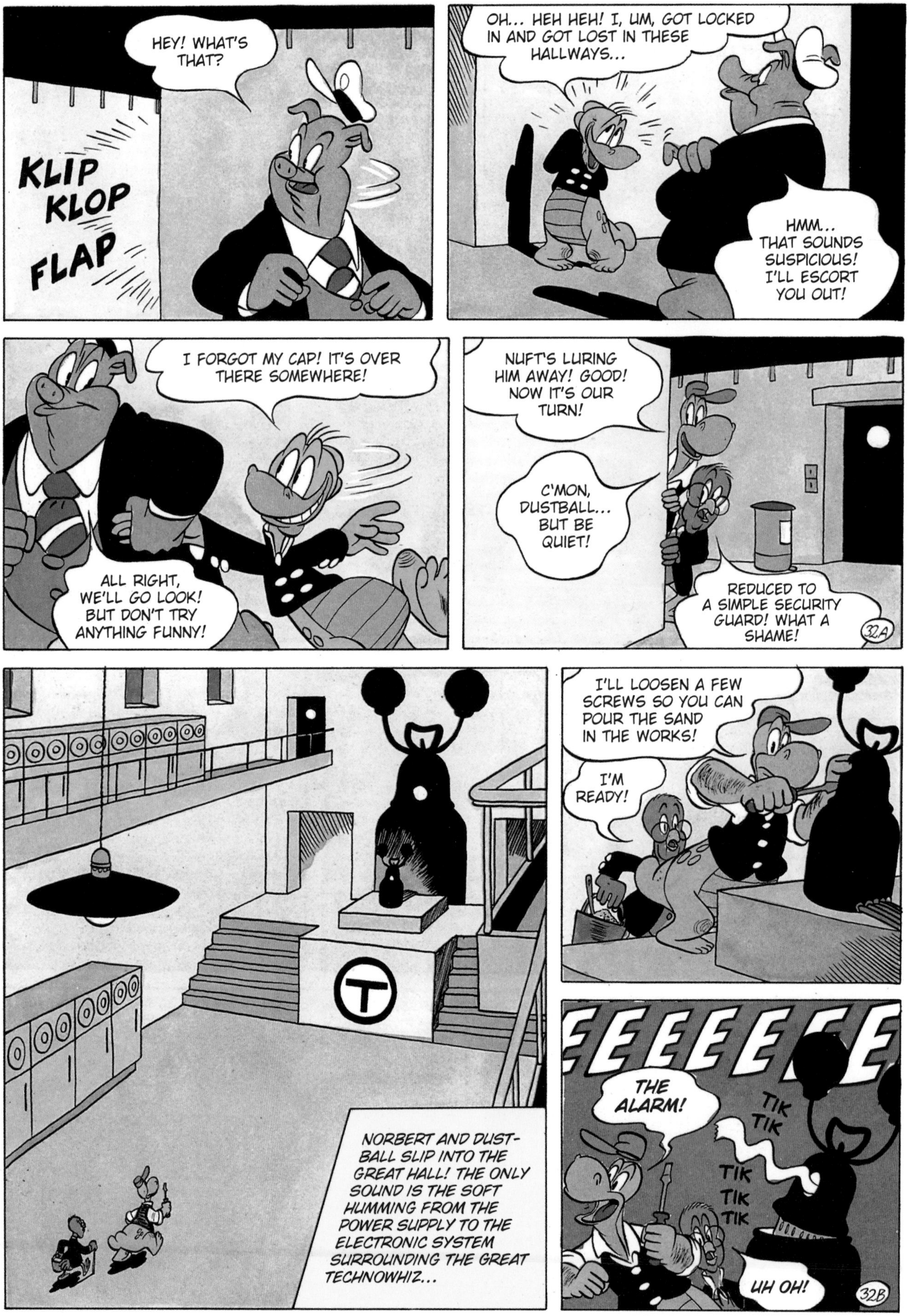
HEY! WHAT'S THAT?
KLIP
KLOP
FLAP
OH... HEH HEH! I, UM, GOT LOCKED IN AND GOT LOST IN THESE HALLWAYS...
HMM.. THAT SOUNDS SUSPICIOUS! I'LL ESCORT YOU OUT!
I FORGOT MY CAP! IT'S OVER THERE SOMEWHERE!
ALL RIGHT, WE'LL GO LOOK! BUT DON'T TRY ANYTHING FUNNY!
NUFT'S LURING HIM AWAY! GOOD! NOW IT'S OUR TURN!
C'MON, DUSTBALL... BUT BE QUIET!
REDUCED TO A SIMPLE SECURITY GUARD! WHAT A SHAME!
32A
NORBERT AND DUST-BALL SLIP INTO THE GREAT HALL! THE ONLY SOUND IS THE SOFT HUMMING FROM THE POWER SUPPLY TO THE ELECTRONIC SYSTEM SURROUNDING THE GREAT TECHNOWHIZ...
I'LL LOOSEN A FEW SCREWS SO YOU CAN POUR THE SAND IN THE WORKS!
I'M READY!
EEEEEE
THE ALARM!
TIK TIK
TIK TIK TIK
UH OH!
32B

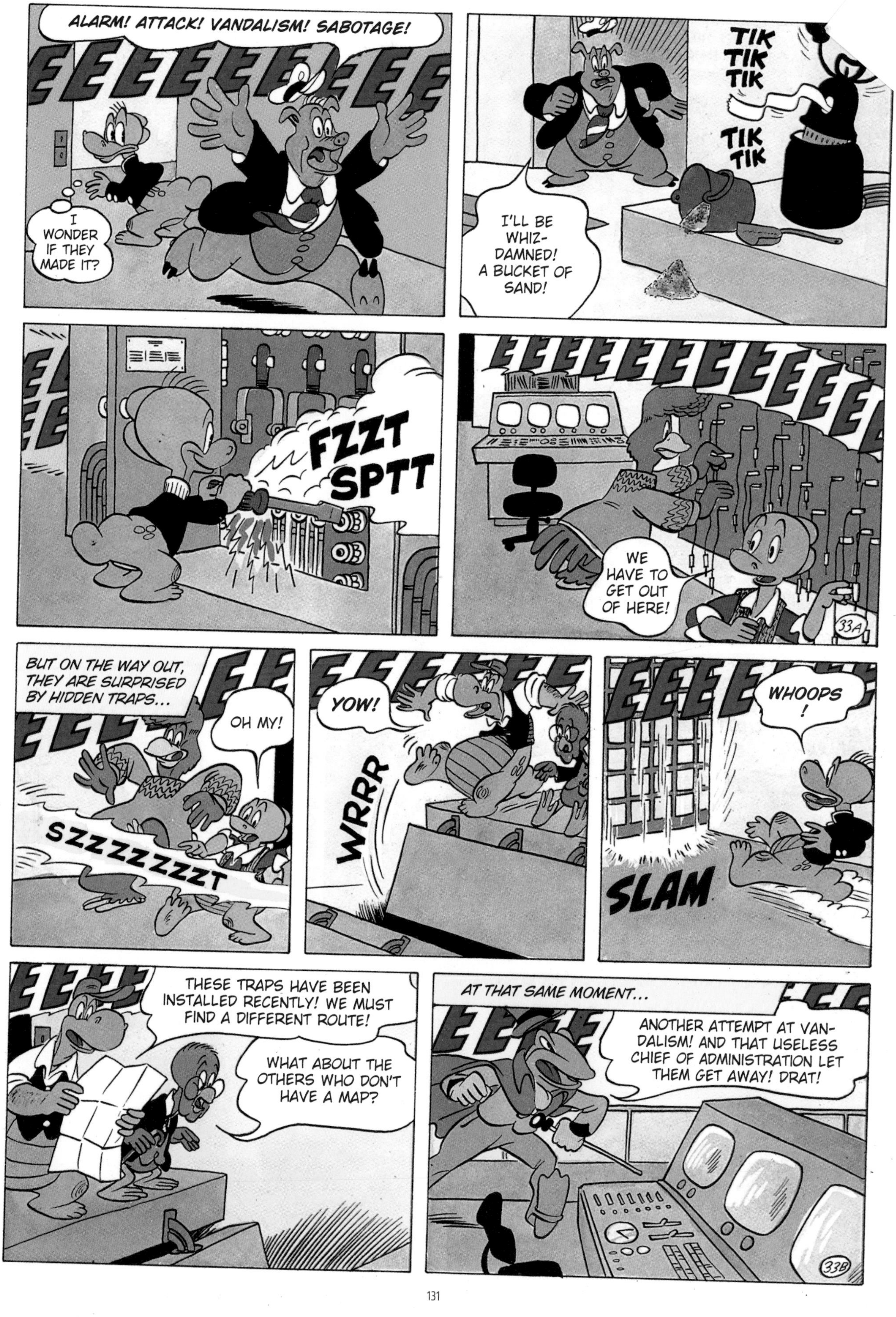
ALARM! ATTACK! VANDALISM! SABOTAGE!
EEEEEEEEEE
I WONDER IF THEY MADE IT?
TIK TIK TIK
TIK TIK
I'LL BE WHIZ-DAMNED! A BUCKET OF SAND!
FZZT SPTT
EEEEEEEEEEEE
WE HAVE TO GET OUT OF HERE!
33A
BUT ON THE WAY OUT, THEY ARE SURPRISED BY HIDDEN TRAPS...
OH MY!
SZZZZZZZT
YOW!
WRRR
WHOOPS !
SLAM
THESE TRAPS HAVE BEEN INSTALLED RECENTLY! WE MUST FIND A DIFFERENT ROUTE!
WHAT ABOUT THE OTHERS WHO DON'T HAVE A MAP?
AT THAT SAME MOMENT...
ANOTHER ATTEMPT AT VANDALISM! AND THAT USELESS CHIEF OF ADMINISTRATION LET THEM GET AWAY! DRAT!
33B

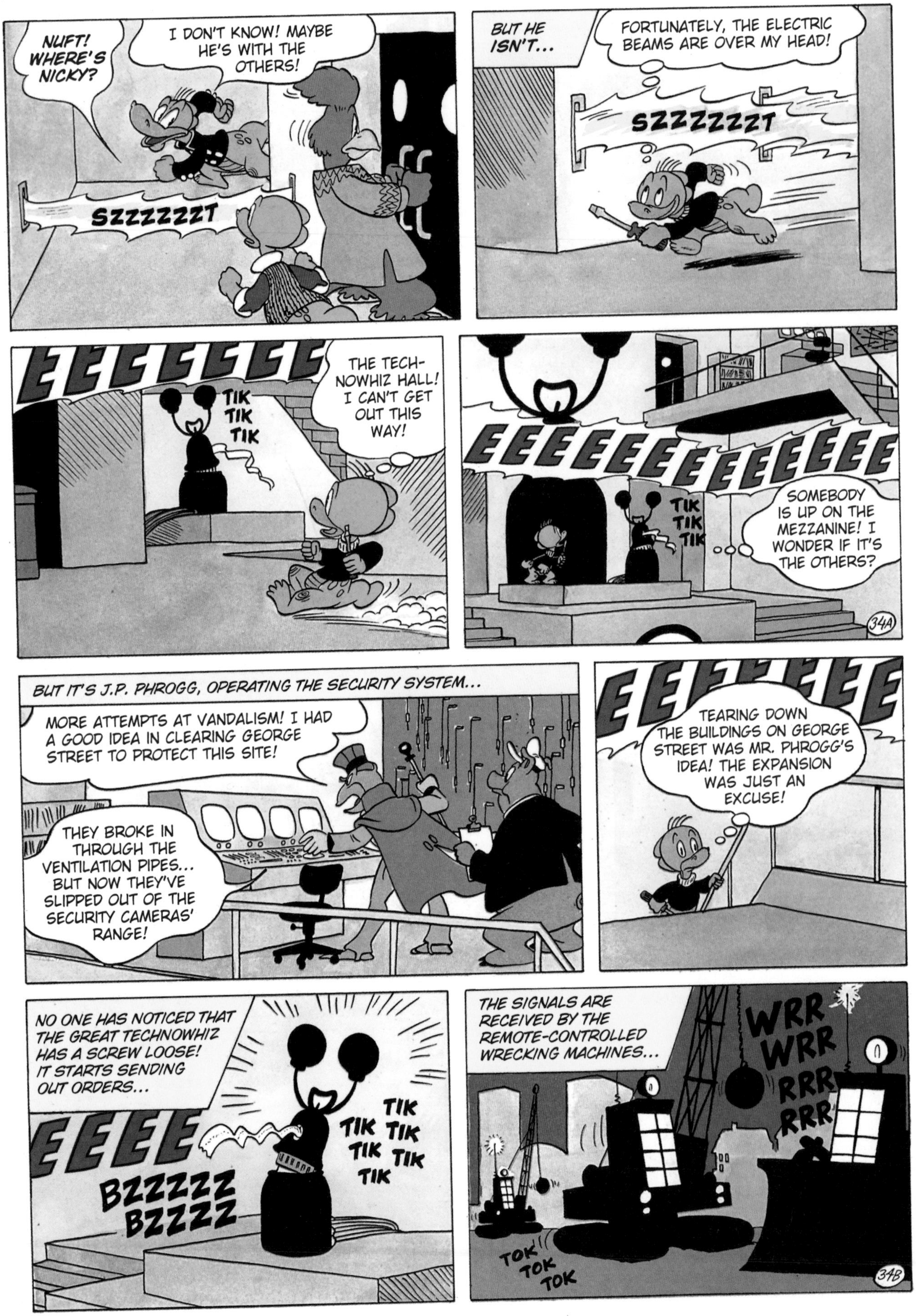
NUFT! WHERE'S NICKY?
I DON'T KNOW! MAYBE HE'S WITH THE OTHERS!
SZZZZZZT
BUT HE ISN'T...
FORTUNATELY, THE ELECTRIC BEAMS ARE OVER MY HEAD!
SZZZZZZT
EEEEEEE
TIK TIK TIK
THE TECH-NOWHIZ HALL! I CAN'T GET OUT THIS WAY!
EEEEEEEEEEEEEE
TIK TIK TIK
SOMEBODY IS UP ON THE MEZZANINE! I WONDER IF IT'S THE OTHERS?
34A
BUT IT'S J.P. PHROGG, OPERATING THE SECURITY SYSTEM...
MORE ATTEMPTS AT VANDALISM! I HAD A GOOD IDEA IN CLEARING GEORGE STREET TO PROTECT THIS SITE!
THEY BROKE IN THROUGH THE VENTILATION PIPES... BUT NOW THEY'VE SLIPPED OUT OF THE SECURITY CAMERAS' RANGE!
EEEEEEE
TEARING DOWN THE BUILDINGS ON GEORGE STREET WAS MR. PHROGG'S IDEA! THE EXPANSION WAS JUST AN EXCUSE!
NO ONE HAS NOTICED THAT THE GREAT TECHNOWHIZ HAS A SCREW LOOSE! IT STARTS SENDING OUT ORDERS...
EEEE
TIK TIK TIK TIK TIK TIK TIK
BZZZZZ BZZZZ
THE SIGNALS ARE RECEIVED BY THE REMOTE-CONTROLLED WRECKING MACHINES...
WRR WRR RRR RRR
TOK TOK TOK
34B

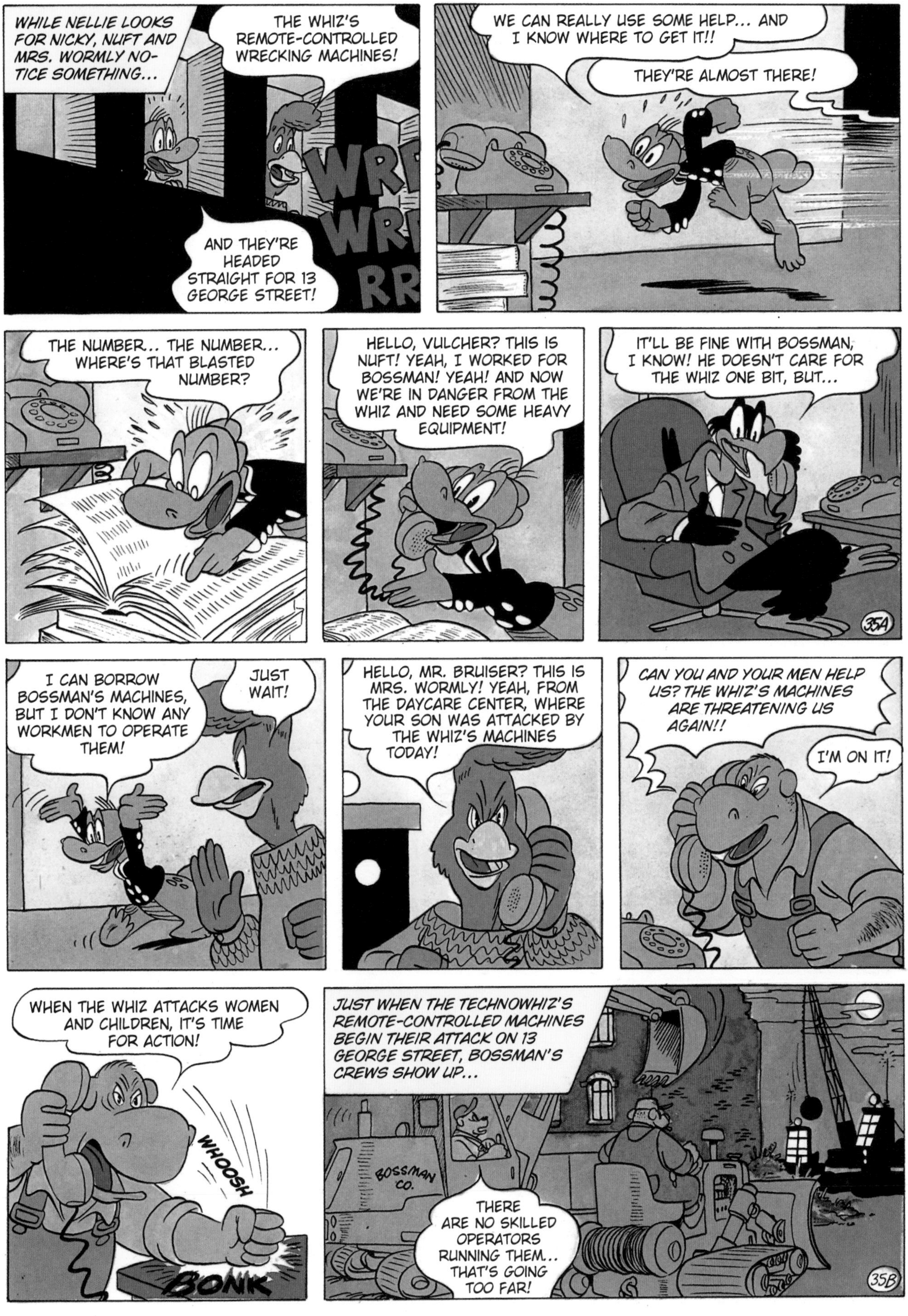

WHILE NELLIE LOOKS FOR NICKY, NUFT AND MRS. WORMLY NOTICE SOMETHING...
THE WHIZ'S REMOTE-CONTROLLED WRECKING MACHINES!
AND THEY'RE HEADED STRAIGHT FOR 13 GEORGE STREET!
WE CAN REALLY USE SOME HELP... AND I KNOW WHERE TO GET IT!!
THEY'RE ALMOST THERE!
THE NUMBER... THE NUMBER... WHERE'S THAT BLASTED NUMBER?
HELLO, VULCHER? THIS IS NUFT! YEAH, I WORKED FOR BOSSMAN! YEAH! AND NOW WE'RE IN DANGER FROM THE WHIZ AND NEED SOME HEAVY EQUIPMENT!
IT'LL BE FINE WITH BOSSMAN, I KNOW! HE DOESN'T CARE FOR THE WHIZ ONE BIT, BUT...
35A
I CAN BORROW BOSSMAN'S MACHINES, BUT I DON'T KNOW ANY WORKMEN TO OPERATE THEM!
JUST WAIT!
HELLO, MR. BRUISER? THIS IS MRS. WORMLY! YEAH, FROM THE DAYCARE CENTER, WHERE YOUR SON WAS ATTACKED BY THE WHIZ'S MACHINES TODAY!
CAN YOU AND YOUR MEN HELP US? THE WHIZ'S MACHINES ARE THREATENING US AGAIN!!
I'M ON IT!
WHEN THE WHIZ ATTACKS WOMEN AND CHILDREN, IT'S TIME FOR ACTION!
WHOOSH
BONK
JUST WHEN THE TECHNOWHIZ'S REMOTE-CONTROLLED MACHINES BEGIN THEIR ATTACK ON 13 GEORGE STREET, BOSSMAN'S CREWS SHOW UP...
BOSSMAN CO.
THERE ARE NO SKILLED OPERATORS RUNNING THEM... THAT'S GOING TOO FAR!
35B

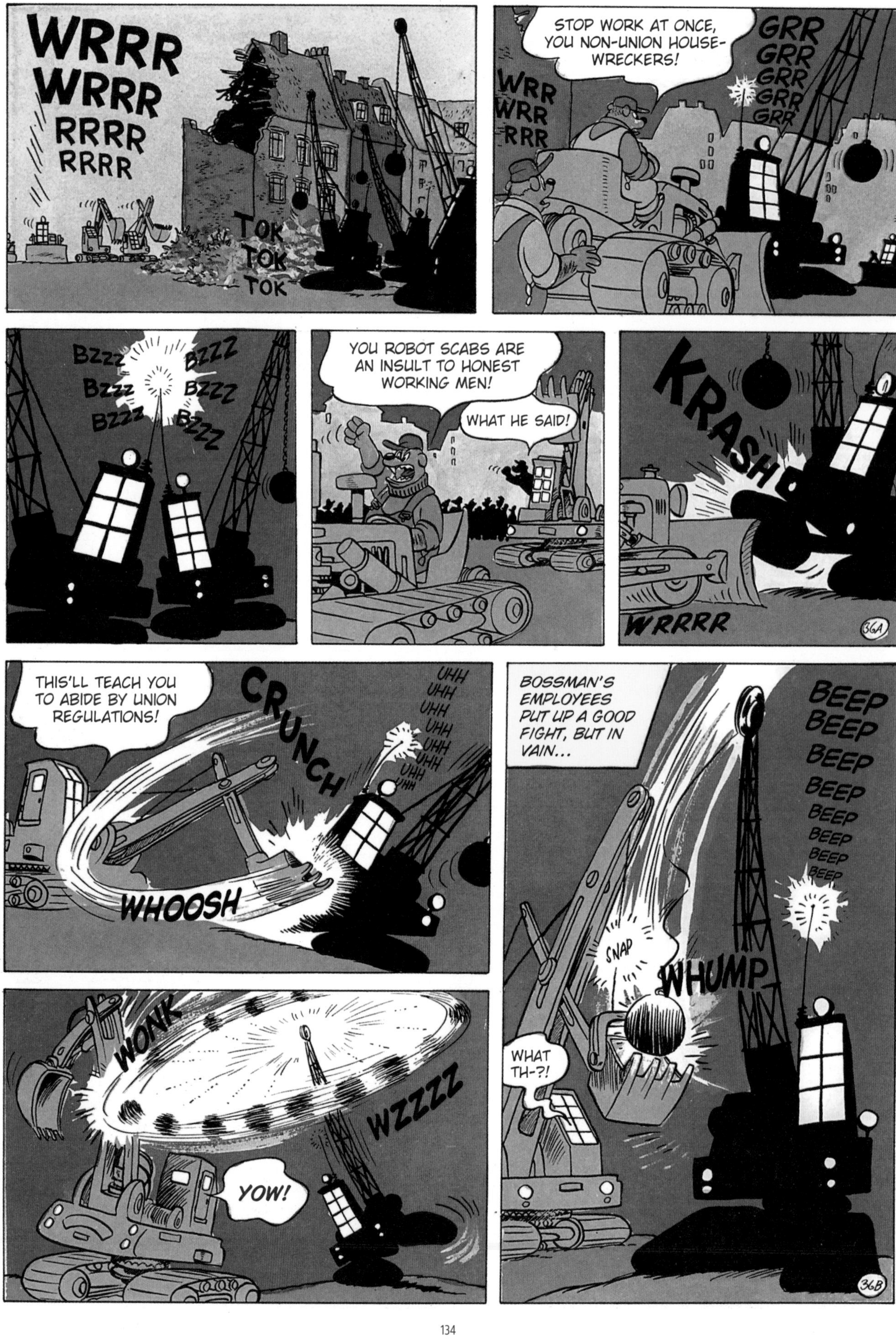
WRRR
WRRR
RRRR
RRRR
TOK
TOK
TOK
STOP WORK AT ONCE, YOU NON-UNION HOUSE-WRECKERS!
GRR
GRR
GRR
GRR
GRR
WRR
WRR
RRR
Bzzz
Bzzz
Bzzz
BZZZ
BZZZ
BZZZ
YOU ROBOT SCABS ARE AN INSULT TO HONEST WORKING MEN!
WHAT HE SAID!
KRASH
WRRRR
36A
THIS'LL TEACH YOU TO ABIDE BY UNION REGULATIONS!
CRUNCH
UHH
UHH
UHH
UHH
UHH
UHH
UHH
WHOOSH
BOSSMAN'S EMPLOYEES PUT UP A GOOD FIGHT, BUT IN VAIN...
BEEP
BEEP
BEEP
BEEP
BEEP
BEEP
BEEP
BEEP
SNAP
WHUMP
WHAT TH-?!
WONK
WZZZZ
YOW!
36B

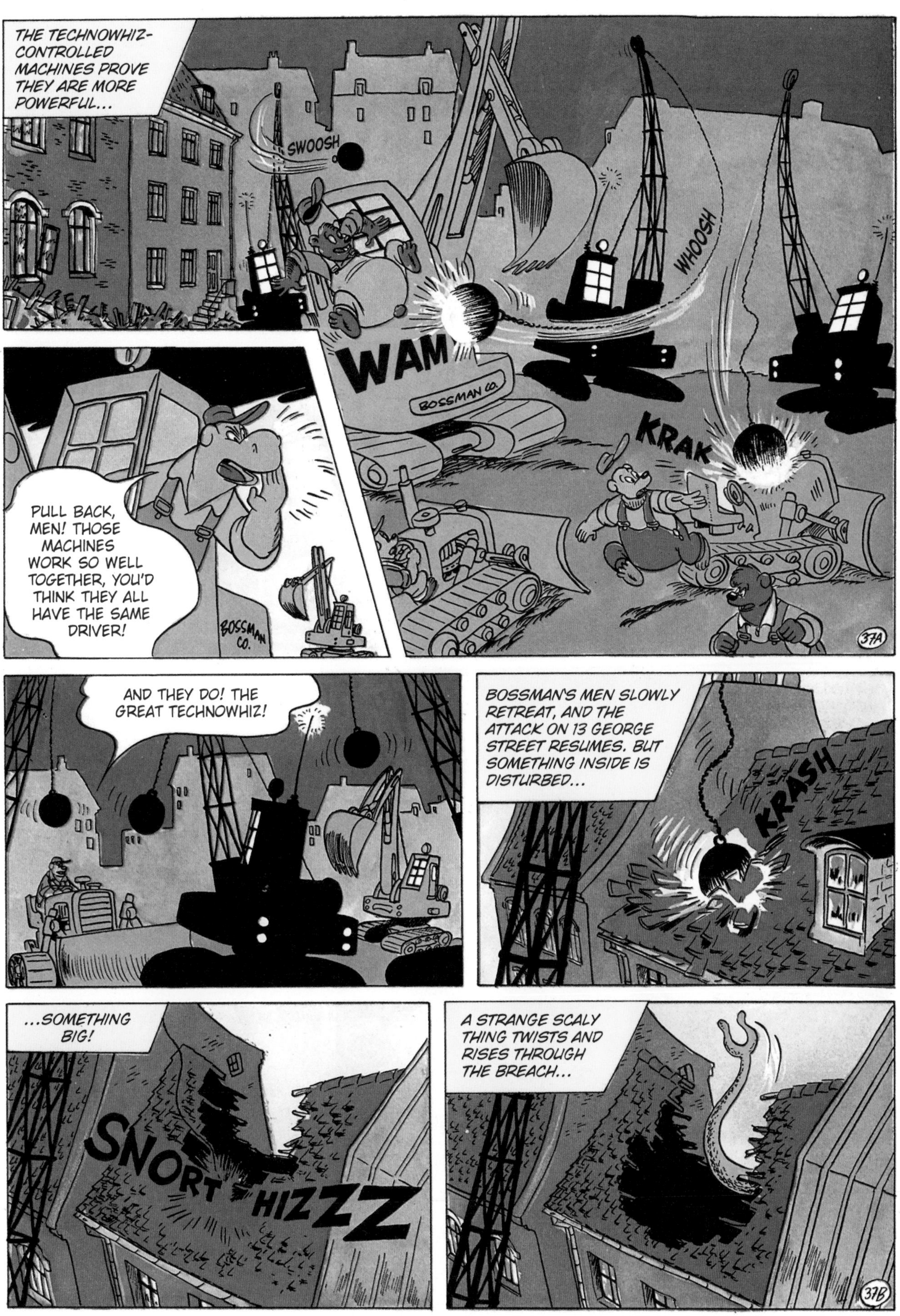
THE TECHNOWHIZ-CONTROLLED MACHINES PROVE THEY ARE MORE POWERFUL...
SWOOSH
WHOOSH
WAM
BOSSMAN CO.
KRAK
PULL BACK, MEN! THOSE MACHINES WORK SO WELL TOGETHER, YOU'D THINK THEY ALL HAVE THE SAME DRIVER!
BOSSMAN CO.
37A
AND THEY DO! THE GREAT TECHNOWHIZ!
BOSSMAN'S MEN SLOWLY RETREAT, AND THE ATTACK ON 13 GEORGE STREET RESUMES. BUT SOMETHING INSIDE IS DISTURBED...
KRASH
...SOMETHING BIG!
SNORT
HIZZZ
A STRANGE SCALY THING TWISTS AND RISES THROUGH THE BREACH...
37B

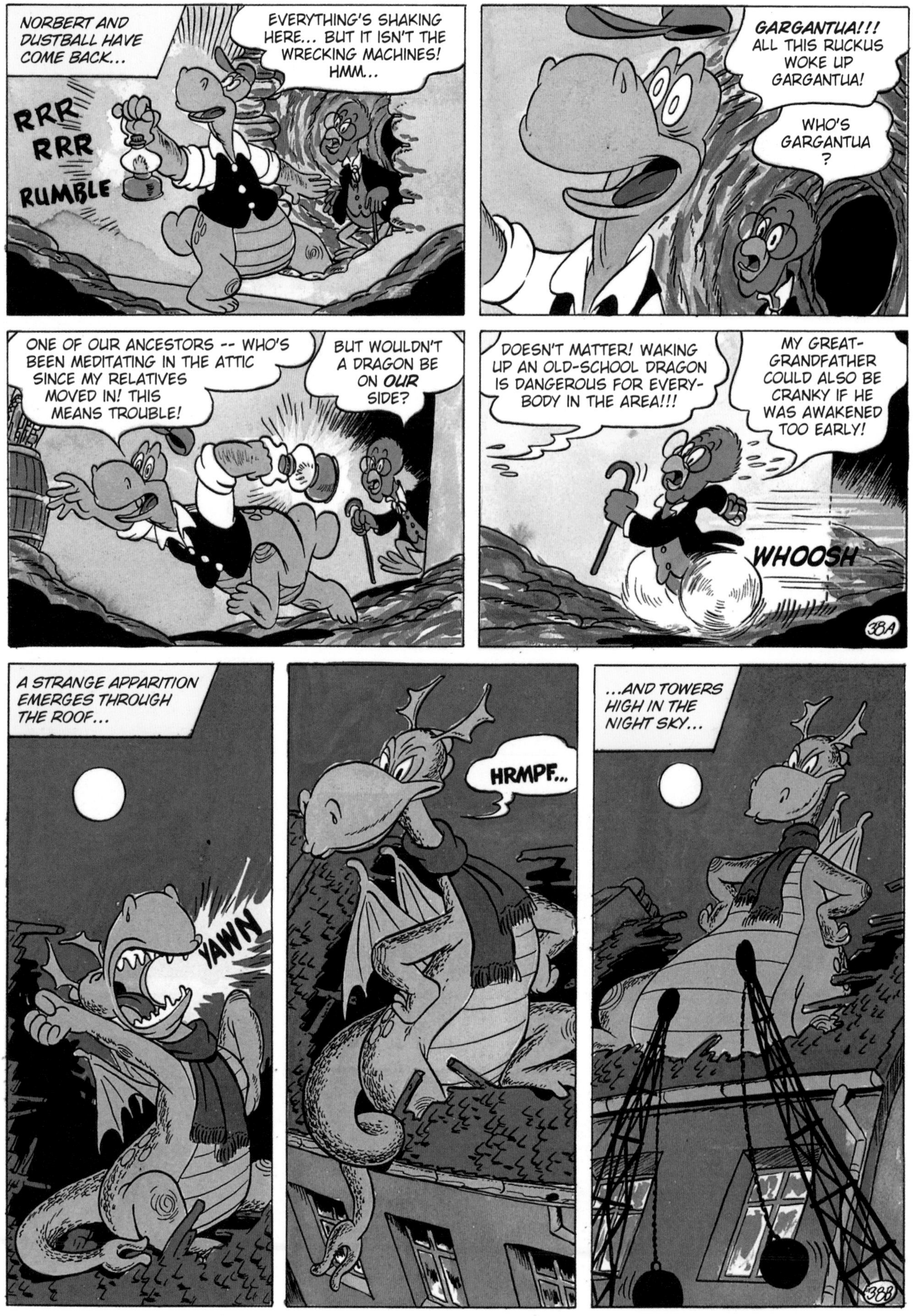

NORBERT AND DUSTBALL HAVE COME BACK...
EVERYTHING'S SHAKING HERE... BUT IT ISN'T THE WRECKING MACHINES! HMM...
RRR RRR RUMBLE
GARGANTUA!!! ALL THIS RUCKUS WOKE UP GARGANTUA!
WHO'S GARGANTUA ?
ONE OF OUR ANCESTORS -- WHO'S BEEN MEDITATING IN THE ATTIC SINCE MY RELATIVES MOVED IN! THIS MEANS TROUBLE!
BUT WOULDN'T A DRAGON BE ON OUR SIDE?
DOESN'T MATTER! WAKING UP AN OLD-SCHOOL DRAGON IS DANGEROUS FOR EVERY-BODY IN THE AREA!!!
MY GREAT-GRANDFATHER COULD ALSO BE CRANKY IF HE WAS AWAKENED TOO EARLY!
WHOOSH
38A
A STRANGE APPARITION EMERGES THROUGH THE ROOF...
YAWN
HRMPF...
...AND TOWERS HIGH IN THE NIGHT SKY...
38B

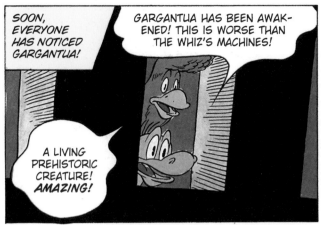

SOON, EVERYONE HAS NOTICED GARGANTUA!

GARGANTUA HAS BEEN AWAKENED! THIS IS WORSE THAN THE WHIZ'S MACHINES!

A LIVING PREHISTORIC CREATURE! *AMAZING!*

A GIANT DRAGON!

UHH... WE'RE CANCELING THE OPERATION!

BOSSMAN C.

EVEN THE SWARMING REPORTERS FALL BACK A LITTLE...

AT LAST! A *REALLY* BIG STORY! AHH!

THIS'LL KEEP THE PAPERS GOING FOR *WEEKS!*

KLIK KLIK

KLIK KLIK

BOSSMAN'S PRIVATE CAB ARRIVES...

THAT TOOK TOO LONG! YOU'RE FIRED, DRIVER!

GASP! PUFF!

SAVE THE MACHINES, MEN!

39A

SIEGEL WANTS TO REASSURE HIS TENANTS, BUT...

MY PROPERTY!!! MY VOTERS!!!

I DON'T HAVE ANY CONTROL OVER THE TECHNO-WHIZ!

HA! HA! SO WHAT YOU'VE BEEN CLAIMING THE WHOLE TIME IS NOW ACTUALLY TRUE!

ZZZZZZZZZZ

T

TIK TIK TIK TIK

TIK TIK TIK TIK TIK

SOMETHING'S HAPPENED THAT'S AFFECTED THE WHIZ!

SNORT! GRUNT!

39B

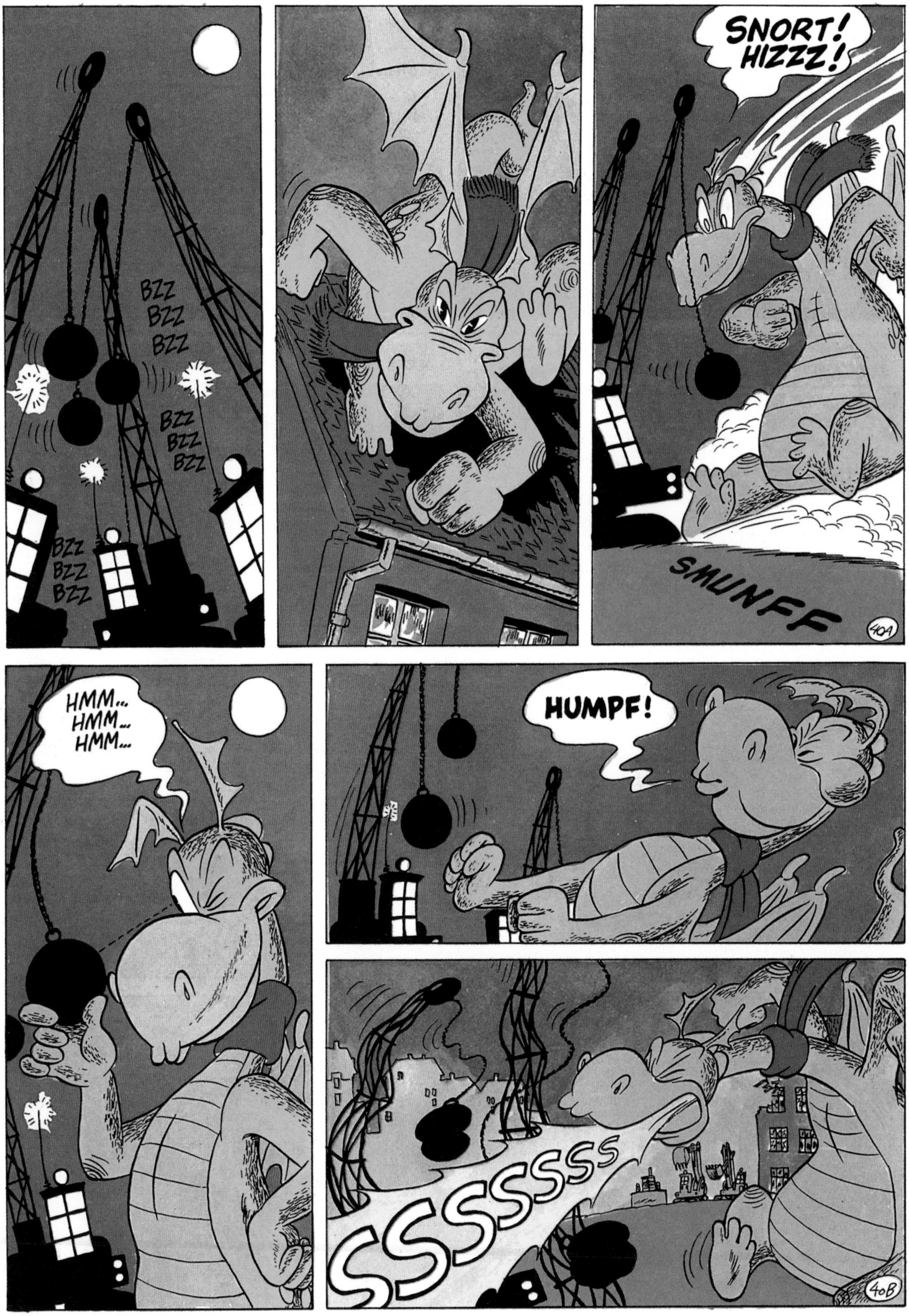
BZZ
BZZ
BZZ
BZZ
BZZ
BZZ
BZZ
BZZ
BZZ
SNORT! HIZZZ!
SMUNFF
40A
HMM... HMM... HMM...
HUMPF!
SSSSSSS
40B

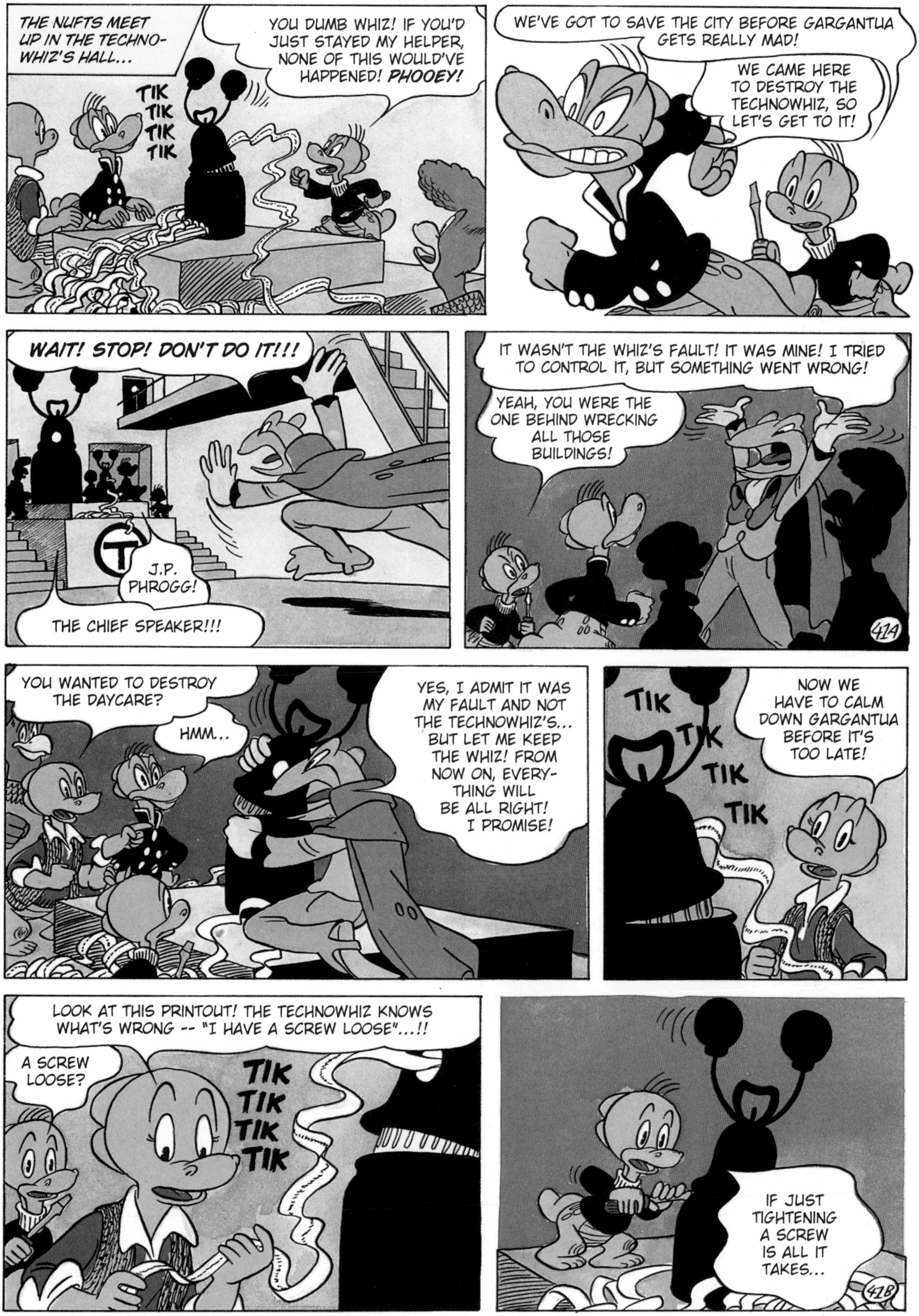

THE NUFTS MEET UP IN THE TECHNO-WHIZ'S HALL...
YOU DUMB WHIZ! IF YOU'D JUST STAYED MY HELPER, NONE OF THIS WOULD'VE HAPPENED! PHOOEY!
TIK TIK TIK TIK
WE'VE GOT TO SAVE THE CITY BEFORE GARGANTUA GETS REALLY MAD!
WE CAME HERE TO DESTROY THE TECHNOWHIZ, SO LET'S GET TO IT!
WAIT! STOP! DON'T DO IT!!!
J.P. PHROGG!
THE CHIEF SPEAKER!!!
IT WASN'T THE WHIZ'S FAULT! IT WAS MINE! I TRIED TO CONTROL IT, BUT SOMETHING WENT WRONG!
YEAH, YOU WERE THE ONE BEHIND WRECKING ALL THOSE BUILDINGS!
42A
YOU WANTED TO DESTROY THE DAYCARE?
HMM...
YES, I ADMIT IT WAS MY FAULT AND NOT THE TECHNOWHIZ'S... BUT LET ME KEEP THE WHIZ! FROM NOW ON, EVERY-THING WILL BE ALL RIGHT! I PROMISE!
TIK TIK TIK TIK
NOW WE HAVE TO CALM DOWN GARGANTUA BEFORE IT'S TOO LATE!
LOOK AT THIS PRINTOUT! THE TECHNOWHIZ KNOWS WHAT'S WRONG -- "I HAVE A SCREW LOOSE"...!!
A SCREW LOOSE?
TIK TIK TIK TIK
IF JUST TIGHTENING A SCREW IS ALL IT TAKES...
42B

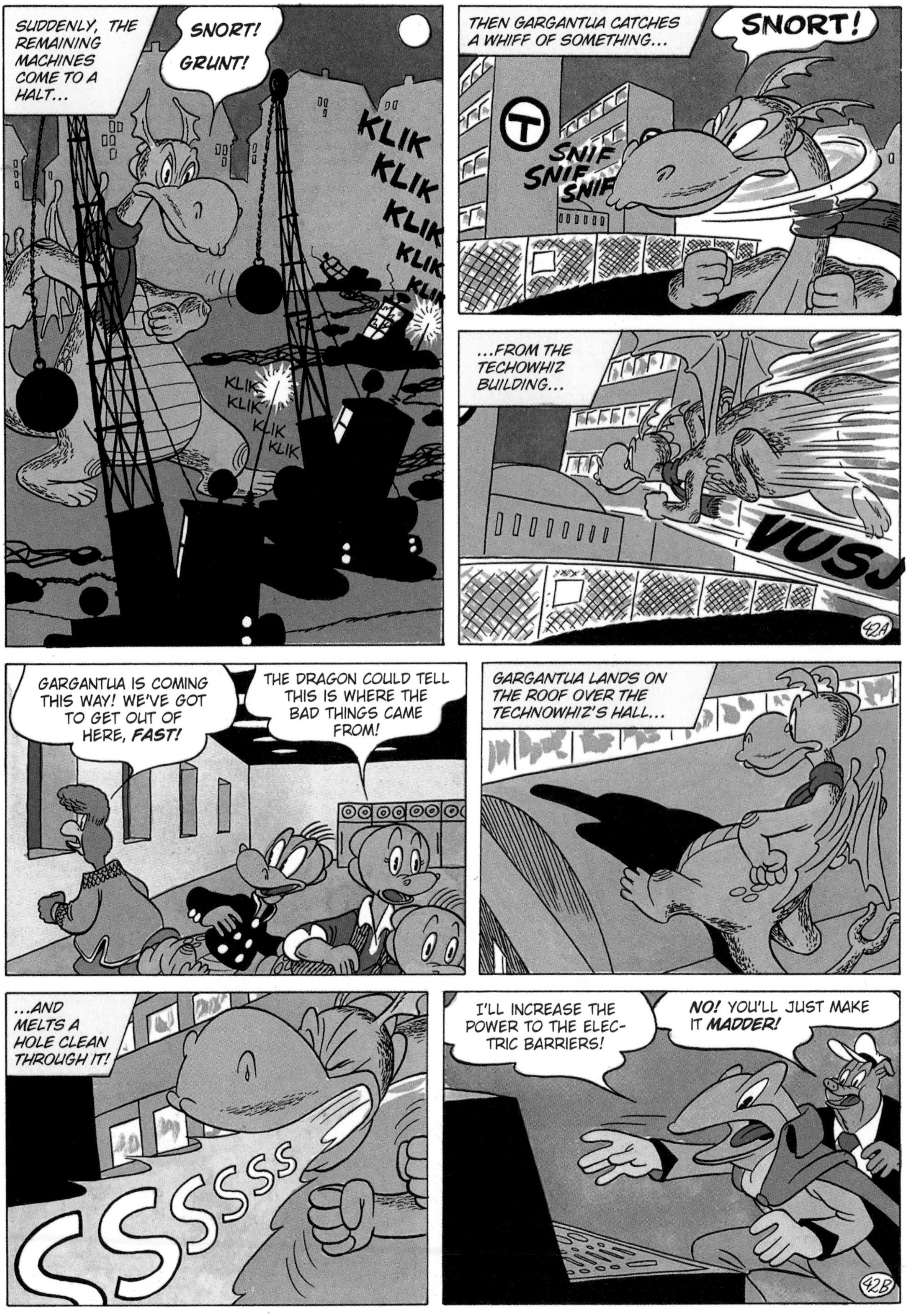
SUDDENLY, THE REMAINING MACHINES COME TO A HALT...
SNORT!
GRUNT!
KLIK KLIK KLIK KLIK KLIK
KLIK KLIK KLIK KLIK
THEN GARGANTUA CATCHES A WHIFF OF SOMETHING...
SNORT!
SNIF SNIF SNIF
...FROM THE TECHOWHIZ BUILDING...
VUSJ
42A
GARGANTUA IS COMING THIS WAY! WE'VE GOT TO GET OUT OF HERE, *FAST!*
THE DRAGON COULD TELL THIS IS WHERE THE BAD THINGS CAME FROM!
GARGANTUA LANDS ON THE ROOF OVER THE TECHNOWHIZ'S HALL...
...AND MELTS A HOLE CLEAN THROUGH IT!
CSSSSSS
I'LL INCREASE THE POWER TO THE ELEC-TRIC BARRIERS!
NO! YOU'LL JUST MAKE IT *MADDER!*
42B

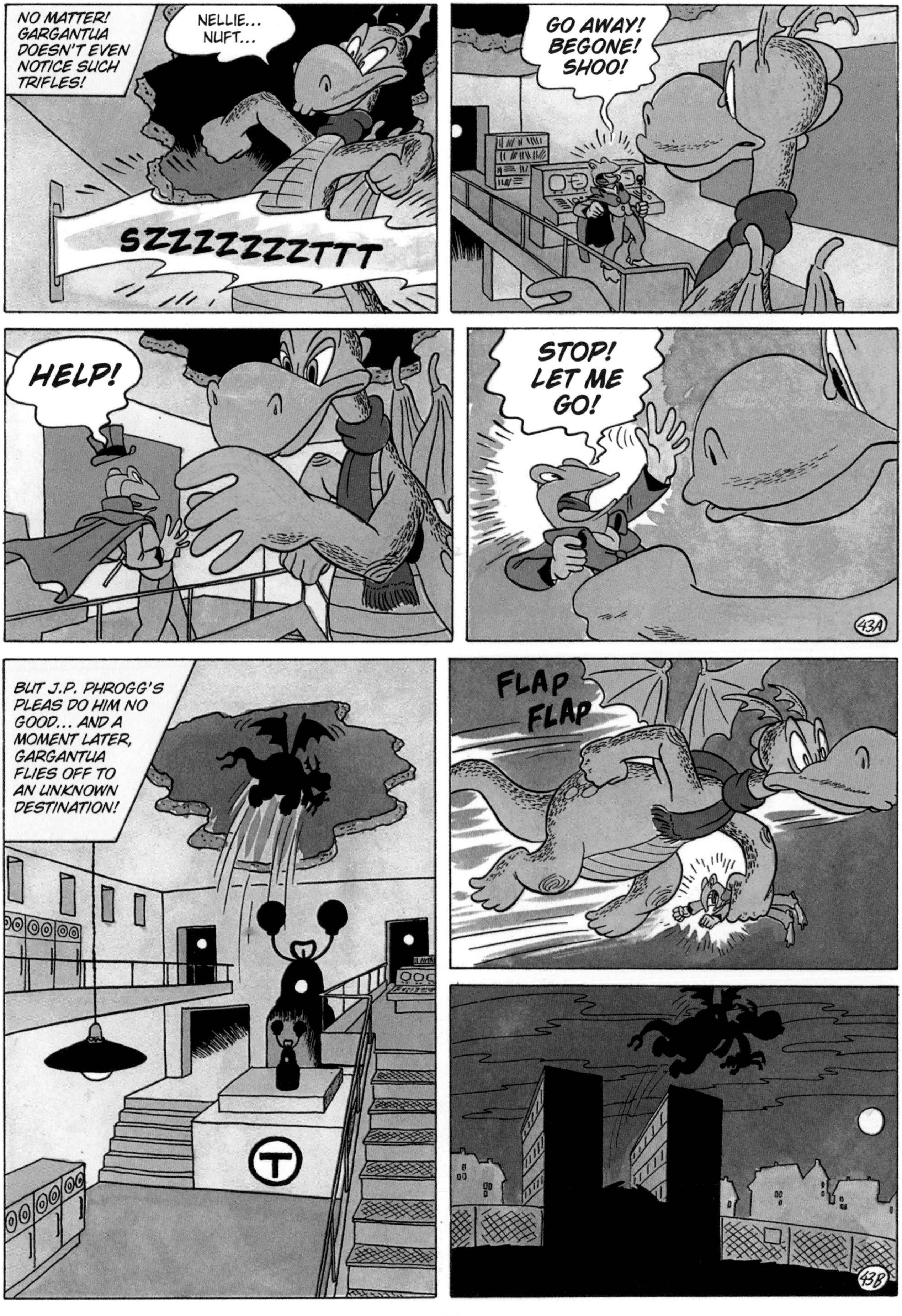
NO MATTER! GARGANTUA DOESN'T EVEN NOTICE SUCH TRIFLES!
NELLIE... NUFT...
SZZZZZZZZTTT
GO AWAY! BEGONE! SHOO!
HELP!
STOP! LET ME GO!
43A
BUT J.P. PHROGG'S PLEAS DO HIM NO GOOD... AND A MOMENT LATER, GARGANTUA FLIES OFF TO AN UNKNOWN DESTINATION!
FLAP FLAP
43B

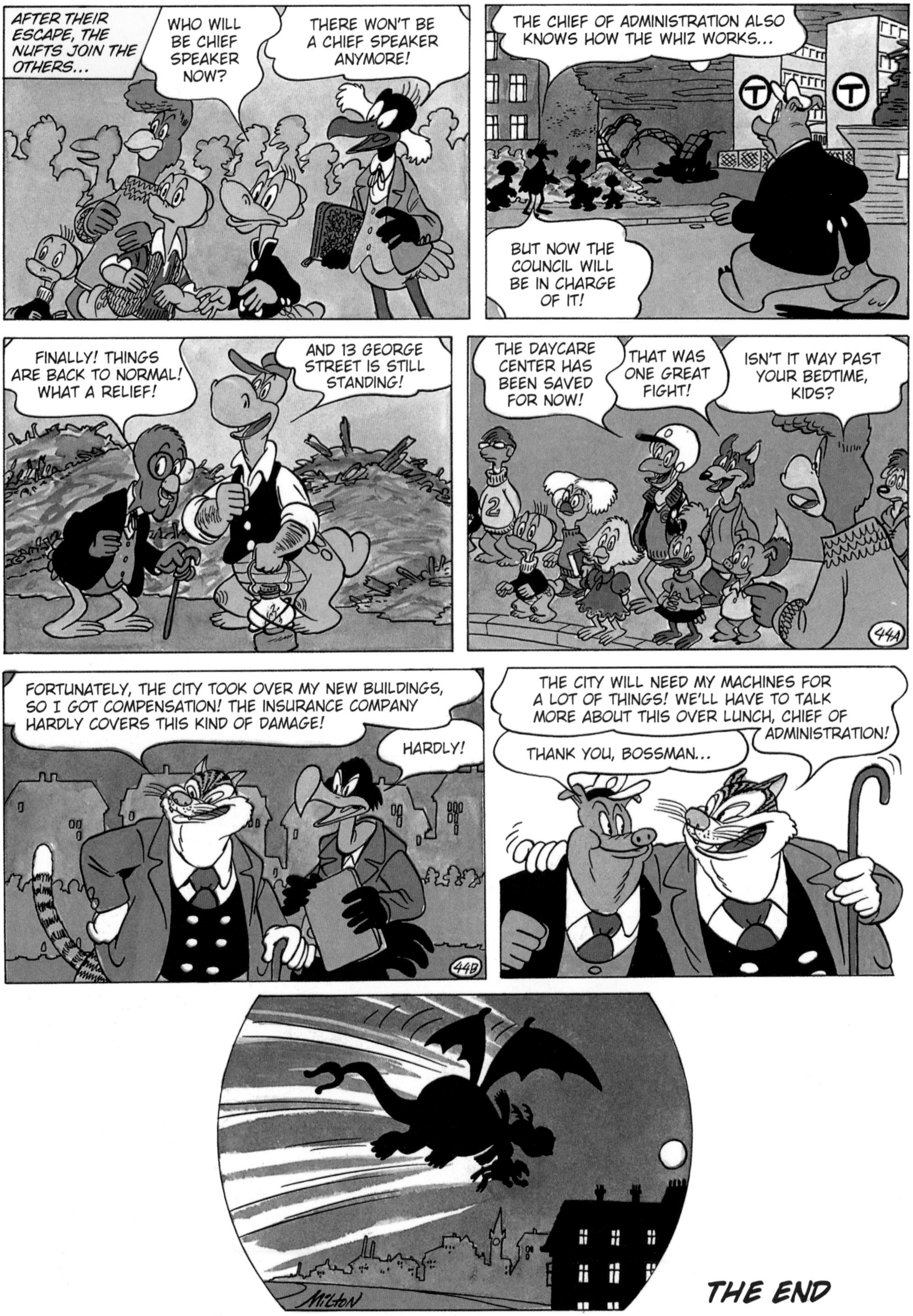
AFTER THEIR ESCAPE, THE NUFTS JOIN THE OTHERS...
WHO WILL BE CHIEF SPEAKER NOW?
THERE WON'T BE A CHIEF SPEAKER ANYMORE!
THE CHIEF OF ADMINISTRATION ALSO KNOWS HOW THE WHIZ WORKS...
BUT NOW THE COUNCIL WILL BE IN CHARGE OF IT!
FINALLY! THINGS ARE BACK TO NORMAL! WHAT A RELIEF!
AND 13 GEORGE STREET IS STILL STANDING!
THE DAYCARE CENTER HAS BEEN SAVED FOR NOW!
THAT WAS ONE GREAT FIGHT!
ISN'T IT WAY PAST YOUR BEDTIME, KIDS?
44A
FORTUNATELY, THE CITY TOOK OVER MY NEW BUILDINGS, SO I GOT COMPENSATION! THE INSURANCE COMPANY HARDLY COVERS THIS KIND OF DAMAGE!
HARDLY!
44B
THE CITY WILL NEED MY MACHINES FOR A LOT OF THINGS! WE'LL HAVE TO TALK MORE ABOUT THIS OVER LUNCH, CHIEF OF ADMINISTRATION!
THANK YOU, BOSSMAN...
MILTON

THE END

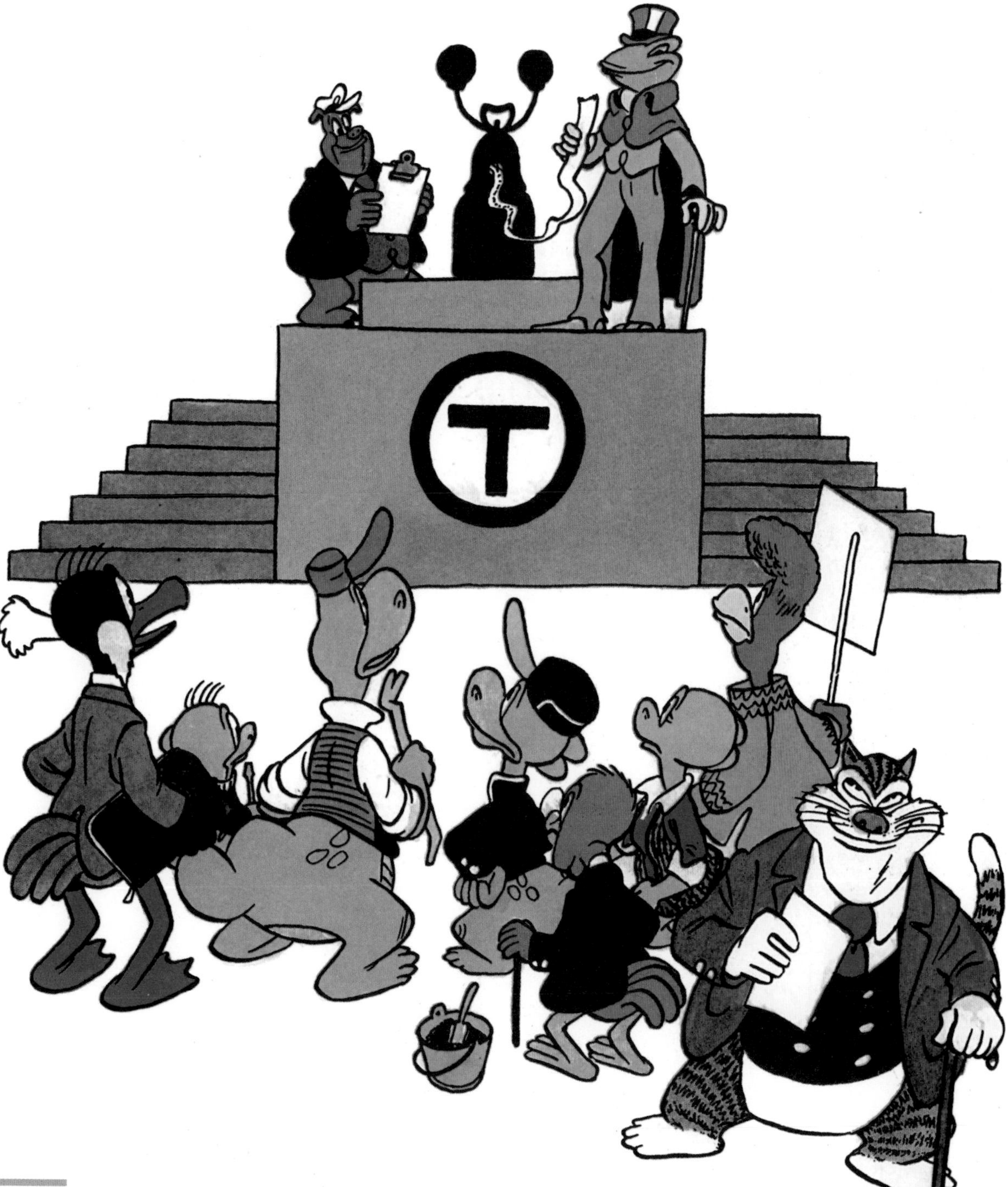

Freddy Milton's frontispiece for the Danish edition of *The Great Technowhiz.*

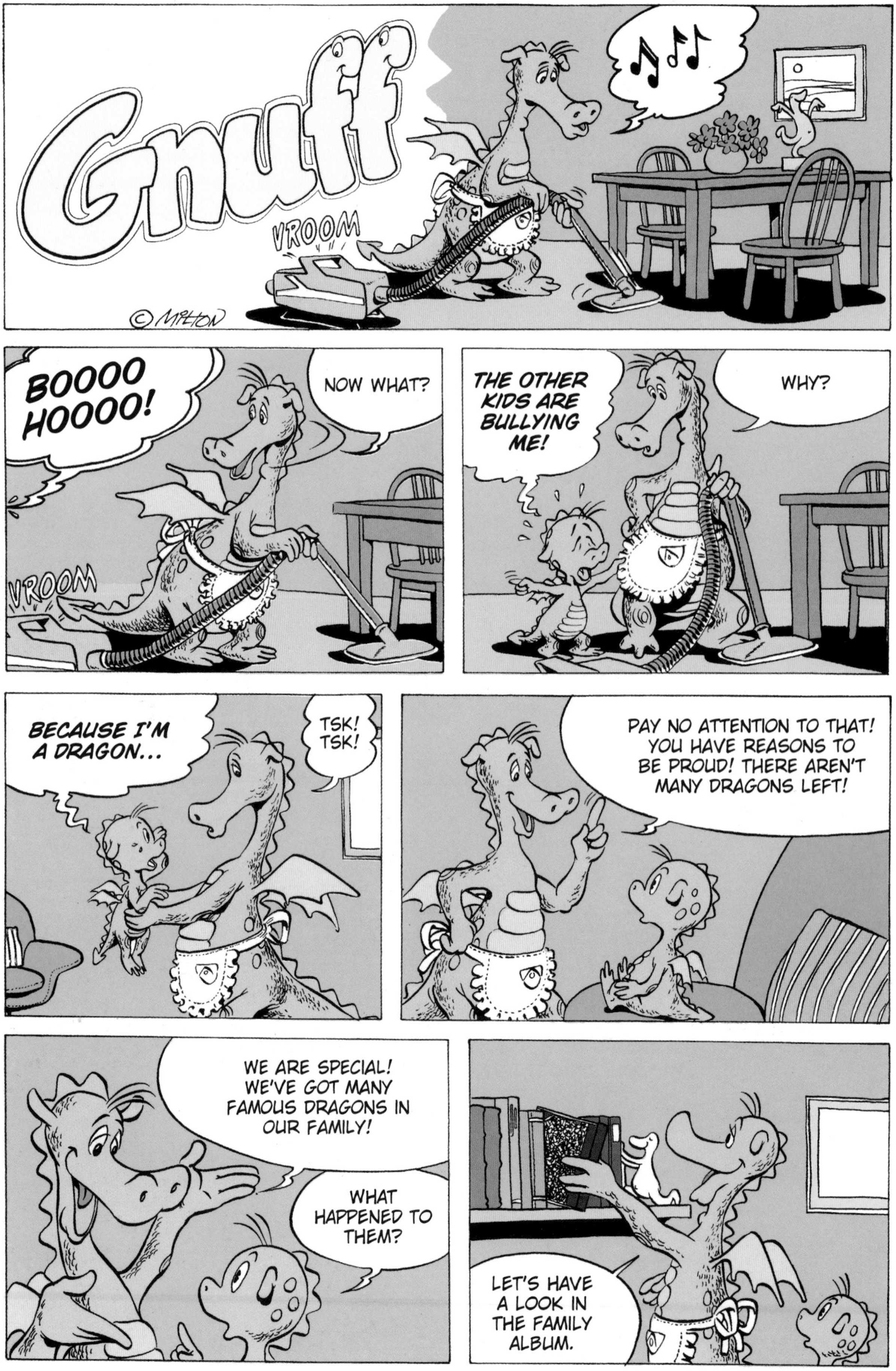
Gnuff
VROOM
© MILTON
BOOOO HOOOO!
VROOM
NOW WHAT?
THE OTHER KIDS ARE BULLYING ME!
WHY?
BECAUSE I'M A DRAGON...
TSK! TSK!
PAY NO ATTENTION TO THAT! YOU HAVE REASONS TO BE PROUD! THERE AREN'T MANY DRAGONS LEFT!
WE ARE SPECIAL! WE'VE GOT MANY FAMOUS DRAGONS IN OUR FAMILY!
WHAT HAPPENED TO THEM?
LET'S HAVE A LOOK IN THE FAMILY ALBUM.

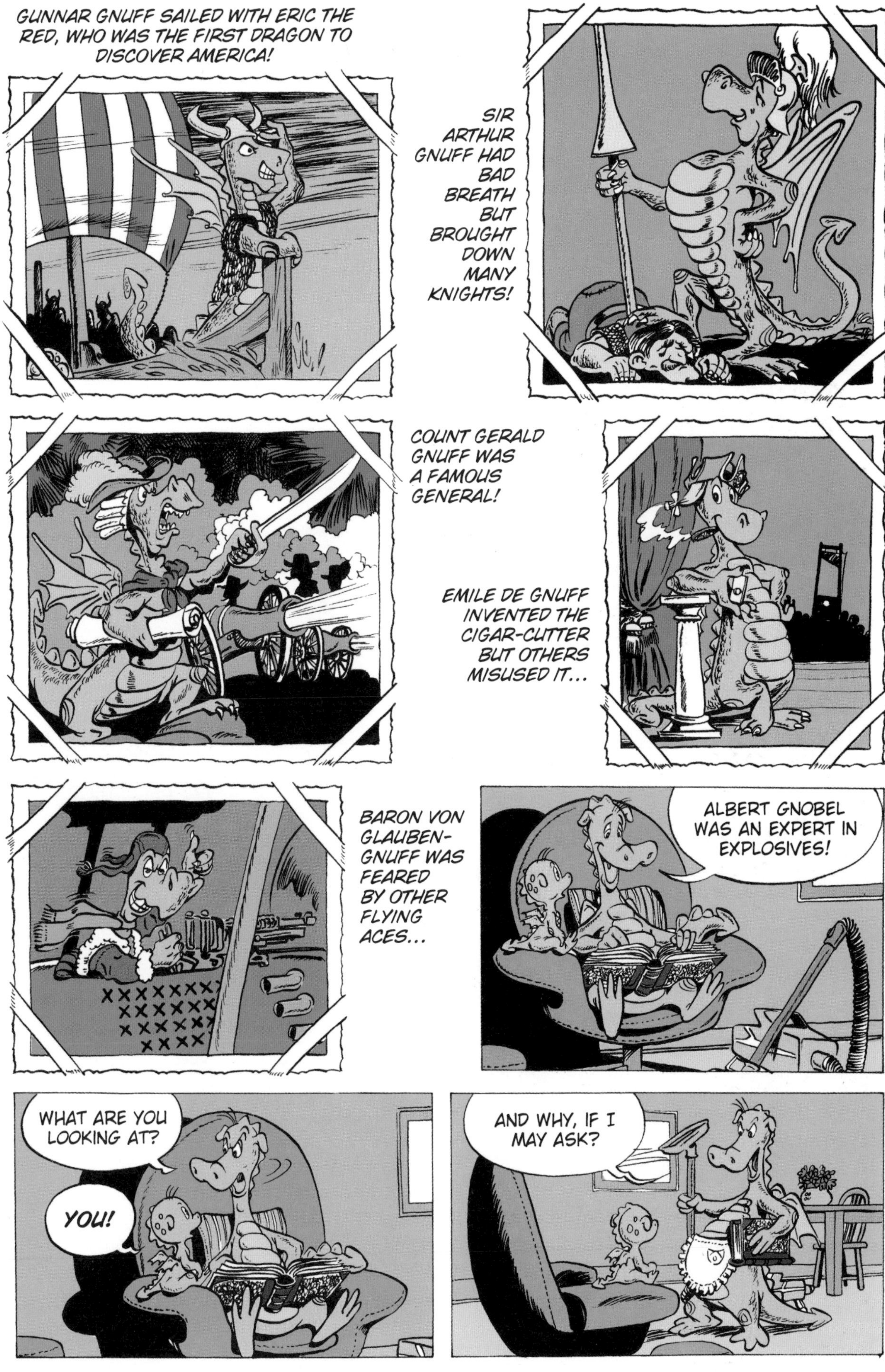
GUNNAR GNUFF SAILED WITH ERIC THE RED, WHO WAS THE FIRST DRAGON TO DISCOVER AMERICA!
SIR ARTHUR GNUFF HAD BAD BREATH BUT BROUGHT DOWN MANY KNIGHTS!
COUNT GERALD GNUFF WAS A FAMOUS GENERAL!
EMILE DE GNUFF INVENTED THE CIGAR-CUTTER BUT OTHERS MISUSED IT...
BARON VON GLAUBEN-GNUFF WAS FEARED BY OTHER FLYING ACES...
ALBERT GNOBEL WAS AN EXPERT IN EXPLOSIVES!
WHAT ARE YOU LOOKING AT?
YOU!
AND WHY, IF I MAY ASK?

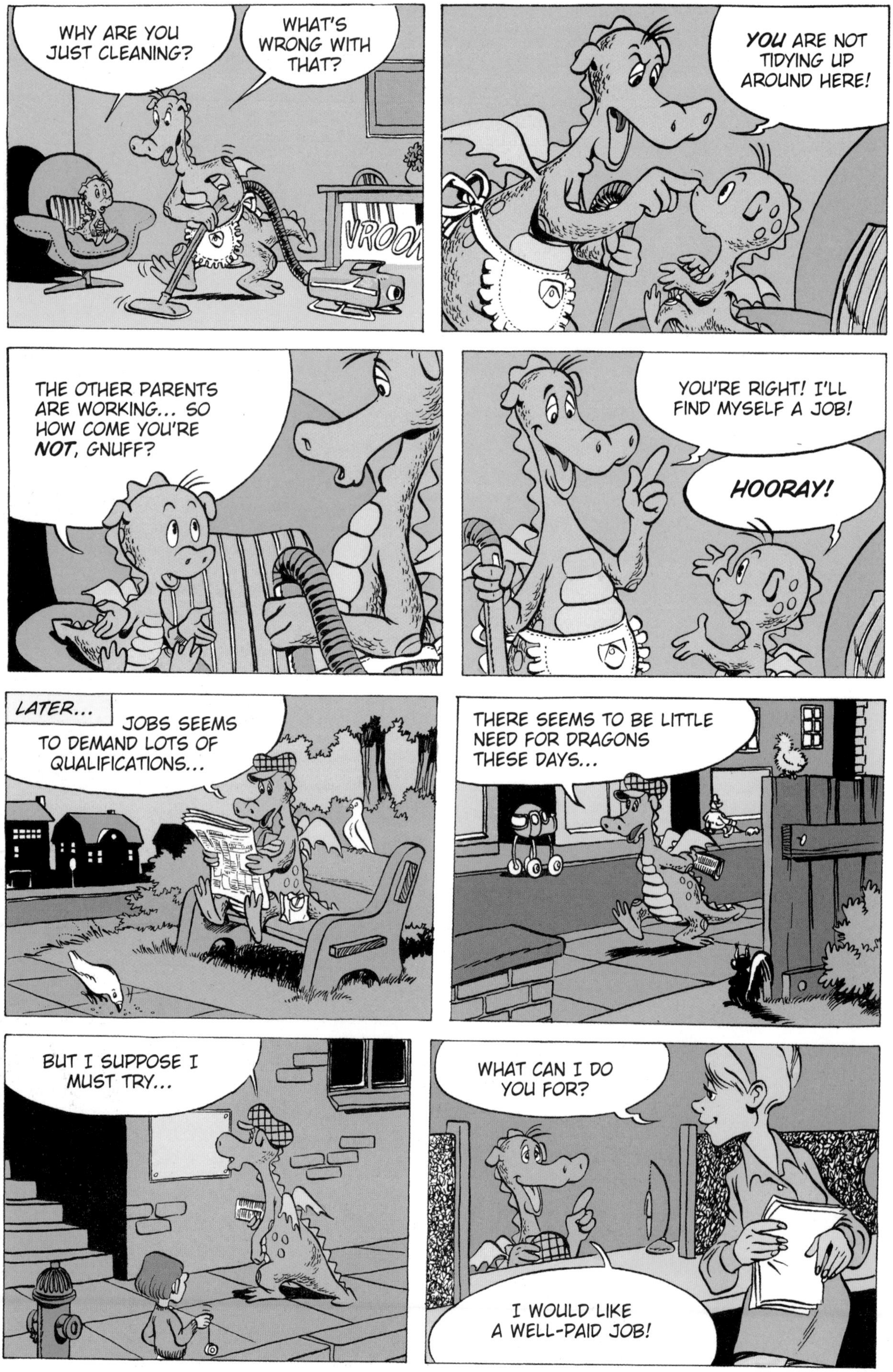
WHY ARE YOU JUST CLEANING?
WHAT'S WRONG WITH THAT?
VROOM
YOU ARE NOT TIDYING UP AROUND HERE!
THE OTHER PARENTS ARE WORKING... SO HOW COME YOU'RE *NOT*, GNUFF?
YOU'RE RIGHT! I'LL FIND MYSELF A JOB!
HOORAY!
LATER...
JOBS SEEMS TO DEMAND LOTS OF QUALIFICATIONS...
THERE SEEMS TO BE LITTLE NEED FOR DRAGONS THESE DAYS...
BUT I SUPPOSE I MUST TRY...
WHAT CAN I DO YOU FOR?
I WOULD LIKE A WELL-PAID JOB!

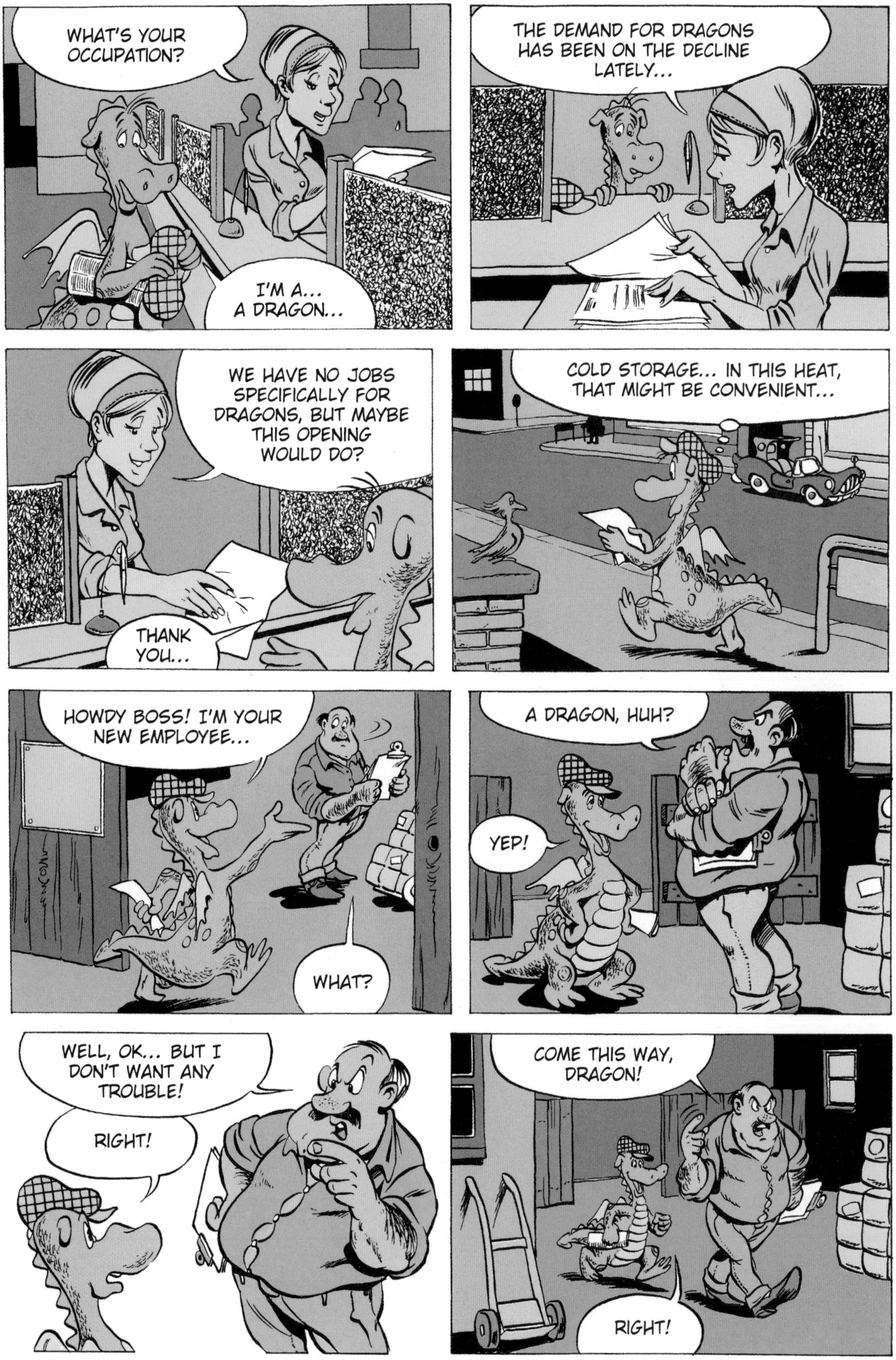

WHAT'S YOUR OCCUPATION?
I'M A... A DRAGON...
THE DEMAND FOR DRAGONS HAS BEEN ON THE DECLINE LATELY...
WE HAVE NO JOBS SPECIFICALLY FOR DRAGONS, BUT MAYBE THIS OPENING WOULD DO?
THANK YOU...
COLD STORAGE... IN THIS HEAT, THAT MIGHT BE CONVENIENT...
HOWDY BOSS! I'M YOUR NEW EMPLOYEE...
WHAT?
A DRAGON, HUH?
YEP!
WELL, OK... BUT I DON'T WANT ANY TROUBLE!
RIGHT!
COME THIS WAY, DRAGON!
RIGHT!

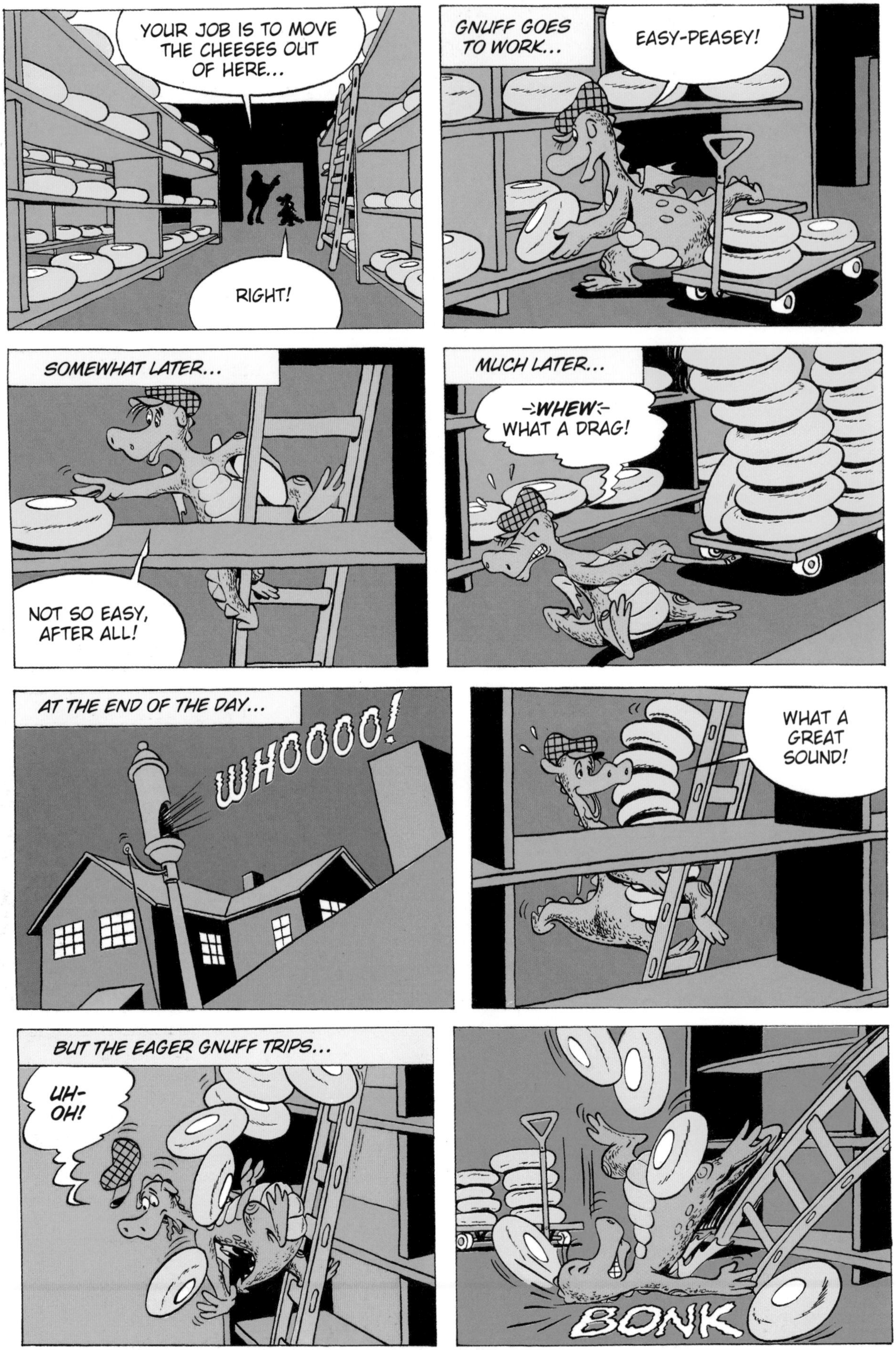
YOUR JOB IS TO MOVE THE CHEESES OUT OF HERE...
RIGHT!
GNUFF GOES TO WORK...
EASY-PEASEY!
SOMEWHAT LATER...
NOT SO EASY, AFTER ALL!
MUCH LATER...
WHEW WHAT A DRAG!
AT THE END OF THE DAY...
WHOOOO!
WHAT A GREAT SOUND!
BUT THE EAGER GNUFF TRIPS...
UH-OH!
BONK

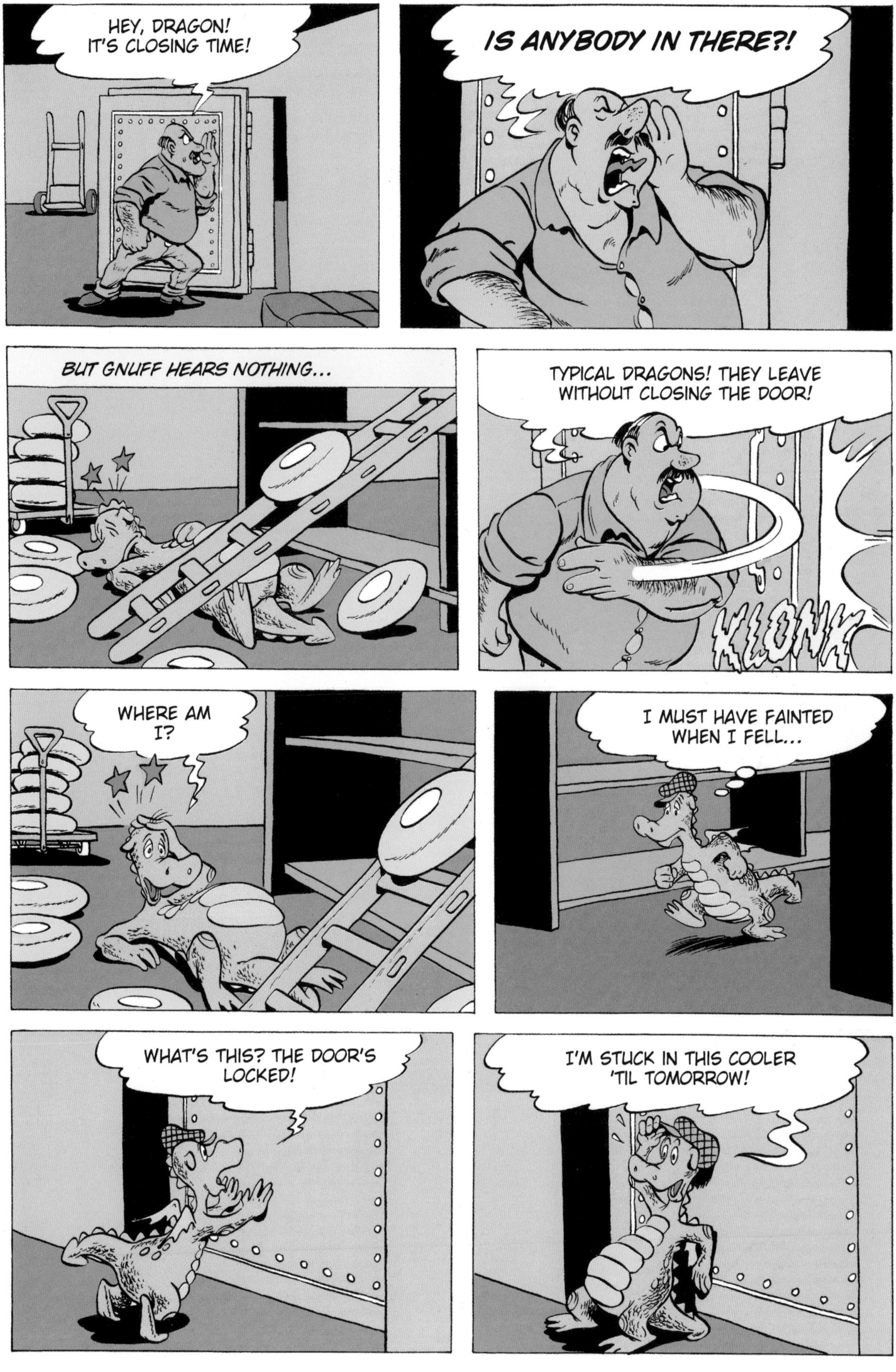
HEY, DRAGON! IT'S CLOSING TIME!
IS ANYBODY IN THERE?!
BUT GNUFF HEARS NOTHING...
TYPICAL DRAGONS! THEY LEAVE WITHOUT CLOSING THE DOOR!
KLONK
WHERE AM I?
I MUST HAVE FAINTED WHEN I FELL...
WHAT'S THIS? THE DOOR'S LOCKED!
I'M STUCK IN THIS COOLER 'TIL TOMORROW!

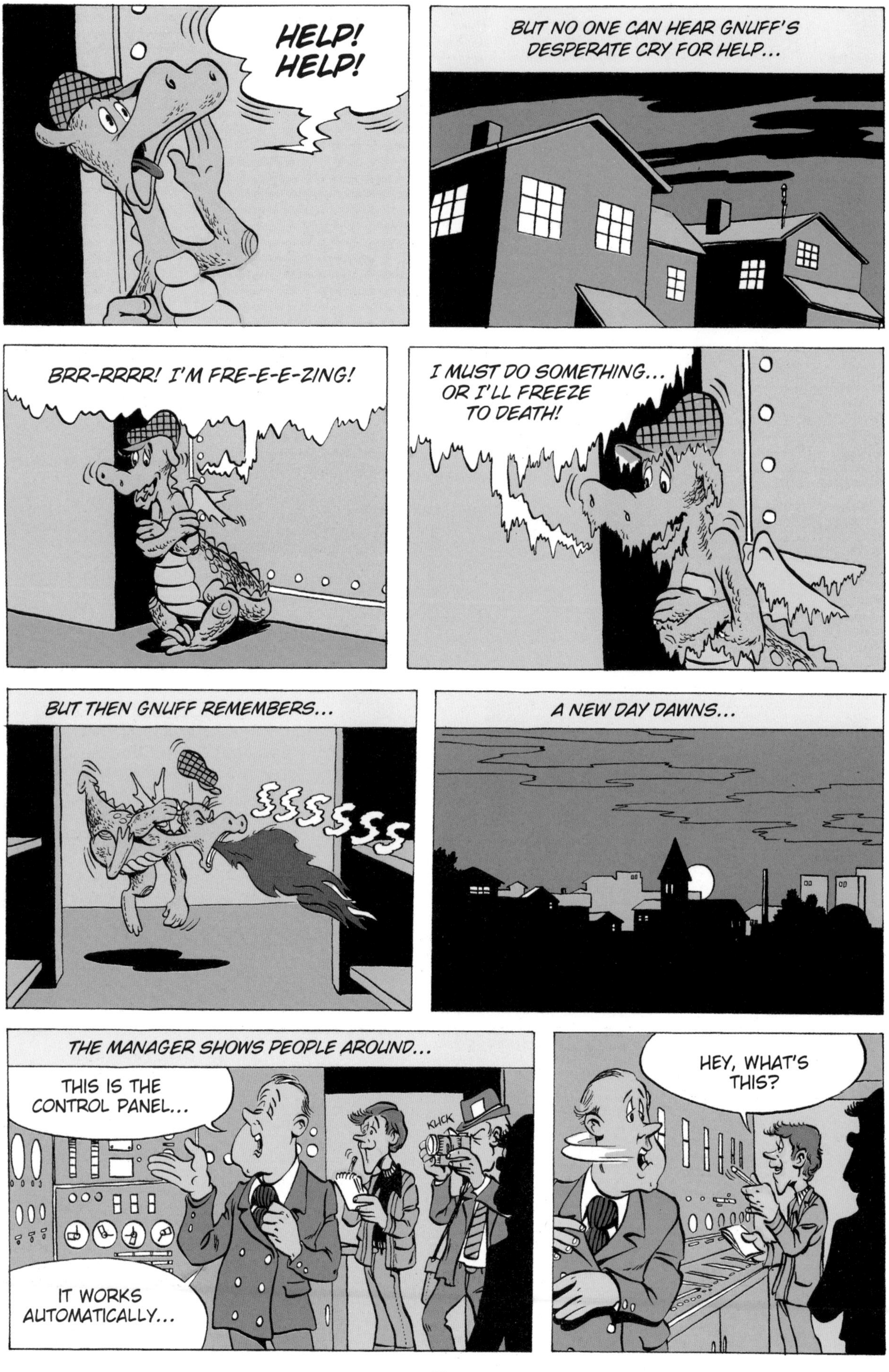
HELP! HELP!
BUT NO ONE CAN HEAR GNUFF'S DESPERATE CRY FOR HELP...
BRR-RRRR! I'M FRE-E-E-ZING!
I MUST DO SOMETHING... OR I'LL FREEZE TO DEATH!
BUT THEN GNUFF REMEMBERS...
SSSSSS
A NEW DAY DAWNS...
THE MANAGER SHOWS PEOPLE AROUND...
THIS IS THE CONTROL PANEL...
KLICK
IT WORKS AUTOMATICALLY...
HEY, WHAT'S THIS?

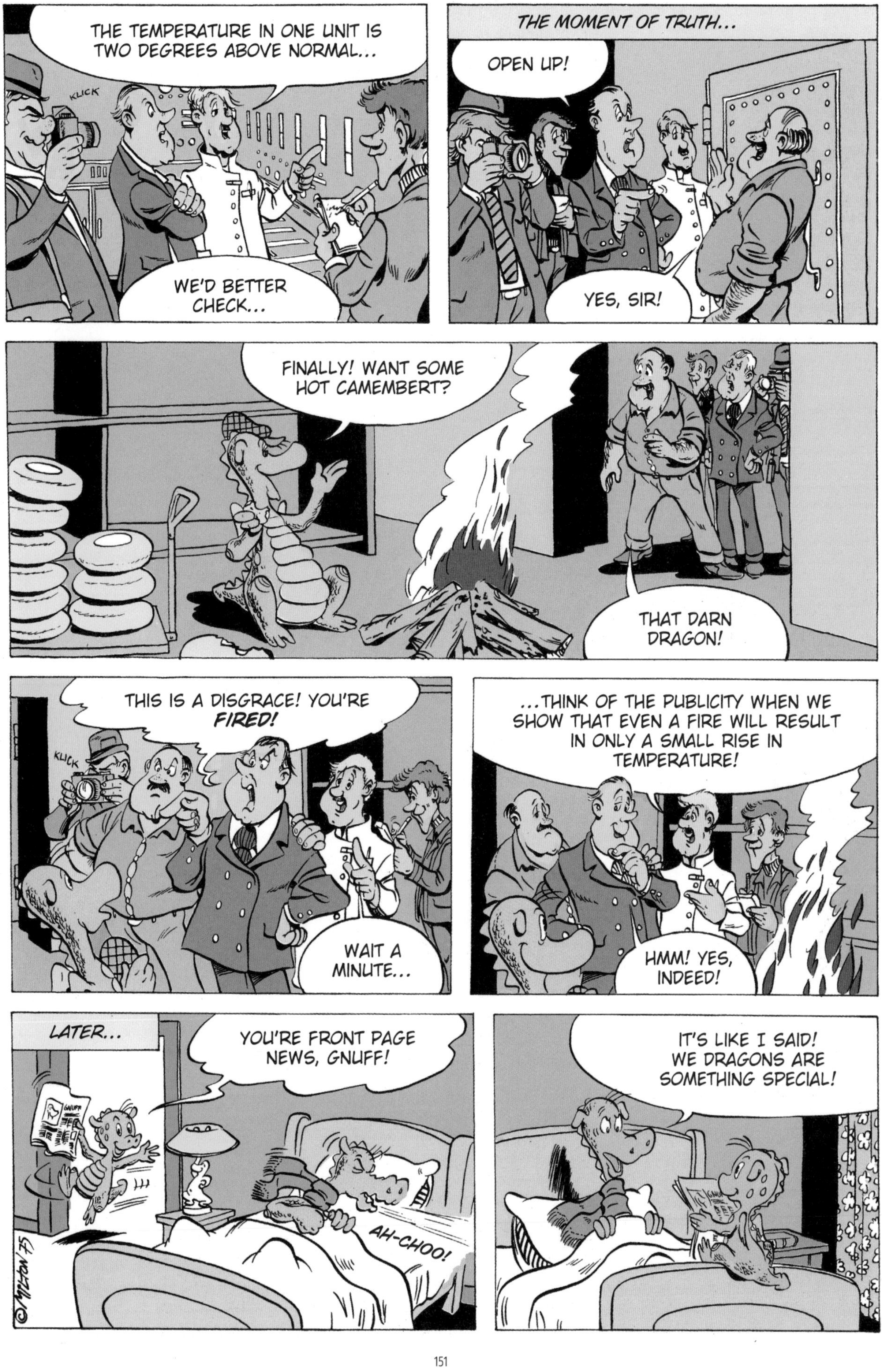
THE TEMPERATURE IN ONE UNIT IS TWO DEGREES ABOVE NORMAL...
KLICK
WE'D BETTER CHECK...
THE MOMENT OF TRUTH...
OPEN UP!
YES, SIR!
FINALLY! WANT SOME HOT CAMEMBERT?
THAT DARN DRAGON!
THIS IS A DISGRACE! YOU'RE ***FIRED!***
KLICK
WAIT A MINUTE...
...THINK OF THE PUBLICITY WHEN WE SHOW THAT EVEN A FIRE WILL RESULT IN ONLY A SMALL RISE IN TEMPERATURE!
HMM! YES, INDEED!
LATER...
YOU'RE FRONT PAGE NEWS, GNUFF!
AH-CHOO!
IT'S LIKE I SAID! WE DRAGONS ARE SOMETHING SPECIAL!

Story Notes

Freddy Milton

The Nufts Move In

"The Nufts Move In" was not the first story I wrote starring the Nufts, but it's the introductory episode — the "origin story," if you will. In Denmark, it was serialized in color in the *Woody Woodpecker* comic, and in America, it was serialized in black-and-white in the much-missed funny-animal comic book, *Critters*. The late great Kim Thompson of Fantagraphics, the editor of *Critters*, gave me the chance to be published in the United States, and he also translated this first installment.

"The Nufts Move In" tells the story of how the dragon family moved from the country to live in the city and what they encountered when they got there.

There are some characters in my stories that I simply cannot do without. I find a lot of humor and drama (and humorous drama) in local political shenanigans. In the Woody Woodpecker series, I had Wally Walrus play the part of the mayor of Peckburg. In *Nuft*, we have city chairman Siegel. In *Nuft*, there are many times when competing interests clash, and Siegel is often torn between one side and the other.

Then there is Bossman, the city's cagiest cat. He's a slick operator who knows the ins and outs of City Hall. He usually gets his way at first, but his big plans always seem to blow up in his face. I get a kick out of imagining how his ventures will eventually backfire.

Nuft's city is well known to me. When I moved to Copenhagen, there was a grocer on the ground floor of my building, and, in my fourth-floor apartment, I had to endure the noise from the compressors in the basement keeping his walk-in refrigerator cool 24 hours a day.

The man on the second floor was a sailor who was seldom home. The man on the third floor was almost deaf. So I had to wage a lone battle to get proper sound insulation for that damned compressor!

That the badger was from Germany was Kim's idea. Also, the doctor has a German accent. I guess it goes back to the idea that psychiatric doctors were regarded as Freudian scholars. There is no such reference in the original text, but I approved it for the English translation.

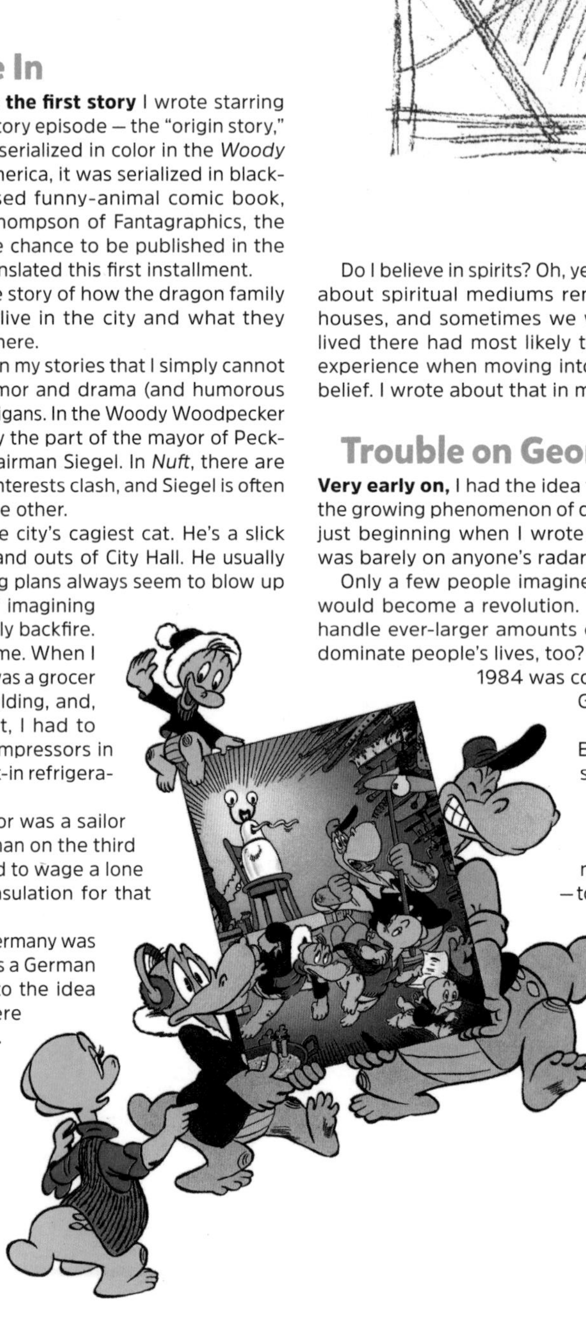

THIS PAGE AND NEXT: Some of Freddy Milton's sketches, layouts, and spot illustrations.

Do I believe in spirits? Oh, yes, indeed! I watched a long series about spiritual mediums removing ghosts from possessed houses, and sometimes we were told that people who had lived there had most likely turned into ghosts. My personal experience when moving into my own house reinforced that belief. I wrote about that in my autobiography.

Trouble on George Street

Very early on, I had the idea that this should be a story about the growing phenomenon of digital technology, which was only just beginning when I wrote this story in 1980. The internet was barely on anyone's radar, let alone smart phones.

Only a few people imagined that the digital breakthrough would become a revolution. We knew that computers could handle ever-larger amounts of data, but could they come to dominate people's lives, too?

1984 was coming closer, but would it be like George Orwell's *1984*?

The look of my version of Big Brother was based on a redesigned Danish vacuum cleaner called Nilfisk. We'd had one in my childhood home, and I combined its design with a calculator—a nice symbolic addition, I thought—to create a serious menace despite its comical appearance. Today, we would say the Technowhiz is a form of artificial intelligence. It was easy for me to whip up science fiction themes. I had read hundreds of science fiction novels when I was young.

The Great Technowhiz

"The Great Technowhiz" is the second part of "Trouble on George Street," and it strikes me now how foresighted I was back then. In those days, it was not at all obvious what the full scope of the digital revolution would be. Nicky's helper here represents the transition from analog methods to a speedy digital technology that can solve all problems, not the least of which is the difficulty of storing all the old paper records at city hall.

One thing I predicted that has not come true is a credit card programmed to prevent unauthorized purchase of alcohol or other restricted items. But that may yet come someday...

These stories are two of my most ambitious, in that they also make references that are quite adult. Yes, these are fairy tales and parables, as are all good funny-animal stories, and there may be bits that not all kids will understand. But maybe some will.

Gnuff

My first Nuft story appeared in the twelfth issue of my fanzine *Sejd*. It was was an 8-pager. We include it in this volume as a bonus, even though the style is a bit different than my later, more polished design. We also decided to keep the "Gnuff" name for this story, to make it more authentic to the original, but I couldn't help myself, and I just had to color it.

Dragons appealed to me, and I was inspired by a design from Claus Deleuran, a talented Danish comics and satirical artist.

The other characters in the story are humans. It didn't bother me to have a dragon living among humans, but I admit it was a bit strange. In this story, I had Nuft demonstrate a classic dragon attribute—breathing fire—for the first and last time.

Some years passed, and I found myself writing and drawing the adventures of Woody Woodpecker. I approached my Danish publisher with the idea that we try an original series, and, naturally, Nuft came to mind.

I redesigned Nuft and Nicky and added Nellie and Norbert to the family to add variety to the kind of stories I wanted to tell. The dragons in Nuft's world are a bit ashamed of their wings, and they normally hide them. Also, Nuft abandoned his fire-breathing ability for good. Fire-breathing appears only once more in the Nuft saga, when Nicky, at his 100th birthday, lights his birthday candles that way.

Last, but not least, a warm thank you to my brother Ingo (who designed the old *Critters* logo and the new *Nuft and the Last Dragons* logo) for all kinds of assistance over the years.

Also available from

FANTAGRAPHICS

DISNEY MASTERS
Donald Duck
The Great Survival Test
DAAN JIPPES AND FREDDY MILTON

by Freddy Milton

DONALD DUCK:
THE GREAT SURVIVAL TEST
Daan Jippes and Freddy Milton
(Disney Masters Volume 4)

Donald Duck
"Under the Polar Ice"
by Carl Barks

by Carl Barks

UNCLE $CROOGE
"Island in the Sky"
by Carl Barks
AIR LOCK
PARTS AND SERVICE
BIG SKY CAFE
VISIT OUR WASHERETTE

WALT DISNEY'S
DONALD DUCK:
"UNDER THE POLAR ICE"
(Volume 23)

WALT DISNEY'S
UNCLE SCROOGE: "ISLAND IN THE SKY"
(Volume 24)

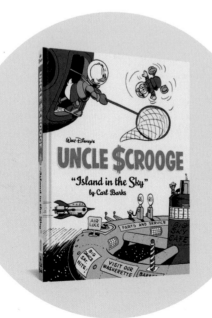

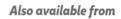

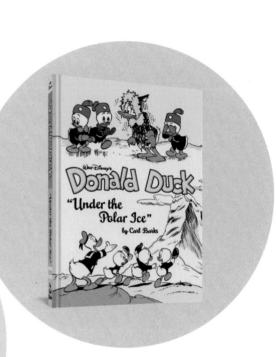

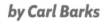

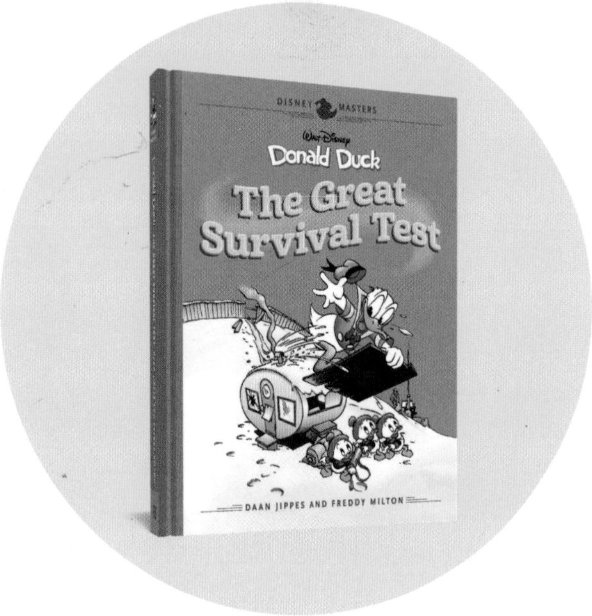